Women and China's Revolutions

Gail Hershatter

ROWMAN & LITTLEFIELD
Lanham • Boulder • New York • London

Executive Editor: Susan McEachern
Editorial Assistant: Katelyn Turner
Senior Marketing Manager: Kim Lyons

Credits and acknowledgments for material borrowed from other sources, and reproduced with permission, appear on the appropriate page within the text.

Published by Rowman & Littlefield
An imprint of The Rowman & Littlefield Publishing Group, Inc.
4501 Forbes Boulevard, Suite 200, Lanham, Maryland 20706
www.rowman.com

Unit A, Whitacre Mews, 26-34 Stannary Street, London SE11 4AB, United Kingdom

Copyright © 2019 by The Rowman & Littlefield Publishing Group, Inc.

British Library Cataloguing in Publication Information Available

Library of Congress Cataloging-in-Publication Data Available

ISBN 978-1-4422-1568-9 (hardback : alk. paper)
ISBN 978-1-4422-1569-6 (pbk : alk. paper)
ISBN 978-1-4422-1570-2 (ebook)

∞™ The paper used in this publication meets the minimum requirements of American National Standard for Information Sciences—Permanence of Paper for Printed Library Materials, ANSI/NISO Z39.48-1992.

Printed in the United States of America

This book is dedicated,
with gratitude, admiration, and love,
to the memory of
Delia Davin
Margery Wolf
and
Marilyn Young
who began this conversation

Contents

Photos

Photo 1.1.   Chinese family, ca. 1875
Source: Photographer unknown. Daniel Wolf Collection, New York City. Nigel Cameron and Philadelphia
Museum of Art, eds., *The Face of China as Seen by Photographers and Travelers, 1860–1912* (Millerton,
NY: Aperture, 1978), 47.

four-generation household.[4] It fell to her to ensure that everyone in the
household was properly fed, clothed, educated, and healthy. It was her
responsibility to care for her widowed mother-in-law, supervise the three
servants, manage the tenants who farmed the family's modest landholdings, marry off her two daughters, and bring in appropriate wives for her
two sons. It was also her task to maintain the family's high standing in
the community as a source of learned advice and occasional material help,
even as their family resources dwindled. Sometimes she longed to discuss
a vexing household issue with her husband, but he worked hundreds of
miles away as the magistrate of a county in another province. A single exchange of letters could take months. For all practical purposes Li Xiuhua
was the head of the household, although in the eyes of the law that was
a position held by a man.

It was not new in the nineteenth century for a married woman to be
responsible for domestic affairs. Life in imperial China had long been
organized by the fundamental principle that "Men rule the outer realm
(*wai*), women the inner realm (*nei*)." Nei and wai were interlocking rather
than separate spheres, because in imperial political thought, well-run
families were the foundation of a flourishing state. In the family, each
member was meant to learn the behavior appropriate to his or her role:
a parent's benevolence and a child's filial duty modeled the obligations
and loyalty that a ruler and his subject could expect from each other. The

domestic was a miniature of the political realm, intimately connected to it by practices of ethical conduct.

Nei and wai cannot easily be mapped onto contemporary ideas about "private" and "public" because households were the site of much quasi-public activity: economic production, schooling, and religious life.[5] As the matron of a respectable family, Li Xiuhua normally stayed at home, in the inner quarters off the back courtyard where the women of the family spent most of their time.[6] She also went regularly to the main hall where the tablets venerating her husband's ancestors were kept, because it was her responsibility to keep them free of dust and to provide appropriate offerings in his absence. But she was not to be found there when male visitors came to converse with her husband during his visits home, because women of her background did not often appear among strangers. Nevertheless, as the person responsible for her family's welfare, Li Xiuhua played an important role not only in her household but also in her immediate community.

Like many other men in the late empire, Li Xiuhua's educated husband was away for years at a time. Beginning more than a thousand years prior to her era, men competed in a civil service examination system. The examinations required years of study to master the classical texts and commentaries, ensuring that men with shared beliefs and a high level of literacy ran the imperial bureaucracy. Elite status was not inherited, nor was it defined by wealth alone; rather, it hinged on the ability of a household's boys and men to study for, take, and pass these exams. Even the wealthiest merchants aspired to government office for their sons and marriage into a scholar-official family for their daughters. A man who succeeded at the higher-level examinations was assigned to a government post far from his home. This "law of avoidance" ideally prevented conflicts of interest between his official duties and demands for special consideration from his relatives or those of his wife. Thus it had long been common for a woman like her, the wife of a successful official, to spend years caring for a man's aging parents, children, and property in his home province while he worked elsewhere, sometimes accompanied by a concubine.

But in the early nineteenth century, this elite wife and mother keenly felt new pressures on her household. The population of the empire, approximately 150 million in 1700, doubled by 1800 and tripled by 1850.[7] Meanwhile, the number of top degree holders remained more or less constant while the sheer volume of material that candidates had to master increased.[8] The competition for official positions was fiercer than ever before. Exam preparation began for young boys as early as age three and went on for decades. The examinations, in theory open to all males, were a realistic option only for boys whose parents could support and supervise their years of preparation. It was most often families with substantial

In the far western regions of Xinjiang and Tibet, Han farmers brought their families to settle after China established a military presence there in the early years of the Qing empire. In Xinjiang the throne actively subsidized settlement by Han farmers from the impoverished northwest, paying their expenses to convert grassland to agriculture in order to supply the military garrisons with millet and wheat.[50] Along this western frontier of Qing control, indigenous girls and women participated in the care and herding of livestock, while the wives and daughters of Han settlers were more apt to produce goods at home for household use.[51] Of the daily lives of these commoner immigrants we know very little. Of the specific challenges for non-Han women pushed out of their traditional lands in the western border region or the southwest highlands, or for Han women in new frontier households, we know even less. It is clear, however, that across the empire, farming households were units of production, and the labor of every household member was necessary.

As a farmer and weaver, Huang's wife rarely left her immediate neighborhood. She was busy all day and often far into the night weaving for the putting-out merchant, working with her family in the fields at sowing and harvest times, and performing the daily domestic tasks of cooking, child care, and needlework for her family's own use. She did not go to the periodic market held every few days in a town an hour's walk away. Women without menfolk went to the market to sell their yarn, but as a skilled weaver working at home she had no need to expose herself regularly to the gaze of strangers. Her husband made that trip whenever the family needed small quantities of matches, oil, salt, tools, pickles, vinegar, sugar, tobacco, herbal medicines, candles, and other sundries. There, too, he could get tools sharpened and repaired for a small outlay of cash. The income from her weaving enabled them to purchase a variety of goods and services rather than relying only on what the household could grow or prepare.[52] Her daily trip to a nearby well and her twice-weekly trips to the irrigation pond to wash the family's clothes gave her a chance to socialize with other women.[53] She could learn about the latest local scandals, impending marriages, and family achievements as she waited her turn and drew water for household use.

Her horizons, however, were not limited to her local community. Her husband brought back news gathered from conversations with other men in the teahouse he visited after making his market purchases. Along with her entire family, Huang's wife went several times a year to a fair at the Buddhist temple in the market town, held to celebrate the Bodhisattva Guanyin's birthday. This excursion provided an occasion to see two of her sisters, who had married into villages an hour outside town in the other direction from her own village. Her favorite activity at the temple fair was to view a folk opera performed by a traveling troupe. The plot

transplanting rice shoots was over, she and her daughters would stay at home, the girls spinning cotton yarn while she wove. Unlike Li Xiuhua's house, with its inner courtyard, formal front hall, and daily patterns of gender segregation, Huang's wife and her family ate and slept in close proximity, sharing two small, adjoined rooms and a small kitchen at the back of the house. Still, except during the busy farming season, women and girls worked inside while men went out to prepare the fields and repair farming tools.

At harvest time, still more than a month away, Huang's wife and her daughters would join her husband and son in the fields. Of course, women were ideally not supposed to be seen outside, but the demands of rice production were so intense at transplanting and harvest time that everyone's labor had to be mobilized.[32] Huang's wife and her daughters were far less vulnerable to gossip or assault than they would have been had she been a widow forced to farm without a male relative at her side. Even though farming women bound their daughters' feet, thereby saving them from social ridicule and preparing them to make a good match, the process began later than in elite families, and feet were bound more loosely among the poor. Mothers and daughters alike walked to the fields on their bound feet when their labor was required.[33]

Bound feet, of course, were perfectly compatible with the spinning and weaving that she and her daughters performed at home, without needing to venture into public space.[34] The ideal household division of labor expressed in the late imperial saying "men plow, women weave" was well within reach for families in her community.[35] Textile production was much praised as a womanly activity and often made a crucial contribution to household income. As a mother taught her daughters to produce new clothes for the family and for sale, she imparted to them as well the womanly virtues of patience, hard work, and thrift. In areas where women no longer knew the skill of weaving, imperial officials wrote earnestly about how to restore that knowledge, expressing their belief that weaving women would contribute to well-ordered households full of virtuous imperial subjects who were prosperous enough to pay their taxes on time.[36]

In the Jiangnan community of Huang's wife, women could be virtuous and secluded while actively spinning and weaving for the market.[37] Merchants, competing with one another for women's labor, regularly supplied her household with raw cotton and yarn, purchasing the finished woven textiles from her as fast as she and her daughters could produce them. This kind of putting-out system did not require her, or her daughters, to market their own products publicly. It was profitable and utterly respectable, though it made for exhausting days of labor that could extend well into the night.[38] Because the putting-out system and

transplanting rice shoots was over, she and her daughters would stay at home, the girls spinning cotton yarn while she wove. Unlike Li Xiuhua's house, with its inner courtyard, formal front hall, and daily patterns of gender segregation, Huang's wife and her family ate and slept in close proximity, sharing two small, adjoined rooms and a small kitchen at the back of the house. Still, except during the busy farming season, women and girls worked inside while men went out to prepare the fields and repair farming tools.

At harvest time, still more than a month away, Huang's wife and her daughters would join her husband and son in the fields. Of course, women were ideally not supposed to be seen outside, but the demands of rice production were so intense at transplanting and harvest time that everyone's labor had to be mobilized.[32] Huang's wife and her daughters were far less vulnerable to gossip or assault than they would have been had she been a widow forced to farm without a male relative at her side. Even though farming women bound their daughters' feet, thereby saving them from social ridicule and preparing them to make a good match, the process began later than in elite families, and feet were bound more loosely among the poor. Mothers and daughters alike walked to the fields on their bound feet when their labor was required.[33]

Bound feet, of course, were perfectly compatible with the spinning and weaving that she and her daughters performed at home, without needing to venture into public space.[34] The ideal household division of labor expressed in the late imperial saying "men plow, women weave" was well within reach for families in her community.[35] Textile production was much praised as a womanly activity and often made a crucial contribution to household income. As a mother taught her daughters to produce new clothes for the family and for sale, she imparted to them as well the womanly virtues of patience, hard work, and thrift. In areas where women no longer knew the skill of weaving, imperial officials wrote earnestly about how to restore that knowledge, expressing their belief that weaving women would contribute to well-ordered households full of virtuous imperial subjects who were prosperous enough to pay their taxes on time.[36]

In the Jiangnan community of Huang's wife, women could be virtuous and secluded while actively spinning and weaving for the market.[37] Merchants, competing with one another for women's labor, regularly supplied her household with raw cotton and yarn, purchasing the finished woven textiles from her as fast as she and her daughters could produce them. This kind of putting-out system did not require her, or her daughters, to market their own products publicly. It was profitable and utterly respectable, though it made for exhausting days of labor that could extend well into the night.[38] Because the putting-out system and

Photo 1.3. Woman weaving, Shanghai, 1870s

Source: Photo by L. F. Fisler. Picture collection, Peabody Museum of Salem, MA. Reprinted in Clark Worswick, Jonathan D. Spence, Asia House Gallery, and American Federation of Arts, eds., *Imperial China: Photographs 1850–1912* (New York: Pennwick Publishing, 1978), 115.

textile production were important features of the Jiangnan economy, the women in her village were all cotton weavers. In some Jiangnan communities, raising silkworms and producing silk were the norm; in others, women made mats, rain hats, rope, baskets, umbrellas, and other handicraft products for sale.[39]

Had Huang's wife been a farming wife in other parts of the empire, her days of labor would have been equally long but different. In areas of central and south China warm enough for double-cropping, women worked in the rice fields during the busy season, transplanting and weeding and harvesting; they also grew a second dry land crop such as beans.[40] Women routinely picked cotton in every area where it was grown. In hilly areas of Anhui, Hunan, Fujian, Taiwan, and across southern China, they picked and processed tea leaves for wages, helping to support their families and, in the case of unmarried women, to earn money for their dowries.[41] Tea harvesting was conducted outside domestic space but nevertheless was accepted as respectable, demonstrating the womanly virtue of diligence.[42]

Photo 1.4. Women making lace, ca. 1890s, Chefoo (Qufu)
Source: Photo by Rev. G. S. Hays. Arthur H. Smith, *Chinese Characteristics* (New York: Fleming H. Revell, 1894), facing 200.

Along the coast in Fujian, women in fishing families took primary responsibility for agriculture, growing sweet potatoes and peanuts, as well as repairing fishing nets and selling the fish their men caught.[43]

In drier, colder north and west China, women spent fewer days in the fields but also spun and wove for the household and the market,[44] in addition to making shoes, tending chickens and pigs, foraging for cooking fuel, husking and grinding millet and other grains, and hauling water. In some areas of Yunnan, women helped transport salt for sale.[45] As the southwestern provinces of Yunnan and Guizhou began to fill up with Han settlers, pushing indigenous residents into hilly, less fertile regions, women mainly were engaged in subsistence agriculture and production for the household.[46]

By the early nineteenth century, Han farmers had begun to settle in the northeast, homeland of the Manchu invaders who had founded the Qing dynasty in 1644, and merchants followed them.[47] Some of the migrants were young men from Hebei or Shandong who stayed a year or two to rent or reclaim land, leaving their wives behind in north China, but eventually whole families of migrants established new settlements.[48] Among the regular tasks performed by women in the northeast were mending shoes and sewing clothes.[49]

In the far western regions of Xinjiang and Tibet, Han farmers brought their families to settle after China established a military presence there in the early years of the Qing empire. In Xinjiang the throne actively subsidized settlement by Han farmers from the impoverished northwest, paying their expenses to convert grassland to agriculture in order to supply the military garrisons with millet and wheat.[50] Along this western frontier of Qing control, indigenous girls and women participated in the care and herding of livestock, while the wives and daughters of Han settlers were more apt to produce goods at home for household use.[51] Of the daily lives of these commoner immigrants we know very little. Of the specific challenges for non-Han women pushed out of their traditional lands in the western border region or the southwest highlands, or for Han women in new frontier households, we know even less. It is clear, however, that across the empire, farming households were units of production, and the labor of every household member was necessary.

As a farmer and weaver, Huang's wife rarely left her immediate neighborhood. She was busy all day and often far into the night weaving for the putting-out merchant, working with her family in the fields at sowing and harvest times, and performing the daily domestic tasks of cooking, child care, and needlework for her family's own use. She did not go to the periodic market held every few days in a town an hour's walk away. Women without menfolk went to the market to sell their yarn, but as a skilled weaver working at home she had no need to expose herself regularly to the gaze of strangers. Her husband made that trip whenever the family needed small quantities of matches, oil, salt, tools, pickles, vinegar, sugar, tobacco, herbal medicines, candles, and other sundries. There, too, he could get tools sharpened and repaired for a small outlay of cash. The income from her weaving enabled them to purchase a variety of goods and services rather than relying only on what the household could grow or prepare.[52] Her daily trip to a nearby well and her twice-weekly trips to the irrigation pond to wash the family's clothes gave her a chance to socialize with other women.[53] She could learn about the latest local scandals, impending marriages, and family achievements as she waited her turn and drew water for household use.

Her horizons, however, were not limited to her local community. Her husband brought back news gathered from conversations with other men in the teahouse he visited after making his market purchases. Along with her entire family, Huang's wife went several times a year to a fair at the Buddhist temple in the market town, held to celebrate the Bodhisattva Guanyin's birthday. This excursion provided an occasion to see two of her sisters, who had married into villages an hour outside town in the other direction from her own village. Her favorite activity at the temple fair was to view a folk opera performed by a traveling troupe. The plot

woman might embellish descriptions of both parties in order to bring the match to a successful conclusion. But luckily, without resorting to the services of outsiders, she had found a suitable match for her son through family connections: the husband of her second sister had provided an introduction to the daughter of a man who had passed the metropolitan exams in the same year he had. So far, she was satisfied with her daughter-in-law, who had married in two years earlier, and even happier that her first grandchild was due later that autumn. She hoped that it would be a boy who could carry on her husband's ancestral line. But even the birth of a healthy girl would reassure the family of the young woman's capacity to bear a son—and an older sister could always help to care for the boys who came later.

At present Li Xiuhua's most pressing concern was safeguarding the health of the young woman during her pregnancy. Here she could draw upon texts by brilliant male physicians who had chosen medicine as an alternative career after failing to pass the civil service exams. They wrote more optimistically about women's health than medical men had done in earlier dynasties. For these doctors, pregnancy was a natural process that would unfold smoothly as long as a woman was careful about her diet, daily activities, and emotional equanimity. The doctors warned against quacks and midwives who were too eager to correct a fetus's position in the womb or extract an infant by force, often injuring both mother and child in the process. But in her own experience, the local midwife knew a great deal about how to assist normal delivery, ease protracted labor, and turn a breech baby in the womb. So far, her daughter-in-law's pregnancy had gone smoothly, and there had been no need to invite a male physician to the household to check the young woman's pulse. In any case men, including physicians, did not attend actual births. Childbirth took place at home, in the women's quarters, assisted by midwives or the older women of the family.[31] Li Xiuhua's task now was to prepare for that event. If all went well, when her husband returned for a visit at New Year's, he could gaze upon his first grandson.

A FARMER-WEAVER

Climbing down from the raised seat of the loom, Huang's wife extinguished the *tong*-oil lamp. It was late. The three children had been asleep since shortly after sundown, and her husband, after smoking an evening pipe outside, had also turned in, because he would need to rise at dawn for early work in the rice paddies. Her father-in-law had died a decade earlier, her mother-in-law the previous spring, so theirs was a two-generation household. In the morning, because the busy season of

in such families roamed the empire on business, sometimes sojourning for years in cities such as Yangzhou, where they consorted with beautiful and musically talented courtesans, while their wives cared for parents and children at home.[29] Li Xiuhua wanted her daughters to marry men with whom they shared values and literary pursuits, even when they were separated. She was grateful that her daughters were most likely to become principal wives rather than concubines. An adult married man who could afford it often later added one or more concubines to his household. Unlike wives, who were chosen by one's parents, concubines were chosen by the man himself with an eye to compatibility, sexual attraction, and the ability to produce a son and male heir if the wife had not done so. But although concubinage could be a step up the social scale for poorer girls, no mother in a scholarly family would prefer this status for her daughter. A concubine's position was of necessity more tenuous than that of a wife, and the children she bore were treated as the offspring of the principal wife.[30]

As she arranged her daughters' marriages, Li Xiuhua knew that she could not control whether in the future they might have to compete with a concubine for a husband's attention. Although she knew of households where a man lived peaceably with a wife and several concubines, Li Xiuhua herself had experienced the pleasures of a close companionate marriage with her husband, one enhanced by affection and shared intellectual interests and without the complications of concubines. It had taken years to develop this intimacy through his periods of residency or visits home, and exchanges of poetry and letters in his absence. Together they worried about his aging mother, the growing children, and one another. That closeness had sustained her during the years when his work separated him from home, and that was what she desired for her daughters. With the eldest daughter successfully married off, she was now in the midst of a search for her younger daughter's match.

Li Xiuhua had already successfully met a different set of challenges in choosing a wife for her son. Because she knew that her daughter-in-law would become a permanent member of her household, eventually succeeding her as the manager of all family affairs, she sought someone skilled at household tasks and able to manage the intricate relationships of an extended family and its servants, with no interest in quarrels and intrigue. Also important was that the young woman be a fit companion for her son and a good mother to her future grandchildren: one who could read the classics, appreciate poetry, and discipline the children, while allowing their grandmother to spoil them a bit. Because elite families endeavored to keep their adolescent daughters out of the public eye, direct reports about likely prospects had been difficult to come by. She had begun by searching for a matchmaker she could trust; otherwise, the

landholdings or commercial wealth who were able to groom their sons for the examinations. An elite boy had only one obligation: to study for the examinations. Freedom from manual labor was a fundamental marker of his social status.

It had helped, when her sons were young, that Li Xiuhua herself knew how to read the classics. This was not unusual in educated families: women's literacy rates in the nineteenth century were somewhere between 2 and 10 percent, with economically advanced areas such as Jiangnan at the high end of the range.[9] She had grown up in a house full of woodblock print books, produced by publishing houses and distributed by book merchants across the empire. Catering to an ever-growing population of literate readers, publishers went far beyond reprinting the classics; they published works aimed at improving manners, offering advice about health and business, and introducing new fiction and essays to interested readers.[10] Among her parents and their relatives and friends, it was generally understood that a girl needed to be literate herself in order to become a wife who could provide support to a promising scholar, as well as a good mother of sons who could be educated to succeed in the exams.

Not that women's literacy was completely uncontroversial. Li Xiuhua's father had told her of a debate among educated men about the purpose of women's learning. He agreed with the position of philosopher Zhang Xuecheng (1738–1801), who emphasized that a classically educated woman could be a moral compass for her husband and an educator of her children. Zhang Xuecheng was far more suspicious of women's poetry, perhaps because some of the more renowned women poets in recent times had been courtesans rather than women of respectable families. Other Qing-era men of letters, in particular the scholar-poet Yuan Mei (1716–1797), celebrated young women as gifted poets.

This debate about the most appropriate status for a woman of learning—moral exemplar or talented poet?—was not resolved, and elements of both models pervaded Li Xiuhua's education.[11] Her own mother had taught her to read, guiding her through the *Instructions for Women* (Nü jie), written seventeen centuries earlier by the woman historian Ban Zhao (45–116 CE), which laid out in detail how women should behave. Her mother also introduced her to a women's version of the Confucian *Analects*, composed by a learned woman of the Tang dynasty (618–907 CE), which outlined proper behavior and tasks for women.

And then Li Xiuhua's father, whenever he came home between stints of his own work as an official, encouraged her to read, recite, and even write poetry. She especially looked forward to the times when her mother received a letter from one of her own sisters. Close in childhood, her mother and aunts had been scattered by marriage, because women of all classes married into the families of their husbands and moved to the homes of their husbands' parents. Now, as adults, her mother and her aunts often exchanged poetry that they admired or had written themselves. The year before Li Xiuhua left her parents' home to marry, her eldest aunt, well-known in her own community as a poet, had sent her a collection of her poetry, which her aunt's grown sons had published in a handsomely bound edition on the occasion of her fiftieth birthday.[12]

Fiction was less commonly found in her parents' household, but the just-published *Story of the Stone*, which portrayed the complex relationships in an extended elite family, captivated her mother and aunts and inspired some of their poems.[13] Also popular were long, rhymed tales called *tanci*, hand copied and later printed. As a child, Li Xiuhua and her sisters especially liked to read aloud one about the heroine Meng Lijun, who disguised herself as a man and rose to be prime minister, and another about the adventures of Meng's daughter.[14] At home in the "inner quarters" where elite girls and women spent most of their time, they imagined and shared a wider world of stories, advice, and adventure through reading.

Curious about what lay beyond the reading list her mother provided, Li Xiuhua had listened in on the lessons her brothers received from a private tutor. Later, when they were adolescents, she trailed them as they put in the nightly hours of memorization required to prepare for the examinations. What she learned came in handy after she had children of her own: she taught them to memorize the *Thousand Character Text* and the *Hundred Surnames*, and then guided them to recite their first passages from the Four Books, the Five Classics, and the *Classic of Filial Piety*.[15] She taught her children their earliest moral lessons, communicating to them the importance of learning, rebuking them when they strayed from the path of conduct presented in the classics. As a mother, she had unparalleled moral authority and responsibility, particularly in a family where the father was absent for years on end.

Li Xiuhua continued to teach her own daughters at home, as her mother had taught her. But as each son turned eight she sent him to the local temple school, and when they reached their teens she found them tutors who could help them attain the high level of classical literacy that the exams required.

Women were not eligible to enter the examination halls, much less aspire to hold office in the empire. Their place was at home. So thoroughly accepted was this gendered division of labor that neither Li Xiuhua nor anyone she knew questioned it. She was well aware, however, that her wifely and maternal labor was essential to the success of her husband and sons. Her acumen in managing the relationship with tenants who cultivated the family land helped to compensate for the fact that her husband's family was richer in learning than in material resources. Had she not taken charge of her sons' early instruction, carefully calculated the household finances, located and paid for the best tutors, and sold her embroidery to supplement the family budget, their chances to pass the examinations would have been diminished.

And the number of competitors was daunting. One year during a trip to visit her cousin in the county seat, from a hidden vantage point at the latticed window of her relative's home, she had seen almost two thousand local men show up to take the lowest level of the exams. They milled about in an anxious crowd before filing into the examination hall, which then was sealed, to be opened only after they had spent three days writing essays. Li Xiuhua had heard from her middle-aged housekeeper, who seized every chance to gossip with servants from other households, that her neighbor went back to the county examinations every few years. Trying with increasing difficulty to make himself appear as young as first-time examinees, he attempted once more to pass.

Her younger son had not yet begun this grueling ritual, but to her great satisfaction her eldest son, at the age of twenty-three, had recently passed the first series of exams. He now held the title of civil licentiate, an honor he shared with half a million men across the empire.[16] Wealthy families sometimes purchased lower-level degrees for their sons—her husband had told her that this provided an important source of government revenue—but her son had earned his by the orthodox and more respected route.[17] Licentiate status brought a man certain tax and legal benefits, and enhanced the prestige of his family, but it was not sufficient to hold government office. Still, she worried, knowing that many young men would go no further, eking out a living as local teachers or, if their families were wealthy, exercising power in their communities as landowners or merchants. Moving on to the provincial examinations, the next hurdle her son faced, was an expensive and uncertain gamble.

Two decades earlier, newly married and installed in the home of her husband's parents, Li Xiuhua herself had prepared the bedding, pots, food, and curtains that her husband would need during the week he was sealed in the provincial examination compound. Now, aided by her daughter-in-law, she was preparing to do the same for her eldest son, so that he might feel a modicum of family comfort as he mingled with fifteen thousand strangers taking the examination in the provincial capital. At this level, the most brutally competitive, only one man in a hundred passed. In an attempt to prevent cheating, no one was permitted to enter or leave during the exam. Water was provided in advance, human waste was collected in tubs, and the corpse of anyone who died was bundled in straw matting and thrown over the wall. Perhaps because the examination compound was an alien place full of the tension generated by thousands of anxious men, it was reported that strange things often happened there. Li Xiuhua had heard terrifying stories in which the ghost of a respectable woman, seduced and abandoned by a young man, appeared in his examination cell and caused him to go insane or die without writing a single word.

Despite the daunting odds, every three years 150,000 men took the provincial exams, even though repeated failure was common and the average age of successful candidates was rising steadily. Some from Jiangnan even migrated temporarily to less populated provinces such as Gansu in the northwest, where more lenient quotas increased their chances of passing.[18] Nor was this the final challenge her son would face in his quest for an official career. Three to four thousand men, including those who had passed earlier rounds, went on to sit for the triennial empire-wide metropolitan and palace exams. Only the several hundred who succeeded at this highest level could be assured of a government job.

Although it would have been unseemly to say so, Li Xiuhua was proud that her husband had attained the highest degree of "presented scholar," held by only fifty thousand men in the entire empire. The path to this achievement had been arduous and difficult for both of them, involving several failed attempts for him and long years of hardship for her. During the two decades between his first county exam and his ultimate triumph, like many of his fellow strivers, he had first worked as a teacher in a nearby private village school for boys. Later, he left home to tutor the sons of the wealthy in the provincial capital, barely making enough to support himself. During that time, Li Xiuhua was compelled to find ways to support her family and maintain its social standing with little or no assistance from him.[19] She made sure that the tenants on the family's land paid every bit of rent they owed. In years when the land rent did not cover the expenses of her growing household, she paid her sons' teachers by selling the jewelry she had brought to her husband's family as part of her dowry, as well as pieces of her own embroidery.[20] At one point she had even discreetly invested in a village business making straw hats for summer fieldwork. But it was also her obligation to maintain the family's social status, and so she would not think of sending her sons out to perform manual labor or let her daughters be seen in public.

At last, at the beginning of her third decade of marriage, their fortunes improved. Her husband had been recommended for a staff position with a Jiangsu official working in the capital, Beijing, and was finally able to send home a portion of his earnings to help support the household. The following year, on his third try, he had passed the metropolitan exam and received an official appointment as a magistrate, enhancing his family's local reputation and easing their financial situation but ensuring that his presence at home was less and less frequent.

Li Xiuhua was satisfied that she had supported her husband during the years when he sought examination success, and when she felt discouraged she consoled herself that her own life was far easier than what her mother-in-law had experienced. Her father-in-law had died when her husband was a toddler, and her mother-in-law had raised her son to adulthood and seen to his education, exhibiting the fidelity expected of a virtuous widow and steadfastly refusing to remarry. In earlier times, widows had been honored by imperial officials if they committed suicide when their chastity was threatened or disfigured themselves to avoid remarriage. But by the Qing dynasty, official praise went instead to widows who refused to remarry and remained alive to perform the daily labor of serving their husband's parents and raising his children. Her mother-in-law had accomplished these tasks, caring for her aged in-laws until they died, ensuring their proper burial, and venerating them through household rituals to honor the ancestors. After thirty years of chaste widowhood and familial duty, she received an imperial commendation. In recent years her vigor had faded. She withdrew to her room, stopped eating meat, and devoted herself to the religious practices of quiet sitting and copying Buddhist sutras. She was finally in a position where she could confidently leave daily household matters to Li Xiuhua.[21]

The success of Li Xiuhua's husband came at an opportune moment, just at the time when they needed to arrange the marriages of their children. His appointment as an official enhanced the family's prestige, making her daughters and sons attractive matches. Betrothing one's child to a mate of appropriate status, whose "doors and windows matched" one's own, as the common saying had it, cemented alliances between elite families. It also involved exchanges of wealth. Li Xiuhua was prepared to send substantial bridal gifts to the families of her sons' future wives. When her daughters married out, they would take a sizable dowry of household goods to their new homes. A bride rode unseen in a curtained sedan chair, the object of much curiosity. But it was important that her dowry be ostentatiously displayed in the bridal procession, signifying to all viewers that a young woman was not being sold into marriage.[22]

With so much family standing and property at stake, it did not occur to Li Xiuhua, or to any adult she knew, to leave the selection of a mate to the young people involved. Her own brother had been betrothed at birth to an infant daughter in the family of her grandfather's best friend. Her oldest sister's future husband had been selected by her parents when the girl was only three years old. And she herself had married a man whom her parents chose after careful consultation with their relatives and friends. Affinal relations—the networks created by marriage—were important to every family, providing people with an economic safety net and a wealth of political connections.[23] If a match could be based on friendships among the senior members of the household, so much the better. Both she and her husband would play important roles in identifying potential families whose children would make good matches for their own.

Much hidden labor was required to raise her daughters to be proper wives. Li Xiuhua had educated them so that they could be effective mothers of literate and high-achieving sons. She had also conveyed to them her love of poetry. Here she was able to draw upon a volume that had not been available when she was a girl: the 1831 poetry anthology published by the woman editor Yun Zhu, titled *Correct Beginnings*, with several thousand poems by women from varied ethnic and social backgrounds. As she read the women's poems Yun Zhu had collected over her lifetime, she thought back to the debate that had roiled her father's generation about the proper uses of women's literacy. To her mind, Yun Zhu's work had settled the matter: a woman could exhibit both talent and virtue in her poetry.[24] In addition, Li Xiuhua had instructed her daughters in the art of embroidery. For a woman of the educated class, embroidering clothing, accessories, shoes, and bedding for one's dowry showed the world, and her new family, that she possessed the virtues expected of a woman—patience, industriousness, and skill.[25]

She had also taken on the unpleasant task of binding her daughters' feet, beginning when they were six. This practice had been common among elite women since the twelfth century and by the early nineteenth century was practiced by almost all Han women.[26] It required perseverance and daily care. A girl's feet were wrapped in long strips of cloth, which were changed regularly and tightened over time, forcing the toes under the feet and buckling the arches, to produce the several-inch-long "golden lotus" feet that marked a girl as cultivated and a proper woman. Of course, neither the feet—normally encased in embroidered leggings— nor the girl herself were meant to be seen in public, because seclusion was an absolute requirement for young unmarried women from respectable families. Footbinding was excruciatingly painful for the child and thus difficult for the mother, even with the various salves her own mother had taught her to make to ease the pain until the process was finished. Even then, throughout a woman's life the diminutive foot size had to be maintained through frequent rewrapping. But Li Xiuhua did not question the necessity of footbinding. It was simply what a loving mother did to prepare her daughter to make a good marriage into a respectable family. Not to bind would be a failure of maternal duty.

As her oldest daughter approached adolescence, she began discreet inquiries through her network of family and friends. Because she and her sisters all had married into their husbands' communities and now lived many miles apart from each other, she had contacts whom she trusted in far-flung places. Her oldest sister wrote that a family of scholars in her neighborhood was seeking an educated, well-behaved, and hardworking fiancée for their eldest son, a promising examination candidate. Her sister was in a poetry circle with the young man's

Photo 1.2.   Woman and servant, ca. 1868
Source: Photo attributed to John Thomson. Elaine Ellman Collection, New York City. Nigel Cameron and
Philadelphia Museum of Art, eds., *The Face of China as Seen by Photographers and Travelers, 1860–1912*
(Millerton, NY: Aperture, 1978), 60.

mother. She reported that the woman was not only educated but kind
and would treat her daughter well.

This was one of the most difficult decisions a parent had to make. Li
Xiuhua's daughter would become part of her husband's family: bound to
continue his family line, serve his parents, and honor his ancestors.[27] A

proper marriage began with the transport of the bride to the home of her in-laws, in which she was carried to the sedan chair or wore disposable paper shoe soles to avoid bringing the dust (and by extension, the attachments) of her natal home into her new family. A daughter was expected to marry out and to return only as a visitor: she was sent off with a ritual spilling of water to symbolize the irreversible nature of the transfer. In elite families, with their far-flung networks, she often moved far away, sustaining emotional ties through correspondence and much-anticipated visits to her parents. Doting parents sometimes offered material assistance if a married daughter fell on hard times, but they were unlikely to take her back: divorce among elite women was rare and stigmatized. The Qing legal code permitted a man to divorce a woman on grounds of inappropriate behavior (gossip, jealousy, adultery, theft, lack of filiality toward in-laws), disease, or failure to bear a son. These rights were not shared by the wife, who could divorce her husband only if her family of origin was willing to sue on her behalf, and then only if her husband had abandoned her, caused her permanent physical injury, or attempted to sell her or force her to commit adultery.[28] In practice, divorce was exceedingly rare. And so, in marrying off her daughter, Li Xiuhua accepted that if the match worked out as she hoped, henceforth the young woman's primary duties and attachments would lie elsewhere.

A new bride's marital home typically included her new in-laws, her father-in-law's concubines if he had any, the brothers of her husband, their wives, and any of her husband's sisters who had not yet married. The bride's relationship with the senior woman in the household—her mother-in-law—might well play a bigger role in her daily life than that with her husband, especially if he was away from home for long periods of work or study. A mother tried to assure a happy life for her daughter in a family of strangers by finding a kindly and fair mother-in-law, one who would not regard the young woman primarily as a competitor for her son's affection. Li Xiuhua knew that her daughter would still need to navigate the relationships with potentially quarrelsome sisters-in-law, and that tensions among the younger women could lead to the formal division of a household's property, even though the socially desirable norm was for multiple generations to dwell together under one roof. And, of course, her daughter would need to develop a relationship with the husband she saw for the first time on her wedding day. Not until she bore a child of her own would her daughter begin to establish herself in her marital home and enjoy close bonds of affection, authority, and filial duty with her own offspring.

Finding an appropriate family was not just a matter of calibrating wealth. A family of newly rich merchants, for instance, might give her daughter more material security than a struggling scholar. But the men

Photo 1.5. A Chinese kitchen, showing method of preparing food, ca. 1890s, Chefoo (Qufu)
Source: Photo by Rev. G. S. Hays. Arthur H. Smith, *Chinese Characteristics* (New York: Fleming H. Revell, 1894), facing 19.

was usually a story based on events from ancient times, with an emphasis on heroic deeds, high moral standards, and karmic rewards or retribution for past deeds. Through those operas she learned about famous women who had protected their chastity, sometimes at the cost of their lives. The temple fairs offered other open-air entertainment as well: storytellers and ballad singers, whose lyrics included moral instruction on how girls and women should behave.[54]

On these trips to town she saw the widow arches dotting the countryside. They had been constructed by government decree to honor women who had served their families for several decades after the death of their husbands. She knew that ideally a virtuous widow should not remarry, though women in her village frequently did so because of financial exigency. Without several able-bodied adults in a household—men to prepare the rice paddies and tend them, women to weave for the merchants and feed and clothe the family—it was difficult for anyone, virtuous or not, to survive.

Although Huang's wife could not read, her husband could recognize enough characters to make it worthwhile, on his trips to the periodic market, to buy a few of the cheap illustrated books sold there. Sometimes over his evening pipe he puzzled out a passage in the farmer's almanac, or a guide to home medical remedies, and read them to her as she wove. She particularly liked the fortune-telling manual he had brought home the previous year, from which they had divined that in the future she would have many grandchildren.[55] A traveling bookseller had told her husband that the woodblocks for these books had been cut by women in south China. The women traced paper impressions of each character pasted on a block, although they could not read themselves. Women and children, the bookseller reported, also did the printing and binding of books, working at home and earning income for their families just as she did through her weaving.[56]

Through the burgeoning book trade, as well as the temple dramatic productions, her family and others like it across rural Jiangnan were exposed to some of the canonical stories and values that their more educated counterparts learned in the course of a classical education. China in the early nineteenth century was not a society sharply divided between worlds of high and low culture. Women across social strata knew what was counted as virtuous behavior. Aspirations, if not always practices, were shared.

But for Huang's wife, some aspirations seemed too far out of reach. She did not harbor dreams that her son could cross into the scholar-official elite, even though in theory the examinations were open to all. The family needed him in the fields, and even sending him to the local tutor, a licentiate who taught some village boys basic literacy, was beyond their means. As for her daughters, her main concern as they approached adolescence was the need to keep them out of the public eye. A young woman who appeared brazenly in public would not be regarded as a desirable marriage prospect—and might expose herself to sexual menace. She had heard of cases where village wastrels or miscreants spied a woman at the village well, or even caught a glimpse of a young woman in her family's courtyard, and proceeded to plot and carry out a sexual assault. When the time came to marry off her daughters, she hoped that her husband's circle of teahouse acquaintances, men he knew from his many trips to the market town, or her own small network of married sisters in area villages, would yield a suitable match not too far away. In many regions of China, though not hers, a new bride continued to spend substantial amounts of time in her mother's home after her marriage, moving to live with her in-laws and her husband only when she bore her first child. But even in her village, a daughter who married nearby would continue to visit home regularly as long as her parents were alive, maintaining close relations with them even as she produced children to carry on her husband's patriline.

Respectable married daughters living nearby was what she hoped for, but Huang's wife was well aware of other possible fates for girls. A desperately poor family who could not afford to raise a girl child to adult-hood might sell her to the family of a future husband, to be raised as a future daughter-in-law and married off to the son of the household when she was of childbearing age. Such girls, young and vulnerable, often were abused by their adoptive families. She felt fortunate that because she and her husband were healthy and worked hard at farming and weaving, they had the resources to raise their daughters until they were ready for marriage. She hoped that her future sons-in-law would be hardworking farmers, for marrying a daughter into a wealthy family was risky. Her neighbor had engineered a match for his exceptionally beautiful daughter to a well-off merchant family in the market town, but the young woman had become a concubine, not a wife, and it was said that the principal wife disliked and mistreated her.

And then there were the women who did not become wives at all. Some girls from poor households, both urban and rural, were purchased by madams to become courtesans-in-training or procured as maidservants for wealthy households. The city of Yangzhou, not far away, was famous for its beautiful courtesans, who entertained officials and merchants in the city on business. The courtesan house was a popular gathering place for scholars and merchants, where extraordinarily beautiful young women sang, played music, recited poetry, played chess, and were both poets and the occasions for appreciative poetry written by their patrons. In return for sustained patronage, a sojourning man of means might also gain sexual access to such a woman and sometimes purchase her as a con-cubine. Elite men often wrote about courtesans as pure lotuses emerging from the mud of the commercial environment, but courtesans were cer-tainly an integral part of that environment, sustained by the commercial ferment and increased male mobility of the late imperial era. Outside the courtesan houses, women who were less beautiful or no longer young plied their trade as ordinary prostitutes on the streets.[57]

Even within a respectable marriage, there were fates no mother would wish upon her daughter. Everyone knew of cases where young married women, after conflicts with their husbands or fights with their in-laws, had hanged themselves, and many ghost stories circulated about such women, who were said to come back to haunt other young brides.[58] And then there were the family crises of the very poor. If a husband became disabled or too ill to farm, his wife might find herself in a polyandrous household, in which the couple invited a healthy man to join the house-hold and do the farmwork in exchange for sexual access to her. In a so-ciety where rich men had access to multiple women—wives, concubines, courtesans, and maidservants—many poor men could not afford to marry at all, becoming what was derisively known as "bare sticks."[59] For them, polyandry was the closest thing to marriage they could hope to attain. As a mother, Huang's wife could only hope that her daughters would never find themselves caught up in a practice so marked by poverty and the loss of all propriety.

All of that, however, was in the future. Her oldest daughter was only thirteen, and she herself was still of childbearing age. The birth of a son after her first daughter, a year before her father-in-law died, had been a relief to her, for only a son could carry on her husband's family line and continue to honor his ancestors. The boy was now twelve, old enough to be a substantial help in the fields. A few years after that, she had borne a second daughter. Both girls were good spinners, and she had just begun to teach the oldest how to climb up on the loom and weave. In a few years, they would make good wives, able to keep house, help in the fields, and bring in a substantial income in textile production. Now midway through her fourth pregnancy, she was hoping for a second son, to help her first son care for her and her husband as they aged, and to fill the house with grandchildren.

Huang's wife had been fortunate. The growing number of merchants buying her woven goods had enabled her family to do well, without the need to limit family size. Unlike some of her neighbors, she did not become pregnant very frequently, perhaps because the herbal tonic she took to regulate her periods had some effect on her fertility.[60] Women with too many pregnancies, she knew, often drowned unwanted girl babies at birth. The practice was condemned by learned men across the empire as a sin and an interruption of the reproduction of future wives and mothers, but such concerns did not guide the reproductive decisions of farming women.[61] Perhaps the wives of educated men could be persuaded to keep every child, but what did they know of the pressures on farming families such as hers? Even in her neighborhood of employed weavers, she knew of several cases of infanticide. Childbirth was a women's business in which the men of the family were not directly involved, and in those cases either the mother had made the decision herself, or the mother-in-law, perhaps encouraged by other women relatives or the midwife, had drowned a newborn daughter. No one condoned it, nor even spoke of it openly, but clearly it happened more often than people admitted. Why else would there be only eight girl children for every ten boys in the village?[62] And would this shortage of girls someday affect her search for a bride for her son?

But she did not dwell on these thoughts. Her household was doing well, in no small part because of her late nights at the loom. That was one reason she could hope that her daughters would end up nearby, in a farming family like her own. The merchants, Huang's wife thought, would always have weaving for them to do.

sources of cultural cohesion for much of this period. By the latter half of the nineteenth century, however, the very meaning of womanhood was being reworked by foreigners and by Chinese working to make sense of their place in a transformed world.

The Taiping civil war that disrupted Zuo Xijia's life was not the first chapter of this intractable crisis. Two decades earlier, China's defeat by Britain in the first Opium War (1839–42) had inaugurated a period of un-settling change. Prior to that war, the Qing dynastic rulers regulated trade through a tributary system in which surrounding lands formally recog-nized the dominant position of the Chinese empire. European and other traders were confined to the southern city of Canton during the trading season each year. Long used in China for medicinal purposes, opium spread rapidly in the late eighteenth century as British traders in China expanded opium imports from India to fund their purchases of tea.[7] Revenues from the tea trade in turn helped fund the British government. By the early nineteenth century, opium smoking had expanded from the China coast to the interior, aided by an active network of Chinese smug-glers, and by the 1830s it was estimated that seven of ten soldiers along the coast used opium.[8] The Qing court, alarmed by the rising incidence of opium consumption and the outflow of silver to pay for it, appointed

Photo 2.1. Women sorting tea in Canton, ca. 1870s

Source: John Thomson, *China and Its People in Early Photographs: An Unabridged Reprint of the Classic 1873/4 Work* (New York: Dover Publications, 1982), vol. 1, plate XIX.

Lin Zexu, one of the most powerful officials in the empire, to bring a halt to the trade in 1838. When Lin destroyed a valuable stock of opium, the British, who were determined to "open" China to trade on their terms, went to war and won.[9]

The Qing state's defeat by Great Britain in the first Opium War inaugurated what Chinese often call "China's century of humiliation." The 1842 Treaty of Nanjing opened five cities as treaty ports where foreigners could live and trade. In the succeeding decades, although China was never fully colonized by a single foreign nation, multiple imperialist powers enlarged their access to the empire's territory. Britain, France, the United States, and other foreign powers won multiple rights through the treaties they imposed upon China. Their citizens were able to reside in China's treaty ports, which expanded steadily in number; to enjoy low tariff rates on goods they imported into China; to be tried under the laws of their home countries for crimes committed in China (a practice known as extraterritoriality); to proselytize as Christian missionaries—after the second Opium War in 1860, anywhere in Chinese territory; and eventually, by the mid-1890s, to invest directly in Chinese industry. When any imperialist power won a concession from China, it was enjoyed by all foreign powers under the "most-favored-nation" clauses of these treaties. Periods of outright war were interspersed with low-level incidents of conflict, as foreign warships ventured up China's waterways to protect European and American traders and missionaries. These foreign activities challenged Qing political control and weakened the state.

At the same time, the foreign presence provided information about the world beyond China and created new knowledge about China itself. Foreigners criticized many long-standing cultural practices, including infanticide and footbinding, as "backward" or "uncivilized." Missionary schools attracted Christian converts, educating boys and girls from poor families. Foreign trading companies employed Chinese interpreters, spreading knowledge of foreign languages into many educated homes. Self-strengthening efforts undertaken by the beleaguered Qing state brought together foreign munitions experts and Chinese trained in new engineering skills. Chinese diplomats, travelers, and students sent home dispatches from Europe, the United States, and Japan describing life abroad.[10] Subjects of the Chinese empire were taught, with varying degrees of coercion, to reinterpret their understanding of their place in the world.

As the Qing state scrambled to cope with infringements on its sovereignty, from the 1850s through the 1870s large-scale uprisings came close to tearing the empire apart. The Taiping and other massive mid-century rebellions—the Nian in north China, the Muslim Rebellion in the northwest, and the Panthay Rebellion in the southwest—were shaped in part by a growing population, shrinking opportunities for advancement, and migration of Han settlers into ethnically diverse borderlands where they came into conflict with non-Han minorities. These sources of strain were intensified by the effects of imperialism: the drain of silver to pay for opium, rising prices and taxes, a punitive indemnity imposed by the British at the end of the first Opium War, a distracted and overwhelmed Qing government, and disruptions in local labor markets and handicraft production caused by the opening of the treaty ports.[11]

In the midst of European incursions, civil war, and severe economic crisis, expectations of how a virtuous woman should behave initially remained intact. As the British moved up the Yangzi in 1841, they were mystified to discover that women in the cities they conquered had hanged themselves or jumped into wells, actions any Chinese would understand as heroic suicide to avoid sexual dishonor.[12] After the Taiping uprising was defeated in 1864, as we will see, devastated communities often commemorated women who had chosen to kill themselves for the same reason. Old ideas about women's virtue helped people to make meaning out of terrible losses.

But a few short decades later the loyal and chaste woman as social touchstone had disappeared. She was replaced by Woman as another kind of symbol altogether: ignorant, slothful, and economically parasitic. This chapter provides the context in which this shift occurred. As chapter 3 will describe, by the 1890s elite male critics began to regard women as an embodiment of everything that was wrong with the Qing empire. Along with a small but vocal number of women writers, they argued that the treatment of women, kept secluded and ignorant, partially explained why the dynasty was unable to repel foreign imperialist powers effectively.

OPIUM AND WOMEN: POETRY, ADDICTION, PRODUCTION

For elite women, the first Opium War was a moment of intensified political engagement expressed largely through poetry. For women of all social backgrounds, opium addiction meant a drain on family resources and a decrease in security. And for the poorest women farmers, the spread of domestic opium cultivation brought new income opportunities.

China's first Opium War brought British bombardment and troops to communities along the coast and in Jiangnan. Women of the elite, although they passed most of their days in the inner quarters, were not isolated from these political discussions. In their poetry, some registered anger at the Qing court for trying to reach a settlement with the invading British forces, praising soldiers and the general populace for resisting. As the British advanced on Nanjing, the woman poet Shen Shanbao wrote from Beijing:

I hear it told that covering the seas is a poison vapor [opium],
Along the river a deadly miasma
[British] ships of war line the Guabu harbor [across the river from Nanjing].
Guns and ships may be fierce and swift
But do we lack river guards and archers?
Stalwart angry braves, hair on end, caps atop;
Students casting down their brushes [to take up arms],
Laughing while they attack the enemy.

Shen concluded her poem with the image of a beautiful concubine in Song times beating drums to rouse the troops fighting the Jin invaders: a woman calling men to war.[13]

The opium question did not end when China lost the first Opium War. A second war in 1856–60, in which China was again defeated, legalized the import of the drug, even as it was banned in Britain.[14] Drug-running networks expanded, and the opium-smoking habit spread from elite men to women and from officials to those of humbler backgrounds.[15] By the late nineteenth century, lower-grade opium was widely grown in China's southwest and northwest regions.[16] Eventually, as the homegrown product supplanted imports, cheap local opium made addiction commonplace.[17]

In 1906, in the last years of the empire, an imperial edict banned the cultivation and use of opium, with partial success. Officials and the elite came to regard opium suppression as a necessary measure to strengthen the nation and enable it to stave off imperialist powers.[18] But even as state officials worked to suppress the opium trade, government at every level grew increasingly dependent on opium tax revenues.[19] By the twentieth century, criminal organizations were competing and sometimes cooperating with state authorities over control of the trade.[20]

China's incorporation into a globalized narco-economy affected women from every walk of life. Late Qing novels blamed opium smoking for the loss of family fortunes, the death of addicts, the birth of weak or addicted children, and the sale of young women into prostitution.[21] Novelists warned that although opium might at first enhance male sexual pleasure during visits to brothels, as a man became addicted the desire for opium would displace desire for sex.[22] Nineteenth-century fiction also made frequent references to women who committed suicide by swallowing raw opium.[23] In spite of such cautionary tales, opium smoking became a normalized feature of elite social life, listed on dinner and wedding banquet menus as part of the festivities. In Shanghai and other cities, women attendants staffed the elegantly furnished opium dens that catered to the wealthy, while cheaper establishments provided opium for transport workers.[24] Unlicensed brothels known as "flower-smoke rooms" provided both women and opium well into the twentieth century; higher-class houses of prostitution also provided the drug to select customers.

As cultivators, smokers, den attendants, and sex workers, some women dealt directly with opium. Alicia Little, a British woman who lived in China for several decades and was active in the movement against foot-binding (see chapter 3), in 1899 described the effects of opium smoking on women in wealthy families:

> The ladies who are regular opium-smokers sit up late at night, and do not get up till five or six in the evening. They mostly have bad health, and generally say they have taken to opium-smoking because of it. Whatever effect opium may have upon men, the various ladies I have seen at ladies' dinners generally return from the opium-couch with their eyes very bright, their cheeks very red, and talking a great deal of nonsense very excitedly. But afterwards they look yellow and unhealthy, mostly with sunken cheeks. They seem no more ashamed of it than ladies are of taking wine in England. But those who do not smoke seem to think it is a rather disgraceful proceeding. . . . But at a good many dinner parties the opium-couch is prepared with all its elegant accessories. And at the only Chinese country house, at which I have stayed, the ladies' one idea was to ask me into their bedrooms to smoke opium.[25]

A 1904 report estimated that in Sichuan half of urban men and a fifth of urban women were addicted, along with 15 percent of rural men and 5 percent of rural women.[26] Rates of addiction appear to have been lower among women than men, although this may have reflected the limited visibility of women in public.[27]

Many more women were wives and children of addicts. Ning Lao Taitai, a household servant in eastern Shandong, provided a rare oral narrative of life with and without her hopelessly addicted husband. Born in 1867, engaged at twelve and married at fifteen,[28] she soon learned to spend as much time at her mother's house as possible, because her husband was "an old opium sot" who did nothing to feed his family.

> He took everything and sold it for opium. He could not help it. . . . I dared not wash a garment and put it out to dry without staying by to watch it. If I hid a copper coin under the matting of the *kang* [a heated brick platform bed common in north China] he found it.

Ning left her husband for the first time after he sold her silver hairpins to buy opium when her oldest daughter was two years old and she was pregnant with a second child. She returned but left him again after he sold their younger daughter for the second time; the first time Ning had found and rescued her. After that she lived apart from her husband for the better part of a decade.

Although a woman going out to work in public was still stigmatized in late nineteenth-century Shandong, her husband's addiction left Ning no choice but to make her living as a crop gleaner, a street beggar, a peddler,

Photo 2.2. Woman spinning cotton, ca. 1868

Source: Photo by John Thomson, Stuart Collection, Rare Book Division, New York Public Library, Astor, Lenox and Tilden Foundation. Nigel Cameron and Philadelphia Museum of Art, eds., *The Face of China as Seen by Photographers and Travelers, 1860–1912* (Millerton, NY: Aperture, 1978), 67.

and a live-in household servant. In some of the wealthy homes where she served, the women lay on their opium couches all day, smoking. When it was time to marry off her oldest daughter, Ning arranged a match with a cobbler, only to learn after the marriage that her new son-in-law, too, was an opium addict and a thief who talked of selling his wife and apprenticing his daughter as a courtesan, and who eventually disappeared to Manchuria.[29]

In addition to creating family instability and hardship, opium provided a potential new income source for rural women. Growing opium was labor-intensive but extremely profitable. Well into the twentieth century, helping with the crop allowed women and children from economically vulnerable households to survive. As a young girl in the

1920s Cao Zhuxiang, daughter of a poor family in central Shaanxi, hired herself out to help with the opium harvest:

> I had collected my own dowry before I reached twelve years old. I got up early in the morning to go to the opium field to harvest opium and was paid according to how much I harvested. At noon I came back to get something to eat. The owner would pay me in opium. I took the opium to the neighbors and exchanged it for cloth and other things. In this way I was collecting a dowry for myself.[30]

For Cao, this source of income disappeared a few years later when opium cultivation was prohibited. But some farmers in her village, both men and women, continued to smoke, even selling their land to finance their habit.

WOMEN'S DISPLACEMENT AND WOMAN AS SYMBOL IN THE MID-CENTURY UPRISINGS

China's nineteenth-century uprisings destroyed communities in large swaths of the Qing empire. These rebellions have captured the imagination of historians for their imaginative ideologies, innovative forms of organization, and individual heroic acts. For the millions of women who joined or were caught up in these upheavals, however, the main effects were hunger, sexual violation, dislocation, and loss.[31]

Of all these upheavals, the most threatening to the survival of the Qing empire was the thirteen-year Taiping civil war (1851–64) in which Zhou Xijia's husband died. The Taiping forces were led by a failed examination candidate, Hong Xiuquan, who was inspired by a missionary pamphlet and a vision to believe he was the younger brother of Jesus Christ. The movement began in Guangxi, an area of south China racked by economic instability and conflict between members of the Hakka minority and their neighbors. The rebels proclaimed a new order known as the Taiping Heavenly Kingdom, with authority bestowed by a transcendent God. Hong considered all Manchus to be devils. The Taiping armies marched north, occupying much of the Jiangnan area, although they never took Shanghai. For a time they threatened Beijing. From 1853 until their defeat in 1864, they ruled from their capital in Nanjing. In the process they occupied, lost, and reoccupied many Jiangnan cities. Initially they attracted a certain amount of fascinated attention from European and American missionaries, who hoped that the movement would help to establish a Christian nation on Chinese soil, but foreign skepticism rose as the movement unfolded. The Taiping finally succumbed in 1864 to internecine warfare and the attacks of regional armies fighting for the Qing.

During the civil war, the gendered features of the Taiping movement drew a great deal of attention and opposition. The rebels' clothing horrified the refined Jiangnan people. Taiping men did not shave their foreheads in the Qing fashion. They dressed in red and in yellow, a color that was supposed to be reserved for the Qing emperor and officials he favored. Taiping officials reportedly sported turbans fashioned from women's pants. Taiping women dressed in brightly colored and flowered clothes and wore pants. People in the areas they conquered were compelled to adopt their hair and clothing styles.[32]

Unorthodox Taiping practices were not limited to modes of dress; the Taiping took aim directly at Chinese patterns of marriage and household formation. In their early years as an army on the march, men and women in the Taiping ranks were required to live separately in hierarchical production units. Sexual intercourse between married couples in the Taiping army was not permitted, although Taiping leaders promised that families would be reunited after the Taiping victory. In some of the larger cities occupied by the Taiping, such as Wuchang and Nanjing, the entire urban population was briefly divided into gender-segregated camps, breaking up established households and provoking popular dismay. But attempts to separate men from women and the ban on marital intercourse were abandoned by the mid-1850s, and marriage was recognized in the form of licenses issued by Taiping officials.[33]

Chinese men who could afford it often took concubines, but in Taiping-controlled areas concubinage was off-limits to all but the highest-ranking Taiping kings, who built up extensive collections of consorts. The Heavenly King Hong Xiuquan reportedly had two hundred wives as well as sexual access to several thousand women officials and maids. Poems Hong published in 1857 suggest that he had trouble managing them. One verse read, "The royal consorts do not know how to follow reasoning; the royal consorts do not take care of the spittoons. The royal consorts secrete evil in their hearts; the royal consorts do not show happiness on their faces."[34]

Some Taiping practices were celebrated by later generations of revolutionaries for promoting gender equality.[35] Historians have suggested that the roots of the Taiping leadership in Hakka culture contributed to a relatively egalitarian view of gender. The Hakka were a migrant subgroup of Han Chinese in southeast China, forced to farm less fertile hilly lands where women's field labor was valuable. Hakka women did not bind their feet. In the Taiping zones women, like men, were expected to labor, and some may have participated in combat. The Taiping planned a special examination for potential women officials, although it apparently never took place. At least one woman attained a high official rank.[36] The Taiping gave women inheritance rights as well, promising in the 1853 document Land System of the Heavenly Dynasty that men and women aged sixteen and older were to be given equal shares of land.[37] Taiping officials proposed that footbinding be banned, declaring, "When men and women all become useful, nothing can stop our country from being strong."[38] The proposed gender rearrangements of households, labor, inheritance, and examination eligibility, even if short-lived or not widely implemented, drew horrified attention from the educated elite in Jiangnan. These measures also have dominated much subsequent writing about the Taiping movement.

But with respect to many aspects of gendered behavior, Taiping rule was more conventional. Adultery, prostitution, and rape were forbidden. Soldiers were banned from hiring women to wash or sew their clothing, on the assumption that illicit sex would surely follow.[39] Violators were to be decapitated. The 1851 Taiping Ode for Youth instructed daughters-in-law to be gentle, yielding, and not quarrelsome, and wives to practice the Three Obediences (to father, husband, and grown son), just as specified in Confucian instructions about family relations.[40] A proclamation aimed at maintaining military discipline from the early 1850s laid out a completely familiar division of labor: men were to engage in scholarship, farming, labor, and commerce; women in needlework and cooking.[41]

Official Taiping gender ideology probably had less impact on daily life than another feature of the Taiping era: its relentless violence. The civil war between the Taiping and Qing forces was more protracted and bloody than the contemporaneous American Civil War.[42] Between twenty and thirty million people died in the course of the Taiping civil war: some at the hands of the Taiping forces, others as a result of the Qing reconquest.[43] Both sides besieged cities and starved out the civilian inhabitants, regardless of their political sympathies. Both sides robbed civilians to provision their troops, kidnapped and raped women, and meted out lethal conqueror's justice to civilians suspected of collaboration with the enemy. Thriving urban centers endured siege and counter-siege accompanied by starvation and cannibalism. They were looted by forces who were supposed to be defending their cities, and endured violence by camp followers who lacked the discipline of the main Taiping and Qing armies. In Canton, the Qing executed tens of thousands of suspected Taiping sympathizers in 1853–54.[44] Graphic accounts circulated in the world press described Qing forces disemboweling pregnant women and murdering infants and mothers who had been taken prisoner in the Taiping areas.[45] Numerous settlements lost half or more of their population and were reduced to rubble-strewn ghost towns overgrown with weeds. Survivors became homeless refugees, wandering the devastated landscape or fleeing to distant cities where they might be taken in by relatives, as Yang Shuhui's poem (see box 2.1) suggests. In 1862, Shanghai alone absorbed 1.5 million refugees displaced by the civil war.[46]

BOX 2.1.
Yang Shuhui Writes to Her Widowed Sister-In-Law

The Yang sisters of Changsha, where much Taiping fighting took place, wrote poems about their lives as refugees. One sister, Yang Shuhui 杨书蕙, wrote of the Taiping battles that displaced them. A poem addressed to her younger brother's widow read in part:

> Shaking the earth, the war has begun,
> Calamity and suffering fill my eyes with anguish.
> The feathered missive flies northward
> Troops and horses race to the south. . . .
> In these strange places I've sojourned for so long,
> My old courtyard—when will I return to it?
> Heaven and earth together shed tears,
> Kinsmen and family, separated so far!
> The land around me overgrown with thorns,
> In desolate mountains we seek sustenance from wild ferns.
> Thinking of you, and failing to meet
> And thinking too how much I miss my mother.

Source: Susan Mann, "The Lady and the State: Women's Writings in Times of Trouble during the Nineteenth Century," in *The Inner Quarters and Beyond: Women Writers from Ming through Qing*, ed. Grace S. Fong and Ellen Widmer (Leiden; Boston: Brill, 2010), 299–300.

This violence affected everyone in combat areas, but it altered the lives of women in particular ways. In the early 1860s, as the Taiping forces were conquering many Jiangnan cities, foreign observers wrote of mass suicides by women who drowned, hanged, poisoned, or stabbed themselves rather than risk being raped by the invaders. In Hangzhou it was said that the number of women dead had reached fifty thousand to seventy thousand in a single week. Similar reports of women's suicidal martyrdom surfaced from Yangzhou and Suzhou.[47] Women displaced by the fighting also considered suicide (see box 2.2), appealing to local philanthropists for support as their menfolk were killed or captured and their property lost.

As communities rebuilt themselves after the conflict, they reasserted traditional gender norms, honoring the chastity suicides of local women. In their commemorations, the individual fates of women who resisted sexual assault were transformed into expressions of Woman, exemplar of the orthodox values of loyalty and chastity. Thousands of women were listed as righteous martyrs in local histories, a martyrdom that was retrospectively labeled as a statement of loyalty to the Qing dynasty. Women became "adjunct honorees" in shrines built by the state to honor the war

BOX 2.2.
The Widow Dong Baohong Threatens Suicide

Dong Baohong lived in the Yangzhou area from 1820 until her death, which may have occurred in 1857. She was widowed at about the age of thirty. In 1856 Dong showed up at a local shelter for chaste widows run by local literati and explained her intention to commit suicide:

I was born in a household of Confucian scholars, and learned the Odes and the Rites when I was young. During the twenty-second year of the Daoguang reign (1842), I was married to Zheng Yue. After nine years (1851), my husband died. On his deathbed he told me to remain a widow in the household because my father-in-law was then travelling outside, and if the latter returned home, I could serve him as if I were his son. I respectfully marked the words of my late husband and dared not to forget. When it came to the third year of the Xianfeng reign (1853), rebels from Guangdong took the city of Jinling (Nanjing), and my father-in-law was trapped there. I had given birth to a daughter, but she had died some years ago. I was therefore all by myself and had no one to turn to. Long I had been thinking of following my husband to the land of the dead! It was only because of the thought of how much he had counted on me to serve his father (that I did not do so). Whenever I met someone who returned from the rebel-taken city, I would enquire about my father-in-law, and someone told me that he was still there. Therefore, although I wished to end my life, I could not allow myself to do so immediately. After the rebels took the city of Yi (Yizheng), I fled to Liu Town. During the following year, the rebels took Liu Town, and I had nowhere else to go but to return to the city of Yi. While my husband was alive, he held a minor government post and we had little savings. Having been plundered time and again by the rebels, what was left with me was all gone. Plus, the famine led the price of rice to soar, and stores were all shut down. The reason, indeed, that I would rather endure hunger than end my life was that my father-in-law might still someday come home. However, he did not in the end, and my situation turned even worse. There was this elderly kinsman from my husband's lineage who constantly insulted me with filthy words. I knew that I could not remain a widow in this household any longer and tried to hang myself, yet did not succeed. Since then, I have been even more determined to commit suicide. The fact that I would choose to do it now rather than on the day when my husband died may give rise to mistaken conjectures. Therefore I list here my reasons so as to inform the Hall for Chaste Widows. If, someday, my father-in-law does come back and I am not here to serve him, I know that I have no excuse for my unfilial behavior, yet perhaps people will understand and forgive me.

The author of this article speculates that Dong had lost all of her property in flights back and forth, was having trouble surviving, and was using the threat of suicide to resist pressure to remarry, which may have been the source of the insults from her husband's relative. She succeeded in winning a small stipend from the local chaste widow shelter so that she would not be pressured to remarry.

Source: Binbin Yang, "Disruptive Voices: Three Cases of Outspoken 'Exemplary Women' from Nineteenth-Century China," *Nannü* 14 (December 2012): 247–51. Translation slightly modified.

dead, or were commemorated in separate institutions specifically for "Chaste and Righteous" women.[48]

Such women's fortitude was celebrated in graphic terms. Yu Zhi's 1864 *Tears for Jiangnan* featured drawings of Taiping soldiers assaulting partially clothed women. In one picture a woman bravely refused the sexual advances of a Taiping warrior, even though her likely fate was clear from the decapitated female corpse at their feet.[49] Another work commemorated a gentry wife who bit a Taiping soldier after he killed her husband, and would not let go even as Taiping troops sliced her to death.[50] A third woman was reportedly killed for defying soldiers who tried to send her to the gender-segregated Women's House, proclaiming, "I am a gentry-man's wife. I know only death. I know not this so-called Women's House!"[51] Local histories featured stories of heroic women who had guarded their virtue unto death, reporting that miraculously their corpses had not decayed after their suicides, remaining "as if alive, eyes and face undimmed."[52]

This celebration of women's virtue even extended to women who had resisted assaults from Qing soldiers rather than Taiping rebels. Huang Shuhua, for instance, was sixteen when Qing soldiers killed her family during the recapture of Nanjing from the Taiping forces, although her family members were not Taiping sympathizers. A soldier abducted her and took her back to his home village in Hunan, intending to marry her. Before he could do so, according to later accounts praising her loyalty and chastity, she wrote her story and several poems, hid one copy on her body, and pasted another to the wall. Then she killed the soldier who had abducted her and hanged herself. Although she had killed a Qing soldier, not a Taiping rebel, the local history praised her as a chaste martyr.[53]

These accounts were testaments to the durability of orthodox values for women in a world gone terribly awry. Women's virtue was a central means by which survivors memorialized their dead and made sense of the material and psychic losses they had suffered. Perhaps it seemed to them that recognizing women's loyalty could redeem and restore the world they had lost. If women had deliberately given their lives to preserve the social order, these accounts implied, surely life in the post-Taiping world could be rebuilt and renewed along old familiar lines.[54]

Other rebellions in China's northwestern and southwestern border-lands had their own trajectories and aftermaths. What they had in common with the Taiping civil war was the violence endured by civilians and the particular effects on women. The Panthay Rebellion (1856–73), an uprising of Muslim Yunnanese (Hui) rebels in the southwest province of Yunnan, was provoked by Han migration into the province and years of officially sponsored Han attacks on men, women, and children in the Hui community, which comprised 10 percent of the province's population. It concluded with a violent Qing assault on the civilian population of Dali in which at least ten thousand died. Women and children were routinely mentioned among the victims of these campaigns, and those women who survived were reportedly sold off to the Han forces to become servants and concubines or to be resold to traffickers. More than a century after the rebellion, Hui in the city of Dali in the 1990s recounted stories of the massacres, passed down through generations, in which women and children were lured out of hiding after the defeat, only to be murdered and thrown into a nearby river.

As with the post-Taiping landscape, women were also credited with reviving the community, this time from the side of the defeated rebels. Stories focused on the heroism of women who were sold into concubinage and threatened suicide unless they were permitted to keep some of the children from the union. Such women reportedly regenerated their communities and raised their children as Muslims. Young women are also credited in these stories with becoming the concubines of powerful Qing officials and convincing them that some Muslim families should be spared.[55]

China's mid-century rebellions permanently altered the late Qing world. Jiangsu and Zhejiang, the economic heart of the empire, saw millions dead and displaced. Shanghai, where foreign business interests were headquartered, became the vibrant new economic center of the region, while cities such as Suzhou and Yangzhou struggled to recover. True, the dynasty restored its formal authority over the empire and showed considerable vigor for almost a half century before its final collapse in 1911. But the regional armies the Qing court had authorized when it was desperate to quell the uprisings grew into decentralized sources of power. The examination system, disrupted by the years of Taiping occupation, was no longer the primary means to upward social mobility, as new kinds of scientific, technical, and military knowledge became increasingly important. In the wake of the mid-century wars, provincial and local elites expanded their own public roles, taking on many functions that an increasingly beleaguered central authority could not handle. One of their concerns was the abduction of widows to become the wives of men who were facing a shortage of women in the post-Taiping years. Elites proposed to address this problem by establishing widow homes where women could maintain their chastity.[56] Unaddressed was the broader demographic and economic crisis behind the gender imbalance.

RETHINKING INFANTICIDE

Another topic of discussion among the post-Taiping elite was infanticide, primarily practiced on infant girls.[57] The Qing legal code did not classify infanticide as a crime, but elites across the empire had long criticized the practice. A famous eighteenth-century essay against drowning daughters was often distributed at civil service examination sites as a way to reach male scholars so that they would spread the criticism in their home communities. Infanticide was widely acknowledged as a gendered act: one of the most common Chinese terms for infanticide was "drowning girls." Members of the elite were not troubled by gender hierarchy and discrimination, only by the lethal form they took. Girls were valued for their filiality and their future roles as wives and mothers, but it was taken for granted that only sons could carry on the family line and that a wife's primary duty was to bear a male heir for her husband's family. In this context, elites regarded female infanticide not as a form of discrimination, but as a practical, if tragic, folk custom produced by ignorance, poverty, and the high cost of equipping daughters with a dowry.

Reformers believed that infanticide could best be eradicated through moral suasion, infant protection societies to provide financial assistance to poor parents, and foundling homes. The Taiping-era reformer Yu Zhi condemned female infanticide through village lectures. He also wrote a play for performance at temple fairs that featured a drowned daughter returning as a snake demon from the underworld to kill her mother and brother.[58] The tales in which a person of high morals intervened to prevent a family from killing its newborn daughter reinforced the gender hierarchy: typically, the person who had spoken out was rewarded by giving birth to a son, or by marrying off her daughter to a scholar who achieved success in the examination system.[59]

Missionaries, whose work in nineteenth-century China is discussed later in this chapter, were active in framing Western perceptions of infanticide. A Catholic publication in France called China a place where "savage mothers throw into the public road and expose to the teeth of cruel beasts the child whose sex should inspire the greatest compassion."[60] The Catholic Church mobilized European and North American children in the 1860s and 1870s to save Chinese children by donating their pennies monthly through the Holy Childhood Association (l'Oeuvre de la Sainte Enfance) to support Catholic work in China.[61] The money went to support orphanages, but as we will see below, the Catholic practice of collecting very sick children in order to baptize them could lead to unintended results.

In 1885 the North China Branch of the Royal Asiatic Society, made up of men who were amateur foreign scholars of China, held a symposium on infanticide. They took Chinese writings condemning the practice as proof that infanticide was common. Bone-collection towers for corpses of the poor, which were philanthropic Chinese projects intended to ensure everyone a proper burial, were incorrectly depicted as places where children, alive or dead, might be deposited to die. Statistics on infanticide were unavailable, but Westerners hazarded estimates anyway, based on anecdotal evidence. American Baptist missionary Adele M. Fielde reported that in her own area around Swatow in eastern Guangdong, forty Chinese women who spoke with her reported ending the lives of a total of seventy-eight daughters, although one of the missionaries in North China she consulted believed that the incidence of infanticide was less than one in one hundred births.[62]

Nevertheless, decisions made by individual families—to drown a newborn daughter, to sell a girl child or a teenager—produced a noticeable aggregate effect in distressed areas. In Xuzhou prefecture in Jiangsu, for instance, the average ratio of men to women in 1874 was 129:100.[63] Such skewed ratios made it impossible for many poor families to find wives for their sons. This meant that about one-fifth of the male population was consigned to the status of "bare sticks," men without stable family networks who were feared as a threat to local social order and safety.[64] By the late nineteenth century, particularly in the treaty ports, Chinese reformers had begun to expand their own analyses of infanticide, reframing the drowning of daughters as a threat to China's population that would need to be addressed in order to strengthen the nation.[65]

WOMEN IN THE TREATY PORTS

In the emergent urban environment of China's nineteenth-century treaty ports, women found new opportunities for study and work, contended with new dangers, and helped to shape new ideas about what women should do and be. The number of treaty ports expanded from an initial five opened by 1852, to nineteen by 1860, and thirty-eight by the beginning of the twentieth century.[66] Foreigners of many nationalities mingled in these settlements, governing and taxing the areas they controlled through municipal councils, creating architecturally distinct enclaves, and constructing amenities such as streetcars, streetlamps, running water, and electric power.[67] They established police forces and built churches and clinics. They published newspapers, chief among them Shanghai's *North China Herald*, which first appeared in 1850 and was distributed to other treaty ports as their number expanded across China.[68] In 1872 an Englishman founded the Chinese-language newspaper *Shenbao* in Shanghai, which became a critical source of information for elites across China.

But the treaty ports were not transplanted foreign cities: their aggregate population was overwhelmingly Chinese. According to 1906 statistics collected by the Customs Office, the total population of the treaty ports was 38,597 foreigners and 6,917,000 Chinese.[69] Shanghai in particular grew rapidly in the mid-nineteenth century, its population swelled by an influx of refugees from the Taiping civil war and other mid-century disturbances. By the turn of the century, more than half a million Chinese lived in the Shanghai foreign settlements.[70]

Men predominated among the Chinese merchants, workers, and sailors who migrated to these expanding cities. But by the late nineteenth century, many Chinese women were drawn to the treaty ports. A small number attended foreign-run schools: from the 1840s on, missionary schools for girls were opened in Ningbo, Shanghai, Fuzhou, Guangzhou, Xiamen, Tianjin, and Beijing. They initially attracted very small numbers of girls, mostly from poor families, but when they expanded their curricula in the 1880s to include instruction in English, physical education, and other topics, enrollment increased, and girls from better-off families began to attend. The Shanghai McTeiyre School for Girls, founded by Methodists in the 1890s, was one such institution.[71]

Other young women found work in new factories. Shanghai did not become an industrial manufacturing center or a major employer of women factory workers until the twentieth century, but from the 1860s on foreign firms operated mechanized silk filatures to process the silk produced in Jiangnan; and women, at first drawn from area villages, formed part of the workforce there.[72] Still other women provided domestic service to the foreigners. The growing number of foreign children in the settlement were cared for by Chinese wet nurses and nannies, often photographed with their young charges.[73]

Many foreign merchants and officials began relationships with local women whom they usually purchased and kept as mistresses, producing offspring who sometimes were sent to Europe or the United States, or to specially established boarding schools, for their education. The census of 1900 in the International Settlement listed three hundred such children. A man might make provisions in his will for his children and their Chinese mother, but marriage between Chinese and Euro-Americans was rare and not generally accepted. (Censure was even more pronounced for foreign women who married Chinese men.) Foreign men working lower-class jobs also frequently lived with local women, but such women had no claims on their property after death, because the relationships were not legally recognized.[74]

Treaty ports could be dangerous places for unescorted women. European residents of late nineteenth-century Tianjin noted that women stayed off of streets full of military men, swindlers, and toughs. Local officials worried about girls and women being kidnapped and sold, a practice endemic even in normal times that got worse in times of chaos.[75]

The treaty ports were also hospitable homes for brothels, and in 1864 the Municipal Council that governed Shanghai's International Settlement licensed 270 of them.[76] The British began health inspections of

Shanghai prostitutes in 1877.[77] Shanghai's foremost illustrated pictorial, published every ten days beginning in 1884, featured short vignettes of urban life illustrated by lithographs. Prominent among them were prostitutes ranging from high-class courtesans to obstreperous streetwalkers, all of them highly visible in the public urban spaces of Shanghai's foreign settlements.[78]

Courtesans, the women who served as companions skilled in song and conversation, were not sexually available to their patrons without extended cultivation of a relationship and complex indirect financial negotiations. The Shanghai pictorial offered glimpses of life in a courtesan house: drawings of customers being ejected from a brothel because they could not pay the fees, men eloping with their favored courtesans, courtesans riding in rickshaws and carriages and hansom cabs, and women cross-dressing as men, sometimes in European garb. These images of courtesans—and their experiments with clothing, new forms of transportation, and interior decorating—introduced new Western goods and practices to the reading public.[79] The courtesan houses were embedded in Shanghai's rapidly expanding lane neighborhoods, which combined residential and commercial buildings. Courtesans in public—not only in rickshaws and carriages, but also restaurants, gardens, and theaters—became an important presence in new forms of urban space.[80]

Reconstructing how women experienced their own daily lives in the nineteenth-century courtesan houses is difficult. The organization of such houses often relied on kinship terms, with the madam as the "mother," the courtesans as her daughters and as sisters to each other, and the servants as aunts and sisters. The familial language masked economic relationships in which the madam and servants relied upon the "daughters" to generate income, and the "daughters" had little say over their initial sale into the house or their eventual exit into concubinage or marriage.[81] But if courtesans lacked control over their own conditions of work, they were nevertheless prominent cultural figures. Famous courtesans enjoyed celebrity status, and their appearances and liaisons filled the pages of the urban tabloid press. The press and late nineteenth-century novels are full of stories in which courtesans cultivated wealthy patrons who might buy them out, or made liaisons with poor but handsome youths who could not afford to do so. These accounts were often quite critical of courtesan behavior, warning that a man could have his pockets emptied and his heart broken by a beautiful but duplicitous courtesan.

The writers of such accounts were men from the Jiangnan elite who had been displaced to Shanghai by the Taiping and other disturbances, or drawn to Shanghai by the possibility of new careers in business, journalism, and literature. Courtesan houses provided a comfortable venue for male literati and merchants to socialize with one another—a

Photo 2.3. Shanghai courtesan, late nineteenth century
Source: Getty Research Institute, Los Angeles (2003.R.22)

home away from home—where they could conduct banquets, rest, or
engage in casual conversation. In writing by these men, the figure of the
courtesan provided a powerful means of describing and assimilating
the changes in their own status and in the wider society of the treaty
ports.[82] The writers often expressed their nostalgia for the vanishing
world of the literate poetry-writing courtesan, whom they saw as being

supplanted by scheming manipulative courtesans on the one hand and crass streetwalkers on the other.

Not all women in the sex trades were courtesans. Lower-class prostitutes, many of them rural migrants who sold sex to the Chinese transport workers, craftsmen, and dock workers of Shanghai, were known colloquially as "pheasants." They were portrayed as voracious monsters or as pitiful victims of trafficking and abuse. Warning that men could easily be assaulted or victimized by such women, illustrators and writers also conveyed their concern that respectable women, such as women workers in a silk filature, might be harassed on the streets by men who mistook them for prostitutes.[83]

MISSIONARIES, FOOTBINDING, AND WOMEN'S EDUCATION

"The Chinese woman does not walk in the street with her husband; she does not eat with him, but takes what is left after the men of the family have finished their meal; she has no legal right to anything whatever, apart from her male relatives," wrote Adele Fielde in 1887.[84]

Among all of the foreigners who flocked to China in the late nineteenth century, Christian women missionaries were the most active in creating new knowledge about Chinese women. Natives mainly of Europe and North America, Protestant missionaries, in particular, credited Christianity for women's attainment of high status in their own societies,[85] and this status was one of the benefits they hoped to promote in China.[86] Missionaries were among the first foreigners to live and work in the countryside far beyond the treaty ports. Many of the English-language books about nineteenth-century China were written by missionaries.[87] The texts they produced for their home audiences—aimed in part at garnering financial support for their work—emphasized the benighted condition of Chinese girls and women. They described and denounced infanticide (as discussed earlier in this chapter), footbinding, concubinage, and arranged marriage. Their writings profoundly shaped worldwide perceptions of the status of Chinese women.

But missionaries had important effects in China as well. First, they brought formal education to a limited number of rural girls and women, initially those from poor families. Missionaries established a network of primary and secondary schools that expanded by the early twentieth century to include a number of colleges. By that time, Christianity had begun to attract upper-class converts, drawn in part by opportunities for education in English and other potentially useful subjects.[88] Second, missionaries converted significant numbers of Chinese women of all classes to Christianity. The activities these women took up—preaching, teaching, practicing medicine—altered the gendered boundaries of acceptable work. Third, missionaries voiced a critique of women's situation that was taken up and elaborated by non-Christian reformers. Their criticisms became part of the Chinese conversation about how women's status might weaken or strengthen the nation.

After the first Opium War, missionaries were permitted to evangelize in and near the five treaty ports. Following the second Opium War and the burning of the Summer Palace, the 1860 Convention of Peking permitted foreigners to travel anywhere in the empire, effectively granting missionaries the right to live, buy property, and proselytize throughout China.[89] For Catholics, this was a return rather than a new beginning. Catholic missionaries had been active in China from the late sixteenth century until 1724, when Christianity was banned and the missionaries expelled. Women converts took the lead in proselytizing other women. Catholicism's long history in China was reflected in its large number of believers: two hundred thousand in the early part of the nineteenth century, perhaps three hundred thousand by 1860, and almost half a million by 1881, most of them in rural areas.[90]

Much Catholic work in China, as suggested earlier, centered on rescuing children from potential infanticide. The Holy Childhood Association gave grants to Chinese bishops contingent on the number of children they had collected. Children were often handed over by parents who signed a contract relinquishing their rights to the child. Infants were farmed out to wet nurses until they were weaned. Those who survived were raised in Catholic orphanages, where it was customary to bind the girls' feet and to find husbands for them when they were grown. When a bride set out from the orphanage for her husband's house, she was expected to engage in the same ritual weeping as a bride leaving her mother's home. The families of many young men competed for these young women, because marriage to an orphanage girl cost much less than a standard bride price, and prospective families knew that such a girl had been strictly brought up. The prospect of an inexpensive bride may have been an incentive for young men to convert to Catholicism.[91]

Protestant missionaries were new to evangelizing in China, but their numbers increased steadily across the second half of the nineteenth century. Women played a prominent role in this expansion, outnumbering men by the 1870s.[92] Of 1,296 Protestant missionaries active in 1890, 707 were women, 316 of them unmarried.[93] Seventeen years later, the number of women missionaries had almost tripled.[94] Protestant missionaries emphasized practical activities such as education, medicine, and social welfare work as means to convey their religious message.

The challenges in reaching Chinese women were substantial. Most of the rural women whom missionaries initially encountered were poor.

Protestants regarded literacy as necessary to spiritual growth,[95] and yet in 1887 missionary Adele Field estimated that perhaps one in a thousand Chinese women could read.[96] Lottie Moon, a Southern Baptist missionary who worked in Shandong in the 1880s, found some women "eager to learn" but most with "minds utterly vacant." She blamed this state of affairs on rural men who told girls and women that they were "too stupid to learn." Rural women could be extremely eloquent, Moon observed, but this usually took the form of defending their own interests through the use of "tongue and temper."[97] When missionary Helen Nevius tried to convince her neighbor, Mrs. Liang, that cursing people was wrong and that controlling her temper would help her go to heaven, Mrs. Liang replied that "reviling people was the only earthly pleasure she had, and that she considered hell fair enough as a possible payment."[98]

But how best to raise the status of women? One of the main obstacles, in the view of missionaries, was the long-standing custom of footbinding.

In the late imperial period, footbinding was taken for granted as something mothers did for their daughters, a prerequisite for a respectable marriage[99] and adult womanhood. Historians have argued that the concealment of both the bound feet and the binding process was integral to making the feet desirable to men.[100] The bound feet of respectable women were conventionally concealed by leggings and artfully embroidered shoes. Perhaps because of this aura of privacy, or its association with personal hygiene, or even the fact that it was regarded as such an ordinary activity, not much was written about footbinding before the late 1800s. Educated men sometimes alluded to the erotic allure of bound feet in their poems. And one satiric novelist, Li Ruzhen (1763–1830), created an imaginary world in which a male traveler suddenly finds himself in a kingdom of gender inversion: the women are in charge of political affairs, and the men are objects of adornment whose feet are tightly bound. But in the nonfictional world of late imperial China, no rituals, prayers, or songs associated with footbinding were recorded. Nor were directions on how best to bind the feet, or the thoughts or responses of the mothers who performed it and the daughters who underwent it.[101] What we know from Chinese sources about the history and meaning of footbinding largely comes from the anti-footbinding movement of the late nineteenth and early twentieth centuries.[102]

In contrast, in writings produced by missionaries and other foreigners, bound feet became an object of horrified fascination.[103] Foreign observers struggled to make sense of footbinding in several ways. Some foreigners hypothesized that it was practiced among the elite as a sign that their women did not have to engage in manual labor.[104] Others, however, observed that poor rural women labored at spinning and weaving, pulled boats on towpaths, hoed cotton and wielded sickles, all with bound feet.[105]

Medical missionaries brought techniques of scientific investigation to bear, detailing how footbinding deformed the leg, covered the skin with cracks and sores, and altered the posture. An 1835 report in the Canton-based missionary journal *Chinese Repository* quoted a Western doctor who had dissected a bound foot taken from the corpse of a Canton woman, adding a sketch of a bound foot's bone structure. Medical missionaries emphasized the pain that the procedure caused to young girls.[106] The Reverend John Macgowan, who arrived in China in 1860, taught that if the body belonged to God, it ought not to be mutilated.[107] At the 1890 General Conference of Protestant Missionaries in China, one Reverend Noyes characterized footbinding as a form of "inhuman, refined cruelty."[108] By the turn of the century, footbinding had been exposed in photographs, X-rays, and detailed textual descriptions, destroying its association with sequestered, respectable women.[109]

When missionaries discussed footbinding, the theme they raised most often was its deleterious social effect on women. As Adele Fielde put it,

> The evils that accrue from this custom are very great. It makes cripples of nearly half the population, and adds immensely to the misery of the poverty-stricken multitudes. It disables women from supporting themselves and from caring for their children, and is one of the causes of the great prevalence of infanticide. It renders women too weak to keep their houses clean, and makes their homes filthy and cheerless. It incapacitates woman for travelling, and keeps her and her thoughts in the narrowest of spheres.[110]

Fielde's linkage of footbinding and women's low status would soon become a standard feature in public discussions of footbinding among many Chinese, Christian or not.

Missionaries encouraged women converts to unbind their own feet and not to bind the feet of their daughters, and they sometimes required girls to unbind their feet before they could enter mission schools.[111] They urged young Chinese Christian men to marry women with unbound feet, and growing networks of Christian families began to arrange marriages among their children, removing footbinding as a criterion for a good match.[112] Nevertheless, missionaries sometimes tolerated footbinding among their students so that respectable families would send their daughters to a Christian school.[113]

Missionaries began to hold classes for girls and women six decades before the Qing dynasty started to experiment with girls' schools in the first decade of the twentieth century.[114] Among their most significant accomplishments was teaching basic literacy to rural girls who otherwise would have had no access to formal education. Beginning with standard Chinese books such as the *Three-Character Classic* and the *Hundred Names*, they proceeded through the *Five Books*, augmented with translations of

Pilgrim's Progress, the Bible, and religious tracts.[115] In 1863, Helen Nevius published the *Mandarin Catechism* (Yesu jiao), which Protestant missionaries taught all over North China into the twentieth century.[116] Later, girls' school curricula were broadened to include history, geography, health, biology, music, physical education, and English.[117] In Fuzhou, a particularly lively center of Christian education, girls could attend elementary day schools in their home communities, then go on to boarding schools in the county seats and colleges in the major cities.[118]

The explicit aim of these girls' schools was to train Christian wives and mothers.[119] Even as they pushed the point that women were equal to men, missionaries placed great emphasis on teaching girls how to cook, sew, and keep house.[120] As Adele Fielde put it, "Chinese mothers will influence the lives and characters of their children far more than any foreign missionary can. If we gain the wives and mothers of this generation we shall have almost secured the next."[121] Missionaries found that when girls reached early adolescence, parents often wanted to withdraw their daughters from school to marry, but they raised no objections to an arranged marriage if the future groom was a Christian.[122] Some young women students, however, did not have marriage on their minds, and welcomed the independence that a mission education could provide.[123] Young women who graduated from mission schools often remained there to teach, establishing a new career track available to Chinese Protestant women.[124] By the end of the century, missionary colleges offering English-language instruction, music, and other subjects drew students from among the daughters of the wealthy; the girls' parents had begun to regard proficiency in English as enhancing both the career options and the marriage prospects of their daughters.[125] And by 1913, Christian brides in Fuzhou were prominently displaying their diplomas on a pole for all to see as part of the dowry procession that transported their goods to the homes of their new husbands.[126]

Missionary efforts targeted adult women as well as children and teenagers. In the nineteenth century, missionary women produced textbooks and fiction in Chinese, and Christian journals aimed at women readers also appeared.[127] By the turn of the twentieth century, women missionaries such as Presbyterian Ada Haven Mateer expanded the literature to include more complex accounts of who a modern Chinese Christian woman should be. Mateer's 1897 book, *The Christian Home in China* (the Chinese title was Collected Pearls of Domestic Learning), included instruction on companionate marriage, child rearing, and hygiene. Helen Nevius in 1902 published her adaptation of the Confucian *Four Books for Women*, taking out all praise of polygamy, chastity suicide, and ancestor worship, Christianizing some of the references, and eliminating a woman's ritual obligation to follow first her father, then her husband, and later her son. These books were meant both for the expanding numbers of girls in Christian secondary schools and for a broader educated reading audience of Christians.[128]

Women, relatively secluded and illiterate as they were, could only be reached by other women, and so foreign women missionaries worked hard to convert Chinese women,[129] training some of them as "Bible women." Many of these were widows who had experienced significant personal hardships before converting. By 1900, forty schools existed to train them. The women learned basic literacy, some math and geography, and how to retell Bible stories. Bible women were freer to move around the landscape than unmarried women or wives with heavy domestic burdens. They received a small salary and travel expenses to visit villages, make house calls, and engage in itinerant preaching. At first they traveled with Western women missionaries, translating and making arrangements for them, but later they began to go out on their own. Some became eloquent public speakers.[130]

As Protestant work in China developed, Chinese Christian women took on many more roles in local churches. Sometimes they married Chinese ministers and took on major responsibility for pastoral work. Women congregants taught Sunday school, led the choir, and attended services. Records of annual missionary conferences show them running meetings, speaking, debating, and voting.

Photo 2.4.   Bible women, south China, ca. 1899–1909

Source: René Antoine Nus. Postcard. China Baptist Publication Co., Canton, China. Reproduced in *Virtual Shanghai*, http://www.virtualshanghai.net/Photos/Images?ID=32818.

Chinese women Christians also became physicians and hospital work-ers, teachers, administrators, and social workers.[131] By 1905, one-third of China's three hundred medical missionaries were women,[132] reflecting in part the fact that Chinese women were reluctant to be treated by male physicians.[133] This led missionaries to establish programs for training women nurses, as well as a smaller number of women physicians.[134] Perhaps the most famous among the latter group were Shi Meiyu (Mary Stone) and Kang Cheng (Ida Kahn, also known as Kang Aide). Kang had been adopted by Gertrude Howe, an American missionary, and Shi was the daughter of a Chinese Methodist minister.[135] The two girls attended a Methodist mission school in China, received medical degrees from the University of Michigan in 1896, and returned to China as medical mission-aries.[136] They went on to train Chinese women nurses and to transform the nursing profession from a demeaned occupation to one represented by the new Chinese term *hushi*, "one who guards and protects."[137] In 1897, the famous reformer Liang Qichao cited Kang and Shi as models of how Chinese women could take part in productive work and thus strengthen the nation, though he did not mention their Christianity.[138]

Missionary work in both city and countryside was punctuated by con-flict. Christian beliefs, both Catholic and Protestant, were not compatible with ancestor worship and concubinage. Chinese who converted were expected to rework family and community relationships in ways that could cause considerable friction and property disputes, particularly if missionaries intervened to support Chinese Christian converts. Foreign consuls and troops were sometimes brought in to support missionary activities and property claims, further inflaming local tensions.[139]

An overriding goal of Catholic missionaries in China was to make sure that every possible child was baptized in order to save its soul, and bish-ops approved payments to Catholics who baptized dying children. For this reason, Catholic clergy and nuns in charge of orphanages frequently paid small sums for children, taking in abandoned children who were desperately ill so that they could be baptized before they died. (During the North China famine, discussed in the next section, Catholics in Shanxi Province baptized 21,460 infants in a single year.) The high death rate among such children led to community suspicions that the foreigners were killing children to harvest their body parts for medicines or potions. The Tianjin Massacre of June 1870 began when a French consul fired at a Chinese official during a negotiation involving a Catholic orphanage, in which the Catholic nuns had been accused of kidnapping and murder. The result was an urban riot, the death of twenty-one foreigners (half of them French nuns) and several dozen Chinese Catholic converts, and a narrowly averted military conflict with France.[140]

FAMINE WITH A WOMAN'S FACE

Most girls and women were rural, poor, and vulnerable in particular gendered ways to catastrophe. In 1876, very little rain fell in the north China provinces of Shanxi, Shaanxi, Zhili, Henan, and Shandong. By 1877 the continuing drought had given rise to the most disastrous famine in Chinese history, which lasted until 1879.[141] Over the course of the North China famine, an estimated nine to thirteen million people died of starvation or diseases aggravated by malnutrition. One-third of Shanxi's population took to the road, desperately attempting to exit the huge drought-stricken area on foot and head for the north China city of Tianjin or other places where they might find work, beg, or qualify for relief.

The famine was closely watched by the Qing court, Chinese elites, and foreign missionaries. In publications and policy arguments, the famine quickly acquired a woman's face—a mother starving so that her son could live, a wife and children sacrificed by a husband so that his mother could live, a mother stealing food for herself and her children, a daughter-in-law whose in-laws threatened to eat her, a righteous widow starving to death rather than engage in improper behavior. The diary entry of missionary Timothy Richards, visiting Shanxi in 1877, read in part:

> Saw six dead bodies in half a day, and four of them were women: one in an open shed naked but for a string round her waist; another in a stream; one in the water half exposed above the ice at the mercy of wild dogs; another half clad in rags in one of the open caves at the roadside; another half eaten, torn by birds and beasts of prey. . . . Met another young man carrying his mother on his shoulders as her strength had failed.[142]

Most common of all was the recurrent image of young women by the side of the road, selling themselves at cut-rate prices as prostitutes or potential wives, or being transported south by the cartload for sale by traffickers in cities outside the famine zone. Some foreign observers noted that the option of being sold allowed women to survive the famine, perhaps even improving their chances over those of men. Of the hundreds of thousands of refugees who reached Tianjin, most appear to have been women and children.[143]

Observers assigned different meanings to these reports. Conservative moralists argued that a decline in filial piety and a rise in women's extravagant consumption and unchaste actions had offended Heaven and caused the famine. Opinion in the Qing court was divided between officials who saw famine relief as a primary imperial responsibility and members of the Self-Strengthening Movement who believed that meeting the foreign threat with military and economic projects had to be the top priority. To missionaries, the reports proved that women would never see an improvement in their status, and would always be vulnerable to being sold, unless China was Christianized.

These reports of catastrophe reinforced the view among Chinese merchants and literati that they needed to take action themselves rather relying only on imperial officials to deliver effective relief. In Tianjin, merchants originally from Jiangnan worked with government authorities to establish the Hall for Spreading Benevolence (*Guangren tang*) (see box 2.3). At the Hall several hundred widows, trafficked girls, adolescent women, and some boys (mainly orphans and sons of widows) could find simple lodging, basic clothing, and food. Boys were given vocational training, and girls and women were expected to work making towels, textiles, and embroidery. Strict limitations on their mobility aimed at ensuring that they would remain virtuous. Men unable to afford a bride could petition for a wife from among the orphan girls and daughters of widows, if they provided a guarantor and had the means to support a marriage.[144]

To a growing community of Chinese reformers, the trafficked women moving south were embodiments of China's weakness and the Qing dynasty's inability to protect and provide for its population. Up to this point, the sale of a woman by her family or traffickers had not generally been regarded as a problem, unless one party was misrepresented or deceived, or a woman was kidnapped or severely abused.[145] But in the

---

BOX 2.3.
How Zhao Xiang Was Trafficked

Zhao Xiang grew up fifty miles west of Tianjin. On a June night in 1880, yamen police making their nightly rounds "noted suspicious activity on the Purple Bamboo Forest docks. The police investigated and found two men hiding a girl inside a horse-cart. The girl was crying bitterly and appeared to have been abused. The police took the girl into their custody. According to her testimony, her parents had sold her as a concubine to a man named Gao Luoqi. Gao did not find her pleasing enough, so he in turn sold her to a man surnamed Zhang. Zhang took the girl to Tianjin, where he sold her to two men from [the southern province of] Fujian. When she cried because she missed her mother, the Fujian men beat her in an attempt to silence her. These men were preparing to ship Zhao Xiang to the South when the police intercepted them. During the questioning the girl constantly cried in a heartrending voice for her mother. She was not willing to return to her mother-in-law, but preferred instead to be sent back to her mother." While awaiting return to her parents, she was sent to the Hall for Spreading Benevolence.

Source: Tianjin dao Zheng to Guangren tang directors, GX 6/6/15 (July 21, 1880), GRT file 130-1-21, quoted in Rogaski 1997, 70, 88.

famine's wake, reformers began to regard these images of women for sale, now circulating throughout China and across the globe in newspapers and missionary publications, as an instance of national humiliation. They called upon a newly emergent reading public to save these women and thus to save China. Across the political spectrum, all of these groups— Qing rulers, literati, merchants, foreign missionaries, and reformers—increasingly linked the fate of women to the fate of a weakened China.

REBEL WOMEN AND MAGIC: SHINING RED LANTERNS

The nineteenth century ended with a series of dismal setbacks for Qing sovereignty. China lost a war with Japan in 1895 and ceded control of Taiwan to the victor. In the war's wake, foreign powers scrambled for spheres of influence on Chinese soil, and Chinese commentators warned that they were threatening to "carve China up like a melon."

The Boxer uprising of 1898–1900 began as a localized Shandong disturbance incited by flood and then drought, by weakened ties to the central state, and by foreign economic and missionary activities. It rapidly became a regional movement attacking missionaries, churches, Christian converts, and other establishments linked to the foreign powers.[146] As the Boxers spread across North China, armed with spears and swords, their fighters claiming that their bodies were immune to foreign weapons, the Qing rulers decided to support them in their attempt to expel the foreigners.

Operating in parallel to the bands of male Boxer fighters were a small number of teenaged girls known as the Shining Red Lanterns. Like the Boxers, they were said to have magical powers, which they deployed to protect the male fighters. "The Boxers would fight down below," recalled a former Boxer, "while the Red Lanterns would watch from above, appearing, suspended in the sky, no larger than a chicken's egg." From up in the air, it was said, they would throw swords to behead the enemy, send forth bolts of fire, and magically remove the screws from the enemy's artillery.[147] One account by a Chinese observer described their reception as they walked through the streets in the Tianjin area: "The people all burn incense and kneel in their presence; they call them female immortals and dare not look up at them. Even the Boxer bandits, when they encounter them, fall prostrate on their knees by the side of the road."[148] Decades after the Boxer movement, legends persisted about their daring exploits and magical feats (see box 2.4). Notable among these stories were several features: the Red Lanterns supposedly did not bind their feet; they could ignite a building merely by shouting "Burn!"; they had healing powers; they could leap up to Heaven, and from there they could reach Japan and reclaim the lands that Japan had stolen from China, putting their powers to a nationalist purpose.[149]

Photo 2.5.   Red Lanterns assist in siege of northern cathedral. Red Lanterns are at left rear (with lantern) and in crossfire.

Source: V. M. Alekseev, *Kitaiskaia narodnaia kartina: Dukhovnaia zhizn' starogo Kitaia v narodnykh izobrazheniiakh* (The Chinese folk picture: The spiritual life of old China in folk graphic art), (Moscow [Moskva], Nauka; Glav. red. vostochnoĭ lit-ry, 1966). Reprinted in Paul Cohen, *History in Three Keys: The Boxers as Event, Experience, and Myth* (New York: Columbia University Press, 1997), 140.

BOX 2.4.
Red Lanterns, Rumors, and Pollution: A Contemporary Account

In Tientsin there were societies of red lanterns, which consisted of young girls, who could walk in the air if they held a handkerchief in one hand and a red lantern in the other, which could help the Boxers to burn the missionary buildings.

Most of the people did not believe this, and considered it superstitious conduct, as others could not see them when they were walking in the air. . . .

A rumour said that some old women were sent out by the missionaries to put dirty blood on the doors of some of the houses, and that if it were not cleaned by the Boxers the inmates of the house would all become fatally mad. . . . Outside the Hai-Tai Gate two women, who were considered to put dirty blood on the door, were killed at once. A rumour said that the red lantern girls could pull down high-storied houses with thin cotton strings, and could set fire to the house simply by moving a fan, and also said they had the power of hanging a rock of several pounds on a hair.

Source: Chuan-Sen, a young Manchu who observed the Boxers in Beijing, quoted in George Lynch, *The War of the Civilizations, Being the Record of a "Foreign Devil's" Experiences with the Allies in China* (London: Longmans, 1901), 102–6.

But such female heroism was not available to all women. Paul Cohen argues that Red Lanterns, as teenagers who were not yet sexually active and perhaps had not yet reached the age of menarche, "were largely if not entirely free of the ritual uncleanness characteristic of adult women in China," and that this enabled others to attribute magical powers to them.[150] In contrast, adult women were regarded by the Boxers as sources of female pollution who could destroy Boxer magic. Women, especially if they were menstruating, were believed to undermine Boxer invulnerability, intentionally or unintentionally. This led to restrictions on the activities of ordinary women, including going to market, leaving their homes after dark, or splashing dirty water in their courtyards.[151]

The Boxer siege of the foreign legations in the capital of Beijing in summer 1900 brought violent military retaliation from an alliance of eight foreign powers. This gave rise to a great deal of civilian suffering, particularly in the cities of Beijing and Tianjin, and again some of it took particular gendered forms.[152] Contemporary reports recorded the grievances Beijing residents expressed about looting, killing of civilians, and rape, the latter being variously attributed to Russian and French forces.[153] War correspondent George Lynch reported, "A story has gone the round that when the French General was remonstrated with by his Allied colleagues about the frequent occurrence of disgraceful outrages upon women, he replied, 'It is impossible to restrain the gallantry of the French soldier.'"[154]

As in earlier conflicts, the imminent threat of rape provoked some women to commit suicide. "I was having a swim one evening," Lynch reports of his march northward with the troops, "when my foot struck against something, and, looking round, I saw the yellow-skinned cheek and shoulder of a corpse drifting past me. It rather put me off bathing for a day or two. It was generally understood that many of the corpses of women were of those who had committed suicide."[155] Later in his account of the expedition, *War of the Civilisations*, Lynch observed,

> News travels fast in China, and in advance of our march the people seemed to be thoroughly aware of the fate that probably awaited them. Although nearly the whole population cleared off before our advance, there were many, especially women, who could not get away, and who were unable to travel with their tiny, compressed feet, except in carts or on the backs of their servants. And it was principally these who, finally in the last extremity, committed suicide.[156]

In Tongzhou on the eastern outskirts of Beijing, 570 women hanged or drowned themselves as the foreigners advanced on the city. Unlike the earlier women martyrs of the Taiping conflict, however, these women were not remembered by all as paragons of chaste virtue, for attitudes among some elite Chinese had begun to change. The future woman revolutionary He Xiangning regarded the women's suicides as a national shame—one that need not have happened if men and women alike had concerned themselves with the fate of the nation before it arrived at their door in the form of a marauding foreign army.[157] In her commentary, women's virtue expressed through suicide was no longer a source of cultural cohesion. It was a sign of cultural trouble and a potential cause of national disintegration.

China's nineteenth-century crisis altered the lives of massive numbers of women. It also reshaped the ways that Chinese thinkers understood the proper practice of Womanhood and its relationship to national strength. Neither the uneven effects of imperialism nor the emergent languages of reform and revolution can be fully understood without attention to gender. By the turn of the twentieth century, chastity suicides as well as female infanticide, footbinding, the traffic in women, and a host of other problems were increasingly interpreted as symptoms of China's weakness.

3

Revolutionary Currents, 1895–1912

Between 1895 and 1911, the Qing empire came apart. In 1911 a revolutionary movement toppled China's last dynasty. The imperial system that had structured political life for more than two millennia was replaced in 1912 by an unstable republic, nominally led by an elected president, that rapidly degenerated into a conflict zone for warlords, while foreign pressure on the new nation intensified. A parliament was elected on the basis of voting rights limited to adult men of property and education, but power slipped into the hands of military men. During the same period, the treaty ports, especially Shanghai, continued to provide partial havens for critics and reformers, while the postal system, the telegraph, and the burgeoning periodical press helped to create something of a national space for the circulation of public opinion.

During these turbulent years, debate about women's status became a central feature of public life. Politically aware people asked how China could maintain its sovereignty and refashion itself into a strong modern nation. Their answers often centered on what came to be known as the "woman question." China was weak, these thinkers argued, in part because Chinese social practices kept women footbound, cloistered, unproductive, and ignorant. They characterized women as economic parasites, narrow-minded, preoccupied with trivialities, and quarrelsome. Drawing upon their knowledge of women's status in other parts of the world, they offered directions for what a modern woman should do and be.

Men inaugurated these discussions, but educated women also joined the debates. Some commentators saw women primarily as the mothers of citizens and opined that they should be educated—preferably at home—in a modicum of modern housekeeping and child-rearing skills so that they could raise the next generation properly. Others envisioned women not just as mothers of citizens but also as citizens in their own right: educated, physically fit, economically productive, and politically active. A few envisioned a global revolution: one that would free enslaved nations from the imperialist powers, workers and peasants from their masters, and women from men. These radicals called for an end to the treatment of women as property and analyzed the effect of the global spread of capitalism on women's living conditions. This was a period of great intellectual ferment and varied opinions. Many of the elements associated with later Chinese political movements first appeared during these years, including feminism, nationalism, eugenic concerns with strengthening China's people, and globally inflected visions of revolution.[1] Central to all of them was the idea that the status of women would help to determine the fate of China. All along the political spectrum, debates about what role women should play helped set the agenda for action on Chinese territory.

This chapter begins with a brief account of high politics between 1895 and 1912. Then it traces the ideas of seven people who saw the situation of women as key to the future of China in the world: male reformers Kang Youwei and Liang Qichao, anti-footbinding activist Alicia (Mrs. Archibald) Little, feminist publicist Xue Shaohui, anarcho-feminist He-Yin Zhen, revolutionary martyr Qiu Jin, and republican activist Tang Qunying. Together, they offer a glimpse of how elites at the end of the empire viewed the connections between social change, China's survival, and women's status. Because sources are scarce and scholars have much work left to do, this chapter has relatively little to say about the daily life of poor working women in cities and villages, who appeared in the public discussion mainly as oppressed subjects in need of uplift.

Each of the activists discussed here helped to create new institutions, ranging from political parties and journals to schools and commercial publications. In these venues women became publicly visible in unprecedented ways. They unbound their feet; attended school in China or abroad; read, wrote for, and published new journals; and discussed education, childbirth, foreign relations, working life, new modes of scientific inquiry, and commercialization. The public activities of these elite educated women marked a fundamental reshaping of what was considered appropriate womanly conduct. Key to public discussion by both men and women was the emergence of Woman as a central symbol in debates about the nation's future.

THE POLITICS OF CRISIS

For many centuries, Chinese elites had seen Japan as a peripheral king-dom. It thus came as a profound shock when, after several decades of energetic reform in Japan beginning with the 1868 Meiji Restoration, China lost a war to Japan in 1895. Defeated by Japan's larger and better-trained land forces and better-organized naval power, China lost Korea as a tributary state and ceded Taiwan, which became a Japanese colony. A subsequent series of land grabs by competing foreign powers deepened fears that the empire would be carved up. Japan's emergence as a suc-cessful and expansive empire convinced Chinese reformers that techni-cal and military strengthening was not enough; the situation demanded profound institutional change.

Chinese intellectuals, chief among them Yan Fu, began to translate the works of Thomas Huxley, Herbert Spencer, and others into Chinese, introducing social Darwinism and the concept of "survival of the fit-test" into the debate about China's survival.[2] During the Hundred Days' Reform of 1898, reformers convinced the young Guangxu emperor to inaugurate changes in education, the diplomatic corps, the military, and government promotion of economic development. But the Empress Dow-ager Cixi, one of the most powerful (and subsequently reviled) women in two millennia of imperial history, called a violent halt to the reforms.[3] She confined the young emperor, who was her nephew, to house arrest in the palace and executed several of the leading reformers, while others fled into exile. Among the exiles, with a price on their heads, were Kang Youwei and Liang Qichao.

In 1900 the Eight Nation Allied Expedition sent to defeat the Boxers (described in chapter 2) occupied Beijing and Tianjin, as the Empress Dowager and her entourage fled the capital. The punitive indemnity im-posed as part of the peace agreement further weakened the Qing capacity to rule. In 1904–5 the Qing dynasty was a bystander to a war fought on its own soil between Japan and Russia. Japan won, taking effective control of northeastern China, or Manchuria.

In what turned out to be the final decade of Qing rule, the Qing regime under the direction of the Empress Dowager introduced what was called the New Policies. Many of these were similar to the measures for which reformers had been exiled or executed a few years earlier. The civil ser-vice examination system, for more than a thousand years the accepted route for men to attain political office, was abolished in 1905. Replacing it were the beginnings of a modern school system, which included special schools opened for girls and young women.

As the basis for their new curriculum, Chinese intellectuals increasingly turned to Japanese translations and adaptations of Western works. Thousands of Chinese students flocked to Tokyo, and in smaller numbers to Europe and the United States.[4] Overseas Chinese communities became lively centers of political critique. Sun Yat-sen (Sun Zhongshan), born in a village near Guangzhou and educated in Honolulu and Hong Kong, founded his Revolutionary Alliance in Tokyo in 1905. For the first time, radical students and intellectuals from the different provinces of China came together on the basis of their shared belief that the Manchu Qing empire needed to be replaced by a modern republic. Qiu Jin and Tang Qunying, both in Tokyo at the time, were early members. A small but vocal group of anarchists was also active in Tokyo, among them the woman anarchist and feminist He-Yin Zhen.

In China, the Qing New Policy reforms proceeded. Opium use was suppressed, although never eliminated, and British opium imports were tapered off by diplomatic agreement.[5] New constitutional assemblies, new military forces, and new schools all became venues for political activity. Popular unrest intensified in the last decade of the Qing, partly because rural people resisted the new taxes imposed to pay for these reforms. But the revolution that transpired was not a mass uprising. It began in October 1911 with an unplanned and uncoordinated revolt among the Qing's own troops in Wuhan. After several months of violent conflict, the last emperor, a three-year-old child named Puyi, abdicated. Both the Qing dynasty, founded in 1644, and the much longer-lived dynastic system came to an end. The Republic of China was established on January 1, 1912.

The Republic got off to an unpromising start with Sun Yat-sen as the first president. Sun was well connected abroad but unaccustomed to militarized politics in China. He quickly handed over the presidency of the new Republic to Yuan Shikai, a former Qing military man. Women republican activists, Tang Qunying among them, were denied the vote. Many concluded that the republic was a failure and that further political action, along with a revolution in the culture, was necessary to save China.

LIANG QICHAO AND KANG YOUWEI: MEN WORRY ABOUT WOMEN

One of the first male reformers to articulate what became known as "the woman question" was Liang Qichao (1873–1929), a scholar, journalist, and political reformer in the last years of the Qing dynasty. Liang began his career as a child prodigy, passing the lowest level of the civil service examinations at eleven and the provincial level at the age of sixteen. He was twenty-two when China lost the war with Japan. In 1897 he published "On Women's Education" in a journal he had founded and edited. He argued that China was not faring well in the international realm because its women were uneducated:

> In this great wide world, there are some four hundred million people who have round heads and square toes [and are thus Chinese]. . . . There are also nearly two hundred million who have round heads but bent toes [i.e., women], among whom there are no officials, scholars, peasants, artisans, merchants, or soldiers; since ancient times they have never been educated. What is more, those officials, scholars, peasants, artisans, and merchants whose lives are almost like those of beasts are nevertheless ashamed of that fact; but women who are not officials, scholars, peasants, artisans, or merchants and are almost like beasts feel no such shame! Not only is this so, but all of humanity simply takes this state of affairs to be the natural, fixed order of things. Alas! How painful it is! . . . When I seek out the root causes of national weakness, I find that they inevitably lie in women's lack of education.[6]

Liang believed that if women were educated, they would teach their children well, determining "whether a nation will survive or be destroyed and whether it will prosper or languish in weakness."[7]

Even as Liang recognized women's centrality to the survival of China, he belittled or ignored much of their history. A minority of elite women, in fact, had been educated, some achieving great distinction as painters, calligraphers, and poets. But Liang derided ancient women poets for wasting their talents writing about "the beauty of the wind and moon, verses describing the flowers and the grasses, or poems lamenting the passage of spring or the loss of a friend. Such activities cannot be called learning." Liang declared that among the nation's two hundred million women, "all are consumers and none are producers," erasing with one phrase women's contributions to the household economy and production for the market. It was because they could not support themselves, he believed, that men treated them as slaves.[8] This misrecognition of women's labor is particularly puzzling in light of the experience of Liang's own mother. A 1915 article by Liang's daughter suggests that the labor of Liang's mother was largely responsible for the success of Liang and her brothers, and that she also taught embroidery to village women, prepared meals for ten hired laborers on the family estate, and did much of the housework.[9]

In Liang's view the problem of women's ignorance affected their personalities and behavior. Because they were uneducated, Liang said, women were prone to narrow-minded quarrels, making it impossible for men to enjoy domestic peace:

Today most women are disadvantaged because they know nothing about the world and therefore devote all their energy to fighting daily over trivial matters. . . . Because of this, among hundreds of millions of people and tens of millions of families throughout the land, there is not one family that is at peace inside and out. . . . And all these family conflicts begin with women— the mothers-in-law, daughters-in-law, and sisters-in-law. . . . Are women evil by nature? If you throw together a bunch of untamed, uncivilized hollow bodies and lock them up in one room, do you expect them to get along with each other? Unable to provide for themselves, these women become men's burden by wearing men down bodily and physically. Even worse, if the family is in chaos all day, causing a man to become agitated and upset as soon as he enters the room, the degree to which this undermines and exhausts his spirit and aspirations cannot be underestimated. Hence, even for an outstanding and charismatic hero, the mundane trivialities of domestic life can scarcely fail in a short time to confine and to undermine his ambition and talent. If so, women really are poison and men should not be united with them. Instead of ingesting and enjoying this poison, perhaps men should pay some attention to finding the antidote.[10]

Liang's teacher Kang Youwei, fifteen years older than Liang, took a more radical line on the woman question. Kang had led protests after China's 1895 defeat by Japan and became a tireless advocate for reform. His ideas about women and social transformation were much more utopian than those of Liang but were not widely circulated. Kang believed that gender inequality had historically been a problem everywhere, not just in China. Unlike Liang Qichao, he recognized women's labor on farms and in factories, as well as their literary talent. His *Book of the Great Community* (Datong shu) depicted an ideal society in which all divisions would disappear, including those of gender. Men and women would be free to make and terminate short-term marriage contracts, children would be reared communally, and public dorms and dining halls would replace home and family. Kang finished *Book of the Great Community* in 1902, but he regarded many of its ideas as too advanced to circulate broadly, and it was not published in its entirety until 1935, after his death (see box 3.1).[11]

BOX 3.1.
Kang Youwei Denounces the Treatment of Women

In the more than ten thousand years of human history, taking all nations of the whole earth together, incalculable, inconceivable numbers of people have had human form and human intelligence; moreover, each man has had some woman with whom he was most intimate, whom he loved the most. Yet men have callously and unscrupulously repressed women, restrained them, deceived them, shut them up, imprisoned them, and bound them. Men have prevented them from being independent, from holding public office, from being officials, from living as citizens, from enjoying participation in public meetings. Still worse, men have not let them study, or hold discussions, or make a name for themselves, or have free social intercourse, or enjoy entertainments, or go out sightseeing, or leave the house. And worse even than that, men have forced them to distort and bind their waists, veil their faces, compress their feet, and tattoo their bodies. The guiltless have been universally oppressed, the innocent universally punished. Such actions have been worse than the worst inhumanity. And yet throughout the world, past and present, for thousands of years, those whom we call good men, righteous men, have been accustomed to the sight of such things, have sat and looked and considered them to be matters of course, have not demanded justice for the victims or offered to help them. This is the most appalling, unjust, and unequal thing, the most inexplicable theory under heaven.

I now have a task: to cry out the natural grievances of the incalculable numbers of women of the past. I now have one great desire: to save the eight hundred million women of my own time from drowning in the sea of suffering. I now have a great longing: to bring the incalculable inconceivable numbers of women of the future the happiness of equality, of the great community and of independence.

Women are not different from men; men are not different from women. For this reason women are equal with men in their ability to handle the occupations of agriculture, industry, business, and commerce. In the country villages today, there are none among the farmers' wives who do not help with the tilling. In various countries women are already being much used in industry and commerce. Women are equal with men in their ability to study for official positions. There have already been many women writers in China. And so far as holding office and managing affairs is concerned, those who have done so with clarity, decisiveness, and real sagacity according to the historical biographies are innumerable. . . .

From the point of view of the individual nation, to throw away the talents of half of the population is surely a stupid policy. In America some progress has been made in admitting women to serve in the professions, but it is far from adequate. . . . Nowadays the women of Europe and America are generally free in studying, talking, entertaining, traveling about, and sightseeing, choosing their husbands or getting divorces. In other things they still do not rank with men. As for all the nations of Asia and Africa, they all bind and restrict their women. . . .

Now, when we consider the earliest societies, it is certain that it was women, and not men, who discovered and originated all of the arts and crafts of civilization. This is because the men were hunters, who had no time to sit at home, thinking, and finding new methods of doing things. So it must have been the women, who stayed at home, who originated such techniques as cooking, agriculture, house-building, weaving, silk-making, cloth-weaving— and including the fine arts, music and writing—while men were still brutes who spent all their time and energies in the hunt.

Source: Kang Youwei, *Datongshu*, 193, in *Ta T'ung Shu: The One World Philosophy of Kang Yu-wei*, ed. and trans. Laurence G. Thompson (London, 1958), 149–55, portions adapted and cited by Jonathan Spence, *The Gate of Heavenly Peace* (New York: Penguin Books, 1981), 72. On the history of this book, see Thompson, 26–57.

Liang Qichao and Kang Youwei were among the organizers of the Hundred Days' Reform of 1898. When the Empress Dowager moved against the reformers, they fled for their lives; Kang's younger brother was executed. Liang spent more than a decade in Japan, while Kang traveled through Hong Kong, Japan, Canada, England, Singapore, India, the United States, Sweden, and a host of other places. Both men were advocates of constitutional monarchy, and by the time of the 1911 revolution, they were no longer on the cutting edge of radical thinking. But it was Liang Qichao's 1897 arguments, not Kang Youwei's imagined utopian community, that became an article of faith among reformers and revolutionaries. China's weakness, reformers argued, was in part the fault of how Chinese society treated women. Changing this situation was key to creating a strong nation in a global context where China's very existence was threatened.[12] Kang's assessment that it was "women, and not men, who discovered and originated all of the arts and crafts of civilization" was not prominent in this discussion. Instead, it was Liang's assumption that women had never been economically productive, and that their subordinate status had left them deficient in personality and character, which was widely accepted. Woman activist Hu Binxia affirmed the connection, writing in 1903, "Stupid as deer and pigs, doltish as blocks of wood and stone, is it any wonder that men see them as a low form of animal life?"[13]

Such descriptions of women appeared well into the 1920s.[14] Even at the dawn of the People's Republic of China in 1949, the Women's Federation would echo Liang's assumption that the key to women's equal status was to transform them from consumers into producers.[15] Liang had put into circulation a powerful, if incomplete, notion of how gender arrangements worked in China. His masterful writing ensured that the figure of Woman emerged into public conversation as deficient, in need of uplift, and potentially a danger to the survival of China—not as a laborer whose contributions were essential to families, communities, and the nation.

ALICIA (MRS. ARCHIBALD) LITTLE AND THE CAMPAIGN AGAINST FOOTBINDING

Much of the new critical portrayal of women, by foreigners and Chinese alike, centered on footbinding. For centuries, footbinding had been regarded as an unremarkable practice of self-cultivation that shaped the body appropriately and as preparation for a proper marriage.[16] In less than a generation at the end of the Qing, many Chinese came to see it as monstrous.

As chapter 2 detailed, this assessment began with Christian missionaries. It continued with Alicia Little, who was not a missionary but a novelist married to a British merchant. Arriving in China in 1887, Mrs.

Little lived in southwestern Sichuan for two decades.[17] She published several accounts of her travels and activities under her married name, Mrs. Archibald Little, including *Intimate China: The Chinese as I Have Seen Them* (1899) and *In the Land of the Blue Gown* (1909). Footbinding played a prominent role in these recollections. Recounting her first journey up the Yangzi River to Chongqing, she described how Chinese women would flock to inspect her:

> Then some old woman is sure to squeeze my feet, to see if there is really a foot filling up all those big boots: for, of course, all the women here have small feet—that is, they have them bandaged up; and astonishingly well they get along upon their hoof-like feet.[18]

Photo 3.1.   Archibald and Alicia Little, Shanghai, 1894

Source: Sze-Yung-Ming & Co, albumen cabinet card. © National Portrait Gallery, London.

Mrs. Little was a shrewd observer. She was quick to notice what Liang Qichao ignored and missionary commentators failed to mention: that women labored in the fields with bound feet, even working as track- ers hauling boats attached to ropes up the Yangzi. No one in China, she wrote, had ever suggested that footbinding was explicitly intended to keep women from moving about.[19] She described regional variations in how soon or how tightly girls' feet were bound.[20] She also observed that footbinding was performed by women and that some elite men opposed it: "For though it is to please men and win husbands of good social posi- tion for their daughters that women bind their little girls' feet, it is again and again the case that the elder men, especially amongst the learned classes, object to the practice as barbarous."[21]

Mrs. Little was inspired by missionary opposition to footbinding, but her own objections to it were scientific rather than religious. She wrote in graphic terms of girls who developed gangrene, whose skin sloughed off when tight bandages were removed, whose feet hung by tendons or dropped off entirely, who suffered damage to internal organs or died because of footbinding complications. Even when the procedure went normally, Little asserted, during the two-year period of binding "their mothers mostly sleep with a big stick by the bedside, with which to get up and beat the little girl should she disturb the household by her wails; but not uncommonly she is put to sleep in an outhouse."[22] In Little's writings, footbinding was recast as an unscientific and incomprehen- sible form of child abuse.[23]

In 1895, Alicia Little and nine other foreign women founded the Natu- ral Feet Society. Aiming to build opposition to footbinding from the top of the social scale down, the organizers prepared their written appeals in classical language that could persuade the Chinese elite.[24] The Society even submitted an 1896 memorial to the emperor proposing that the dy- nasty abolish the practice, but the Foreign Affairs Ministry rejected it on the grounds that this was a matter of custom rather than law.[25]

When Alicia Little undertook a speaking tour for the Natural Feet Society in Central and South China at the turn of the century, she found that opposition to footbinding was no longer limited to Christians.[26] In every city, upper-class Chinese women attended meetings, often accompanied by their large-footed women servants. There they could hear anti-footbinding speeches, read anti-footbinding literature, sign petitions, and testify about their own experiences.[27] Little, who spoke to the crowds in English translated by missionaries and others, showed X-rays of bound and unbound feet, presenting physician testimony on the deleterious effects of footbinding, while addressing the question of marriageability and matchmaking for the unbound.[28] In Hanyang, she invited women who had already unbound their feet to stand up and exulted when "one after another they slowly rose till the whole number were standing. . . . that was the crowning finish."[29] Much of the discussion in such meetings centered on how to unbind the feet, a painful process that could be eased through the skilled use of cotton wool, massage, and bed rest.[30] Unbinding required consistent effort and could only partially undo the effects of footbinding.

Alicia Little's writings were popular among Western audiences, but she was not the prime mover advocating an end to the practice in China. By the time she began her campaign, many educated Chinese men already shared the goal of ending footbinding. In 1883 Kang Youwei had established an Anti-Footbinding Society in Guangdong.[31] Kang petitioned the emperor in 1898 to abolish footbinding because it led to foreign ridicule:

> In our country, houses are shacks and clothes are rags. In addition, our air is polluted by the smoke of opium and our streets are lined with beggars. For some time now, foreigners have taken photographs to circulate among themselves and to laugh at our barbaric ways. But the most appalling and the most humiliating is the binding of women's feet. For that, your servant feels deeply ashamed.[32]

Kang was in exile by the time of Little's speaking tour, but in Hankou Viceroy Zhang Zhidong was on record denouncing the practice, and Little's group

> had taken care to decorate our hall with huge red placards containing his words against footbinding, in which the reasons for doing away with this most damaging custom are so well stated it seems almost needless for anything further to be written.[33]

Another prominent Qing viceroy in Guangzhou, Li Hongzhang, inscribed Little's fan with an endorsement of unbinding. Nevertheless, he reportedly worried aloud to Little, "You know if you unbind the women's feet you'll make them so strong, and the men so strong too, that they will overturn the dynasty."[34]

More frequently, however, elite Chinese worried that if Chinese women continued to bind their feet and remain sequestered at home, China would collapse. In a document posted in the civil service examination halls in Suifu, a local scholar pointed out that women in Europe and the United States "have natural feet; they are daring, and can defend themselves; whilst Chinese women have bound feet, and are too weak even to bear the weight of their own clothes." Unbound women, the author said, could "even be trained in military exercises."[35] In 1906, writing for the *Beijing Women's News*, essayist Zhao Zhiqian linked bound feet, reproduction, and racial demise, warning that footbinding caused difficult childbirth and weak children. If it continued, Zhao worried, "the race will be gradually enfeebled and finally extinguished."[36] In the emerging consensus against footbinding, the contrast between strong martial foreign women and weak footbound Chinese women stood in for the relative strength of foreign nations and China.

Observing the revulsion expressed by foreign commentators, elite Chinese rapidly came to understand footbinding as barbaric, painful, harmful to women's health and childbearing capabilities, unscientific, injurious to the Chinese "race" (in the social Darwinist language of the day), and detrimental to the national standing of China in the world.[37] In the process footbound women became the embodied symbol of where China had gone wrong and why it had become vulnerable to the European powers and Japan. Concerns about women's status and well-being were articulated primarily as they affected China's survival.[38] No longer a foreign project, the anti-footbinding movement was taken up by Chinese elites as a form of concern about national strength, a marker of their own modernity relative to their compatriots, and a sign of the uplift they hoped to accomplish among the uneducated and largely rural population. In 1902, the Qing government issued a decree urging an end to footbinding.[39]

The residents of smaller cities and villages did not abandon footbinding as early as the upper classes and the inhabitants of large cities. The process was uneven and nonlinear, what Dorothy Ko calls "a confusing period of bind-unbind-bind-unbind."[40] Campaigns to end the practice, intended to rescue peasant women from an abusive practice, often brought them humiliation instead. In 1906, a reform official in a small Sichuan city had members of a youth corps escort all of the women who had come to watch an athletic meet into his office, where he compelled them to remove their bindings and then burned them.[41] In the 1982 film *Small Happiness*, a trio of women recalled that in the 1910s and 1920s, warlord soldiers and local officials would maraud through their villages, fining families who had bound their daughters' feet and sometimes hoisting the bindings on the tips of their bayonets. The women remembered such moments as invasive and frightening, not liberating.[42]

Footbinding came to an earlier end in some rural areas than in others. Some scholars have argued that the eventual abandonment of the practice in some areas by the 1930s was linked to the decline of sedentary handicraft production performed in the home by footbound women and the accompanying rise in factory production of yarn and cloth, rather than the exhortations of elite writers and activists.[43] In other areas, such as Yunnan in the southwest, footbinding continued into the 1940s and 1950s, eventually coming to an end only after active intervention by the Communist Party–led government established in 1949.[44]

Photo 3.2. Famine survivors, North China famine of 1920–21, Liaozhou, Shanxi, ca. 1922

Source: Photo by Isaiah E. Oberholtzer, courtesy of Joseph Wampler. Used with permission of the Brethren Historical Library and Archives, Elgin, Illinois.

XUE SHAOHUI AND THE RISE OF GIRLS' SCHOOLS

In the last years of the Qing empire, women filled the pages of China's new journals and newspapers.[45] The press showcased courtesan escapades, the establishment of girls' schools and the behavior of girl students, anti-footbinding meetings, and the activities of women revolutionaries. Women wrote some of these stories, and they certainly were among the readers of these publications. But for men, too, writes Barbara Mittler, "To read and talk about women was to be fashionable and modern."[46]

Not everyone agreed on what modern women should be and do. From the 1880s on, editorials in Shanghai's *Shenbao* called for an end to footbinding, concubinage, and the confinement of women so that foreigners would no longer despise China as uncivilized.[47] At the same time, newspapers, tabloids, pictorials, and women's magazines all continued to publish stories of chaste widows and other virtuous women, sometimes with the suggestion that it was just this kind of familial self-sacrifice that a strong nation required.[48] Women's magazines and the commercial press encouraged women to contribute to the nation as mothers and homemakers, reimagining the home as a modern, scientifically managed space.[49] Advertisements urged women to purchase medicines that would regulate their menses and ensure their fertility, while preserving their beauty with specially formulated shampoo and skin cleansers.[50] Sometimes the role of woman consumer was linked directly to national politics. Advertisements in 1905, for instance, encouraged women to save the nation by boycotting American goods in protest of the U.S. Chinese Exclusion Act.[51]

Pictorials featured drawings of women bicycling, selling goods, riding around in rickshaws, and strolling on the street, even as reporters and editors warned women about the dangers of leaving domestic space. *Shenbao* editorials fretted in the 1880s about what might happen if women workers, housemaids, and prostitutes continued to move around freely in public. In news reports, women appeared as victims of brutality and kidnapping. Courtesans and streetwalkers were portrayed in a variety of roles: avatars of fashion, targets of abuse by cruel madams, thieves, and occasionally murder victims. Scandals involving prostitutes sold papers, of course, but at the same time they served as cautionary tales for all readers about the consequences of improper behavior.[52] Controversies about women's attendance at theatrical performances roiled a number of cities in the early twentieth century.[53]

Officials and elites moved toward a consensus that women needed to be educated in public schools. But should that education be aimed at training women to be citizens, or mothers of citizens?[54] It was in the pages of the press that the educator, poet, essayist, and translator Xue Shaohui

(1866–1911) staked out her disagreement with Liang Qichao's statement that women were ignorant and narrow-minded. Xue Shaohui had a tart reply to Liang Qichao's 1897 argument that women needed education to overcome their idle uselessness. Xue agreed with Liang that women should be educated. But she rejected the idea that they were ignorant to begin with or that classically educated women had nothing to offer to the contemporary world. Liang had mocked the classical poetry of learned women as frivolous, concerned only with the moon, the flowers, and the grass. But Xue saw something different in their poems: women expressing their "love of the land, the people, and the culture," as well as criticism of rulers who did not protect the people.[55]

Xue was a child prodigy, born into a family of scholars in Fujian. According to family lore, she narrowly escaped being given away when her father learned through divination that she would grow up to be a scholar of significant accomplishment. Orphaned at eleven, locally famous as a poet by thirteen, married at fourteen, she became a member of an elite cultural network of Fujian intellectuals. Her brother-in-law Chen Jitong was a Qing reformer who had spent sixteen years in Europe, returning to China with two French wives.[56] In 1898, Xue helped found a women's journal, the *Chinese Girl's Progress* (Nü xuebao).[57] In her own poetry she expressed judgments about the actions of European monarchs and commented on the Sino-French war of 1884 and China's loss to Japan in the war of 1894–95.[58] Women should not be required to give up poetry for practical matters, Xue believed; the two were intertwined.

But Xue did not limit her defense of women to a tiny cohort of patriotic poets. She argued that all mothers, by virtue of their authority in the household, could help to renew China. In the first issue of the *Chinese Girl's Progress*, she wrote:

> Today new knowledge from all countries has been glamorously and beautifully developed, going beyond the scope of the masters and the one hundred schools [in the Chinese tradition]. If we women, staying in the inner chambers all day long, still . . . limit our learning [within a narrow field], how can we talk about getting knowledge so as to fit ourselves to the principle of the "new people"(*xinmin*)? . . . Known to every household, this new knowledge will enable our women in assisting their husbands and teaching their children. This is because the skills of managing a household contain that of governing the state and harmonizing all under Heaven. Laozi said: "The Dao is the mother of all things." Mothering the world is precisely our women's business. Who says that the female Dao cannot achieve anything?[59]

Here Xue skillfully deployed a classical adage—that a well-run family ensured a well-run state—to justify the new idea that Chinese women should master foreign learning. She also deployed the concept of a "new people" or "renewing the people," an ancient classical trope that Liang Qichao adapted to describe the qualities of modern citizens.

In 1899, Xue Shaohui and her husband, Chen Shoupeng, turned their attention to compiling a book that would introduce the lives of foreign women to Chinese readers. Their method was for Chen to read the original works in European languages and translate orally, while Xue transformed his words into exquisitely crafted Chinese. The *Biographies of Foreign Women*, published in 1906, introduced women as sovereigns, consorts, courtiers, gentlewomen, writers, scholars, righteous and heroic women, holy women, mistresses, actresses and courtesans, with two appendixes on wicked women and goddesses.[60] Many other writers in the last decade of the Qing also published biographical collections about foreign women, and prominent women's journals included such biographies in each issue.[61] Joan of Arc, Anita Garibaldi, Madame Roland, Harriet Beecher Stowe, and Florence Nightingale became familiar figures to literate Chinese women and men.[62]

Xue Shaohui and other authors made editorial choices that rendered their heroines in forms familiar to Chinese readers. In *Biographies of Foreign Women*, Elizabeth I and Queen Victoria were praised for showing motherly love for their subjects and promoting education, while Athena appeared in a Confucian scholar's turban rather than a warrior helmet, and Venus contributed to conjugal harmony rather than erotic abandon. In works by other authors, Joan of Arc was praised for her nationalism, whereas her religious beliefs were barely mentioned.[63] A heroine of the French Revolution might be singled out for extending domestic virtues into the public sphere or for leaving family ties behind in her zeal for political engagement.[64] In these works foreign women of the past formed a new composite image of Woman, exemplifying the qualities the authors wanted Chinese women to display in the present.[65]

All of these writers assumed that Chinese women, and the Chinese nation, needed to work out their place in a modern global situation currently dominated by Western powers. The question on which they divided—the source of Xue Shaohui's disagreement with Liang Qichao— was what kind of break with the Chinese past would be required in order for women to contribute to strengthening China.[66] Xue believed that Chinese women needed to draw on their own cultural repertoire as poets as well as every example that foreign nations had to offer. Her writing and others of its kind were later forgotten or dismissed as "traditional," but the problem that interested Xue was what kind of modern to become and what kinds of cultural resources might be useful in figuring that out. She and other late Qing intellectuals engaged in what Theodore Huters has called "bringing the world home"⁶⁷—selectively reworking foreign knowledge in a local context to deal with China's crisis.

New women required a new type of schooling. In 1897, prominent intellectuals in Shanghai, including Xue Shaohui, began a campaign to open the Chinese Girls' School (*Nü xuetang*), the first such school established by Chinese.⁶⁸ One hundred women and an equal number of men participated in this campaign.⁶⁹ Xue proposed a curriculum drawing on both Chinese and Western knowledge, including poetry.⁷⁰ The school opened in May 1898 with an all-women staff. It survived the crushing of the 1898 Reforms but closed in the face of conservative opposition in the fall of 1900.⁷¹

As part of the New Policy reforms of the early 1900s, the Qing court approved the creation of a new state school system, but initially made no provision for girls' schooling.⁷² The school regulations of 1904 stipulated that girls should be taught—at home—the skills required of wives and mothers, including how to teach their future children. On no account should they

> go to school in groups or parade in the streets and markets. If they read too many Western books and are unfortunately misled by foreign customs and manners, they will [insist on] freedom of marriage and grow arrogant against their parents and husbands.⁷³

But by 1907, following the lead of several provincial governments, the Qing government reversed itself and established a system of elementary schools and secondary teacher training institutes for girls and young women.⁷⁴

The central government hoped to reinforce old standards of behavior, not endorse new ones. Regulations for the new schools, published in *Shenbao* in March 1907, decreed that they should teach "the 'beautiful virtues' of filial piety, submission, compassionate love, propriety, reverence, and chastity and the 'feminine virtues' of honesty, diligence, and frugality."⁷⁵ Girls should obey their parents and husbands, were not permitted to select their own spouses or to give political speeches, and were expected to use their education to become good mothers and homemakers.⁷⁶

To that end, girls in the upper grades of elementary school were to spend five to six hours per week learning "women's work" (*nügong*), which included sewing, embroidery, handicrafts, and sericulture. This was as much time as they spent studying history, geography, and science.⁷⁷ They were not to study foreign languages, the Confucian classics, or business.⁷⁸ Their required course of study was shorter than that for boys—eight rather than nine years of elementary school, four years of teacher training school versus five years of middle school, and no options for high school, college, and graduate study comparable to those for boys.[79] Coeducation was not permitted, and women's teacher training schools required students and faculty to live at school under highly supervised conditions.[80]

In 1902, two private girls' schools were founded in Shanghai. The Patriotic Girls' School (*Aiguo nüxiao*), a project of the politically radical Chinese Education Association, was directed by Cai Yuanpei, who would later become the president of Peking University. The mission statement of the Patriotic Girls' School emphasized that girls would be educated to become the mothers of citizens. School regulations stipulated that they should dress modestly, behave appropriately at home, and not "flock like birds and wander in public unsupervised." Nevertheless, it was rumored that the girl students also studied the history of the French Revolution, anarchist theories, and bomb making.[81] The anarchist writer He-Yin Zhen (see below) briefly was a student there.[82]

At Wuben Girls' School (*Wuben nüshu*), students aged ten to twenty studied scientific household management along with Chinese, foreign languages, math, history, geography, drawing, and physical education. Girls were provided with instructions on how to unbind their feet and given special shoes. They were not allowed to wear jewelry or powder their faces, and were required to wear simple cotton clothing of white or light blue.[83]

The female figure who caused the most anxious commentary in late Qing public discourse was the schoolgirl dressing or behaving inappropriately.[84] Beijing girls' schools forbade students to spit, write graffiti, adopt modern fashions, cut their hair short, or engage in political discussions or "unrestrained and foolish" conduct.[85] In 1910, the Ministry of Education decreed that women students should wear gowns that reached two inches above the ground, with one-inch borders on the sleeves and in front, in prescribed shades of blue that varied with the season, made of domestic rather than imported cotton and linen. This was not a return to older ways of presenting the female body—footbinding was prohibited—but with its ban on students wearing Japanese or Western fashions, or applying cosmetics, it was not an embrace of the new.[86] (One source of conflict between girls and their women teachers was bangs: the girls liked them, the teachers did not.)[87]

More disturbing, or possibly titillating, to the general public was the sight of young women students driving carriages or riding horses through the streets of Beijing, or talking and laughing by the school gates, oblivious to the leers of rickshaw pullers loitering nearby.[88] More than a tinge of class anxiety suffused these accounts. Girls from well-off families, who in the previous generation would have been secluded at home, were now as visible—and in the eyes of worried commentators, as vulnerable—as women from more humble backgrounds.

In spite of such reservations, by the last years of the Qing the debate was no longer about whether girls and young women should go to school, but rather about what they should do with their education. The predominant view, expressed by Qing officials and many reformers including Xue Shaohui, featured women as the "mothers of citizens." Girls needed to become physically fit and scientifically knowledgeable wives and mothers who would run a clean modern home with a regular schedule and a clear budget, give birth to healthy children, and raise them to become citizens of a strong and powerful nation.[89] By the early twentieth century, this vision of the home as the key source of national strength was becoming a transnational ideal. In Japan, the ideal of "good wives and wise mothers" underpinned much thinking about women's education, appealing to both Qing officials and Chinese students studying in Japan.[90] Chinese women who were sent by Qing officials or by missionary educators to study in the United States in the early 1900s encountered this ideal in the form of home economics, which exalted the domestic sphere and women's place in it.[91] For a Chinese woman to manage the home—or to teach girls to manage their future homes—was understood as a modern activity.[92]

Photo 3.3.   Beijing Muzhen girls' school, 1904

Future mothers of citizens needed to cultivate their own health, and many schools took up the challenge of providing physical education for girls and young women, sometimes with military drills. Like the campaign to end footbinding, physical culture for women was from its inception entangled with an emergent worldwide discussion about eugenics on the one hand and concern about China's national strength on the other.[93] The earliest modern song about women, published in a collection of school songs in 1904, was titled "Physical Education—for Women's Use":

> The nice name of "tender and charming,"
> we absolutely do not want it.
> We want not only knowledge,
> we also want good body and health.
> We are not afraid of the white people who are so tall,
> we are not worried about the shortness of the yellow people,
> Our head touches the sky and the sky rises high,
> our feet stand on the ground and the ground is not shaking.
> Exercise, exercise, in the twentieth century,
> we women also are bright and outstanding.[94]

An essay in *Women's World* (Nüzi shijie) began with specific exercises for each part of the body. It decried the lack of physical training for Chinese women, and ended with an acerbic description of them as footbound, lazy, sickly, preoccupied with adornment, and unable to produce healthy offspring, in contrast to Western women, who were likened to "supernatural beings" with superior children.[95] Newspapers such as Beijing's *Shuntian Times* editorialized that as the future mothers of citizens, girls needed to acquire scientific knowledge and physical strength because "A strong mother will have a strong son. A strong race will make the country powerful."[96]

Some women, however, had aspirations beyond becoming the mothers of citizens.[97] Seventeen-year-old Liu Shurong, a teacher at a new girls' school, declared at the opening ceremony in 1906:

> Both men and women are of equal importance to the country. Women are also citizens; if they do not understand what a nation is and what duties they have for the country, the country will have half of the population as apathetic citizens.[98]

Lü Bicheng (1883–1943), a young assistant editor at the *Dagong bao* who would go on to a long career as a reformer, wrote that women should "fulfill the same obligations, possess the same political consciousness, and enjoy the same rights as male citizens."[99] Some male educators also argued that although it was fine to teach young women cooking and sewing as a supplement to the curriculum, women should have access to the same educational opportunities as men.[100] Only in this way could they help China compete with Western nations where, as one women's journal commented in 1907:

> Their women receive the same level of education as men. The ideals of love of country and the duties of citizens are poured into their brains, so daily their female citizens diligently consider national affairs their responsibility. . . . No wonder their national strength has advanced, and no one dares insult them![101]

Girls' schools became an important feature of the early twentieth-century landscape. By mid-1907, Shanghai alone had more than one hundred girls' schools in operation, most of them privately funded with some official support.[102] Nationally, the Qing government counted more than four hundred such schools.[103] A women's medical college was founded in Shanghai in 1905 to train women gynecologists and obstetricians in both Chinese and Western medicine.[104] Across China, a variety of vocational schools taught girls and women sericulture, midwifery, and handicrafts.[105] Women carved out new career paths as teachers and administrators in both government and private schools. Nationwide, the number of all students remained small, and 70 percent of all girl students were concentrated in the four provinces of Zhili, Jiangsu, Zhejiang, and Sichuan.[106] Catering mostly to students from elite families, girls' schools emerged as places where students and teachers tried new activities and roles. Ultimately, the schools produced new types of women—educated to be mothers of citizens but also aspiring to an enlarged political world for themselves.[107]

REVOLUTIONARY MARTYRDOM: QIU JIN

Qiu Jin is the best known of all revolutionary women active in the last years of the empire.[108] Executed in her early thirties by the Qing after a failed 1907 uprising against the dynasty, she has had a long afterlife. Since 1907 she has been laid to rest nine separate times, most recently in 1981 in a grand tomb by West Lake in Hangzhou.[109] In spite of the unique circumstances of her death and posthumous fame, she had much in common with other educated young women of her generation. Qiu's life was profoundly shaped by new-style education, exposure to Western and Japanese ideas, anti-Manchu political convictions, close family and friendship ties, and work as a teacher in new girls' schools.

Qiu Jin was born into a wealthy Zhejiang family in 1875. It is said that as a girl she was drawn to horseback riding and martial swordplay.

At twenty-one she entered an arranged marriage to a merchant, bore a daughter and a son, and lived for several years with her husband in Beijing, observing the city under foreign occupation after the Boxer uprising. Her marriage, never a happy one, disintegrated during her stay in Beijing. In 1904, with financial support from her mother, Qiu left her husband and children to study in Tokyo.

Even as Japan's armed forces encroached on Chinese territory, Japan offered Chinese a model of how to strengthen the nation and avoid a colonial fate. By 1906, twelve thousand Chinese students, about a hundred of them women,[110] were living in Tokyo. There it was possible to engage in anti-Qing political activity too dangerous to conduct in China. Many of the women's organizations, teacher training protocols, periodicals, and revolutionary activities described in this chapter had their origins among Chinese students who spent time in Tokyo.[111] They drew upon works translated from European languages into Japanese, and then into Chinese, to spread the new ideas they encountered to a wider reading audience back in China.

Qiu Jin enrolled in the Jissen Women's School run by educator Shimoda Utako[112] and then in the Aoyama Vocational Girls' School. She joined the intense political debates among Chinese students, arguing that women's status was linked to the fate of the Chinese nation. In a 1904 essay, Qiu denounced the devaluing of girl children, footbinding, and arranged marriage. An enthusiastic proponent of physical activity, Qiu had already unbound her own feet and favored military drills.[113] She helped found the Encompassing Love Society, a women's group that promoted women's education and protested the Russian presence in northeast China.[114] She established a society to train revolutionary organizers in effective public speaking, which she saw as an effective way to reach "even illiterate women and children."[115] Qiu herself became a compelling orator who addressed men and women, exhorting them to change the fate of China.[116]

In 1904–5, Qiu Jin published a monthly women's journal in Tokyo that called for the overthrow of the Manchu-led Qing dynasty. Her writing reflected a growing anti-Manchu sentiment among the predominantly Han elite, many of whom had concluded that China's current suffering under European imperialism would not cease until the Qing dynasty was brought to an end and the Manchus expelled.[117] In 1905 in Tokyo, Qiu Jin joined Sun Yat-sen's Revolutionary Alliance, the umbrella group of Chinese from various provinces based on anti-Manchuism and republicanism. Already known as a calligrapher and poet, she described herself as "tossing aside the brush to join the military ranks," echoing Liang Qichao in encouraging educated women not to waste time on poetry, but instead to engage in direct action.[118]

Yet she did not toss aside the brush: much of her own action took the form of writing about and for women. Between 1905 and 1907, Qiu Jin began to write a novel called *Stones of the Jingwei Bird* in traditional ballad (*tanci*) form, a type of literature often composed by women for women audiences.[119] The novel, a lightly fictionalized polemic, describes the friendship among five wealthy young women who decide to flee their families and the proper arranged marriages awaiting them, in order to study and join revolutionary activities in Tokyo. Most of the dialogue takes the form of speeches in which the women denounce the bitter fate that awaits them as lavishly adorned footbound brides. They declare their desire for an education and pledge to help build a strong China. The young women proselytize their new beliefs to their serving maids, one of whom helps them run away. Titles for the uncompleted later chapters suggest that the women will go on to engage in education, manufacturing, military activities, speechmaking, and direct political action, eventually overthrowing the Qing dynasty and establishing a republic.[120]

Returning to China in early 1906, Qiu Jin lost her first job teaching Japanese and science at a girls' school in Zhejiang for encouraging the students to become revolutionaries. A year later she became principal of the Datong School in Shaoxing.[121] There she attracted unfavorable attention from local authorities by directing girl students to practice military drills. In 1907 she founded the *Chinese Women's Journal* (Zhongguo nübao). It folded after two issues, but not before she had published "An Urgent Announcement to My Sisters," exhorting women to throw off their fate as slaves and become self-supporting:[122]

> While our two hundred million male compatriots have already advanced, our two hundred million female compatriots are still mired in the utter darkness of the eighteen layers of hell. They cannot even envisage a way of climbing up one layer, with their feet bound so small, their combed hair glossy and inlaid with flowers, their bodies wrapped in silks and satins, and their white powdered faces smeared with rouge. They pass their entire lives knowing only how to depend on men. . . . They are meek, subservient and fawning. . . . They live the life of obsequious servility.[123]

Qiu urged that women be awakened to act on behalf of themselves and the nation:

> When there is danger, and yet people are not aware of it, this then is indeed great darkness. . . . If we can arouse people from their drugged state and activate their minds, then the people can themselves make plans against all sorts of dangers. . . . I think of the darkness of our China . . . what is to be done? What is to be done about the dangers in China's future? And what is to be done about the darkness of the women of China or the dangers in their

future? When I think of this I am agitated and saddened; disconcerted, I stand up and hurry around, shouting to my sister comrades. For this purpose I have established the *Chinese Women's Journal*.[124]

Qiu Jin helped plan an uprising in Zhejiang in 1907. When her fellow revolutionary Xu Xilin failed in an attempt to assassinate the governor of Anhui, a nearby province, Qiu Jin's activities were exposed. Qiu refused to flee her teaching post, waiting five days to be arrested by Qing officials. She was taken into custody in July 1907 and beheaded on July 15, her body abandoned at a crossroads in Shaoxing.[125]

In some respects Qiu Jin has remained a mystery to subsequent generations. Why did she choose to remain at her school and die? Was she hoping that her actions would inspire others to begin an immediate uprising? Was she impelled by the culturally powerful figure of the woman martyr?[126] Was she attracted by the possibility of public acclaim for her sacrifice—ending up, as the famous writer Lu Xun later suggested, "clapped to death"?[127] Were her choices shaped by a profound melancholy, or even what would now be understood as mental illness? She seemed to suggest as much in a poem she reportedly wrote just before her execution that played on her surname Qiu ("autumn"): "Autumn rain, autumn wind, I die of sorrow."[128] Her motivations for allowing herself to be captured and executed remain opaque.

Qiu Jin nevertheless has seemed familiar to later feminists. Her writings prefigure their social critique of women's restrictive gender roles, exhorting them to break out of those roles and take political action, as in her 1903 poem:

> Alas, they sent me off by force to be mere "rouge and powder,"
> How I despise it!
> My body will not allow me
> To join the ranks of men,
> But my heart is far braver
> Than that of a man.
> All my life, has not my liver and gall
> Burned for others?
> But how could they with their vulgar minds understand me?[129]

As she explained to a Japanese educator, "I want to become strong like men. First I want to look like a man in appearance, and then I will become like a man in my psyche."[130] Qiu is usually shown in one of three photographs. In the first, taken in 1904 in Beijing, she wears male Western dress, suggesting a transgressive gender bending that later generations have found attractive. The second, in which she appears in Japanese kimono carrying a small dagger, commemorates her days as a Tokyo student. In the third, she is dressed in the gown of a Chinese male scholar in 1906.[131] In a poem addressed to her own image dressed as a man, she writes:

> Who is this person, staring at me so sternly?
> The martial bones I bring from a former existence regret the flesh that covers them.
> Once life is over, the body itself will be seen to have been an illusion,
> And the world that has not yet emerged—that will be real.
> You and I should have got together long ago, and shared our feelings;
> Looking out across these difficult times our spirits garner strength.
> Someday, when you see my friends from the old days,
> Tell them I've scrubbed off all that old dirt.[132]

During Qiu's time at the Datong school, she apparently dressed in men's attire and rode to town, causing consternation among local notables.[133] In all of these portrayals, and in her explicitly articulated desire to shock,[134] Qiu Jin has appealed powerfully to subsequent generations of women activists.

Photo 3.4.   Qiu Jin, ca. 1905

She has also become a familiar hero to twentieth-century Chinese nationalists. Her feminism might have been deliberately transgressive, but her nationalism drew upon a very old figure—that of the knight-errant—to justify her dramatic actions. The knight-errant, a prototypically male figure already established in the Han dynasty works of historian Sima Qian (ca. 145–86 BCE), was known for swordsmanship, bravery, faithfulness to his word, and self-sacrifice, even when his worth was not recognized by contemporaries.[135] The names Qiu Jin adopted suggested her desire to play such a role: she called herself Female Knight-Errant of Jian Lake, as well as Vying for Heroism. Hu Ying has argued that Qiu Jin, and friends who later wrote about her, drew upon the culturally familiar knight-errant figure as a conventional means of portraying Qiu's unconventional behavior, making her actions legible to a wider public.[136] Qiu Jin also was attracted by the stories of Western heroines who sacrificed themselves for a larger cause—Joan of Arc, Anna Garibaldi, Madame Roland, and Sophia Perovskaya, who was executed in Russia in 1881 after planning several assassination attempts and succeeding in one.[137]

Qiu Jin criticized Chinese family practices, but remained close to her brothers and drew support from her mother. When her mother died in 1906, Qiu commemorated her by composing the kind of couplet conventionally written by filial sons, linking her heartbreak at the loss of a beloved parent to a nationalist vow:

> The tree wants to be still though the wind blows on; her descendants would like to support her but Mother hastily departs. It would be much too short if I were to serve you for a whole millennium. Sadly you were ill for some years and now you are gone—your life spanning just a brief sixty-two years.
>
>   Loving my nation my intent is not yet fulfilled; for the one who gave me life, I have not yet repaid the debt. This insignificant body of mine, perhaps one day it may be recorded in history. But by then I will not see your kindly face—it will be hard to find you in that heavenly land of immortals.[138]

Qiu drew support as well from two close friends, Xu Zihua (1873–1935) and Wu Zhiying (1868–1934), both of whom had earlier sworn sisterhood with her.[139] In the months after her execution, with the Qing rulers still in power and Qiu classified as a criminal, her two sworn sisters stepped forward to memorialize and honor her. Wu wrote three essays mourning Qiu. She criticized Qing officials for the execution and argued that Qiu had been slandered and her actions unjustly besmirched.[140] Then the two friends set out to bury Qiu properly near West Lake, fulfilling her wish to be buried near heroes of earlier periods. Her memorial service in 1908 became a political event. Xu Zihua's younger sister spoke, denouncing the Manchus for their brutal conquest of China in 1644. Qing officials ordered the tomb razed, but Qiu's brother retrieved her body and Wu Zhiying carried off the memorial stele, installing it in her own house and selling stele rubbings as a way to commemorate her fallen friend.[141]

Qiu's self-styling as a lone misunderstood hero, and the circumstances of her death, mark her as a unique figure in the history of modern Chinese women. And yet, in most respects she was quite typical of educated women grappling with the challenges of the time. Qiu was by turns student, teacher, proponent of unbound feet and physical education, journalist, and political activist. Like many others, she articulated a feminism that quickly became indivisible from anti-Manchu nationalism. Her actions, her very public stylings of her own gender identity, and the circumstances of her death were unusual. The content of her critique and the arc of her public activities, however, were increasingly shared by many elite urban women.[142] After her death, she was elevated posthumously to the status of nationalist martyr. She remains important as well for the visual and written record of her struggle with the meaning of gender in the last years of the empire.

RADICAL CRITIQUE IN TOKYO: HE-YIN ZHEN

If Qiu Jin differed from other educated women mainly in the manner of her death, He-Yin Zhen was distinguished from other women activists by the content of her feminism.[143] Unlike most of her feminist cohort, she did not believe that a nationalist revolution would solve women's most fundamental problems, which she saw as rooted in the spread of global capitalism. For her, gender was inseparable from class. Although He-Yin soon faded into obscurity, parts of her anarchist critique of capitalism and gender oppression survived to become an important, if often unacknowledged, feature of China's revolution.

He-Yin Zhen was reportedly raised in such a conservative Jiangsu home that as a girl she never met anyone who was not a family member. She married Liu Shipei in 1904, and as a student at the Patriotic Girls' School, she changed her given name to Zhen, meaning "Thunderclap."[144] In 1907, He-Yin and her husband joined the activists who gathered in Tokyo. Well-educated in the Chinese classics, and at the same time deeply involved in a worldwide anarchist conversation, He-Yin was also a feminist who adopted the unorthodox practice of hyphenating her paternal surname (He) with her maternal surname (Yin).[145] She was a founder of the Society for the Restoration of Women's Rights and editor of the anarchist journal *Natural Justice* (*Tianyi*), which in 1907–8 published influential essays about Marxism, anarchism, and feminism aimed at Chinese students in Japan.[146]

He-Yin's pieces in *Natural Justice* were dazzling in their erudition and uncompromising in their politics. Her essay "On the Revenge of Women" denounces the devaluing of women from ancient times, supported by dozens of quotations from Chinese classical writings. The Manchus should be overthrown, she said, but this would not end the oppression of women, which long predated the Manchus and involved cloistering, corporal punishment, kidnapping, abandonment, and enforced chastity for women only.[147] A transition from the Qing empire to a Chinese republic, she felt, would only replace one form of oppression with another. Liberation depended on the destruction of both the state and capital.

Unlike virtually all of her fellow activists, He-Yin was not interested in improving the position of women merely in order to strengthen the Chinese nation. "Our purpose," she declared, "is to destroy the old society and practice human equality. In addition to women's revolution, we also advocate racial, political and economic revolutions."[148] In her essay "On the Question of Women's Liberation" she voiced her suspicion that now, Chinese male reformers were pushing for women's education chiefly so that the world would praise them for becoming civilized:

> In the past, when traditional rituals prevailed, men tried to distinguish themselves by confining women in the boudoir; when the tides turn in favor of Europeanization, they attempt to acquire distinction by promoting women's liberation. This is what I call *men's pursuit of self-distinction in the name of women's liberation.*[149]

For He-Yin, such superficial reforms would accomplish nothing as long as the bodies of all women were potentially treated as property (see box 3.2). Reform might even increase the burden on women by making them responsible for their own livelihood under conditions of intensifying capitalist exploitation. She did not see a solution in the Western practices of free and monogamous marriage, divorce, and women's education, pointing out that in the West women continued to marry for money and status, monogamy existed in name only, and men still ruled.[150]

He-Yin followed the progress of feminist suffrage movements in Northern Europe and the United States, but she was not impressed. She did not believe that giving propertied women the vote would solve fundamental problems for the poor and laboring majorities in those places. Suffrage was not a priority in the future she envisioned for China.[151] She believed that the best hope for women's liberation required abolishing private property and guaranteeing a viable livelihood for all, based on communal property.[152] In "The Feminist Manifesto," she envisioned a future where gender itself would disappear:

> If sons and daughters are treated equally, raised and educated in the same manner, then the responsibilities assumed by men and women will surely

---

BOX 3.2.
He-Yin Zhen on Women's Subjugation

I address myself to the women of my country: has it occurred to you that men are our archenemy? Are you aware that men have subjugated us for thousands of years? . . . It is true that men can be subjugated and must submit to an alien group, the will of a king, or some capitalists. . . . With women, however, the subjugation takes on a whole different character. One cannot deny that an empress occupies a highly esteemed position, but she never questions her own subjugation to men. At the other end of the hierarchy, one finds beggars whose social position cannot be more degraded, yet even a female beggar would not question her subjugation to men. This situation is by no means confined to the ancient world and is just as prevalent in the modern world. . . . Nor is it uniquely a Chinese situation, since the same thing happens in foreign lands as well. . . .

The level of self-awareness among the women of China is very low, and those who have attained a notch slightly higher rush to pick up the crumbs of men's fallacious discourse of a racial revolution. There is no doubt that the Manchu court [of the Qing dynasty] should be overthrown, but I would like to point out that a Han sovereign or regime could be a disaster worse than the ones wrought by foreign rule. I argue that the more successful a Han-dominated regime is, the worse their oppression of women. . . .

Surely, the main culprits were despotic rulers and their cruel officials, but also responsible is men's treatment of women as their private property. Men have caused many a woman's untimely death. If you are a man, would you not take a hard look and admit the extent to which you owe the women?

Source: He-Yin Zhen, "On the Revenge of Women," originally published in *Tianyi*, 1907. Translated by Dorothy Ko in Liu, Karl, and Ko 2013, 105–6, 167.

---

become equal. When that happens, the nouns "men" and "women" would no longer be necessary. This is the "equality of men and women" of which we speak.[153]

It is unclear what became of He-Yin Zhen after *Natural Justice* ceased publication in 1908. Following a split with other revolutionaries, she and Liu Shipei were accused of collaboration with the Manchu regime. After Liu's death in 1919, it was variously rumored that He-Yin had suffered a mental breakdown and/or entered a Buddhist nunnery, dying at the age of about thirty-six and leaving no historical trace beyond her brilliant essays. Many of the anarchist ideas first put forward in her essays were later incorporated into Marxist thinking in China. Years after she stopped writing, her naming of the family as a site of women's oppression surfaced anew in writings of the New Culture movement, and her argument that women could not be liberated under capitalism was incorporated into the Communist movement.

TANG QUNYING AND THE WOMEN OF 1911

By the first decade of the twentieth century, discontent with the Manchu rulers of the Qing dynasty was widespread. Elite critics, as we have seen, blamed the Manchus for China's suffering at the hands of European and Japanese imperialism. They also were beginning to attribute China's weakness to cultural practices such as footbinding and sequestering women that long predated the Qing. Under the Qing New Policies, property-owning men were now permitted to elect provincial assemblies and then a national assembly, which they promptly used to press for more reform measures. Local elites found new opportunities to expand their power and wealth. Meanwhile, many of the urban poor and farmers objected to the reforms that Qing rulers promulgated after the Boxer Rebellion. New military forces, new constitutional assemblies, and new schools all had to be paid for—chiefly through taxes that disproportionately affected the poor. Well over a thousand protests were reported in the decade preceding the 1911 Revolution, with women playing prominent roles in several of them.[154]

The Revolution of 1911 began by chance in October. A bomb accidentally detonated in a secret revolutionary headquarters in the Qing's military garrison in the city of Wuchang. Facing discovery, revolutionary soldiers had no choice but to come out fighting. At first, this seemed to be just the latest in a long list of futile uprisings, but the revolutionaries this time were quickly able to take control of the provincial capital. Revolutionaries in other cities responded. Sun Yat-sen himself read about the outbreak while he was in Denver, where he had gone to raise money for the cause. He returned to China via Europe, where he continued to raise funds for the new Republican government. For several months localized violence spread across China, including attacks on Manchu ethnic enclaves. As cities and provinces declared their independence from the Qing, much local leadership fell into the hands of reform-minded—but far from radical—men of educational attainment and property. In January 1912 the Republic of China was declared in Nanjing, ending not only the Qing dynasty established in 1644 but also the dynastic system that had united China intermittently since 221 BCE.

Women joined in the events leading up to 1911, often drawing upon their capacity for disguise.[155] Male revolutionary leader Zhang Ji recalled: "In every uprising there were female comrades participating:

playing the roles of brides, sitting in sedan chairs carrying bombs, or carrying small children to transport bombs, or protect [male] comrades. How great was their courage!"[156] Students at girls' schools were an important source of recruits.[157]

The number of women directly involved in the 1911 fighting was small.[158] Among them was the Canton-trained doctor and educator Zhang Zhujun (b. 1879), who had established a girls' school in Canton in 1901 and cofounded Shanghai's first medical college for women in 1905. Famous for dressing like a man and enjoying political discussions with male revolutionaries, in 1911 she helped organize a Red Cross volunteer corps and provided cover to three prominent revolutionaries who were wanted by the Qing authorities. She transported medicine and wounded soldiers between Wuchang and Hankou, braving Qing fire and sustaining a minor wound.[159] Because of her outspoken commitment to gender equality, she was sometimes called the "female Liang Qichao."[160] In Shanghai, Suzhou, Hangzhou, and Yangzhou, women founded militia units, mobile medical teams, and associations to provide the revolutionary soldiers with provisions and clothing.[161]

Not every revolution results in a profound reordering of the social landscape. Military men from the New Armies of the late Qing ended up in control of the new Republican government. By spring 1912 Sun Yat-sen had ceded the presidency to Yuan Shikai, a military man interested in maintaining order. Finally able to return to China fourteen years after he had been forced into exile, Liang Qichao sardonically observed that the Revolution of 1911 was like a freshly opened bottle of beer, producing a momentary fountain of bubbling foam that dissipated quickly.[162] Still, at first it seemed national elections contested by new political parties would determine the course of the new republic. But the position of women in political life remained uncertain.

In late August 1912, feminist and revolutionary Tang Qunying (1871–1937) delivered the most famous public slap in China's history.[163]

Members of Sun Yat-sen's movement had gathered in Beijing to found the Nationalist Party, which was to carry the ideals of the Revolutionary Alliance into the era of Republican governance. One of those ideals was full citizenship for women, which Sun had initially supported, including the right to vote. But in negotiations with conservative politicians before the meeting began, Sun Yat-sen and his younger male comrade Song Jiaoren traded away their commitment to women's rights in return for conservative support. The Three People's Principles put forward by Sun—nationalism, people's power, and especially people's livelihood—were

Photo 3.5.   Tang Qunying

Source: Gardner L. Harding, *Present-Day China: A Narrative of a Nation's Advance* (New York: Century Company, 1916), plate facing 42. Reprinted in David Strand, *An Unfinished Republic: Leading by Word and Deed in Modern China* (Berkeley: University of California Press, 2011), 112.

rearticulated to blunt their revolutionary potential. Conservative power brokers demanded that the new party's charter not include a clause about the equality of men and women.

As the Beijing meeting proceeded, Tang Qunying and two of her women comrades, Shen Peizhen and Wang Changguo, entered the meeting hall and mounted the stage. Tang and Shen slapped Song Jiaoren's face with their fans. From the podium, the women denounced the disappearance of women's rights from the Nationalist Party's proposed constitution, bringing the meeting to a halt. When the meeting reconvened later that day, women members of the party made further speeches on the topic. But women were only several dozen of the thousand or so Party members present, and in the end the assembly voted against inclusion of the male-female equality clause. Sun Yat-sen, struggling to get the Republic off the ground in a highly militarized environment, tried to calm the women by promising that Chinese women eventually would get the vote. Tang Qunying and her fellow activists were not appeased.

The image of a group of angry women storming a meeting of men to demand their rights lends itself to easy interpretation: outsider feminists assail entrenched power brokers. This is misleading. The women were not outsiders: they were longtime revolutionary allies of the men, and members of the new Nationalist Party. It was precisely the fact that they had been betrayed by close political associates that most angered the women.

Tang Qunying, the leader of the protests, exemplified changes in elite women's lives that were already well underway by the time of the 1911 revolution. Tang was forty-one years old when she slapped Song Jiaoren. The third daughter in a prominent Hunan family, educated in the classics and poetry, she had resisted her mother's attempts to bind her feet, removing the binding strips so often that her feet never achieved their intended lotus shape. Her father taught her to wield a sword and ride a horse. Married at nineteen into another famous Hunan family, she made the acquaintance of Qiu Jin. At twenty-six, Tang returned to her natal family after the successive deaths of her toddler daughter and her husband.

Tang read the works of Kang Youwei and Liang Qichao. In 1904, with Qiu Jin's encouragement and her own family's support, she made her way to Tokyo to study at the women's school run by Shimoda Utako. Tang joined Sun Yat-sen's Revolutionary Alliance in Tokyo when it was founded in 1905, becoming one of its first woman members, and she worked for the revolutionary cause after her return to China. In rural Hunan she cooperated with local secret society members; at one point she dressed as a tea picker and gave directions to Qing troops that sent them into an ambush. David Strand describes her as "gifted in areas as diverse as bomb making, poetry, battlefield tactics, and public speaking."[164] In 1911 she fought in Wuchang and Nanjing.[165]

After the Republic was founded, in early 1912 Tang and others formed a group known as the Women's Suffrage Alliance, drawing directly from the military units they had formed during the conflict.[166] Membership rapidly expanded into the thousands.[167] Citizenship, they argued, was both their natural right and something they had earned on behalf of all women through their actions as revolutionaries.[168] Women including Wu Zhiying, one of the sworn sisters who had buried Qiu Jin, argued forcefully for women's equal political rights in 1912.[169] Not all women agreed that women should get the vote immediately; some advocated an extended period of women's education first. But Tang and her associates persevered, buoyed by their own history of political activism and their awareness of suffragist struggles in Britain and the United States.

In the months before the slap, Tang and others stormed the Senate in Nanjing several times. Tang and some of the others carried pistols, heckled the legislators, pushed and pulled them, and on one occasion broke windows and teacups in the empty Senate chamber. They reminded male legislators that they were skilled bomb makers. Strand points out that the women were deliberately rejecting conventional standards of womanly behavior: their actions were "appalling by design."[170] By August, when Tang and her two fellow suffragists mounted the stage, the assembled men knew full well why they were there.

Song Jiaoren, the man Tang Qunying slapped, had been her friend since her Tokyo days. He usually addressed her respectfully as "Elder Sister Tang." Both were veteran revolutionaries devoted to republican principles. But their opinions diverged on the suffrage question. Tang said that women had fought for the revolution and should have full rights. She was determined to ensure that the revolution fulfilled its promises to women: that they be empowered to act "in the public realm of parliaments, the press, and the street"[171] rather than confining their sphere of influence to the home. What brought her to the stage in August 1912 was not the rage of an outsider. It was a commitment to women's full political rights, upheld by women who had fought side by side with men as revolutionaries. These women continued their activism in suffrage groups and other women's organizations in the years after Tang denounced Song from the podium.

As the radical voices in the revolution were suppressed, a general conservatism gripped politics in general and attitudes toward women's rights in particular. Much ink was spilled on the training and behavior of girl students. Government guidelines on schools issued in January 1912 specified that girls should study the same curriculum as boys but should also be trained to embroider and run a household. Reports in the press focused on outlandish fashions worn by female students, and commentators worried that it was difficult to tell students from prostitutes on the basis of what they wore or how they comported themselves in public.[172] Yuan Shikai's minister of education made it clear that girls' schools were

not there to promote equal rights, women's suffrage, or new careers for women. Rather, he said in 1914, "the proper direction of women's education is to make them able to be excellent wives and virtuous mothers. . . . able to maintain the household—and that is all."[173]

The argument over suffrage continued. In late 1912, a women's journal commented in an editorial, "Today our country is not the Republic of China, but the Republic of Chinese Men. If this is not so, then why haven't women obtained the vote?"[174] But the efforts of women activists were ignored by the government. Regulations issued in 1914 rewarded women with plaques and ceremonial arches for the same sorts of virtues praised in the Ming and Qing dynasties, including filial behavior, chastity, thrift, and charitable work. In 1917 two new categories for reward were added: arts and crafts, and maintaining harmonious relations with one's relatives.[175]

Song Jiaoren, the slapped Nationalist Party leader, also became a victim of the conservative turn. He was murdered in spring 1913, almost certainly by agents of Yuan Shikai. In spite of her earlier disagreement with Song, Tang Qunying eulogized him, saying "his heart beat only to strengthen China."[176] She went on to attack Yuan Shikai as a traitor to the Republic. The Beijing government put out a ten-thousand-yuan reward for her arrest, and she had to flee to Shanghai and then to her hometown in Hunan, traveling via Hanoi to avoid detection. Meanwhile, Sun Yat-sen himself was compelled to flee the country.

Tang Qunying went on to found several publications and organize for women's rights and suffrage in the 1910s and 1920s.[177] She continued to use violence when she felt it was warranted. In 1913, for instance, she and several associates invaded the *Changsha Daily* offices to protest a slanderous news story accusing her of a sexual relationship with a man.[178] For Tang, it remained important to maintain a reputation for virtuous conduct, partly in order to preserve her political effectiveness—a standard that did not apply to male reformers and revolutionaries.[179] The American suffrage activist Carrie Chapman Catt visited China in 1912 as part of her work in international suffrage for women, declaring that Tang and others were an inspiration to her.[180] (Women in the United States did not win the right to vote until 1920.) Tang Qunying died in 1937, just before the Japanese invaded North China and a decade before the Nationalist government finally gave women the vote in 1947.[181]

The Revolution of 1911 ended the dynasty, but it fell far short of the revolutionaries' aspirations. Tang Qunying's slap marked a revolution betrayed—but it also demonstrated women's unprecedented boldness in publicly responding to betrayal. Her life as Tokyo student, bomb maker, fighter, educator, and political organizer mapped out one set of new possibilities in the lives of early twentieth-century women. In China of the 1910s and 1920s, the visions of change introduced in the late Qing continued to alter both representations of Woman and the life trajectories of Chinese women.

4

Imagined Futures, 1912–27
The May Fourth Story

In 1919, a suicide galvanized a generation of young activists. Riding in a bridal sedan chair to an arranged marriage she did not want, Zhao Wuzhen removed a razor from her footbindings and slit her own throat, sending a powerful message to her parents and the family of her fiancé. Suicide was commonly regarded not only as a sign of despair, but also as the ultimate form of personal revenge. It doomed those who had wronged the dead person to disgrace, potential financial ruin, and perpetual haunting by an angry ghost.[1]

But the young women and men who commented on Zhao Wuzhen's death in the press saw the suicide as something else: a call to arms against an oppressive family system. Tao Yi, a young woman activist who for a time was involved romantically with Mao Zedong, and who later became an educator,[2] pointed out that a young man could refuse his parents' choice of a fiancée for him. But a young woman, she wrote, "has no freedom to decide anything other than whether to hang herself; she has no possible answer besides the words 'I would rather die.'" Without her family's support, Tao added, "there will be nowhere on earth for her to go."[3] Mao Zedong, later to become head of the Chinese Communist Party, wrote in 1919 that Zhao had been killed by a society in which Chinese parents forced their children into unwanted marriages, thereby "all indirectly raping their sons and daughters." Mao called for radical change, saying that "the army of the family revolution will arise *en masse* and a great wave of freedom of marriage and freedom of love will break over China."[4]

This call for family revolution—an end to coerced arranged marriages and an increased say for young people in determining their own lives—

came at a time when the political revolution had failed. Yuan Shikai had suspended Parliament, rewritten the constitution, sponsored assassinations, and attempted his own coronation as emperor, but he was unable to establish effective control over the new nation's finances and territory.[5] In 1915, Japan presented China with what was called the Twenty-One Demands for expanded economic rights and the placement of Japanese administrators at many levels of government. Yuan was forced to yield to most of the economic demands. The revolution had produced neither stable government nor a defense from imperialist forces.

After Yuan's death in 1916, central government institutions nominally remained in place, but actual control passed to regional and local military men. The most powerful among them became warlords who engaged in dozens of major armed conflicts and hundreds of smaller skirmishes for control over more territory and, ultimately, the central government. China's warlords were an eclectic group who enacted various policies affecting women. One forbade footbinding in his territory and sponsored a conference to examine how to ensure "constancy and regularity of sexual intercourse between husbands and wives" as a means of combating prostitution.[6] Another pursued urban reform in Sichuan and was known for what Kristin Stapleton describes as "his collection of well-educated, short-haired, fashionably dressed wives [who] appeared frequently in public, sometimes on bicycles."[7]

Warlords brought much suffering to the people under their control, particularly in rural areas. Their demands for revenue and men, military campaigns, arms deals with imperialist powers, and shifting alliances ensured a constant state of instability. Warlord armies often were poorly paid and fed, undisciplined, and inclined to steal and rape. (This was one career path for "bare sticks" during this period; another was banditry, which was also endemic.) The warlord era persisted for more than a decade, until the Nationalists under Chiang Kai-shek (Jiang Jieshi) nominally unified China in 1928. But traces of warlord control, as chapters 5 and 6 will show, continued to mark national politics throughout the 1930s and 1940s.

Many writers and activists concluded that a political revolution alone could not change China. They believed that a cultural revolution was needed, and that what they called New Culture should begin in the most fundamental of social units: the family.[8] In the family, they said, people learned habits of subservience. This prevented them from becoming autonomous individuals and free citizens, which, in turn, weakened the Chinese polity. Furthermore, many argued, the emancipation of women was key to overthrowing the Chinese family system.

Initially, most who wrote on this subject were men. The magazine *Xin qingnian* (*New Youth*, with the French title of *La Jeunesse*) began publication in 1915. Its founder, Chen Duxiu, and others praised the virtues of youth over age, individualism over family authority, science over superstition, and democracy over authoritarian rule. Family elders, they said, wielded authority like despots, with the old oppressing the young and men oppressing women. Repeating criticisms made during the last years of the Qing, Chen wrote that most women did not participate in politics, as modern civilization required, because they were "bound by the Confucian teaching that 'to be a woman means to submit,' that 'the wife's words should not travel beyond her own apartment,' and that 'a woman does not discuss affairs outside the home.'"[9] He criticized teachings that mandated widow chastity, kept men and women from interacting, required a daughter-in-law to serve her husband's parents, and prevented women from making their own living outside the home. In focusing on the need for cultural change, Chen and other progressives targeted Confucianism and "superstition"—many popular religious practices—as the chief sources of China's backwardness. The liberation of youth and women from familial and customary strictures, they argued, would lead to a fairer and more democratic China.

This New Culture narrative about women and the family quickly became popular among young intellectuals. The benighted, ignorant, confined, and victimized figure of Woman, who could only be liberated by new ways of thinking and new political action, became a standard image in fictional writing, polemics, and news reports. In 1919, dissatisfaction about China's vulnerability in a world of rapacious imperialist nations gave rise to the May Fourth Movement, conjoining this discussion with national politics.

China had been on the side of the winning Allied powers in World War I, and more than one hundred thousand members of the Chinese Labor Corps had supported the war effort in Britain and France. When Germany lost the war, Chinese expected that German rights in Shandong Province would be returned to China, but the Treaty of Versailles granted those rights to Japan. Angry students protested in Beijing. They burned the residence of a government negotiator, demanding that the Chinese government reject the treaty. Protests spread throughout Chinese cities, accompanied by labor strikes and a boycott of Japanese goods.

The May Fourth Movement, which absorbed the New Culture critique, is now regarded in China as the origin point of China's 1949 revolution. Chen Duxiu, the editor of *New Youth*, went on to cofound the Chinese Communist Party (CCP) in 1921. In the early 1920s, with help from the Communist International (Comintern) in the newly established Soviet Union, Sun Yat-sen's Nationalist Party reorganized itself in south China. By 1923 the Nationalists and the CCP had entered into an alliance known as the United Front. Communists joined the Nationalist Party as individuals and played key roles in its propagandizing and organizing. Political mobilization of workers as well as students intensified after May 30, 1925, when British police in Shanghai's International Settlement killed thirteen demonstrators who were protesting the shooting of a worker in a Japanese-owned cotton mill.

In 1926, leaders of the Nationalist-CCP United Front mounted a military expedition from south China to oust the warlords and reunify China. As the United Front army marched north, young Communists organized worker strikes. Among rural dwellers, they publicized an agenda of lower land rents and introduced the notion of marriage freedom. Women soldiers joined the campaign, while women organizers began to create a mass women's movement. But when the United Front reached Shanghai, the Nationalists engineered a bloody coup that decimated the Communist leadership, followed by what became known as the White Terror, which ultimately drove the CCP out of the cities deep into the Chinese countryside.

New Culture/May Fourth writing has given us our most familiar images of Chinese women and the "woman question." Both the Nationalists and the Communists perpetuated what historians call "the May Fourth story": Chinese women had always been oppressed creatures who suffered terribly in families guided by Confucian values, and only a strong nation, governed by a strong state led by a dominant party, could ensure their liberation. The May Fourth story also specified what women needed to become in order to contribute to the Chinese nation: educated, employed, and free to choose their own spouses. Women's emancipation became part of the origin story of the CCP. Feminism emerged as a set of practices that could unify and strengthen China, helping to deliver it from warlordism and imperialism.[10]

But we need to reconsider the May Fourth story of an oppressed woman who had no recourse but suicide and was waiting for a political movement to liberate her. Like Liang Qichao's image of the parasitic ignorant woman, the May Fourth story makes many Chinese women and much of their daily activity invisible. This chapter cannot bring all women equally into view: sources about cities in this period are much richer than those describing the countryside, and rural areas were not much affected by the New Culture and May Fourth discussions. But many urban factory workers, sex workers, and domestic workers came from rural families, and it is possible to piece together a picture of why and how girls and women entered the cities. Women were subjects of public discussion not only in their role as homemakers, but also in offices, schools, factories, and brothels. These discussions sometimes echoed the May Fourth version of Woman, but the sheer variety of women's circumstances shows why that story is inadequate. By the early 1920s some women joined the revolutionary CCP and the United Front army, where women of both the Nationalist and Communist Parties briefly worked together to support the National Revolution of 1925–27.

Before tracing the entanglement of women, Woman, and revolution, however, we begin with a fictional Norwegian woman named Nora.

FINDING NORA

Nora was the heroine of the 1879 play *A Doll's House* by Henrik Ibsen. Unlikely as it may seem today, for many Chinese intellectuals in the late 1910s Nora embodied what women needed to become. *A Doll's House* was translated into Chinese in 1918, published and discussed in *New Youth* magazine, and widely performed in Chinese cities. In the play, Nora becomes aware of her own infantilization by her narcissistic husband, reinforced by broader social limitations on women. After a dramatic confrontation with her husband, Nora leaves home. The play ends with the sound of her slamming the door.

Chinese readers were enthralled by Nora's rejection of a cloying family system and her assertion of self. For Hu Shi, who had received his PhD in philosophy from Columbia University in 1917 and returned to China as a leader of the New Culture movement, "Ibsenism" highlighted the development of the individual's unique personality and social obligations alike. And of all the Confucian institutions that suppressed the individual, the family system was the most overbearing. Although Nora's problems stemmed from her social and legal role as wife and mother, Vera Schwarcz observes that "the predicament of women thus spoke most directly to the emotional needs of young men trapped in social duties not of their own choosing. Nora . . . fired the imagination of Chinese sons."[11] And given the strictures against women appearing onstage, it was most often young men who played Nora in productions of *A Doll's House*.

Lu Xun, a prominent writer of fiction and critical essays, cautioned readers not merely to admire the defiant gesture that ended the play. "What Happens after Nora Walks Out?," he asked in a 1923 talk to some of his students at a women's teacher training college in Beijing. Lu Xun observed that without education or employment, Nora would have three unattractive choices: return to her husband, "fall into degradation" (i.e., become a prostitute), or starve to death[12] (see box 4.1).

Lu Xun's point was that individual heroic gestures alone could not change society: broader transformation was required. But the Nora question had other dimensions. What became of all the Chinese women— some not yet married, but all from families with considerable authority

BOX 4.1.
Lu Xun, "What Happens after Nora Walks Out?"

What happens after Nora walks out? . . . Logically . . . Nora really has only two options: to fall into degradation or to return home. A bird in a cage lacks any kind of freedom, no doubt, but should it leave its cage, dangers lurk outside: hawks, cats, and so on; and if it has been shut up for so long that its wings have atrophied or it has forgotten how to fly, then truly it has no way out. There is another possibility—that is, to starve to death—but since starving means departing from life, it's no solution to the problem and so is not a way out either. . . .

And yet once Nora had awakened, it was not easy for her to return to dreamland, so her only recourse was to leave; but after she'd left, she soon faced the inevitable choice between degradation and returning home. Otherwise, we are obliged to ask, what did Nora take with her apart from her awakened mind? If she had nothing but a crimson woolen shawl like you young ladies, it would be completely useless, whether it was two feet wide or three feet wide. She would still need something more substantial that could go in her purse; to be blunt, she would need money.

Dreams are fine, but otherwise money is essential. . . .

So for Nora, money (or to put it more elegantly, economic means) is crucial. It is true that freedom cannot be bought, but it can be sold. Human beings have one major defect: they are apt to get hungry. To compensate for this defect and avoid acting like puppets, economic rights seem to be the most important factor in present-day society. First, there must be a fair division of property between men and women in the family; second, there must be an equal division of power between men and women in society at large. Unfortunately, I have no idea how to obtain these rights, other than that we will have to fight for them, perhaps with even more violence than we have to fight for our political rights.

Source: Lu Xun, *Jottings under Lamplight*, ed. Eileen J. Cheng and Kirk Denton. Translated by Bonnie S. McDougall (Cambridge, MA: Harvard University Press, 2017). Reprinted in "What Happens after Nora Walks Out," China Channel, September 29, 2017. https://chinachannel.org/2017/09/29/lu-xun-nora.

over them—who already had left home as students, white-collar workers, factory workers, prostitutes, teahouse hostesses, entertainers, domestics, activists, and revolutionaries? And what sorts of transformations were beginning for women within Chinese homes? Many women, particularly in urban areas, were not confined in the ways suggested by the May Fourth story. In women's magazines, housewives read about global ideas of modernity and scientific household management. They engaged in patriotic campaigns to boycott the products of aggressive foreign powers and buy nationally produced rather than imported goods. Some women forged illustrious careers as educators and writers. Poor women sought employment in new factories and small workshops, contributing to the support of their parents, siblings, and children. Some women, like Qiu Jin in the last years of the Qing, did slam the door, engaging in protracted struggles with family members who opposed their political activities or personal choices. Still others, particularly prostitutes, would have fallen into Lu Xun's category of "falling into degradation." Nevertheless, these women were not the socially isolated victims so prominent in New Culture/May Fourth writing.

AT HOME AND IN THE OFFICE

In the 1910s and early 1920s, portrayals of what a home should be were reconfigured, and even in many conservative writings the married woman was depicted as a skilled custodian of the modern home, crucial to the stability of the new nation. Prescriptions for how to navigate daily life inside and outside the home appeared in new magazines such as the *Women's Eastern Times* [Funü shibao], the *Ladies' Journal* [Funü zazhi], and *Chinese Women* [Zhonghua funü jie].[13] All of their titles incorporated the term *funü*, a classical word that originally had referred to wives and daughters but now was used to refer to women in respectable public roles.[14] Joan Judge calls the women who were the subjects of these magazines "Republican ladies"—teachers and other professional women, students, and older women from genteel families who were active in philanthropy and civic-minded public life.[15]

Women appeared in, read, and sometimes wrote for these magazines, although male readers likely far outnumbered women, in part because educated men regarded discussion of women's issues as a quintessentially modern practice.[16] Men wrote for the journals too, often using female pen names. Much of the didactic literature directed at women—unbind your feet, get educated, teach, get out and see the world—was crafted by men.[17] Both the *Ladies' Journal* and *Women's Eastern Times* showed what women were wearing, how they were making a living, what they were learning in school, what sorts of physical exercise they did, how they were advised to keep house and give birth, and where lines were drawn or blurred between respectable sexuality and sex work. As a group, these magazines depict how an emergent vision and practice of urban modernity, inside and outside the home, were changing the possibilities for women.[18]

Women's Eastern Times and the *Ladies' Journal* offered their readers foreign models of womanly achievement: author George Eliot, educator

Photo 4.1. Woman out and about, 1914

Source: *Funü shibao* (Women's Eastern Times), 13 (April 1914), cover. Courtesy of Joan Judge.

Mary Lyon, Queen Victoria, the wives and daughters of emperors and presidents, and martial heroines including Joan of Arc. *Women's Eastern Times* also described the lives of American college women at places such as Bryn Mawr, highlighting their social interactions, physical fitness, and participation in student government.[19] *Fiction Monthly*, its title notwithstanding, offered nonfictional accounts of successful businesswomen in Europe and the United States, including gold miners in the Yukon Territory and boat captains in Scandinavia.[20] *Women's Eastern Times* also published classical poetry by women celebrating Qiu Jin and other heroines of the 1911 revolution and denouncing Japan's Twenty-One Demands of 1915.[21] The language in these journals mixed classical Chinese, terms imported from Japan, and the vernacular language of daily life, which language reformers were beginning to incorporate into publications aimed at broadening the community of readers. Some of the content was translated or adapted from Euro-American and Japanese publications, bringing global discussions about reproduction, sexuality, eugenics, and scientific household management into domestic circulation.[22]

The imagined woman reader of the *Ladies' Journal* was, above all, the expert manager of a small modern household. The new science of home economics in the United States provided a model, conveyed through translations about hygiene, home economics, and the benefits of the Parent-Teacher Association from the U.S. *Ladies' Home Journal* and other publications.[23] Women were introduced to newly invented objects, such as toasters and hair dryers, and given directions for keeping bees and raising chickens, making paper, fashioning hats and gloves, tending a garden, and pruning fruit trees.[24] They were instructed to learn to use a sewing machine, master the science behind household chemistry and home health care, and keep meticulous household accounts.[25] The science underlying household management was portrayed as ever-changing, and it was the duty of the modern housewife to keep up with rising standards.[26]

The *Ladies' Journal* offered—indeed prescribed—what Helen Schneider calls the "happy family ideology," centered on "the middle- and upper-class urban fantasy of a two-parent family with a few children in a clean, well-managed home." The lady of such a household would expertly manage a domestic space in which "contented families" would form the foundation of a stronger China.[27] Some writers opined, Paul Bailey says, that a woman's "role in the household was as significant for national well-being as a man's role in the military."[28]

To play this role, a woman needed to be healthy, and women's health was defined as a matter of national importance. Articles in the *Women's Eastern Times* decried the "hunchbacked" posture and "ashen complexions" of Chinese women in contrast to tall and sturdy American women. Authors warned that breast binding would damage both respiration and breast-feeding. They promoted the use of fabric menstrual pads rather than rags and portrayed menstruation as a normal bodily process determined by women's physiology. But menstruation was also conceptualized as a time of vulnerability, in which lack of care could lead to later illnesses.[29] A 1919 *Ladies' Journal* article translated from Japanese in two parts explained that menstruating women were more likely than other women to engage in criminal behavior, that pregnancy could make them susceptible to a variety of deadly diseases, and that sexual difference was firmly rooted in nature.[30] Here the desire to participate in the circulation of modern scientific knowledge worked at cross-purposes with the desire to establish women as fully educated citizens of a strong China, because much of the translated material suggested that women were naturally inferior to men in physique and intellect. One male author writing for the *Ladies' Journal* in 1918 listed eight shortcomings of Chinese women: "self-indulgence, laziness, licentiousness, bias, stupidity, narrow-mindedness, jealousy, and viciousness."[31]

As the May Fourth Movement expanded, the *Ladies' Journal* turned its attention to the goal of women's emancipation. Readers were offered translations of Japanese feminist writings and Euro-American feminist and socialist essays.[32] Authors, many of them male, continued to admonish women to reform themselves so that they could help reform China. The *Ladies' Journal* also discussed obstacles to women's emancipation in special issues devoted to divorce, reproductive health, love and marriage, chastity, and the women's movement.[33]

Women's journals offered frequent discussions of how a modern woman should navigate romantic love and sex while also strengthening the nation through eugenics: the pursuit of desired genetic traits through selective reproduction.[34] In 1922, the *Ladies' Journal* editor argued that the sexual liberation of women would lead to improved motherhood and thus "the evolution of the race and the advancement of humankind."[35] He drew on the thinking of Swedish feminist Ellen Key, who emphasized a biological basis for gender difference, extolled women's capacity for motherhood, and saw love itself as biologically based and eugenic because "when love was given free rein devoid of any ulterior motives, both the individual and the race would benefit."[36] The journal continued this discussion in its first issue of 1925 on "the new sexual morality," in which the male editors and writers argued for an individual's sexual pleasure, the importance of love, the right to divorce, and the idea that sexual arrangements would "benefit the future generations of a nation."[37] Writers linked sex to a recurrent global discussion, circulating in China since the late Qing, in which strengthening the nation and "the race" were overlapping projects.[38] Feminism thus became entangled with eugenics and attention to women's reproductive role, as it was in many other parts of the world during this same period.[39] When the American birth control activist Margaret Sanger gave several public lectures in China in 1922, she found her audience as interested in the idea that planned births could improve the quality of the Chinese people as they were in its benefits for women.[40] The assumption was that if people were free to choose their own partners, sexual satisfaction would rise along with the quality of children, putting Chinese society on a trajectory of improvement.[41]

But this trajectory was not assured. Women writers did not always agree that the "new morality" advocated by male feminists was good for women, nor did they find male notions of the New Woman capacious enough. In an acerbic piece titled "To Men" published in the journal *New Woman* at the end of 1926, woman writer and journalist Chen Xuezhao opined that marriages between educated men and educated women were often unhappy ones. The men wanted good mothers for their children and entertaining wives for themselves, she said, but they "cannot meet these women's psychological and physiological needs." In a follow-up piece, she elaborated that once educated women had to stop working outside the home to care for homes and children, their husbands would soon "forget how intelligent and accomplished their wives once were and how active they could be in society had they not chosen to take their roles as wives and mothers so seriously." Chen also published two short stories about educated women who found marriage and life at home confining and unsatisfactory.[42]

The New Woman, a social category portrayed in journals and the press, was educated, concerned about national political events, and perhaps politically active. She was self-supporting, most commonly working as a teacher or in an office, bank, department store, publishing house, telephone company, or law firm.[43] She possessed personhood (*ren'ge*), which meant she could think for herself and act with integrity.[44] She was, in short, the woman that Nora might hope to become.

And yet, just as the visibility of women students made commentators uneasy, the appearance of working women in workplaces dominated by men occasioned anxious and sometimes sensationalistic public discussion. This was the case with Xi Shangzhen, a young woman secretary at a business journal who hanged herself with an electric tea-kettle cord in the office one evening in 1922.[45] Xi had given five thousand yuan to her male employer, Tang Jiezhi, to invest in the Shanghai stock market. She lost the entire sum when the market collapsed. This was her third suicide attempt. Her family accused Tang, a U.S.-educated, politically active reformer, of fraud and of pressuring Xi to become his concubine, charges that he vociferously denied.

After Xi Shangzhen's death, Tang Jiezhi was tried and imprisoned for fraud, in spite of scant evidence. The case occasioned an outpouring of essays in newspapers and tabloids, as well as poems and a play. As Bryna Goodman points out, commentators drew varying lessons from the suicide. Conservatives focused their criticism on Tang, whose political activities had made him many enemies. Xi's suicide also became an opportunity to criticize the stock market, a new and unstable institution widely regarded as mysterious, dangerous, and possibly "death-inducing."[46] Men active in the New Culture discussions looked upon Xi "as a gender pioneer who was victimized by an insufficiently reformed society."[47] Some feminist commentators, drawing on the powerful historical connection between suicide and women's virtue, opined that Xi had committed suicide to preserve her chastity.[48] This was a complicated claim: it voiced anxiety that women's presence in public would inevitably expose them to sexual threat, but at the same time it asserted that women did not lose their sense of virtue by going out to work, as conservative critics feared.

Before and during the New Culture movement, many writers cautioned educated women to navigate carefully between an active cosmopolitan public life and adherence to "the old principles of calmness, quiet, frugality, domesticity, and attentiveness to educating the young,"[49] as one male writer for *Women's Eastern Times* put it. This was not the call for family revolution made by the fans of Nora, who had emphasized autonomy and choice, but it was a persistent set of prescriptions for women voiced by both men and women writers for the new journals.

DOMESTIC SERVANTS

For many women, of course, the home was not a scientifically managed unit where they presided. It was a workplace where they were employed as domestic servants to perform household labor.

Of the servants employed by wealthy families, bondmaids or slave girls engendered the most discussion in the press. These were young girls, often between eight and twelve years old, typically bought from destitute rural families and transported for sale into wealthy urban households. Bondmaid contracts specified the amount that the seller would receive in return for the girl. The purchaser had absolute authority over her and the right to resell her to another owner. She was to live and work in that household in return for room and board until she reached marriageable age, at which time the contract specified that her owner should find her a mate—which could mean either that she was married off or that she was given as a concubine to a wealthy man. During the early Republic, critics of the bondmaid practice pushed for its abolition, pointing to the domestic confinement of the girls, unlimited working hours, and potential for physical and sexual abuse. In response, defenders of the bondmaid practice portrayed it as a form of benevolent employment and protection that saved girls from starvation or prostitution and later ensured them permanent sustenance as a wife or concubine.[50]

Bondmaids were only one type of household servant. Wealthy households in the Zhejiang city of Ningbo employed scullery maids from poor families who cleaned and cooked and washed, as well as attendants who assisted with personal grooming.[51] When married women worked as servants, either under a contract or a more informal arrangement, they usually lived in. In addition to room and board they received a regular wage, which in 1920s Beijing might be three to six *yuan* per month, as well as bonuses and tips. Employment agencies, often run by older women, connected job seekers with households who wanted servants. Their duties included housekeeping, mending, child care, and errands such as shopping.[52]

Servants were often new immigrants to the city or urban women who had fallen on hard times—abandoned when a husband left home to seek work and disappeared, or impoverished by a husband's opium addiction. In her first-person account Ning Lao T'ai-t'ai, the Shandong woman who began to work as a maid after her husband twice tried to sell their daughter to support his opium habit, expressed her shame at having to work outside the home. To her it was more difficult than begging. "For a year I had begged for my food but had lived in my own home. Now I could not live in my home and must 'come out,' even though women of my family had never 'come out' before."[53] In the homes of her various employers, Chinese and foreign, she sewed clothing for the children, cooked, did the family's laundry, waited on table, combed the mistress's hair, and cared for a baby. She emphasized that she knew how to behave properly in any circumstances, having been raised in a respectable family, in contrast to some of her employers who were former bondmaids and prostitutes.[54]

STUDENTS

In 1916, when Xie Bingying was ten years old, her mother defied conventional opinion in their Hunan village to enroll her in a private school where all of the other students were boys.[55] But her mother balked when Xie, encouraged by her older brother, asked to attend the Datong Girls School in Changsha. She relented only after Xie refused to eat for three days. At Datong, against her mother's explicit orders, Xie unbound her feet at the age of twelve. She went on to attend two other girls' schools and a teacher training institute, eventually becoming famous as a soldier during the Northern Expedition (see below), a war reporter, and author of a well-known autobiography.

Not every girl student went on to become a revolutionary or a writer. But the growth of girls' education produced an alternative social universe to the family, an incubator for political activity, and a refuge for students and teachers fleeing family constraints and parentally arranged marriages.[56] Girls' middle schools, teacher training schools, and the small number of universities open to young women became sites for new social relationships and the spread of new ideas, particularly about feminism, nationalism, and revolution.

The number of girls attending school at all levels continued to increase in the 1910s and 1920s, from 141,130 in non-mission schools in 1912–13 to 417,820 in 1922–23. But girls remained a small minority of students nationally, in the range of 5 to 7 percent.[57] The number of women university students nationally was small: 847 in 1923 and 1,495 in 1928, or 8.5 percent of the total university student population.[58] Nonstudents far outnumbered students at every level. In the North China province of Zhili, for instance, one-third of all boys attended school in 1916, but only 1.24 percent of girls.[59]

Young women who attended teacher training schools studied tuition-free, and graduates were expected to teach in primary and middle schools. As the public education system expanded, so did positions open to women teachers, who gradually began teaching at higher levels of education as well.[60] Chen Hengzhe (1890–1976), who studied at Vassar and the University of Chicago, in 1920 became China's first woman university professor, briefly teaching history at Beijing University.[61]

The curriculum at girls' schools was in flux during the early Republic. In middle schools, students attended courses in Chinese history, foreign history, Chinese geography, foreign geography, and civics. Boys did military training, while girls were given classes in home economics, gardening, and sewing. Girls spent fewer hours on mathematics, foreign language, and physical education than boys.[62] By the early 1920s, critiques of Chinese family practices and women's status were making their way into some national language textbooks.[63]

Girl students usually boarded at middle schools, and the experience built a new sense of identity. Young women who published articles often identified themselves by school, and class portraits of women students filled the pages of women's magazines.[64] Girl students performed dances on National Day and other occasions, participating in new rituals of citizenship.[65] Outside the classroom, students were exposed to New Culture and political ideas through lectures, study societies, and journals.[66]

The appearance of young women students in public spaces continued to engender significant anxiety. Officials and conservative reformers continually proposed that girls' schools should be the place where students learned how to manage a household, including the skills of cooking,

Photo 4.2.   Students, 1913

Source: Funü shibao (Women's Eastern Times), 9 (February 1913), cover. Courtesy of Joan Judge.

needlework, nutrition, hygiene, budgeting, and child rearing.[67] *Women's Eastern Times* featured many articles cautioning women students to dress simply, reject the fashions set by courtesans, exercise restraint in relationships with men, and avoid the perils of same-sex love, reportedly endemic in girls' schools.[68] Embedded in many of these criticisms was the fear that women were becoming Westernized, a catch-all category that included haircuts with bangs, gold-rimmed glasses, high heels, skirts without trousers worn underneath, public displays of affection with young men, same-sex relationships with fellow students, rejection of parental authority over marriage, and showing greater interest in international affairs than in keeping house.[69]

On campus, students often struggled with adult authorities over restrictions on their behavior. They criticized school administrators for opening women students' mail to search for inappropriate contacts with young men.[70] Xie Bingying and her classmates pressured an older woman teacher to resign after she warned them not to laugh or talk with their friendly young male science teacher, causing him to quit in anger.[71] When a male principal forbade women students at Beijing Women's Normal School to read newspapers in 1913, the students wrote protest letters to the Ministry of Education and prominent periodicals.[72]

In 1925, students at the same school, now called Beijing Women's Normal University, succeeded in forcing the removal of their woman chancellor, Yang Yinyu. Chancellor Yang, who had been educated at Columbia Teacher's College, imposed many restrictions on students and expelled politically active young women. She had consistently portrayed herself as a mother to the students, but Lu Xun, who taught there, wrote that she was more like an autocratic mother-in-law oppressing a child bride.[73] Activist women students occupied Yang's office in a confrontation that went on for half a year before Yang was dismissed and the school temporarily closed, with the police removing the resisting students from campus by force.[74]

Girl students were active off campus as well. Some taught in literacy programs established by their schools for poor people in the vicinity, a first step toward political mobilization of the poor.[75] More than a thousand women students marched in demonstrations during the May Fourth Movement.[76] Xie Bingying was expelled from a missionary-run school in 1920 for organizing a parade on National Humiliation Day to recall the Twenty-One Demands imposed by Japan in 1915. As she commented sardonically in her autobiography, "At twilight that day I departed God's school, rewarded with expulsion only because I loved my country."[77] In 1925 she joined other Changsha students in a citywide parade protesting the May 30th killing of protesters in Shanghai.

But when student protestors moved their activities off campus, they entered a danger zone. In March 1926, six women students were among the forty-seven demonstrators shot and killed in Beijing by the troops of warlord and provisional president Duan Qirui. Lu Xun had taught one of the slain women, Liu Hezhen, at Beijing Women's Normal University. His mournful elegy for her, full of political despair, found a small sign of hope in the courage of the women students:

> Only last year did I begin to notice how Chinese women manage public affairs. Though they are few, I have often been impressed by their ability, determination and indomitable spirit. The attempt of these girls to rescue each other amid a hail of bullets, regardless of their own safety, is a clearer indication of the courage of Chinese women which has persisted through the thousands of years of conspiracies against them and suppression. If we are looking for the significance of this casualty for the future, it probably lies here.[78]

FACTORY GIRLS AND HANDICRAFT WOMEN

Women workers in modern industrial factories such as cotton mills, silk filatures, and tobacco-processing plants were a new phenomenon in the early twentieth century. Machine-powered industries were concentrated mainly in a few treaty-port cities, with Shanghai the dominant center of manufacturing. By 1915, one study estimated that 620,000 women nationwide were working in industry.[79] Government statistics put the number of women much lower, at roughly a quarter million—slightly more than one-third of the total number of industrial workers nationwide.[80]

Perhaps the numbers varied in part because who counted as a "woman worker" (*nügong*) and what counted as a "factory" changed from survey to survey. Many women working in industry were not actually in factories. Some women in Shanghai, for instance, collated books at home for bookstores, which would send an agent to drop off printed pages and collect the collated manuscripts.[81] Others labored in workplaces with no mechanized equipment, such as the several thousand Beijing women in 1918 who, a contemporary observer said, sat "on the floor all day long" in an "immense building" founded by the Ministry of War, earning a few coins a day sewing military uniforms.[82] Some women, such as Shanghai's cotton mill workers, worked in sprawling complexes full of imported mechanized machinery. And some were not adult women, but girls as young as five laboring in the silk filatures of Shanghai, where children and adolescents beat cocoons over basins of very hot water to loosen the threads, often burning themselves in the process. The thread was then

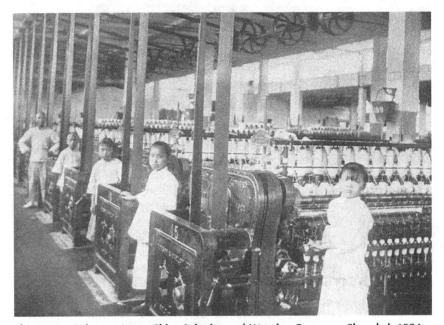

Photo 4.3.   Spinners, Japan-China Spinning and Weaving Company, Shanghai, 1924
Source: Far Eastern Review (August 1924), National Archives and Record Administration. Reproduced in
Virtual Shanghai, http://www.virtualshanghai.net/Photos/Images?ID=35154.

reeled by adult women.[83] "Woman worker," in short, was a flexible and
somewhat blurry category.

What is clear is that from the 1910s on, the figure of the woman
worker became the subject of growing public concern. Chinese researchers trained in American social science methods sought to quantify her
wages and household expenditures.[84] Missionaries and Chinese reformers deplored her working and living conditions and sometimes worried
about her virtue in factory settings, where she could be preyed upon by
men. Left-wing essayists wrote about the need for a proletarian revolution to free her from appalling factory conditions.[85] Like the figure of
Woman more generally, the woman worker emerged in print mainly as
a social problem that needed addressing. As with most nonelite women,
accounts in their own words of how women workers understood their
lives remain extremely rare.

The circumstances of women factory workers in Shanghai, China's
biggest industrial city, are easiest to reconstruct from the surviving
historical records. Chinese-owned factories expanded there while foreign powers were occupied elsewhere during World War I, but modern
cotton mills through the 1920s remained dominated by foreign capital.

Japanese companies increased their number of mills from eleven to thirty-two between 1919 and 1925.[86] By the late 1910s, about thirty thousand women were working in Shanghai cotton mills, silk filatures, and paper mills.[87] By 1929, the number of women in these industries, as well as tobacco, matches, food processing, and others had reportedly grown to 173,432. At that point women were 61 percent of the total Shanghai factory workforce and about three-fourths of the workforce in cotton mills and silk filatures. More than 84,000 adult women were cotton spinners, more than 22,000 were cotton weavers, and more than 12,000 worked in silk filatures.[88] Women comprised a much lower percentage of the workforce in other industrial cities.[89]

Most women workers in Shanghai were new arrivals from the countryside.[90] Some had followed family members to the city, drawn by stories of plentiful jobs or propelled by economic or political distress in the villages.[91] Women workshop supervisors played a key role in hiring new women workers, drawing on kinship or native-place connections.[92] By the 1930s, some rural women were being recruited from their villages by labor contractors. This could often shade over into trafficking.[93] The woman's parents would sign a contract and accept a payment in several installments. In return, the broker agreed to take their daughter to Shanghai, find her a factory job, and take responsibility for her housing and safety. The young woman's wages were paid to the contractor.

An agreement with a contractor may have lessened the worries of rural parents about the fate of their daughters in the city. But under this contract labor system, young women were often confined by the contractor at all times when not at work, forced to provide unpaid domestic labor, and sometimes sexually assaulted. If the factories were not hiring when a broker brought a new group to Shanghai, he might decide instead to sell them to brothels that catered to lower-class customers.[94] Because contractors often belonged to the Green Gang, a secret society network with underworld connections whose members controlled much of the Shanghai economy by the late 1920s, contract laborers were in no position to dispute the terms of the contract.[95]

Living conditions in Yangshupu and other Shanghai mill districts were not necessarily an improvement over the villages.[96] Women and child workers lived in "unending rows of dingy, sunless little houses," American observer Margaret Burton noted in 1918.[97] Their two-story mud-floor dwellings did not have running water or electricity. Nearby creeks provided water for cooking and washing. Some recent migrants lived even more simply in shack settlements along Suzhou Creek or the Huangpu River.[98] Each morning and evening, groups of women walked to the mills or rode to and from work on wheelbarrows. Burton wrote:

Some of them had come a distance of two, three, even five miles. How it is possible to sleep on such squealing, bumping conveyances, I do not know, but it is done. We counted thirteen women on one of them, six on one side, seven on the other, most of them asleep with their heads on each other's shoulders.[99]

Inside the mills, the shifts were twelve hours long, and the factories ran day and night, with workers changing shifts on alternate weeks. Each step in the production of thread and cloth required dexterity and attention.[100] Wages, hours, working conditions, and safety measures were left up to factory owners. The machinery set the pace, noise and dust were ubiquitous, and lunch or bathroom breaks were rare. Sometimes a woman contrived to take a nap on the shop floor while someone else substituted for her.[101] Mistakes in the work were punished with fines, deducted from the daily wage. Dire safety conditions and grisly industrial accidents, particularly those involving sleepy children and mechanized machinery, filled the pages of missionary publications, women's magazines, and political broadsides.[102] Labor regulations were impossible to enforce.[103] Many accounts also highlighted the threat of sexual harassment and sexual assault in the silk filatures and cotton mills.[104]

In this challenging environment, women cotton mill workers relied on networks of people from the same native place for support. Workers from different native places often had trouble communicating and did not get along. Women often felt that they had more in common with their shift supervisors from the same native place than with fellow workers from another region. Mill hands born south of the Yangzi River predominated in the weaving departments and often derided those born north of the river, known as Subei or Jiangbei people, who worked in the lower-paid and dirtier spinning process.[105] Women from Subei also tended to concentrate in Japanese-owned mills, where apparently managers were more willing to hire them than in Chinese-owned factories.[106]

The mills had a clear gendered division of labor, and although the specifics changed over time, some tasks were routinely assigned to men and others to women.[107] Unless she had a male relative or knew a fellow villager working elsewhere in the mill, a woman worker did not generally socialize with male mill hands because of concerns about sexual advances and reputation. All of these factors hindered the emergence of a unified working class.

Strikes roiled Shanghai's cotton mills between 1922 and 1927, but women generally were not the leaders. In some instances where women were recorded as striking, it appears that they were blocked from entering their workplaces by striking male workers.[108] In search of docile workers, mill managers expanded the hiring of women, and by 1929 women predominated in the industry.[109] They were more likely in the 1920s to join sisterhoods for mutual protection than to become union members or political activists. This situation did not change until the 1940s.[110]

Women silk workers were more militant than cotton mill hands, even though the industry was dominated by Chinese capital and so nationalist protests against imperialism were not a factor. The main grievances in the silk filatures were economic.[111] Strikes tended to erupt in summer, when the heat in the filatures became unbearable. In August 1922, women in more than forty silk filatures struck for four days for a shorter (ten-hour) workday and better working conditions. At one point in this strike, a disagreement over whether to extend the strike occurred between the footbound but more militant women migrants from Yancheng and the unbound but more conservative women from Taizhou. Silk workers did not participate in the general strike of the May Thirtieth Movement in 1925, but by mid-1926 they went on strike with the support of the CCP. Strikes over pay and working hours continued in the silk filatures even after the 1927 suppression of CCP organizers (see below).[112]

Many striking silk workers got little support from their families, however, because a woman active outside the home was suspected of immoral activity. One Communist woman organizer described the problem in terms that echoed Nora's dilemma:

> Brave and enthusiastic young women workers who wanted to strive to maintain the strike could of course sever family bonds and march courageously forward. But sooner or later they had to return home. It was said that when they went home they were scolded, scorned, and beaten by parents, elder brothers, and sisters-in-law. Given nothing to eat, they were left to starve to death. The other family members said, "Not having come home for several days, you must have been shacking up with somebody. This kind of girl can go away and die." One worker's father gave her a length of rope and a knife, asking her to make her own choice.[113]

Right up to 1949, Communist organizers in Beijing reported that factory work still carried such a stigma of unrespectable behavior that some "chose to hide their occupations" and "attempted to disguise themselves as students by adopting students' dress styles, hairstyles, and behavior."[114]

For many women, factory work was a temporary expedient. They left the mills upon marriage. Matches were generally arranged for them by their relatives or the women shift supervisors, methods that bore little resemblance to the new marriage practices envisioned in *New Youth* and other publications.[115] After marriage, former mill workers returned to the countryside or turned to housework and child care in their urban homes, interspersed with stints of casual labor.

In the households of the urban poor, men's earnings as peddlers, rickshaw pullers, or itinerant laborers were not enough to support a family.[116]

Women contributed to household income by entering handicraft work-shops to embroider or make matchboxes, or assisting in small family busi-nesses such as street vending or recycling.[117] Some took in mending and laundry, or earned a piece wage sewing clothes, spinning wool, embroi-dering, making lace, or fashioning artificial flowers at home with material provided by merchants. One study estimates that in the 1930s more than fifty thousand Beijing women earned money by embroidering.[118] None of these women would have been counted as having an occupation (*zhiye*) in formal social surveys; they would likely have been classified as unem-ployed. And yet, like the many poor women who helped their husbands run small businesses, they helped to sustain themselves and their families by working at home.

COURTESANS AND STREETWALKERS

The worst fate Lu Xun could imagine for Nora, short of starving to death, was "falling into degradation"—that is, becoming a prostitute. Hundreds of thousands of women did sex work in 1910s and 1920s cities, where male residents and sojourners greatly outnumbered women.[119] Prostitutes ranged from high-class courtesans, who sang and provided dinner com-panionship for elite men at restaurants, to streetwalkers known in Shanghai as "pheasants," who lurked in alleyways and often pickpocketed their cus-tomers.[120] The elaborate hierarchy of prostitution had a niche for Chinese men of every income level, as well as separate groups of women servicing Western sailors and Japanese businessmen.[121] In Shanghai, the most beauti-ful and highly valued courtesans were said to come from Suzhou, and the streetwalkers who serviced lower-class customers were said to be natives of Subei. In Beijing, women from Jiangsu dominated the high end of the market, and Hebei and local Beijing women filled the cheaper houses.[122]

This variety makes it difficult to generalize about the lives of prosti-tutes. We do know that some came from impoverished farming families and were trafficked to brothels. Press reports in mid-1920s Beijing warned of gangsters who abducted young women for sale to brothels and de-scribed desperately poor men who sold their wives to brothels to settle debts.[123] Whether a young woman ended up as a contract worker in a cot-ton mill or a prostitute in a low-class brothel depended on many factors: a city's employment structure, job vacancies, trafficker networks, physical attractiveness, and chance.

Some women came from educated families who had fallen on hard times, but even a girl with no previous education might be purchased by the madam of a courtesan house. She would be trained to sing and recite

poetry and eventually have her virginity sold to a wealthy patron, because some men believed that sleeping with a virgin brought good luck in
business. Sex in courtesan houses could be expensive, but it was seldom
a straightforward cash-for-services transaction. A man had to present a
courtesan with gifts and win her favor, and that of her madam, in order
to become a regular patron and possibly gain access to her sexual services.
Guidebooks warned men newly arriving in Shanghai that they needed
to comport themselves correctly according to the rituals and etiquette
of courtesan houses, or else the women would ridicule them as country
bumpkins. Courtesans became the arbiters of sophisticated urbanity.

The most famous courtesans became minor celebrities of the tabloid
press, where literary men published their praises. From the 1860s to 1920,
when a reform campaign intervened, the city's most famous courtesans
were awarded mock official titles by tabloid newspapers in a recurrent
contest, based upon how many patrons wrote flowery letters of recom-
mendation describing their beauty and singing skills. The titles mimicked
those granted to men who garnered top scores in the Qing civil service
examinations, and later were renamed after Republican government
positions such as president and prime minister. Gossip columns traced
courtesans' love affairs, rivalries, financial troubles in which they pawned
jewelry to pay their bills, and their attempts to flee their madams by running off with handsome but impoverished suitors.

The degree of control that a courtesan had over her own working life
depended upon her age and her relationship with the madam, who might
have purchased her as a child and raised her, and whom she would then
address as "mother." A courtesan had to hand over a portion of all her
earnings to her madam or the brothel owner. If she wanted to redeem her
contract, she also had to pay a substantial sum to the madam, and the
most common way to do so was to take up with a wealthy patron who
might then take her as a concubine. Clearing one's debts by becoming a
concubine was known colloquially as "taking a bath."

Courtesans lived their working and personal lives in public. Their
photographic portraits, in elaborate costumes ranging from Chinese op-
eratic dress to Western gowns and floral hats, adorned the windows of
picture studios, and courtesan albums circulated widely. Often the props
in these pictures included Western-style furniture, automobiles, and even
airplanes, with the courtesans serving as a medium to introduce all of the
accoutrements of modern urban life to a viewing audience.[124] Popular literature in the early Republic was full of descriptions of their lives, loves,
and travails, told with detail and sympathy (though not in their own
words) by male authors writing fiction for popular magazines, newspapers, and publishing houses.

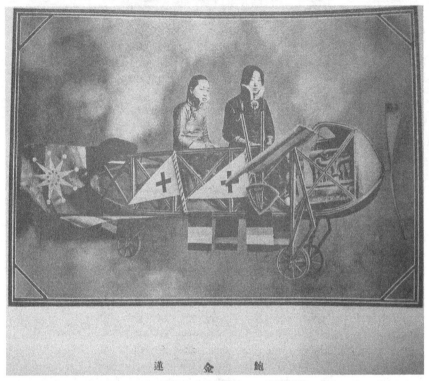

Photo 4.4.   Courtesans in mock airplane at photography studio, 1914
Source: *Xin jinghong ying* (Shanghai: Youzheng shuju, 1914). Courtesy of Joan Judge.

Writers talked differently about prostitutes who serviced lower-class customers: as emblematic figures of urban disorder and distress. Guidebooks and the press described how impoverished women found themselves scrabbling to survive not only as "pheasant" pickpockets, but also in opium brothels known as "flower-smoke rooms," tawdry "salt-pork shops" where the "meat" was not quite fresh, and other colorfully named low-class brothels. Streetwalkers were portrayed as both dangerous and victimized: trafficked, prone to petty crime, and at risk for tumbling further down the hierarchy as they aged or contracted sexually transmitted diseases. The only places where we can read fragments of their own testimony are in press reports, where they usually were portrayed as lurching from one crisis to the next, and in police interrogations, where women arrested for solicitation invariably claimed—often in identical formulaic language—to be supporting widowed mothers, impoverished young siblings, and children of their own.

To many writers of the May Fourth era, prostitution was emblematic of wider social problems. In 1919 Li Dazhao, who was soon to cofound the

CCP, denounced prostitution as an insult to human values, a debasement of love, a threat to public health and racial survival, an affront to personal freedom, and a sign of the low status of women.[125] In 1922, Christian groups in Guangzhou demonstrated against prostitution as a threat to public safety.[126] During the United Front years, feminists within both the CCP and the Nationalist organizations called for abolition of prostitution.[127] Social scientists, reporters, and other urban observers regarded prostitutes as the embodiment of everything that could go wrong in a nation experiencing rural economic crisis and rapid urbanization.

Attempts to confine, regulate, and license prostitution began in many Chinese cities even before the end of the Qing, as part of the project to bring a modern order to rapidly growing cities. Such campaigns generally failed, and continued to fail during the early years of the Republic.[128] The Beijing municipal police, like those in other cities, issued detailed regulations on how to license and regulate brothels, register prostitutes and examine them for sexually transmitted diseases, and monitor their public conduct.[129] In the late nineteenth century, residents of the foreign-controlled Shanghai International Settlement, modeling their efforts on Britain's Contagious Diseases Act of the 1860s, had attempted to institute health inspections for prostitutes. In 1920, the Settlement government, under pressure from the newly formed Moral Welfare League, began to require that all brothels be licensed, with the aim of reducing the number of licenses over five years. Such efforts met resistance from many quarters. Merchants protested that courtesan houses promoted commerce; courtesans protested that they were not prostitutes; some brothels moved to the French Concession where prostitution was permitted, while others went underground; unlicensed prostitution soared. The campaign was declared a failure by 1924, with one Chinese observer likening it to an attempt "to mop up the Huangpu River with a bath sponge."[130]

In the Republican period, attempts to ban prostitution fizzled because it was more profitable for local governments to license and tax brothels. As one commentator put it in 1936, "Mr. Morality could not triumph over Brother Cash."[131] Unlicensed ("secret" or "dark") prostitutes invariably outnumbered their licensed sisters.[132] Working in less formal establishments or receiving clients in their own homes, they avoided government fees and surveillance.[133] Prostitution provided a way to survive for many women, even as it engendered debates about social decay and suffering.

THE GENDERED COMMUNIST SUBCULTURE

In the early 1920s, several women's associations continued the struggle of Tang Qunying for women's rights. The Women's Suffrage Association agitated for suffrage, inheritance rights, and an expanded curriculum for girls' schools, and got women elected to public office in the provinces of Hunan and Guangdong.[134] The Women's Rights League advocated legal equality for women, an end to prostitution and concubinage, educational access, and legislation to protect women factory workers.[135]

Some women activists, however, saw no point in struggling for the vote and legal reform while China was controlled by warlords. These women turned to the broader project of remaking Chinese politics and culture. Among many theories circulating in Chinese intellectual circles at that time, Marxism and Lenin's theory of imperialism offered an analysis of why China continued to be targeted by expansive foreign powers. A collection of urban reading groups devoted to Marxism coalesced into the Chinese Communist Party (CCP). Founded in 1921, its initial membership consisted of fifty-five men and two women.[136] It is estimated that one hundred women joined the CCP between 1921 and 1925, comprising about 10 percent of the total membership. During the first four Party congresses, no voting delegates were women.[137]

The CCP was founded with the support of the Communist International (Comintern), based in Moscow with the goal of fostering revolution worldwide. Lenin believed that in colonized countries with weak working classes, the bourgeoisie might lead resistance against the imperialist powers, thus weakening the global capitalist system. The Comintern, therefore, gave much support to Sun Yat-sen's Nationalist Party, which had a considerably broader base than the fledgling CCP. It urged the two parties to cooperate, and they formed a United Front in 1923. By that time, the reorganized Nationalist Party had endorsed gender equality and women's rights, the very position that the party had declined to adopt at the time of the famous slap, and it promised that universal suffrage would follow.[138] Both the Nationalists and the CCP established women's bureaus; and as individual Communists joined the Nationalist Party, the Nationalist Women's Bureau came to be dominated by women Communist organizers.[139] The two political parties, with Communists taking the lead, worked to mobilize women factory workers and farmers.

Most young women activists, whether Nationalist or Communist, came from elite or middle-class families. Many had studied at teacher training schools. Their critique of family relations picked up themes that He-Yin Zhen had voiced before the fall of the dynasty. They cited the observation of Marx's colleague Engels that women's oppression was rooted in the emergence of private property relations. Some Chinese Communist writers linked class and gender oppression. They pointed out that women, who seldom had control of property, had much in common with workers, who possessed nothing but their labor power (and in the words of Marx, had nothing to lose but their chains).[140]

Nevertheless, in the CCP view, feminist goals—raising women's status, providing education and employment, and reworking family relationships—could not be separated from the primary tasks of a worker-peasant revolution to overthrow the bourgeoisie, eliminate the warlords, and throw out the imperialists. Any feminist project that threatened to divide the revolutionary ranks was regarded with suspicion by Party activists. Taking class revolution as their primary objective, the CCP gave support to women's suffrage as an interim but insufficient goal.[141] What was needed was thoroughgoing political change. Without such change, commented Communist organizer Xiang Jingyu in 1924, the efforts of suffragists "will result in the whole bunch of them entering the pigsties in the capital and the provinces where, together with the male pigs, they will preside over the country's catastrophes and the people's calamities."[142]

In the early 1920s, CCP activists established a journal titled *Women's Voice* and ran a school for young women in Shanghai. Both the journal and the school quickly foundered and closed because of intra-party differences and organizational problems.[143] CCP efforts to organize the working class encountered obstacles as well. It quickly became evident that the Party needed women organizers to effectively reach the many women who labored in Shanghai's cotton mills and silk filatures. But when the students from the Communist women's school went out to support a cotton mill strike in 1922, they discovered that sometimes they could not communicate because they spoke different dialects.[144]

In spite of these problems, young women activists found within the Party sustenance and a degree of freedom from the gendered constraints of the wider society. The CCP produced a series of meetings, decisions, campaigns, and institutions, but it fostered something more intangible as well: a new cultural milieu that Christina Gilmartin has called a "Communist subculture."[145] For young men and women Communists, the personal and the political were inseparable. The activists were products of the New Culture/May Fourth ferment, and they brought into the Party their advocacy of unfettered love and free-choice marriage, equality in the family, and women's right to be active in the public sphere. They denounced the treatment of women as playthings who were forced to adorn themselves to appeal to bosses, acquire husbands, and maintain their social standing.[146]

But young men and women also brought residual notions of gender hierarchy into the Party with them, and some aspects of that hierarchy remained unexamined in the hectic years of United Front organizing.[147] Leadership was the preserve of Party men. In the daily division of labor among Party activists, women usually were assigned either to organizing women—for which there were good practical political reasons, because gender segregation made it difficult for men to mobilize women—or providing logistical background support. They did not design or implement overall strategy. When men debated Party ideology, they had no hesitation about speaking on behalf of women and articulating what shape women's emancipation should take. Nevertheless, women in the early CCP sometimes emphasized different women's issues from men—for instance, the right to birth control and the need for women to become political activists on their own behalf.[148]

Women usually gained prominence in the Party organization when they became the wives or lovers of Communist men. The founders of *Women's Voice* and the girls' school in Shanghai, Wang Huiwu and Gao Junman, were not formal members of the Party but were in relationships with top male leaders Chen Duxiu and Li Da. The two women hatched their plans for the CCP women's program while preparing dinner for their husbands in a house the two couples shared in the Shanghai French Concession.[149]

When a male Communist leader fell from power, or a liaison between a powerful man and a woman activist ended, the women's leadership positions tended to evaporate.[150] Although free-choice marriage and divorce was a common theme in New Culture discussions, women Party members who engaged in serial sexual relationships were criticized and even denounced, unlike the men they slept with; the double standard continued to operate. Everyone assumed that women would take responsibility for raising the children who resulted from intra-Party relationships (unless their in-laws could do so), while men went on with their organizing work.[151]

Perhaps the most famous woman who sought to navigate these contradictions during the United Front period was Xiang Jingyu.[152] Born into a Hunan merchant family in 1895 and educated at a girls' school, she became a teacher and political activist during the May Fourth Movement. She spoke at a memorial meeting organized in Changsha for Miss Zhao, the young woman in the sedan chair who had committed suicide to protest her wedding. Xiang then traveled to France in 1919 and married fellow political activist Cai Hesen. Their wedding portrait pictured them reading Marx's *Capital* together. While in France, Xiang published an essay arguing that women would only be liberated when collective institutions replaced the family. A small nuclear family, she warned, was just going to shrink and individualize the shape of the prison.[153]

Back in Shanghai in 1921, Xiang joined the Communist Party, although there are no records of a formal admissions process for her, as there were for men who joined. She directed the Communist Women's Bureau from 1922 to 1925, organizing girl middle-school students and building a coalition of women's groups. She pushed for a larger Party presence among women factory workers and persuaded several hundred women workers to enroll in Party-run night schools.[154] She often

Photo 4.5.   Women workers coming out of a meeting, 1927
Source: Archives of the French Ministry of Foreign Affairs. Reproduced in *Virtual Shanghai*, http://www
.virtualshanghai.net/Photos/Images?ID=25255.

found herself at odds with her male comrades over their suspicion of
the noncommunist women's movement and their slowness in recruiting
women to join the Party. At the same time, the men were happy to have
her run daily operations for the CCP's Central Committee because they
saw her as more organized than themselves—a characteristic, Gilmartin
suggests, that "was an extension of women's traditional roles as mothers and housekeepers."[155] Xiang Jingyu and Cai Hesen had a daughter
and a son, born in 1922 and 1924, respectively. Cai's mother raised them,
enabling Xiang to continue her organizing.

Beginning in 1924, during the United Front, Xiang also led the Nationalist Party's Shanghai Women's Movement Bureau and edited its journal *Women's Weekly*, in which she published articles about women silk
workers. She worked actively to marshal women's groups to support
Sun Yat-sen in his call for a National Assembly to unify the country,
and to press for women's rights in the constitution and laws they hoped
would come out of that new government. This effort soon foundered
on political disagreements with Duan Qirui, the warlord in charge of
the national government, and was abandoned after Sun Yat-sen's death
from cancer in 1925.[156]

When Xiang Jingyu had an affair with another Communist, Peng Shu-
zhi, she was criticized by her comrades as unvirtuous and had to step

down as head of the Women's Bureau.[157] She separated from Cai in 1925, and they remained separated even when both of them were sent by the Party to Moscow to study in 1925. Her departure damaged the growth of the Communist women's movement in Shanghai and resulted in the closure of *Women's Weekly*. Xiang returned to China in 1927, working with the United Front in Wuhan. In early 1928, she was arrested by the Nationalists during the White Terror and executed at age thirty-three.

WOMEN SOLDIERS AND THE NATIONALIST REVOLUTION

By the mid-1920s, the south China province of Guangdong had become the Nationalist Party's base, as United Front forces prepared to organize a military expedition to oust the warlords and unify China. Veteran woman revolutionary He Xiangning directed women's mobilization.[158] Her Central Women's Bureau published a monthly magazine titled, like its Communist predecessor, *Women's Voice*, and operated night schools for women workers. The Bureau also ran a Women's Movement Training Institute. It sent activists to tour factories and hospitals that employed women, and trained graduates in propaganda strategies aimed at women. The resemblance of this Nationalist program to earlier Communist-sponsored activities in Shanghai was not coincidental. He Xiangning was not a Communist, but women's mobilization was largely shaped by women CCP members. Among them was Deng Yingchao, a May Fourth student activist and feminist who in 1925 married fellow Communist Zhou Enlai (later to become one of the CCP's most prominent leaders). Cai Chang, a former teacher and sister-in-law of Xiang Jingyu, also came south to Guangzhou to work under the banner of the Nationalists.[159]

Beginning in 1924, revolutionaries in Guangzhou celebrated International Women's Day, a holiday with origins in international socialism that was observed in the Soviet Union and the international communist movement. He Xiangning and a woman Comintern adviser, Tanya Borodin, initiated planning for the day's activities. Large rallies featured pronouncements about women's education, wages, and voting rights. Thousands of leaflets were distributed calling for the abolition of arranged marriage, concubinage, child marriages, prostitution, and bonded servitude for girls. Photographs of the German socialist Rosa Luxemburg appeared everywhere during the holiday.[160]

The following year, the May Thirtieth Movement of 1925 exploded after a Shanghai worker was shot and International Settlement police opened fire on demonstrators protesting his death. In the organizing surge that followed, women CCP members increased tenfold to about a thousand women; a much larger number of women attended rallies and demonstrations around the country.[161] By the end of 1926, the Party had 1,892 women members.[162]

Communist and Nationalist women were active in women's associations formed in south and central China. They called for an end to imperialist power in China and advocated for women's rights in marriage, education, the workplace, and the political sphere.[163] As John Fitzgerald points out, "Women *and* men recognized themselves in the symbol of the awakening female, and both invested in her struggle to free the suppressed hopes of a captive nation." Women's emancipation was presented as inseparable from the Nationalist Revolution being organized by the United Front.[164]

The Guangdong Women's Emancipation Association, founded in 1925 with girl middle-school students as its core organizers, soon fanned out into the countryside to establish local branches, beginning with girls' schools in rural locations.[165] The association's drama troupe performed revolutionary skits in towns and villages across the province, and by early 1926 an estimated 1.5 million women had become involved in the women's movement.[166] Women also were drawn into the peasant associations established by the revolutionaries; by mid-1926, eighty thousand rural women reportedly had joined.[167] Women workers also founded unions of telephone operators and sewing workers.[168]

When the Northern Expedition set out from Guangdong in the summer of 1926 in the name of the "Nationalist Revolution," women marched with the army. A small number were in combat roles, but more worked as medical personnel, propagandists, community organizers, and spies. Three lines of march took them into Hunan, Jiangxi, and Fujian Provinces, organizing women's associations along the way in dozens of county towns. The propaganda distributed by women organizers promised that the revolution would enable women to take on new public roles and protect them from the depredations of warlord armies. Young women students and teachers at teacher training schools, as well as recent graduates, were particularly responsive to the propaganda, volunteering to prepare food, assist with medical care, and provide calligraphy for political rallies. Many women became soldiers through their schools, regarding military service as an extension of their struggles for women's freedom. As the Northern Expedition gained ground, many of these local activists organized new women's associations, mobilizing women for troop support but also agitating for marriage freedom and an end to polygamy, child brides, and bondservants.[169]

Xie Bingying, the young student activist who had staged a hunger strike to go to one school and been expelled from another for patriotic activity, was not a Communist. But she did join the army, as, in her words, "brave young men and women one by one discarded their books, shed their long gowns, and joined the revolution."[170] In her own case, the personal and the national were entwined. She describes herself in 1926 as besotted by classical love stories and attracted to a young man. But then her elder brother berated her:

> Women are truly useless. The alarm bell for the era has run, and yet here you are, still snoring in your dreams. . . . You should have stopped reading such stuff long ago, and dumped it all. You are an intelligent young woman and very fond of modern literature—so why don't you read writings about revolution?

She was also aware that if she remained at home, her mother would compel her to marry a man to whom her parents had betrothed her when she was still a toddler. Her brother, himself in an arranged marriage, advised her that "only by joining the revolution will you solve your marriage problem and your problem of finding a future." Xie estimated that nine out of ten girl students who joined the Northern Expedition army had a similar mixture of motivations. As another young woman put it in a public speech to new recruits, "We escaped from our families in order to offer ourselves to the revolution. Our goal is to save the suffering people—and our suffering selves."[171]

Xie was one of the women admitted to the first class of the Wuhan Central Military and Political Institute in early 1927. The women students dressed in military uniforms when on duty and men's clothing when off duty, carried arms, trained with their male classmates, and eschewed romance.[172] When they graduated they were assigned to a propaganda corps.

Accompanying the troops as they marched through Hubei and Henan, women soldiers participated in the violent struggle meetings against members of the local landowning elite. They guided local women to form women's associations, encouraged them to unbind their feet and cut their hair (a powerful sign that they had rejected older gender norms), and publicized the Nationalists' revolutionary program of marriage freedom and an end to the commodification and abuse of women.[173] When the left wing of the Nationalists established a government in the city of Wuhan, they guaranteed women rights in marriage, divorce, and inheritance. They banned footbinding and the sale of women, and supported the Hubei Women's Association, which counted seventy thousand members by 1927.[174]

The issue that proved most divisive in rural areas through which the revolutionary United Front armies passed was marriage freedom. Because accumulating a bride price was expensive, many men worried about being able to afford a bride at all, not necessarily about choosing one themselves. The prospect of free-choice marriage raised the possibility that no woman would choose to marry a poor peasant. And the danger of losing a wife to divorce, when one's family had paid hard-earned resources to bring her into the family, was even more disturbing to rural men and their parents. As the CCP would later learn during its many years building a revolutionary force in rural areas, active discussion of marriage freedom could threaten peasant political support.

In April 1927, the United Front ended violently as Chiang Kai-shek's forces murdered Communists and labor organizers in Shanghai. Communists were expelled from the Wuhan-based left wing of the Nationalist Party in July. The White Terror that followed the 1927 coup affected women activists of every political stripe. In the immediate aftermath, hundreds of known women Communists and activists were summarily arrested and executed.[175] Mao Zedong's wife, Yang Kaihui, was arrested and shot in 1930.

Communist or not, women with bobbed hair were in particular danger, because that hairstyle was understood to be proof of radical political leanings.[176] Lu Xun in 1927 commented darkly:

> A likes it short, C likes it long. A has the long hair cut; C has the bobbed heads cut off. These seem to have been unlucky years for the young, especially for the fair sex. The newspaper described a district where short hair was encouraged; but another army came in, and wherever they found a bobbed-haired woman they would slowly tear out her hair and cut off her breasts.[177]

As Xie Bingying put it when her company of women soldiers were disbanded, her friend's

> head was shaved almost like a potato. So no matter how expert we were in applying makeup, people could tell at a glance that until recently we had been female soldiers who had been walking around carrying guns and sticks. Sun had dried and darkened our skin. Months of gripping gun butts had calloused our right palms. These were two other signs by which people recognized us. . . . Because our heads were not fit for public view, we . . . went to a department store and each of us bought a foreign hat of woven straw.[178]

Even if they escaped political reprisals, women organizers ejected from the Nationalist ranks faced considerable challenges reintegrating into the communities they had left behind. Xie Bingying arrived home to find her parents' views on women's marriage freedom unchanged. They were determined to marry her off to the husband they had chosen when she was three. When Xie resisted, her parents did not blame her stint as a soldier, but rather her years in school. "What kind of devil's den is a school?" her father asked. "All those who enter it become bewitched. When they return home, they all make an outcry and beg to break off their marriage contract." Although he did not mention Miss Zhao, he also blamed his daughter's intransigence on newspaper accounts publicizing the suicides of young women who died protesting their arranged marriages.[179] Xie's parents were not opposed to the prospect of Xie taking up a teaching position after marriage. But refusing to marry the man they had chosen would, they felt, rupture their family relationships and damage the position of their family in the wider community.

Xie's mother confined her to a small room, where she considered and rejected suicide (see box 4.2). After six months and three failed attempts to run away, she went through with the wedding ceremony but refused to consummate the marriage. Her eventual escape from what she called "the family prison" happened when she was offered a teaching position at the Datong Girls School she had once attended. With the consent of her

---

BOX 4.2.
Xie Bingying Considers Suicide

Tossing and turning, I considered my problem. Certainly it was not one that could be resolved peacefully. . . . Mother would insist on carrying through the law of the feudal society. . . . But I happened to be a rebel who opposed feudal society. With mother and daughter two eras apart in their ideals, how could they avoid clashing? No question about it, only by risking my life in a struggle with my family could I finally prevail and gain my freedom. . . .

Rather than offer this vigorous life of mine to be butchered by others, let me sacrifice myself. I might as well die by my own hand, to my own satisfaction. My life is mine and I have the right to do with it as I please. Death, my final peace, will be also my final victory. . . .

Death? Is it true that this is the only road to follow? . . . You have often blamed those who commit suicide for lacking courage, for being too weak and too useless. To search for life is the instinct of all living creatures. So how can a person filled with the spirit of all things, who has the intelligence to create all things, be seeking death instead of striving for life? . . . Think: you have been baptized by revolution. You have the mission to change society. You have been to the front line and worked under fire to kill enemies and save comrades, and you once swore to struggle for the liberation of millions of workers of the world who have been repressed. You are not a weak and old-fashioned female who lacks abilities. Rather, you are a modern woman, resolute, courageous, strong willed. . . . Also, consider a little further—suicide is a stupid act. When you are dead, the old society will have one less rebel. . . .

All night, Life and Death struggled in my brain. And finally Life won.

Source: Xie Bingying, *A Woman Soldier's Own Story: The Autobiography of Xie Bingying*, translated by Lily Chia Brissman and Barry Brissman (New York: Columbia University Press, 2001), 102–5.

in-laws and parents, she left for Datong—and kept going for Changsha, a teaching job in Hengyang, and then eventually Shanghai and Beijing. Her departure carried a high price: a break in her relationship with her parents that lasted several years and the immediate need to find a way to support herself.

Xie's subsequent career, after her stint as a soldier and her unwilling marriage, might be understood as an answer to the question, "What happens after Nora walks out for the second time?" She went on to work as a teacher, writer, editor, and university teacher. When Japan invaded China in 1937, she organized a women's service corps that served on the front lines. Her adult life was far more complex than the stark choices laid out by Lu Xun for Nora, but it was not an easy one: marked by intermittent poverty, romantic liaisons, confinement as a political prisoner in both China and Japan, a child out of wedlock, marriage, more children, and near-constant mobility occasioned by political upheaval.

In the years of the White Terror, as part of a broad campaign to discredit their former political partners, the Nationalists accused Communist women of sexual promiscuity. Just before the Communists were expelled from Wuhan, a satirical poster circulated in the city saying:

> The women's association suggests to have a naked body procession on the 1st of May in promoting the principle of freedom. If any one wishes to enter into this naked body procession an examination of body is necessary. The choice will fall on the one who has a snow white body and a pair of swollen nipples.[180]

In government policy and local propaganda, the United Front agenda for women's emancipation was reduced to a crude sexual joke. The Nationalist government established in Nanjing in 1928 closed its women's department.[181] In the decade that followed, the gender and sexual mores featured in public political discussion in Nationalist China became markedly more conservative.

NORA'S LEGACY

In the late 1910s and 1920s, Nora, the Norwegian housewife who left home, came to embody acute dilemmas for Chinese intellectuals. How could a fully formed modern individual emerge from the Chinese family, become an independent self-supporting citizen, and help a weak and divided China take its proper place in the world? Most of the intellectuals who wrote about Nora were not women. But in identifying their dilemma and China's situation with the figure of Woman, they continued the conversation Liang Qichao had begun in the last years of the Qing. If China was to become modern, in their view, women's emancipation would be an important part of the process.

The term most often used for "feminism" in this period of intense political activity, *nüquan zhuyi*, literally translates as "women's rights-ism." New Culture writers, most of them male, continued the advocacy by late Qing intellectuals for women's right to be educated, own property, open a business, move freely in society, and choose their own spouses, adding the right to vote. But for them, in contrast to their Qing predecessors, the precondition of women's emancipation was the emancipation of the individual from Confucian family authority and social hierarchy. In some respects, these men saw themselves as spokesmen and guides for oppressed Chinese women awaiting emancipation. They hoped that once emancipated, women would be able to fulfill their duty to reform and strengthen Chinese society.[182]

As more women joined in public political activity during and after 1919, all of these elements remained part of the conversation: individual personhood, education, economic independence, and strengthening the nation. This was not a conversation confined to China, and local writers drew upon and transformed elements of global discourses about gender, sexuality, eugenics, and feminism, adapting them to local circumstances.

In the early 1920s, Communist Party activists focused their discussion on the oppression of working-class women and the difficulty of cross-class organizing. Much as He-Yin Zhen had done in 1907, Communists saw women's emancipation as contingent upon a thorough change in the social order. In the context of the United Front with the Nationalists, that meant organizing women to help overthrow imperialism and the warlords, aiming to establish the conditions in which private ownership would come to an end. Only in the context of this revolution, Communist organizers argued, could women's productive and reproductive labor be emancipated.

Even after the United Front was violently dissolved, all of these elements remained part of the public conversation about women. As the next two chapters show, feminism became incorporated into the project of saving the nation, embraced by both the increasingly conservative Nationalist government and the Communist revolutionary movement that took shape in the countryside. Within the feminism-nation-revolution nexus, discussions about women's role in free-choice love, reproduction, and the strengthening of "the race" persisted. The emphasis in these discussions was not women as "a state of being," as Tani Barlow puts it, but rather women as "a name for potentiality"—not what women were, but what they "will have been" in a future still under construction.[183] Long after Nora ceased to be intellectuals' favorite embodiment of refusal and resistance, women and Woman remained central to debates about the family, the individual, the polity, the nation, the race, and the revolution.

5

Regulatory Regimes, 1928–37

Gender was central to the state-building projects of the new Nationalist government. In the decade between 1928 and Japan's full-scale invasion of China in 1937, the Nationalist Party had the most extensive control over Chinese territory it was ever to enjoy. From the new capital of Nanjing, the Party's national government attempted to protect China's sovereignty and govern effectively. The state issued a revised legal code in 1930. It sought to broaden educational access, improve public health, prevent flooding and drought, and raise agricultural and industrial productivity. Leaders wanted a disciplined population that understood the rights and duties of a modern citizen. The Nationalist Party was to guide and educate the people in a period of political tutelage that would, in the indefinite future, be replaced by constitutional government. Social revolution was off the agenda.

The Nationalist Party was not united internally. Some leaders emphasized military elimination of the Communists, who had begun to build a rural base in Jiangxi (see chapter 6). Other leaders advocated rural reconstruction and urban industrial development, in the belief that economic expansion was the best way to avoid the perils of a revolution. As Japanese invasion loomed, the Nationalist Party drew on some features of European fascism to promote popular militarism, autarkic economic development, and the anti-Communist New Life Movement.[1]

State visions of Woman incorporated elements of the late Qing reforms and the May Fourth critique, minus the popular activism. State planners envisioned men and women who could be mobilized for economic production and patriotic displays—not oppositional activity.[2]

Determined to minimize social conflicts of all sorts, Nationalist authorities did not seek a thoroughgoing change in women's work, political activity, and domestic roles.

Instead, state authorities approached the woman question by means of regulation. They aimed to produce woman citizens whose most fundamental role was to be modern, educated, productive wives and mothers. New civil and criminal laws introduced changes in marriage, divorce, and women's property rights. The state attempted to modernize childbirth through licensing midwives, ban prostitution by withdrawing brothel licenses, and specify some features of women's dress and adornment. Much of this regulation was ineffective because the state's reach beyond the capital was limited. But the idea that modern gender practices could be regulated into existence persisted into the war years and the establishment of the People's Republic (see chapters 6 and 7).

By the Nanjing Decade, acknowledgment of women's labor outside the home was routine. The educated and employed New Woman was less controversial than she had been a decade earlier. But her mischievous younger sister—the irresponsible, seductive, and duplicitous Modern Girl—emerged as a new figure of unease on the urban cultural landscape. In rural areas, the reach of the state and the lure of New Womanhood and Modern Girlhood were limited. But village life was changing, too, as many rural women produced goods for export, suffered the effects of the Great Depression, and coped with a growing outflow of male laborers from farming.

State projects and broader social change during the Nanjing Decade were disrupted repeatedly. Political factionalism, remnant warlord powers, endemic banditry, major and minor natural disasters, global economic depression, an extended military campaign against the Communists, Japanese occupation of Northeast China (Manchuria) in 1931, and constant Japanese incursions into north China all limited the effectiveness of the Nationalist regulatory regime. But the vision of state-directed social development, and the centrality of women to that vision, remained important well beyond 1937.

LIVING WITHIN THE LAW:
LEGAL CHANGES AND SOCIAL PRACTICE

Regulating Marriage and Divorce

Even after it purged the Communists in 1927, the Nationalist state retained some traces of the New Culture movement that had informed the United Front agenda. Like New Culture thinkers, Nationalist officials regarded marriage reform as one way to improve the quality of the Chinese people. Their views drew upon the eugenic thinking popular in China and much of the rest of the world at that time. Pan Guangdan, an American-educated professor who was dubbed the "Father of Chinese Eugenics," argued in the 1930s that the only way for China to improve the quality of its citizens was to encourage genetically superior people to marry early and produce many children.[3] Arranged marriage was seen as an obstacle to eugenic progress: one Nationalist lawmaker believed that it "had resulted in many, many unfortunate couplings in which talented women were hitched to idiotic men and led to the production of subpar offspring." Free marriage, lawmakers hoped, would strengthen the Chinese nation, one improved child at a time.[4] The Nationalist government loosened the control of the patriarchal family over marriage. It claimed the authority to issue marriage certificates and monitor the conditions under which marriages were contracted and dissolved.[5]

The Chinese Civil Code, passed in 1930 and implemented in May 1931, granted women equal status with men and displaced the patriline from its central status in the law, replacing it with rights-bearing individuals and the conjugal unit of husband and wife. Daughters were given equal rights to inherit family property, although in practice this seldom happened, and widows were now entitled to a share of their husbands' property.[6] Both parents had rights over children, although in the case of a divorce the husband became the default guardian unless the couple agreed on another arrangement.[7]

In contrast to the provisions of the Qing code, women as well as men could initiate a divorce. The new code specified ten grounds: "bigamy, adultery, spousal intolerable cruelty, in-law intolerable cruelty, abandonment, intent or attempt to murder a spouse, incurable physical disease, incurable mental disease, lengthy disappearance, and imprisonment or the commission of an infamous crime."[8] The definition of intolerable cruelty was expanded beyond inflicting serious physical damage to include other actions that made conjugal life miserable.[9]

Lawsuits filed by women rose in the 1930s and the 1940s, suggesting that ordinary women used the courts to pursue the goal of women's emancipation—not as an abstract ideal but as they wanted to enjoy it in their own families.[10] Intolerable cruelty was often cited in divorce suits initiated by wives. Proving this charge was not easy. Women had to produce witnesses, or provide hospital or police records of abuse, and show that their own improper conduct had not provoked a beating. Even with such evidence, the courts often refused to grant divorces on these grounds.[11] Alimony was possible, but the court charged higher fees for a case involving alimony, discouraging most women from seeking support.[12]

When men initiated lawsuits, they most often were attempting to compel wives who had left an abusive or economically untenable situation to return. Runaway wives often went back to their families of origin. It was no longer a crime for a wife to leave, as it had been under Qing law. Now it was a matter of civil contract, in which the court could order a woman to return. But a runaway wife might find employment in another city, refusing to return home even when a court ordered her to do so.[13]

Republican law did not mention concubines at all, leaving it to the courts to sort out their status. The judges concluded, as Lisa Tran puts it, that "concubinage was to be prohibited, but concubines were to be protected."[14] Courts treated concubines as family members. Whereas Qing law had given a principal wife parental authority over a concubine's children, Republican legal practice gave a concubine full parental rights. Under Qing law, a concubine could be expelled from the household at any time, but in the Republican period she could not be expelled except under one of the legal grounds for divorce. She could, however, demand to leave at will and successfully sue for support after a relationship had ended, as long as her conduct had not been the cause of the separation. If she remained a household member, a concubine also had the right to demand support from the man's wife after his death.[15] Sometimes concubines tried to gain legal recognition as wives in court by proving that they had been married in a ceremony with at least two witnesses, which was the definition under the law of a valid marriage.[16]

Although concubines now enjoyed increased legal protection, for a man to take a concubine became less acceptable. The new code effectively regarded it as adultery on his part.[17] Thus, a wife could divorce her husband if he took a concubine after the Civil Code went into effect in May 1931, but not if he took a concubine before that date. Although a wife could not force a husband to abandon his concubine, she could seek a judicial separation rather than a divorce, so that she would not have to live under the same roof with him but would not be stigmatized as a divorcée.[18] By 1935, pressure from women's groups opposed to concubinage resulted in adultery being named as a criminal offense in the revised Criminal Code for men as well as women. But the courts showed little inclination to prosecute men who took concubines.[19]

Under the 1931 Civil Code, women, just like men, were now rights-bearing subjects who possessed "legal personhood." Drafters of the code hoped that categorizing women as persons with legal status would help to reinforce the move toward women's rights. And yet, even as the Civil Code did away with older gender distinctions based on the patrilineal family, it installed new gender distinctions based on biology and the conjugal tie between husbands and wives. Men had to attain the minimum age of eighteen in order to marry, but for women the age was sixteen. (The gender gap persists in contemporary Chinese marriage law, although the ages have been raised to twenty-two and twenty, respectively.) The reasoning behind this was eugenic: it was assumed that females reached sexual maturity earlier than males and that marriage before sexual maturity might adversely affect one's body, the quality of one's offspring, and one's ability to support them.

The revised Civil Code did not challenge the prevailing practice of patrilocal residence. Given the fact that a wife often lived with her husband's family, intolerable cruelty by in-laws effectively became a gendered ground for divorce. No one thought it was necessary to specify that a man could seek a divorce if his in-laws mistreated him. Men also retained more control over marital property, exclusively on the basis of gender.[20] Nevertheless, in urban areas notions of what a marriage should be began to change, and women's access to the courts improved.

In the countryside, where more than 80 percent of the population lived, the Civil Code's marriage provisions had very little effect on women. The sale of women, arranged marriages, forced remarriage of widows, the purchase of child daughters-in-law, and sons' primary claim to inheritance of property remained common. Rural marriage reform started later, under the aegis of the CCP, and took decades to change social practice.

Regulating Reproduction

Like other modern states, the Nationalist government linked the health of citizens directly to the health of the nation. New public health measures tried to regulate the bodies of Chinese citizens, promoting what Ruth Rogaski calls "hygienic modernity." In the cities, officials created municipal health departments and public hospitals. They campaigned to vaccinate the public and provide health care to the poor. They lectured about the bacteria that caused cholera and the need for quarantines during epidemics. This was a new realm of state regulation, even though it was limited by lack of funding and inconsistent administration.[21]

In the countryside, the state's reach was much more limited and intermittent, and nongovernmental reform played a larger role. One ambitious experiment was in Ding County in Hebei Province, a model reform site partly funded by private American foundations. A Chinese-run organization called the Mass Education Movement (MEM) directed its efforts mainly at rural women, who were identified as key participants in bringing modernity to the villages. MEM took new health practices to every village home: treatment of trachoma and ringworm in school children, epidemic control, an opium detox program, and rural clinic construction. Health workers trained local community volunteers in first aid, vaccination, digging wells far from the latrines, and moving livestock out of the

Photo 5.1.   Church of the Brethren missionary, Nettie Senger, local officials, and graduates of her women's literacy class, Qinzhou 1932. The women studied mass education primers on new citizenship.
Source: Photograph courtesy of Joseph Wampler. Used with permission of the Brethren Historical Library and Archives, Elgin, Illinois.

house. The emphasis on clean, ventilated, well-lit homes brought the principles of home economics out to the countryside.[22]

One central question for rural health reformers was how best to manage pregnancy and childbirth. Fetal education (*taijiao*)—the practice of exposing the unborn child to beneficial influences—had a long history in Chinese medicine. But by the 1930s, as Nicole Richardson comments, the modern discourse of fetal education "incorporated the language of eugenics and nationalism," drawing upon biology, psychology, and European theories of sex difference. It was said that women were more emotional than men because they had fewer red blood cells per cubic meter and their reproductive organs, especially the womb, controlled their emotions. Popular writings continued to warn that pregnant women needed to control their emotions, because a woman's emotional state could affect her body and thus the health of her fetus.[23] New strictures on pregnant women were recommended: stay away from violent scenes in films, hang portraits of famous people in the bedroom, take medications such as Three Friends Nourishing Pills to enhance fetal health, and avoid heavy farm labor—a virtual impossibility for rural women. As Frank Dikötter comments, "women were given a responsibility over the uterine environment," but they were also installed at the lower end of a gender hierarchy now believed to be scientifically grounded in reproductive biology.[24]

Government officials and reformers regarded rural childbirth practices as particularly backward and unsanitary.[25] Rural women gave birth at home, either unattended or under the supervision of an older woman relative or a midwife. Village midwives were usually women who had borne children themselves and who had learned how to deliver babies from relatives or older midwives. Formal training in midwifery was rare, and complications from difficult births, postpartum bleeding, and the use of folk remedies were common.[26] Neonatal tetanus, often caused by cutting the umbilical cord with an unsterilized instrument, was a leading cause of infant death and maternal infection.[27] Public health personnel denounced old-style midwives as charlatans who were ignorant of sterile practice and apt to resort to brutal and even lethal methods of extracting a baby. Government reports, medical journals, and the popular press criticized common midwifery practices such as using cow dung to dress the umbilical cord. But in most rural areas, local midwives were the only medical personnel available to deliver babies.[28]

In response, the Nationalist government established a National Midwifery Board and announced its intention to standardize midwifery training across the country. Yang Chongrui, a woman obstetrician and public health official, directed the First National Midwifery School in Beijing. Her agenda was to train midwives who could, in turn, train others to staff a comprehensive network of rural clinics. Most midwives who received training, unlike the village midwives, were young, unmarried women from educated, urban backgrounds. Some old-style midwives took short retraining courses. They were taught sterile technique and how to identify and get medical help with difficult births.

Midwives were supposed to pass state examinations and be entered in a registry, but this law was unenforceable even in the cities, let alone the rural areas.[29] In Ding County, the MEM hired a woman nurse, only to find that the villagers would not accept a young woman as a midwife. Retraining older midwives turned out to be somewhat more effective, just as it would be for the People's Republic government in rural areas after 1949 (see chapter 8).[30] A 1935 study of Ding County found that more than 90 percent of births were attended by old-style midwives.[31] Even in Beijing, the epicenter of new midwife training, half of all babies were delivered by untrained midwives and another quarter by relatives.[32] The Nationalist government's transformative visions for the field of midwifery loomed much larger on paper than they did in practice.

The government public health program also included family planning, a novel concept that did not spread widely during the Republican era.

Cultural norms called for the production of sons to carry on the patriline. In Ding County, young women and men responded favorably to
information about birth control methods such as douching with soap or
using a tampon soaked in vinegar to swab a woman's vagina before and
after intercourse. But diaphragms, available in the cities, were regarded
in rural areas as too expensive, and other methods such as condoms,
pessaries, and intrauterine devices were not part of the rural conversation. MEM public health workers found that rural men and women were
receptive to the idea of birth control, but its effective practice often remained beyond their reach.[33]

Women did attempt to limit their pregnancies, as poverty created
pressure to restrict family size. In addition to practicing infanticide, they
turned to folk remedies that were often ineffective or downright harmful.
Some ate large amounts of water chestnuts to prevent a pregnancy. Others drank herbal concoctions that were supposed to induce sterility. Some
women tried to induce miscarriage by repeatedly pulling the beater bar
of a handloom with great force against their abdomens.[34] Abortion was
against the law but commonly performed by means including chopsticks,
long needles placed in acupuncture points, and abortifacients of poison-
ous insects, musk, and other ingredients. Often bleeding and infection
were the result.[35]

Regulating Indigence

Women refugees and beggars featured prominently in Nationalist efforts
to regulate the poor. The Nationalist capital of Nanjing was supposed
to be a showcase city with modern infrastructure and amenities, inhabited by well-educated, productive citizens.[36] But Nanjing had a housing
shortage, deadly respiratory illnesses, low wages (especially for women
laborers), and an unemployment rate of about 50 percent.[37] Early in the
Nanjing Decade, the municipal government began campaigns to label
and reform the many residents who did not live up to its ideal. It tried to
prevent refugees from entering the city, demolish squatter settlements,
control the activities of disorderly rickshaw pullers, and abolish prostitution. None of these efforts was successful.

Refugees by the thousands, including large numbers of women and
children, streamed into the city after a drought in Henan and Anhui,
and again after floods in the summer of 1931. The overwhelmed and
underfunded municipal government first distributed limited amounts of
relief and then began to deport refugees back to their devastated home
provinces. Some managed to stay, putting strain on limited housing
stock: a fifth of the capital's population lived in shantytown huts made of
straw and scrap materials. City planners wanted to relocate them to more

remote areas where they would not ruin the visual image of a modern city. But poor people resisted these attempts because they wanted to stay where they might find work as peddlers, rickshaw pullers, junk recyclers, launderers, and day laborers.

The city also had a sizable population of beggars. Some were well organized into professional begging guilds. Others, including women and children, had been forced into mendicancy by family disaster. The municipality sought to remove them from city streets and tourist sites and offer them job training in a newly established Vocational Training Institute for Vagrants. But the blurry line between refugees and beggars confounded their efforts. A 1929 municipal report commented, "Now there is no big street or small alley that doesn't have [the] elderly, [the] weak, women and children, scattered about like stars, begging along the roads."[38] Attempts to corral them into shelters preoccupied the city government throughout the decade.

The aim of regulating the poor was to prevent them from becoming a source of social instability and reform them into productive citizens.[39] The effect was to stigmatize and even criminalize large numbers of people. In 1930 about 15 percent of Beijing's population, more than 247,000 residents, were classified as "very poor." The Nanjing Decade brought to the poor what Janet Chen calls "an uneasy combination of charity and coercion, help and punishment." The state found them, in her words, "guilty of indigence."[40]

Indigent women presented the authorities with a special set of problems. Poor women were reportedly two-thirds of the clientele of Beijing soup kitchens in the winter of 1931–32. Some social critics worried about men and women mixing inappropriately in the soup lines. Beijing city authorities tried to create a relief home with separate workhouses for men, women, and children, where each group could receive vocational training. Women beggars, drug addicts, and prostitutes were referred by the police or charities to the Women's Welfare Institute.[41] Other poor women, unable to support themselves, applied to enter the home voluntarily. Some, whose husbands had disappeared, brought along their young children. Their days were highly regulated in the same manner as jail inmates, with daily work requirements, communal meals and bath times, and limits on visits by outsiders.

When the residents wanted to leave, they had to petition for release and prove that they would be able to support themselves, usually by marrying someone. Marriages were arranged by the institute, which displayed photographs of eligible women residents for men who were seeking wives to inspect. The underlying assumption was that the institute could contribute to the greater social good by providing poor men with inexpensive brides who could contribute their labor to the household economy.

Marriage ceremonies were performed at the institute after a background check of the prospective grooms. The institute agreed to take women back if the marriages proved abusive.[42] Most of these arrangements anticipated methods that the Communist government used in reforming prostitutes in the early 1950s (see chapter 8). During the Nanjing Decade, however, relief efforts reached only a tiny fraction of women and were not always welcomed by the poor.

Regulating Prostitution

The 1930s saw a decline in the courtesan houses, with their expensive ritualized encounters. Meanwhile cheaper sex-for-money transactions featuring streetwalkers, flophouses, and thinly disguised forms of sex work performed by masseuses and waitresses expanded.[43] Working as a prostitute under the Nationalist criminal code was not against the law, as it had been under the Qing.[44] But it was only legal to be a prostitute in a licensed brothel, and police regularly targeted street soliciting and unlicensed establishments.[45]

Throughout the Nanjing Decade, women's groups and other reformers argued that prostitution demeaned women, threatened public health, and injured national strength. In the would-be model capital of Nanjing, the city attempted to ban prostitution outright in 1928.[46] The mayor proposed to put prostitutes to work in textile factories, encourage them to get married, or shelter them in a Women's Relief Institute. But the financially strapped municipal government did not provide adequate funding for clinics and rehabilitation facilities. After the ban went into effect, prostitutes could be seen selling sexual services in every neighborhood of the city. Arrested prostitutes usually were fined and released.

The ban garnered little popular support. One satirist suggested that if the ban were lifted the government would be more efficient because officials would stop wasting time going to Shanghai to patronize prostitutes and might instead stay in the capital and do their jobs.[47] Nevertheless, the ban remained in place until the mid-1930s. In 1934 the national government named prostitution one of the "three evils," along with gambling and opium, to be eliminated by the New Life Movement, which linked personal comportment to national welfare.[48] In spite of New Life propaganda, prostitution continued to be a major source of livelihood for poor women in the nation's capital.

Many other city governments tried to regulate prostitution during the Nanjing Decade. Light regulation, practiced in Hangzhou and many other places, entailed registering and taxing brothels and prostitutes, along with some efforts to protect public health and reform prostitutes. Coercive regulation, practiced in Kunming, confined prostitutes to des-

ignated areas and kept them under surveillance. This approach was relatively rare. Revenue-intensive regulation, practiced in Guangzhou and
the surrounding province of Guangdong, entailed high licensing fees for
prostitutes and taxation per encounter, including singing appearances at
banquets. Prostitution was a crucial revenue source: in one Guangdong
County, the prostitution tax provided more than half of government revenue in 1929, while in the city of Guangzhou, the prostitution industry
generated 10 to 30 percent of municipal tax revenues. The funds financed
road building, vocational education, and poverty relief.[49] By 1935, the city
and the province shifted their approach, announcing that they would
abolish prostitution by gradually withdrawing licenses. It appears that
this step was never fully implemented. Meanwhile, many women turned
to unregistered sex work.[50]

In Shanghai, prostitution was concentrated in the two foreign-controlled
areas of the city.[51] In the International Settlement, prostitution was banned
in 1920. But courtesans and courtesan houses were exempted from the ban,
licensed, and taxed, providing a healthy revenue stream for the foreign-
controlled Municipal Council.[52] Meanwhile, unlicensed prostitutes and
brothels continued to operate. Nearby, the French Concession permitted
licensed prostitution. In these two areas as well as the Chinese-controlled
sections of the city, enforcement fell to the police, who arrested "pheasant"
streetwalkers for unlicensed soliciting. Prostitutes routinely were detained
overnight, fined a nominal sum, and released back onto the streets.[53]

Even while licensing prostitution, regulators attempted to control the
spread of sexually transmitted diseases. By 1933, Shanghai's French Concession required medical inspections of prostitutes.[54] In the Japanese Concession of Tianjin, prostitutes were examined by health officers in a local
clinic every seven to ten days. More than one-third of them were found to
be infected. They were forbidden to work while they were being treated,
although an infected woman was most likely simply to leave the brothel.[55]

Guidebooks, scandal fiction, and newspaper advertisements aimed
at urban readers warned that a sexual encounter, even with a beautiful
high-class courtesan, could leave a customer syphilitic. Streetwalkers
were portrayed as even more dangerous: their brothels were nicknamed
"fruit stores" because one could acquire strawberry-shaped syphilitic le-
sions there. Prostitutes were understood not only as a disease vector, but
as a dangerous weak point in China's defenses. Connecting to broader
eugenics concerns, writers warned that sexually transmitted diseases,
passed down to offspring, would weaken the Chinese "race" and make
the Chinese nation more vulnerable.[56]

No matter what mix of policies a city adopted, prostitution continued
to flourish and even expand. The reliance of local governments on licensing fees, taxes, and fines helped to perpetuate the profession. Regulation

was not successful at controlling sexually transmitted disease. Nor did it ensure the protection of prostitutes, many of whom worked for madams under exploitative contracts.[57] One study estimated that Shanghai residents spent more than sixty million yuan per year on licensed prostitutes alone.[58] Official regulators and nongovernmental reformers continued their efforts to limit prostitution, but it persisted as a major employer of urban women until the early 1950s.

Regulating Customs

Perhaps the most far-reaching Nationalist attempt to control daily life was the campaign to regulate customs and behaviors regarded as harmful to women. Such efforts preceded the Nanjing Decade. In the mid-1920s, reformers and social activists in South China had tried to emancipate women from what they regarded as harmful social customs. A series of campaigns sought to eliminate indentured servitude (*binü*), child daughters-in-law, concubines, and prostitutes. Activists also denounced breast binding—the wearing of tight undergarments to constrict the breasts—as unhealthy and unmodern. In 1927, the Nationalist government in Guangdong outlawed the practice.[59]

But what started out as an attempt to free women from family and bodily restraints took a conservative turn during the Nanjing Decade. By the early 1930s, Guangzhou authorities stopped trying to overturn what they saw as social customs and instead attempted to control women's behavior. The main threats to social morals, in their view, were women who came from the economically distressed countryside to the city. Unable to find factory employment, they entered sexualized service jobs that could shade over into clandestine prostitution. The Guangzhou press published reports, illustrations, and fiction about women teahouse singers (*nüling*) and waitresses (*nü zhaodai*), asking whether they were social victims or social threats who might become pickpockets, seductresses, and disguised prostitutes. The Guangzhou city government undertook to license teahouses and restrict the hours that women could work there.[60] In the mid-1930s, it also launched a campaign to criticize makeup, short sleeves and skirts, plunging necklines, bright nail polish, and other "strange costumes," which were finally banned outright in September 1935.[61] Similar initiatives, which generally were ineffective, took place in other cities as well.

The Nationalist state also promoted reform of wedding ceremonies. State authorities hoped to replace a marriage ritual celebrating the bride's absorption into the patriline with a ceremony centered on the conjugal couple and their role as modern citizens. When Nationalist leader Chiang Kai-shek married Wellesley-educated Song Meiling in late 1927, Chiang told the newspaper *Shenbao* that he had divorced his previous wife from an arranged marriage, taking the opportunity to criticize the practice. He and Song, a Christian, married in two ceremonies: a small Methodist service and a public gathering at a Shanghai hotel. The couple wore Western-style wedding attire: a white gown for the bride, a dark morning coat for the groom. This new-style wedding, sometimes called the "civilized wedding," was linked to marriage reform, cosmopolitan consumption, and the idea that a modern ceremony was the sign of a modern nation.[62]

Chiang and Song were not creating a new trend with their wedding. They were providing a state endorsement of practices favored by young, educated urban dwellers. New-style weddings were publicized by urban popular magazines aimed at young women, such as *Linglong* (Linloon Magazine). They moved the rituals of marriage away from parental control and toward a union of conjugal equals witnessed and sanctioned by the state.

But the cost of such weddings, including portraits, clothing, rings, a cake, a venue, and a banquet, could be prohibitive. By the mid-1930s, the Nationalist Party was requiring officials to set a frugal example when they married. City governments began to promote less expensive group weddings, in which several dozen festively dressed couples married before a portrait of Sun Yat-sen. The ceremony typically featured orchestral music, the national anthem, marriage certificates, official speeches, and a group photograph. The promotion of group weddings was part of the New Life Movement's drive to instill frugal and responsible conduct at a time of national peril (see below). Even group weddings, however, required a financial outlay beyond the means of many urban residents.[63]

Regulating Religion

During the Nanjing Decade, intellectuals continued to criticize popular religious practices as superstitious and a fundamental cause of China's backwardness.[64] The Nationalist state named rural women as particularly vulnerable to superstition. One woman Nationalist organizer called for the reeducation of nuns, women diviners, and women spirit mediums, along with midwives, women healers, matchmakers, and other backward elements.

Many government officials sought to nationalize temples and temple lands, and convert them to schools, a recurring goal of campaigns since the late nineteenth century. Nationalist Party activists in the lower Yangzi region and Guangdong detained Buddhist priests, led groups to smash statues of deities, and seized land and monasteries controlled by Buddhist and Daoist temples. In central China, women's mosques and women clerics, which had been established features of local Muslim religious life for centuries, were also targeted for reform.[65] Arguing that popular religion promoted harmful customs, authorities prohibited many local festivals and rituals, including customary celebrations associated with the Lunar New Year.

Anti-temple activity provoked a military uprising in 1929 by the Small Sword Society and the Red Spears, both secret societies with many rural adherents. They attacked Nationalist government offices in northern Jiangsu and at least one girls' school that was identified with the modernizing and antireligious stance of the state. They even detained a number of women teachers and students identified by their short hair.

And yet this was not a clear-cut case of modernizing officials versus feudal-minded believers. Both the government activities and temple resistance to them were deeply entangled with local political and economic interests, and women appeared on both sides of the conflict. In Gaoyou, a town in northern Jiangsu, Party activists smashed the temple of the city god in early 1931. Several hundred protesters led by women in their fifties and sixties known as "temple grannies" assaulted party officials at their headquarters and their homes. They installed paper images of the gods to replace the statues. Then they deployed their organizing skills to petition county authorities, leaflet the local population, and force local businesses to close, duplicating many political tactics used by student protesters. The grannies raised funds from thousands of people in the area to restore the temple. Their techniques for defending the temple were no less modern than the Nationalist move to destroy it.[66]

In response to this and many other protests, the Nationalist government curtailed antireligious activities, declaring that religion was permitted and only superstition was forbidden. The net effect was that the Nationalists required religious groups to register and pledge loyalty to the state. Secret societies, redemptive societies promising salvation, and popular religious practices that were less easily controlled remained off-limits. But they were never successfully eliminated.

WOMAN AS SYMBOL: THE NEW WOMAN AND THE MODERN GIRL

The New Woman and the Modern Girl were globally circulating figures. Their careers, personal comportment, and consumption habits embodied urban modernity. In 1930s China, both took on particular localized features. The New Woman was a representation of what women should do and be, and the Modern Girl often embodied what women should not do and not be. Both should be understood as symbols—Woman with a capital W—that were constantly under discussion, engendering differences of opinion and social tensions. These symbols did not merely hover in the discursive atmosphere; they became reference points, ideals, and warnings about where a woman might go wrong.[67]

The New Woman

The New Woman already had been a fixture on the Chinese urban cultural scene for several decades, but by the 1930s she had acquired some new features. The illustrated women's magazine *Linglong*, or Elegance, outlined her characteristics: eager to acquire knowledge and attain economic independence, trained in a profession, not subservient to men, frugal, modest in dress and self-presentation, politically informed, attuned to contemporary social problems.[68] The New Woman was supposed to do and have it all. After education in a new-style school, she would pursue a career in business, education, medicine, journalism, or the arts,[69] at least until she married a modern, forward-looking New Man. In the workplace, she would avoid any hint of scandal—no gossip about seduction or extramarital affairs. After marriage—an aspect of New Womanhood that became more prominent in Nanjing Decade writings—she would run a scientifically managed home, supervise the preparation of healthful meals, educate the children, and make sure the domestic space was tastefully decorated in a cosmopolitan mode. As a politically aware consumer, she would honor the frequent boycotts of Japan and buy products produced in China. In all of these respects, the New Woman was a worthy descendant of the virtuous woman of the late Qing. Both types of Woman were expected to work hard, sacrifice themselves, and show sexual restraint. Both were seen by the elites of their day as key to the well-being of the larger polity—the threatened empire during the Qing, the imperiled nation during the Republic.

Many of these prescriptive features of the New Woman were formulated by men.[70] They do not tell the whole story of this powerful symbol. The careers and self-conceptions of several self-identified New Women born in the first decade of the twentieth century show how new ideas about womanhood could be understood, altered, and enacted in many different ways.[71]

Some who understood themselves as New Women chose careers in physical education. Lu Lihua established her own teacher training institute to train women physical education teachers. She also founded China's first women's basketball team and led it to competitive play in Japan and Korea. Lu married twice—she divorced one husband and another died in 1932 during the brief Japanese assault on Shanghai—and had another long relationship with a man during the war.[72] Chen Yongsheng also taught physical education at a number of teacher-training schools, graduated from Baylor College in Texas in 1927, and after her return to China continued to teach physical education to girls and young women. Repelled in childhood by the fact that her educated, politically progressive father and uncles took concubines, Chen Yong-sheng chose not to marry.

For many women in Lu and Chen's generation, physical fitness was not merely a spare-time activity. It was a means to save the nation and thus the Chinese "race" through strengthening individual bodies, while at the same time creating a "healthy beauty" in women that could contribute to gender equality. Woman gymnasts, swimmers, track stars, and basketball and tennis players became minor celebrities in newspapers and maga-zines, especially when five women athletes joined China's delegation to the 1936 Olympics in Berlin.[73] Women's teams had to contend with zeal-ous spectator interest in the bodies of the players, as when the audience repeatedly shouted "Legs!" during a basketball tournament in 1931.[74]

Other women chose self-consciously feminist lines of work. Zhu Su'e, a lawyer, graduated from the Patriotic Girls' School in Shanghai and Shanghai Law College, with the express intention of advocating for wom-en's rights. She joined the Nationalist Party, representing many women clients in domestic abuse and family property complaints. At age thirty Zhu married a physician she met through a friend, raised two children, organized the Chinese Women's National Defense Organization, edited a women's magazine, and practiced law until 1949. Wang Yiwei studied journalism and in 1932 founded *Women's Voice* (Nüsheng), a biweekly journal aimed at educated women readers. Along with *Women's Monthly* (Nüzi yuekan) and *Women's Life* (Funü shenghuo), the magazine pub-lished fictional and nonfictional portrayals of women's contemporary dilemmas.[75] Wang Yiwei published *Women's Voice* until financial and censorship difficulties forced it to close in 1935. She was dismayed by the increasing diversion of New Woman ideals into homemaking, believing that women should help make a social revolution.[76]

The New Woman figure was a common, if still controversial, feature of 1930s urban life, even though the number of white-collar career women remained small.[77] Occupying the role was difficult, however. Popular suspicions about the personal characters of career women continued to proliferate. Lu Lihua, for instance, became the subject of gossip that she had sexual relations with men in order to raise funds to support her teacher training school.[78] In the 1930s, even if a woman had a job she was not free from the effects of economic instability, gossip, or direct threats to her person and her virtue. For New Women, remaining single or leaving a difficult marriage offered alternative paths through adulthood, but both required extreme vigilance about one's reputation.

Melodramatic films enjoyed by a large audience often showed New Womanhood culminating in a damaged life or a tragic death. In 1935, film star Ruan Lingyu starred in *New Women* (*Xin nüxing*), a film based on the life of an actress who had committed suicide.[79] Ruan herself was a product of the new possibilities available to women. The only surviving child of a widowed mother, she attended a mission school for girls and in 1926 responded to a Shanghai newspaper advertisement placed by a film company. Eventually she ended up at the left-leaning Lianhua film studio, and by 1930 she was nationally famous.

The plot of *New Women* revolves around the travails of Wei Ming, a divorced woman writer who suffers the loss of her job, the illness and death of her young daughter, and the unwanted advances of several men. Wei composes "The Song of New Women" for a woman friend who is a factory worker and organizer. But then, driven to despair by her circumstances, Wei commits suicide. The film's final scene shows women workers marching together as they sing the triumphantly militant song she has composed. The song, actually composed by Communist musician Nie Er, suggests that collective solidarity among working-class women may render them stronger New Women, shielded from the forces that felled Wei Ming.[80]

The film *New Women* soon became caught in a tight circuit of life imitating art. After it was released, Shanghai tabloids pursued exposés on star Ruan Lingyu's personal life: her failed relationship with a gambler who sued her for support and her later relationship with a wealthy merchant. Media accounts denounced her behavior as scandalous and damaging to society. Under relentless pressure, and possibly responding to problems in her relationship with the merchant, she committed suicide at age twenty-four on International Woman's Day in 1935. That day she had planned to talk to middle-school girl students about what the holiday meant and how they themselves could become New Women.[81] She left behind a note (although the authorship is in doubt) that read, "Gossip is a fearful thing," inspiring the writer Lu Xun to publish an essay by that name denouncing tabloid coverage for contributing to her death. It was reported that more than one hundred thousand people lined the route of Ruan's funeral cortege.

During the Nanjing Decade, the New Woman struggling in the professional world was joined by a domesticated avatar, the modern scientific housewife. For Nationalist state authorities, as for their late Qing and early Republican predecessors, promoting women's domestic skills was a priority. The government mandated that girls' schools devote substantial classroom time to instruction in sewing, cooking, child care, and other household arts, all based on the latest in scientific knowledge.[82] Educated in a new-style school, after marriage the New Woman was to apply her education to household management, considering outside employment only after the children were raised successfully.[83] Sometimes the domestic version of the New Woman was promoted at the expense of the career woman. One educator commented in 1934, "The reality is that except for a few genius women who devote themselves to their careers and apply what they have learned to their work, most women put what they have learned on the shelf once they marry and have children." The writer concluded that it was a waste of resources to educate girls in general subjects rather than domestic skills.[84]

Urban magazines and newspapers portrayed an idealized modern housewife who could create and preside over a domestic environment with all of the accoutrements of modern consumer culture, while also maintaining a family savings plan.[85] Some writers affixed the modifier "new" in front of the phrase "good wife and wise mother" to emphasize that they did not want a return to Confucian family arrangements.[86] The New Culture's family revolution—the transition to a companionate, freely chosen marriage—was presented as a finished process, already taken for granted. The new good wife and wise mother did not live in the extended kinship household of previous generations, but rather in the "small household" of a couple and their children.[87]

In the 1930s, business people joined the discussion about family reform, seeking to shape the family as a unit of consumption.[88] To keep the household clean and conflict-free, while providing her productively employed husband and children with well-prepared meals in a properly decorated domestic space, this new housewife required new products and the educated good judgment to distinguish among them. The business community was happy to provide guidance. The milk entrepreneur You Huaigao produced a free magazine, *Family Weekly*, which was distributed with his milk deliveries. It instructed women on everything from home decorating and family budgets to wholesome leisure-time activities and the duties of husbands and wives.[89] You Huaigao emphasized a housewife's role as helpmate to her hardworking husband:

> You must respect yourself and you must respect your husband's work. . . . Help him with his work as much as you can, giving him every kind of convenience. No matter what his success at work, you should be the first to praise him. When he fails, you will be the only one to comfort him. . . . So, if you make up your mind to be a virtuous and intelligent wife, you cannot let your husband have only hard work and no comfort.[90]

New clothing was central to a New Woman's self-presentation. The *qipao*, a one-piece garment with a high collar, modeled in part on the long gowns worn by late imperial male scholars, became popular in the mid-1920s. It was worn by urban middle-class women in part because it suggested women's equality and perhaps a degree of androgyny. The Nationalist government formally endorsed the qipao in 1927 as appropriate dress for women. By the 1930s it had become shorter and more tight-fitting, with a high slit in the skirt, telegraphing the desirability of the woman wearing it. The New Women featured in print advertising often combined Chinese-style clothes with Western-style shoes, gloves, or purses.[91]

Also required were new protocols of personal hygiene and health products, some of foreign origin. Dr. Williams' Pink Pills for Pale People made appearances in many magazines.[92] Beginning in the mid-1920s, Kotex, Modess, and Tampax sanitary napkins were touted in articles and advertising for their scientific design, cleanliness, comfort, and lack of odor. Authors graphically contrasted them to older-style menstrual cloths denounced as "'filthy,' 'coarse' and 'prone to scraping women's private parts.'" Women were instructed to use these new products in a regimen that also included exercise, rest, and frequent ablutions.[93] By the 1930s, advertisements for soap featured film stars and models, promoting clean, glowing skin free of bacteria and odor. Women were advised to pour a few drops of the cleaning fluid Lysol in their bathwater to kill bacteria on the skin and deodorize the vagina.[94] Modern hygiene required a woman to become a discerning consumer.[95]

Anti-imperialist boycotts in the 1920s and 1930s affected the use of foreign products, particularly those from Japan. The domesticated New Woman was encouraged to buy "national products" in a movement sponsored by the Nationalist government with the support of urban manufacturers and bankers.[96] Like foreign imports, national products were marketed as components of a modern home environment in which members of the family exercised and showered regularly, now using Chinese-made soap and wearing a Chinese-made bathrobe.[97] The modern housewife directed the flow of goods that linked consumerism to patriotism. A housewife who consumed unwisely—for instance, seeking low prices or high quality even if the goods were not Chinese-made—was pilloried as a direct threat to the nation.

In 1934, organizers of Women's National Products Year decreed that national salvation hinged upon the choices of women consumers. "A woman who commands her family to use national products," ran one campaign slogan, "is the equivalent of someone commanding officers and soldiers on the battlefield to kill the enemy for the country." Some women objected to the incessant emphasis on national products as the most important focus of women's political activity, pointing out that many threats to China had nothing to do with women's consumption. Most frequently, however, women registered their discontent with the high-pressure tactics of Women's National Products Year by quietly buying what they pleased.[98]

Photo 5.2.   Woman in 1930s Victory Cigarettes ad

Not all features of urban advertising were directed at virtuous wives and mothers upholding the nation. The domestic space had erotic potential as well. Commercial calendar posters rendered the faces and limbs of women in sumptuous detail, lingering on the revealing fabrics they wore and the array of fashionable jackets and shoes, furniture, and appliances in their surroundings.[99]

The Modern Girl

The Modern Girl can be understood as the mischievous, irresponsible, and vaguely dangerous younger sister of the New Woman. As the New Woman was increasingly domesticated in the form of the new good wife and wise mother, the social disquiet attached to her was redirected onto the Modern Girl.[100]

Unlike the New Woman, a term that dates from the early twentieth century, the Modern Girl first appeared in the 1930s, in the context of urban consumer culture. Her very name, "modeng nülang" or "modeng nüzi," with "modeng" appearing as the transliteration of "modern," referred to the circulation of "the modern girl around the world" at this time.[101] If improving society and saving the nation were the tasks of a New Woman, and responsible consumerism was the hallmark of a domesticated modern housewife, reckless behavior and wasteful consumption were the characteristics of the Modern Girl.[102]

The figure of the Modern Girl was prominent in Shanghai advertising and fiction in the 1930s. Every aspect of her bodily self-presentation was depicted: permed hair, high heels, fashionable (often imported) clothing—all requiring lavish outlays of money (see box 5.1). When the Modern Girl wore a qipao, it was apt to be sleeveless and made of a flimsy fabric that revealed every feature of her breasts and much of her legs. Unlike respectable urban women, she smoked cigarettes in public as a sign of rebellion and sexual availability.[103] Cautionary tales warned men to stay away, lest the Modern Girl cause their financial ruin. Unmarried Modern Girls appeared as deceitful, flirtatious, and greedy, and a man credulous enough to marry one would find her uninterested in housework and motherhood, leaving him to manage the home while she continued her free-spending, sexually promiscuous ways.[104] Her love of imports, especially cosmetics and perfume, was blamed for the minimal success of the national products movement and for China's trade deficit. Although some essays about her in women's magazines attempted to redeem her image, more commonly she was portrayed as a threat to personal morality, financial health, and national strength. Her fundamental error was that she misunderstood modernity, equating it with anything Western.[105] When a woman sported the Modern Girl look, a man could never be sure exactly who she was: college student, factory worker, secretary, recent rural migrant, or prostitute.[106]

One place where women dressed in the Modern Girl mode could be found was the cabarets of Shanghai. There male students, literary men, film actors and directors, journalists, officials, gangsters, and other urbanites went at night to listen to jazz and dance the Charleston and the Black Bottom. Customers would purchase a book of dance tickets and redeem

BOX 5.1.
The Modern Girl's Outward Appearance and Essence, 1933

Modern (*modeng*) means contemporary. It used to be that as long as one lived in present times, one could be considered modern. Ordinary people never used to say "this girl is modern" or "that girl is so un-modern." I believe that anyone with a little bit of knowledge cannot deny this statement. But, haven't people today misinterpreted modern? There are people who say that there is nothing good about modern girls. In fact this is too unjust.

Basically what ordinary people call modern is based solely on outward appearance. A girl wearing the latest fashion of 1933, her hair set in a "permanent wave," blood red lips, and leather shoes 6 or 10 cm high is seen as the modern girl. Indeed it is so. From her appearance she seems to represent the meaning of contemporary. But if this kind of person does not have brains, then isn't it a joke [to call her modern]? It is most unfortunate that today there are in fact so many of this kind of empty, superficial person. As a consequence, modern girls are subjected to strong attacks.

Therefore our explanation of modern must use, at the very least, two standards:

1. Her outward appearance, while it should be contemporary, should not be extravagant. Being constrained by old-fashioned things is not really a moral virtue.
2. Her spirit and brains are most important. How does she think? What is her outlook on life? What are her convictions? Of course, it is not that we expect all modern girls to be extraordinary characters, but at the very least they should measure up to the standard of a contemporary person.

Of these two conditions, without a doubt, the second condition is much more important; after all, isn't the modern girl's inner substance always more important than her external appearance?

Source: Shi Lili, "The Modern Girl's Outward Appearance and Essence," *Linglong* 3, no. 99 (1933): 882–83, English translation from https://exhibitions.cul.columbia.edu/exhibits/show/linglong/about_linglong/woman/modern.

them for dances with women partners, or "taxi dancers," employed by the dance halls. Taxi dancers incurred considerable expenses to look the part of a sophisticated ingénue, with appropriate clothing, shoes, accessories, hairstyles, and cosmetics. Exotic Western dances with attractive young hostesses began to replace courtesan performances at dinner banquets as the entertainment of choice for Shanghai's gilded youth. Courtesans even began to work as taxi dancers, and stories of cabaret hostesses filled the city's films, fiction, and gossip columns.[107] But in spite of their glittering public image, many taxi dancers were hired from the countryside and made marginal incomes in the cabarets, especially as Shanghai fell into a deep recession after the Japanese bombed part of the city in 1932.

Some dance hostesses entered into long-term relationships with their patrons, and others supplemented their income by selling sexual services. Dancers were known in local slang as "locomotives," and their patrons were called "cabooses."[108] In the 1930s media, dance hostesses embodied the full range of images of the Modern Girl: beautiful, mysterious, alluring, victimized, dangerous, and duplicitous. Less often emphasized was their role as service workers in an urban economy shaped by the world depression, Japanese aggression, and the influx of impoverished women from the countryside.

WOMEN WORKERS

The New Woman was remote from the daily existence of the estimated 160,000 women working in Shanghai's textile mills, silk filatures, and tobacco factories.[109] The Modern Girl as a style of presentation was less distant: many journalists commented on the fashionable dress of the better-paid young women in Shanghai's silk industry. Nevertheless, neither the New Woman nor the Modern Girl tells us much about the daily experience of urban women workers during the Nanjing Decade.

Their world was shaped by global depression, China's 1931 loss of Manchuria to Japan, and ongoing military conflict with the Communists. These events shrank the market for cotton textiles, silk, and other goods, leading to factory closings and lockouts.[110] Many labor disputes recorded during the 1930s were defensive in nature: workers demonstrated or occupied factories in order to keep their jobs. They were not in a position to agitate for improved pay or working conditions.

Worker militancy was also limited by the Nationalists, who installed corporate ("yellow") unions in the larger factories, run by officials connected to a far-reaching urban network with ties to the underworld known as the Green Gang.[111] Union membership encompassed both management and workers, and every effort was made to suppress union activity based on a notion of class struggle. Women workers were further constrained by the contract labor recruiting system in the cotton mills, which expanded during the 1930s. Young rural women were indentured for a period of several years to contractors who usually also were affiliated with the Green Gang. Women contract laborers had no direct access to the wages they earned, and outside of working hours were often confined to the housing controlled by the contractors.[112]

Photo 5.3.   Factory women on their way to work, Shanghai, 1933
Source: Agnes Smedley, *Chinese Destinies; Sketches of Present-Day China* (New York: Vanguard, 1933), facing p. 266.

In spite of these limitations, women played an important role in labor activism during the Nanjing Decade.[113] One potential basis for solidarity was the practice of pledging sisterhood, in which a group of six or eight women who had sworn loyalty to each other looked out for each other in the mills, kept harassers at bay inside the factory and on the street, lent each other money when necessary, and socialized during their off hours.[114] Mill hands also learned techniques of political organizing in night schools for workers run by the Young Women's Christian Association, many of whose organizers, foreign and Chinese, were committed to strengthening the labor movement.[115]

In spring 1928, silk workers from many different filatures organized a strike in response to the dismissal of four workers and the fatal beating of a fifth. The workers demanded that the police and manager involved in the initial incident face trial, and reportedly 6,000 men and 111,600 women in ninety-three filatures joined this strike. When the manager and one police sergeant were acquitted, the workers struck again for a month in the summer, seeking economic gains for themselves and compensation for the family of the man who had died. An estimated fifty thousand women participated in this second action.[116]

Six years later, at the height of the world depression, workers at the ten Meiya silk weaving factories went on strike to protest a 15 percent wage cut, the second in two years. Meiya workers were skilled and relatively well educated, and they made good money, even though the women weavers earned less than male weavers who did the same job. Meiya workers were known to spend their spare income on Western clothing and shoes, as well as urban amusement houses and dance halls. It is possible that the women among them resembled the Modern Girl figure more than other Shanghai workers did. But by 1934, Meiya's exports of woven silk to India and Southeast Asia were being squeezed out of the market by Japanese competition. Strike activity began among male skilled craftsmen and weavers, of whom some were members of the underground CCP, which had been operating clandestinely in Shanghai since the suppression of the Party in 1927.[117] Workers organized through a committee structure of their own making, rather than the "yellow" union.

Throughout the protest, women militants played key roles. The first fatality of the strike was a woman worker killed in a standoff at one of the factories by French Concession police armed with machine guns and tanks. Worker demands for compensation to the injured and the family of the dead woman fueled an extension of the strike. When plainclothesmen arrived at the factories to take ringleaders into custody, Elizabeth Perry writes, "An alert member of the strikers' security force managed to sink her teeth into the hand of the policeman before he could complete his assignment." The arrest of a woman weaver led to a vigil at the police station by workers at Meiya, other factories, and university students. At one point two hundred women engaged in a hunger strike. One of the strike demands was equal pay for men and women. The strike was suppressed after fifty-one days, many activists were arrested, and worker pay was cut by 30 percent.[118] Although not a memorable labor victory, the Meiya strike nonetheless illustrates the active participation of women workers in labor protest at a time of economic crisis.

RURAL WOMEN AND THE WORLD ECONOMY

Women's Agricultural Labor

For many New Culture and later leftist writers, the rural woman embodied everything that was most backward about China. She inhabited the corner of Chinese life that was most difficult to reform—the family—in an agricultural sector that urban intellectuals often portrayed as unchanging. The rural woman, in their view, was a sign of China's deep troubles. Her powerlessness and feudal attitudes were a drag on the modernity sought by urban Chinese intellectuals and activists.

Their portrait of rural women was not completely inaccurate, but it was certainly incomplete. Village women comprised roughly 40 percent of the total Chinese population during the Nanjing Decade, and it is important to ask an additional set of questions about their lives, even though the documentary record on rural women is much sparser than it is for urban

women. What sorts of labor did rural women perform in different regions? How were their lives affected by the integration of some of China's
rural areas into the global economy and by the collapse of that economy
during the worldwide Great Depression? Did expansive Nationalist state
projects or nongovernmental reform efforts touch their lives? In short,
what changed in the 1930s, and where, for China's village women?

Women across all of China's agricultural regions worked.[119] They went
to the fields during the busy seasons, doing so year-round in households
that were short of male labor. In areas well beyond the one described by
Mao Zedong in 1930 (see box 5.2), they could be found weeding corn, harvesting barley, transplanting cabbage, picking peanuts, tending sweet potatoes, hoeing and picking cotton, planting and hulling and threshing rice
and other grain, sharpening and wielding sickles, raking the fields, picking tea, pushing water carts and irrigating the fields one ladleful at a time,
working the foot pedals of waterwheels, driving the oxen that powered
some water pumps, and guarding the irrigation ditches.[120] Women poled
boats downstream and hauled them upstream along towpaths. In more

---

BOX 5.2.
Mao Zedong on Women's Work

In 1930, Mao Zedong skipped an important conference in Shanghai to spend
a month investigating life in a remote corner of Jiangxi Province, where he
was beginning to develop a rural strategy for the CCP. One of the things he
noted in Xunwu County was the relentless demand for women's daily labor:

> Strictly speaking, in terms of farming, women's duties are much heavier than those
> of men. Because certain tasks require physical strength, men are more likely to
> take charge of plowing and raking the fields and carrying the muck and grain.
> However, women assist men in carrying the muck and grain, transplanting rice
> seedlings, weeding fields, uprooting the weeds in the paths between the fields and
> on the edges of the fields, turning over the soil, and cutting the grain. But although
> men help out, women are chiefly responsible for hulling grain, polishing grain,
> watering gardens, transplanting vegetables, cutting wood, mowing grass, making
> tea, cooking meals, raising pigs and other domestic animals, washing and iron-
> ing clothes, mending clothes, making shoes, sweeping floors, and doing dishes.
> Besides these tasks, raising children is also a woman's duty; thus, the toil of women
> is harder than that of men. Women's tasks come one after another, and their work
> never ends. They are appendages of the male economy. . . . Although men are no
> longer serfs, a woman is still a man's serf or semi-serf, without political rights and
> personal freedom. No one suffers more than women.

Source: Mao Zedong, *Report from Xunwu*, translated by Roger R. Thompson (Stanford,
CA: Stanford University Press, 1990), 212–13.

commercially developed regions such as Jiangnan, they produced textiles and handicraft goods for the market under the putting-out system.[121] In north China, they spun and wove for home consumption and sometimes for sale.[122] They also were responsible for domestic labor: cooking, washing, spinning and weaving and sewing the family's clothing, making cloth and felt shoes and shoe soles, and caring for children, who generally were not in school and were put to work as early as possible. Whether or not women had bound feet, whether they worked indoors—the preferred location for reasons of respectability—or in the fields, rural women's labor was crucial to household survival.

Rural women's production in economically more developed areas was increasingly shaped by international markets.[123] In silk-producing rural areas of Guangdong Province, women's labor was particularly valuable. With the support of their families, women delayed cohabitation with their husbands after marriage, or declined to marry altogether, contributing to the upkeep of their natal (and sometimes marital) families through their work in silk filatures.[124] In the Wuxi area, women raised silkworms at home. They remained respectably out of public sight, selling the cocoons to urban filatures in Shanghai and elsewhere that produced silk yarn for export to European and U.S. factories.

Raising silkworms was extremely demanding work. The voracious creatures had to be carefully arranged on bamboo trays in a warm moist environment and fed round the clock with a steady diet of mulberry leaves in order to spin their cocoons without damage during the brief spring season. Women were often blamed if the cocoon spinning went awry. It was widely believed that menstruation, pregnancy, or postpartum bleeding could pollute the environment and cause the silkworms to die. Raising cocoons was also a financially risky business, because prices were unstable, and a fall in price could ruin a farming household.

Women who raised silkworms formed a crucial node in China's capitalist production for an international market—and were vulnerable to market vicissitudes. When the global depression spread to China in the early 1930s, prices for agricultural goods dropped rapidly, and foreign markets for Chinese exports collapsed. This ruined the livelihoods of farmers who produced raw cotton, handwoven cloth, silk cocoons, and other products. Prices for silk cocoons in Jiangsu and Zhejiang Provinces fell by more than two-thirds between 1930 and 1934. With the drop in their cash incomes, farmers in highly commercialized areas had trouble purchasing rice and other food supplies. Many were forced to take out high-interest loans to finance daily expenses, production supplies, and life-cycle events such as weddings and funerals.[125] Reports of dozens of rice riots filled the press, and mobs of farmers attacked and robbed wealthy households.[126]

During the same period, more than one hundred thousand women in Guangdong who had worked in silk production lost their employment and headed for the cities to look for work as servants.[127]

The stigma attached to women's going out to the fields remained strong, yet women routinely performed farm labor. In the northern Yangzi Delta, which produced raw cotton for mills in Shanghai and other Jiangnan cities, and cotton cloth for China's northeast, large commercial farms began to emerge by the 1920s. Men increasingly left their shrinking family farms to weave for the market or find other jobs. Women took their place, weeding and picking the cotton crop on the family farms, and hiring out as wage laborers for larger farms run as commercial enterprises. Some women, bought by wealthier families as child daughters-in-law and concubines and wives, doubled as unpaid farm laborers.[128] Women also hired out as farm laborers in parts of Zhejiang and in Guangzhou to the south.[129]

The partial feminization of agriculture was not limited to China's most commercialized regions. In Yunnan, some women spent more days in the fields than men; in coastal Fujian, women were deeply involved in agricultural production while the men fished.[130] As a child, Xie Bingying encountered many child daughters-in-law among Hunan tea pickers: "Every day each girl had to pick at least 140 or 150 pounds of tea leaves, yet her pay was only twenty or so copper coins. She had to give this money to her future mother-in-law."[131]

In inland rural Shaanxi, when able-bodied men left home in search of work or to avoid conscription, or became disabled, or died, women replaced them in the fields. Cao Zhuxiang, who married in the mid-1930s, did field labor from the minute she became a wife:

> That's why I was never really a daughter-in-law. For a daughter-in-law, there were many restrictions in better-off families. She was not allowed to go out of the door easily. But in my situation, I went to work in the field right away.

Later, as a young widow, she even learned to plow, normally a task reserved for men: "I was ashamed that the land that I plowed was not as good looking as other people's plowed land, so I plowed my land at night." Working alone made her vulnerable to criticism and even assault. But she felt that employing a hired hand would expose her to scandal:

> I didn't call in anyone, and didn't hire anyone. I was afraid that others would make idle talk. My neighbors said that my family had never before had such a capable person. In the fields I quietly threw myself into the work. I didn't gossip or waste time. So they had no basis for idle talk.[132]

Women's increased involvement in agricultural work clearly enabled them and their households to survive. But it did not necessarily raise their status or loosen the control of family authority.

Rural Instability and State Regulation

When Chiang Kai-shek unified the country in 1928, the warlord era nominally came to an end. But in Hebei, Sichuan, and many other areas, episodic conflict continued between his regime and military factions, or among sub-factions that sought to expand their own power.[133] Marauding bandits and remnant warlord troops were not always easy to distinguish. Newspapers in 1928 reported that farmers in areas twenty miles from Nanjing, where state control might have been expected to be strongest, were paying protection money to bandits and being kidnapped for ransom. One farmer in the area said,

> Those who are as poor as we have neither means to move to other places, nor work at home, but close the door at night and hurry away to hide with their children wet and cold, in the bushes and streams of the mountainsides, in spite of the mosquitoes and snakes.[134]

The Nanjing Decade was marked by natural disasters. During a 1928 drought in Shandong, children and women reportedly were being sold for a few dollars or traded for a sack of grain.[135] In summer 1931, floods on the Yangzi and Huai River systems affected one hundred million people in seventeen provinces. Several million people drowned or died from cholera and typhus, and massive numbers of refugees in Hubei, Henan, Jiangxi, and Jiangsu fled their homes for higher ground and treetops, or sought escape in small boats, rafts, washbasins, and hastily emptied coffins.[136] The 1935 Yellow River flood was estimated to affect four to five million people.[137]

Rising waters endangered all in their path, but the social aftermath was often gendered. During the 1935 Yellow River flood and resulting famine in Shandong, for instance, the sex ratio of children born to mothers in flood refugee shelters was 151 males to 100 females, suggesting that women were practicing female infanticide. This practice may have been even more common among refugees who were not in the shelters, where women were provided at least a minimal food allotment for each new child.[138]

In 1935, an article in the popular Chinese journal *Eastern Miscellany* (Dongfang zazhi) elaborated on the consequences of the rural crisis for women. As men left—for the cities, overseas, the army, or banditry—Chen Biyun wrote, "over 99 percent of them leave their wives and their children (if they have them) behind." Remittances were rare, and so

> the married woman who remains in the countryside faces a hopeless situation. If she has only herself, it is easier. If she has children, short of starving and waiting to die, or fleeing famine and wandering abroad, she has few options.

Women who left for the cities would find that many cotton mills and silk filatures had closed, and that the market for nursemaids, maids, and prostitutes was saturated. "As a result," Chen observed, "most of these women have no escape; they must resign themselves to hunger and cold." When food was short, rural women ate less. When debts were due, "moneylenders have been known to accept a wife or daughter as collateral on a loan as if she were a piece of livestock." Women suffered domestic violence from their hard-pressed and angry menfolk and, Chen said, were more likely to die in China's floods and droughts, both because bound feet made flight difficult and because they were responsible for children. She noted press reports of markets in many provinces where women and girls were sold for a pittance. One account described young women selling sexual services in drought-stricken areas, advertising their services with a placard that read, "Drought household, gentlemen welcome."[139]

Rural women in the 1930s received some attention from the state. The Nationalists banned footbinding and set a schedule of fines for households that violated the regulations. Enforcement was not consistent, and the ban probably had less effect on the decrease in footbinding than the spread of girls' schools and changing economic patterns.[140] Women sometimes were incorporated into ambitious state development plans for the countryside. One approach led to various experiments with rural cooperative industry in model counties, supported by the government, academic institutions, and sometimes by foreign funding.[141]

Just outside the new national capital of Nanjing, the government in 1933 established the model county of Jiangning where, it boasted, women were given literacy training and vocational classes while their children were cared for in county government facilities.[142] But this rosy picture was overdrawn. Nationalist party leaders did not agree about the best approach to the rural crisis, and so support was inconsistent.[143] Local officials spent far more on their own operations than on farmers. Intervention in land ownership or marriage practices, which might have addressed the rural crisis and its effects on women, was unthinkable.

WOMEN WITHIN AND BEYOND THE NEW LIFE MOVEMENT

Throughout the Nanjing Decade, the Nationalist government struggled to reformulate the radical agenda that had characterized the official women's movement during the United Front years. Attacks on patriarchy, involvement in political activity, and support for social revolution were no longer official goals. During the Nanjing Decade, women were mainly exhorted to support the Nationalist regime in their role as wives and mothers.[144] Women active in the Nationalist Party, as well as non-Party reformers, had some success in sending more than a dozen nonvoting women observers and representatives to the citizens' convention of 1931, at which a provisional constitution was formulated. Tang Qunying's vision of universal suffrage, however, remained unfulfilled.[145]

In early 1934, in the midst of a military campaign against the Communists and intensifying Japanese encroachment, Chiang Kai-shek inaugurated the New Life Movement. New Life, which drew on fascist practices in Germany and Italy, sought to involve every citizen in nation building, down to the level of bodily habits. Chinese citizens were exhorted not to spit, urinate in public, scratch, gamble, or smoke opium. They were enjoined to stand up straight, shower regularly, trim their nails, button their top buttons, shine their shoes, comb their hair, air out their bedding, and purchase domestically produced goods.[146]

Women had gender-specific roles to play in the New Life Movement. Chiang Kai-shek's wife, Song Meiling, presided over the New Life Women's Guidance Committee (WGC). Its monthly magazine, the *Women's New Life Monthly*, promoted model homemakers who were also deeply concerned about the nation, poor urban and rural women who contributed to the survival of their families, and women who had put aside idle pleasures to join the war effort—a portrayal that preceded the national outbreak of war in 1937.[147]

As students, girls and young women were to be offered an education that cultivated housework skills, industriousness, frugality, and mothering.[148] As housewives and mothers, they were expected to bring modern hygienic practices into the home and impart them to their children, reordering family life in the service of a mobilized nation. With the wives of high-ranking Nationalist officials directing the effort, the WGC sponsored public lectures and ran seminars on how to run a model household and how to be a model domestic servant, while also conducting disaster relief and running civics classes for women. But attendance at all of these early activities was spotty, and local police were enlisted to round up people and deliver them to the meetings.[149]

The New Life Movement discouraged personal adornment and consumption in a time of national crisis. Government regulations, which were widely disregarded, decreed that the qipao should fall four inches below the knees, with a side slit that extended no more than three inches above the knees. Revealing clothing and permed hair were prohibited, with police sometimes enforcing these regulations. The Modern Girl was repudiated. Model New Life women were to be athletic and healthy beauties like the champion woman swimmer Yang Xiuqiong, who was recruited to help publicize New Life in appearances across China.[150]

Not everyone found New Life initiatives adequate to meet the growing political crisis. A commentator in *Women's Voice* observed, "Thousands of square miles of Chinese territory have been occupied by the Japanese without any resistance, but if a woman offends public decency, she must

be expelled."[151] Women responding to the various restrictions on dress
and behavior invoked the state's own ideal of "healthy beauty," which
required physical activities such as swimming and a certain amount of
exposed flesh, as intrinsic to nation building.[152] Like other Nationalist
initiatives, the New Life Movement had limited effect on the daily lives
of urban residents, reaching people mainly through their schools or workplaces, and no effect on those in rural areas. And its message about wom-
en's societal roles was not consistent: in addition to their crucial domestic
duties, women were encouraged to work in teaching, public health, and
handicraft production at home. Then, with the outbreak of full-scale war
in 1937, the movement shifted to mobilization for the war effort.

It is tempting to conclude that the Nanjing Decade marked the end of
a national politics entwined with feminism. Women's rights in marriage
were expanded by state decree rather than by social activism. Refugees,
poor women, prostitutes, women workers, and labor activists were regulated and contained, albeit with limited success. The ideal of domesticity
was reconfigured on a scientific and hygienic basis, to be presided over by
new good wives and wise mothers who would guide consumption, reduce
the trade deficit, and raise a new generation of strong citizens. The rebellion
of the Modern Girl centered on profligate consumption and sexual allure,
not on political engagement. Rural women, beleaguered by an economic
crisis whose origins lay far beyond their local communities, seemed to
dwell in a universe untouched by the radical questions of the late Qing period and the New Culture debates. And the state's response to intensifying
political threat from Japan and from the Communist movement entailed
militarizing all social arrangements, with a largely unrealized vision of
disciplined unity in which women were chiefly responsible for the home.

And yet, in the daily practices of new institutions, the range of activities considered normal for women continued to expand. Teacher training institutes proliferated, drawing women from inland cities and rural
areas, and offering them a road into teaching and other professions: law,
journalism, literature, and the arts. Radical educators urged women to
become politically active, decrying educational goals that taught them to
be consumers who were dependent upon men and isolated from broader
social movements.[153] At secondary schools in the lower Yangzi region,
both male and female students participated in extensive self-government
activities: managing the school cafeteria, organizing cooperatives, coor-
dinating work in the school garden, regulating student behavior, taking
sick classmates to get medical attention, and organizing sports meets as
well as extracurricular clubs for the arts and home economics.[154] Almost
every week, girl students in lower middle schools attended civic rituals and ceremonies to honor Sun Yat-sen, raise and lower the flag, and
mark various holidays, although celebrations of the May Fourth and
May Thirtieth Movements, common during the United Front period,

were curtailed.[155] Government-sponsored Girl Scout troops, established in secondary schools during the 1930s, taught young women martial drills, outdoor skills, and first aid. A group of Girl Scouts who rescued a drowning young woman was widely publicized. The scouting program

Photo 5.4. High school Girl Scouts, 1933

Source: Linglong magazine, 123 (December 6, 1933), cover. Courtesy of C. V. Starr East Asian Library, Columbia University.

closely paralleled the activities organized for young men, but when male students attended their mandatory military training class, young women were sent to learn nursing.[156] Thousands of young women wrote for school journals in secondary schools across China, far outnumbering the small number of literate women whose work had seen print under the Qing. In some of these writings, they expressed a commitment to discipline themselves, build up their physical strength, learn to work hard, and contribute equally with men to saving the nation.[157]

Such declarations could be understood as an obedient response to the state's New Life Movement. But as the decade wore on and a growing student movement advocated increased resistance to Japan, student activists found themselves at loggerheads with the Nationalist authorities. By late 1935, American reporter Agnes Smedley wrote,

> each week-end men and women students gathered by the hundreds in the Western Hills [outside Beijing] on what they called "picnics." . . . What they were really doing was practicing mountain-climbing and guerrilla warfare. Sticks were their weapons, and stones were their hand-grenades.[158]

The December Ninth Movement of 1935 began with a rally of two thousand students in Beijing to protest Japanese encroachment in North China. Among the marchers were students from a girls' middle school.[159] Hundreds of marchers were attacked by police and injured, and several dozen were arrested, setting off similar protests in other cities and garnering significant support from labor unions and prominent intellectuals. A week later, a young woman student from Qinghua University named Lu Cui briefly became the face of the protest movement. Arriving at a locked city gate with five thousand student demonstrators, she rolled under the gate to try to unlock it and was arrested. Her supporters won her release by conducting a sit-down strike. Foreign journalists dubbed her "China's Joan of Arc."[160] Enacting their citizenship, students asserted their critical judgment. In doing so, the women among them asserted their full rights and duty to act politically, just as their male classmates did.

In 1935, outraged by Chiang Kai-shek's continued policy of nonresistance to Japan, He Xiangning, former head of the Nationalist women's bureau (and future high-ranking official in the PRC), sent him a cutting poem, written on a woman's skirt. It read in part:

> You claim yourself a man
> But you willingly suffer the humiliation of the enemy.
> You present our mountains and rivers without fighting,
> Thus leaving shame for tens of thousands of generations.
> We, the women,
> Are willing to die on the battlefield.
> I give you my dress,
> To exchange for an army uniform.[161]

Photo 5.5.   Lu Cui, December Ninth student leader
Source: *Dazhong shenghuo* 1.6 (December 1935), cover.

Less than two years later, with the beginning of a full-scale Japanese invasion, war drew all Chinese women into a world where possibilities, as well as dangers, had widened.

6

Wartime Women, 1928–41

War came unevenly to China during the 1930s and 1940s, changing women's lives in every region. The Nationalists surrounded and attacked Communist-controlled rural areas and pursued Communists across China throughout the Nanjing Decade. The residents of remote rural areas in Jiangxi and Fujian were among the first to encounter sustained military conflict. Communist activists driven from the cities after the 1927 coup began to establish bases there, struggling to secure local territory and defend it from the Nationalists. By 1930 they had founded the Jiangxi Soviet as well as a number of smaller base areas.

For much of the CCP and for rural people in these base areas, the 1930s passed in a state of perpetual war. Repeated assaults by the Nationalist army finally drove the Communists out in 1934. Their Long March across China to a base area in Yan'an, Shaanxi Province, became the stuff of revolutionary legend. The chapter begins with the role of women in the peripatetic Communist movement as it decamped to rural areas, built rural soviets, then left most of the women and children behind to undertake the Long March to the northwest.

War arrived in northeast China, too, early in the decade. Occupied by Japanese forces in 1931, the following year the northeast became the Japanese-sponsored puppet state of Manzhouguo (sometimes spelled "Manchukuo"). An influx of Japanese settlers and new policies followed.

The Japanese attempt to occupy the rest of China began in 1937 with brutal assaults on the civilian populations of Nanjing and many rural areas, in which rape and murder played a prominent role. During the Japanese advance across China in 1937–38, millions of Chinese, many of them women and children, were displaced from their homes. The Nationalist government decamped from Nanjing to Wuhan, in central China, and then to the southwest city of Chongqing in Sichuan.

By the early 1940s, collaborator governments were in place in different regions of occupied China, and civil administration was generally in Chinese hands. In the cities, complex dynamics of resistance, collaboration, and survival shaped the lives of women white-collar workers, actresses, prostitutes and cabaret hostesses, as well as women factory workers and the casual laborers of the urban poor. Marriage and divorce remained a means for poor women to improve their living situations. In much of the countryside, Japanese military control was weak, but life was punctuated by campaigns of reprisal against the rural population. Late in the war, Japanese attempts to squeeze more resources out of China to support Japan's faltering war effort brought further hardship to civilians and peril to rural women. And shortly after Japan surrendered, Nationalists and Communists fought a civil war from 1946 to 1949.

For many elite women across the political spectrum, these wars brought disruption as well as expanded opportunities for public activity. For the urban poor, the conflicts intensified their economic vulnerability. And for millions of women both urban and rural, the war displaced them from their homes. The following two chapters trace the effects of war on women, asking how women's labor and other activities shaped various war efforts and how Woman became an important symbol of national vulnerability and resistance.[1]

WOMEN AND THE RISE OF RURAL COMMUNISM: THE JIANGXI SOVIET

How could a small number of fugitive activists make a revolution in a poor and remote rural area? Marxism and Leninism had little to say about this, but after the 1927 coup some CCP organizers, including Mao Zedong, retreated to mountainous rural areas to consider their next step. The Party continued to organize attempts at urban insurrection for several years, and after that maintained an active (if imperiled) underground presence in major cities, but rural organizing became increasingly central to CCP strategy. Mao, believing that peasants could be a revolutionary force, emerged as the de facto chief strategist for Communist activity in rural areas, although other leaders were more important in the Party hierarchy until 1935.

By 1930, the Communist forces controlled considerable territory along the borders of Jiangxi, Fujian, and Guangxi Provinces, and other groups of CCP activists founded more than a dozen smaller bases in other remote areas. In late 1931, the CCP established the Chinese Soviet Republic with its capital at Ruijin.[2]

The 1927 defeat by the Nationalists convinced many Communists that, as Mao put it in August 1927, "political power grows out of the barrel of a gun."[3] Organizing efforts in the countryside were backed by a Red Army under direct CCP control. Revolution from this time forward became a military as well as a political project. Military needs took precedence, and wartime conditions became a way of daily life for civilians in soviet areas.[4] When Communist organizers sought to mobilize women, it was to draw on their labor to ensure the survival of the army and the soviet territory.

To build the soviets, the Communists were determined to redistribute land and other property from rich households to poor. Although in practice land was cultivated by members of the household, not individually, Party policies called for redistribution mainly on a per capita basis, regardless of gender.[5] The CCP encouraged women to join the poor peasant leagues and participate in raids on landlord households and land confiscations.

Xie Peilan was one of those women. Her story of life as a young rural activist in early 1930s Jiangxi, recounted for a documentary film shot many decades later, was unadorned and chilling:

> We smashed the landlord's opium pipes and took away his grain and clothes. We started looking for his money. The landlord wasn't home. His wife was hiding in the attic where rice straw was stored. We found her. We questioned her for several days, and then we killed her.[6]

Did Xie know this landlord or his wife? What particular local factors contributed to the violence? Were women a mainstay of such raiding parties? Was execution of landlord family members a common outcome? This account raises more questions than it answers. But Xie's story does provide an important clue to women's participation in the Jiangxi Communist revolution. She was initially attracted to the movement, she said, because

> people told me if I joined the revolution, I would have my freedom. I could choose who I wanted to marry. If I didn't join, I would have to marry this man who was over thirty. So I thought, if revolution could save me from this, I would join.[7]

This was not an uncommon motivation for young women. The May Fourth message of free-choice marriage had not reached most rural areas, including the poor regions of Jiangxi and Fujian where the CCP was now attempting to survive. Parental control of marriage remained strong. Powerful local landlords could and did demand sexual access to the women in poorer households. When Wan Xiang was a child, she watched the local landlord seize her older sister as a wife. The landlord also demanded to take Wan, who was seven years old, as a maid for his household. Her father refused, and so the landlord demanded one thousand silver dollars to buy a maid instead. Unable to produce the money and unwilling to send a second daughter to that household, her father sold Wan as a child daughter-in-law instead. When the Communists arrived, Wan, now a young woman, became a Party activist.

Mao noticed that for peasant women, land reform was often inextricable from marriage reform.[8] He wrote in 1930, "Women have expressed their appreciation for the land struggle, because it can help dissolve the restrictions on their personal freedom."[9] In Xunwu County, he noted that women had carried wood for Red Army assaults and seized grain from the landlords. Women who had organized themselves into women's associations felt free to stay out later in groups when they went to the hills to cut firewood. With the self-consciousness born in this struggle, many then filed for divorce as soon as soviet township governments were established. Ninety percent of local divorce cases, he observed, were initiated by women, even when their husbands threatened them with death. One township even turned away a propagandist who had been sent to publicize the land reform, saying, "Comrades, please do not give us any propaganda. With more propaganda, the women in our township will all run away."[10]

Mao sympathized with poor peasant men who were worried about losing their wives and the household labor they performed. In a 1930 investigation of Xingguo County, he observed that landlords and rich peasants monopolized the local women, taking wives and sometimes concubines.[11] Middle peasants needed to spend a sum almost equal to their assets to marry, although 90 percent were able to do so by going into debt. But almost a third of poor peasants and 99 percent of landless laborers were unable to muster the resources to acquire a wife.

When the Communists promoted marriage reform in rural areas, it was with an eye to breaking this connection between landed power and control of women. Decrees issued by the precursor of the Jiangxi Soviet government encouraged unmarried men and women to freely choose spouses as quickly as possible, apparently leading to a spate of marriages among the poor. Mao even noted that Jiangxi peasants were beginning to remake the language of marriage. They took the character *you* from *ziyou*, "freedom," and used it as a verb to mean freely choosing a marriage partner rather than engaging in "the old compulsory buying and selling of marriages." But landless laboring men still found it difficult to marry, he said, because "women dislike the fact that the farm laborers have no household utensils or equipment, and they also dislike the fact that they are seldom at home [because they had to hire out their labor to others]."[12]

Concerned Party cadres began to report in early 1931 on "the anarchical situation provoked by the slogan of the absolute liberty of marriage and divorce." They worried, too, about cases of male cadres engaging in sexual relations with women they had been assigned to organize.[13] Mao himself raised criticisms in 1930 about township government officials and their criteria for hiring women: "If a woman is not good-looking, they don't want her even if she is articulate and capable. If a woman is good-looking, they want her even if she is inarticulate and incapable of doing the work." When officials went to the villages to hold meetings, he added, "They talk with the pretty women and won't say a word to those who are not pretty."[14] Additionally, local conflicts erupted when married people took lovers, and wives rallied to oppose their husbands' affairs. At one point, the Xunwu County government briefly felt compelled to forbid affairs involving married people, in order to quiet internal dissension in a county that was still under attack from Nationalist forces.[15] The fear of social conflict in an area increasingly under military siege meant that for the Communists, marriage reform was not always a priority.[16] For Mao, the long-term solution was to push on with land reform so that men would have the wherewithal to find a wife.[17] But fear among poor peasants that marriage reform would lead to the loss of wives continued to trouble Communist organizing across rural China into the early 1950s.

The Party continued its commitment to marriage reform in November 1931, when new soviet marriage regulations established freedom of marriage and divorce, abolished arranged marriage, and forbade the purchase of child daughters-in-law.[18] The Marriage Law of April 1934 formally established monogamy and banned polygamy, polyandry, bride price, and dowry. The legal marriage age was fixed at twenty for men and eighteen for women (two years older than the corresponding provision in the Nationalist Civil Code), and couples were required to register their marriages with the local soviet. In a nod to actual social practice, the law added that a cohabiting couple who had not registered would still be considered married.[19]

The unilateral freedom to divorce was enshrined in law but withheld in the case of the wives of Red Army soldiers, in order to allow the soldiers to fight without worrying that their wives would leave them. An army wife needed her husband's agreement for a divorce, unless she had not heard from him for two years.[20] After a divorce, property was to be divided equally, and a divorced woman who had received land in her husband's village was to be allocated new land in the village to which she moved after the divorce. A man was required to help his ex-wife cultivate her land if he was able to work and she "lacked labor power." Children were to be raised by the woman unless she did not wish to do so, with the man providing two-thirds of the children's living expenses until they turned sixteen.[21] These remained standard features of subsequent Communist marriage laws.

How this law was implemented, and how local people responded, are difficult to assess. Jiangxi Soviet publications mentioned cases of purported sexual chaos and coercion: men forcing women to sleep with them on grounds that this was a way to combat feudalism; tales of forced remarriage of widows within five days of their husbands' deaths; and some cases of sexually transmitted diseases rapidly spreading through communities. Reports were numerous of cases in which local authorities refused to grant divorces to women or even to entertain requests for divorce.[22] Nonetheless, divorce rates rose. The 4,274 divorces registered in only two counties of the soviet during a four-month period in 1932 far outnumbered the 853 divorces granted during the entire year of 1930 in Shanghai.[23]

In a township investigation in late 1933, Mao reported with an apparent mixture of satisfaction and amusement that social behavior was beginning to change: "Husbands curse wives less frequently while, on the other hand, wives curse husbands more now." Parents were beating children less frequently, and children were talking back more when they were beaten or cursed. (Ideally, he noted, no one should be cursing anyone, or beating their children.) Mao contended that the number of women having secret love affairs had declined from 50 percent to less than 10 percent since the advent of Communist control, although he gave no corresponding figures for men. He gave three reasons: women had received land, they now had freedom to divorce, and they were "busy with revolutionary work."[24]

Nationalist propaganda against the Jiangxi Soviet mocked the CCP commitment to marriage reform and freedom to divorce. "The red bandits wish to destroy virtue: they practice free sex. They are savage beasts who abandon themselves to debauchery!" ran one 1934 slogan, while another urged women to take up arms against the "red bandits" in order to "preserve their chastity and enjoy familial happiness."[25]

Under constant attack from Nationalist forces, the government of the Jiangxi Soviet tried to mobilize as much of the population as possible for military support. Women were organized to wash clothes and make sandals for the troops.[26] In June 1932 Mao commented that every revolutionary organization needed women except for the regular forces of the Red Army, which could employ them as nurses but not soldiers.[27] Women could, however, join ancillary military organizations: guerrilla forces, the volunteer army, Red Guard militia armed with spears and an occasional rifle, and youth organizations. Women also could do cultural propaganda: young men and women were trained to perform in traveling drama troupes, with a repertoire of skits about the revolution and the current situation of the soviet areas.[28] Not content with these roles, some young women agitated to join the Red Army as regular soldiers, and in several soviet areas they were organized into all-women units. One of these, in Qiongya on Hainan Island, became the subject of a famous "model opera" in the 1960s titled *Red Detachment of Women*. It was more common, however, for women who received military training to be tracked into medical work or assigned to mobilize village women.[29]

The revolution needed women's political support as well as their labor. Mao called women "a force that will decide the success or failure of the revolution."[30] If women were not convinced that the Red Army was a good thing, he said, they would not let their menfolk join.[31] As the Nationalist campaigns depleted the Red Army's troops, teams of women were recruited to locate more rural men and convince them to join, an increasingly difficult task.[32]

As Nationalist attacks on the soviets intensified, the feminization of agriculture was a crucial element of the CCP survival strategy. In Changgang Township, when adult men went off to join the Red Army, women at home came to outnumber them four to one, taking over most agricultural work. They even "learned to use plowshares," which was a task normally reserved to men. Women also took on responsibility for security in the rear. By late 1933 women predominated in the local Red Guard militia, which comprised 46 men and 120 women, and the youth organization, called the Young Pioneers, had 21 young men and 80 young women. Men and women in the Red Guard and Young Pioneers drilled together, and several of the trainers were women.[33]

In spite of women's value as support labor for the war effort, a 1932 soviet government directive named a daunting series of impediments to women's rights. Working women were supposed to comprise at least 20 percent of the executive committee membership and 25 percent of the total number elected to soviet congresses at the township level and above. And yet, in some places they were being denied the right to vote and run for office.[34] In spite of the Marriage Law, women were still being sold in marriage, forced into marriages they did not want, and physically abused, often with the tacit or active support of local government authorities. Women who divorced their husbands were being denied their rights to land and property. Women workers were earning lower pay than men, even when they did the same job. Labor law provisions protecting pregnant and parturient women were not being enforced.[35] Women who joined the Red Army were not getting the same benefits as male soldiers. Mao proposed that every level of government in the soviet establish a Committee for Improving the Lives of Women to advise local authorities on how to address these and other problems. Particularly crucial, he said, would be part-time schools and literacy classes aimed at women.[36]

THOSE WHO LEFT AND THOSE WHO STAYED

By late 1933, the Jiangxi Soviet was being choked. More than half a million Nationalist soldiers methodically constructed rings of blockhouses to surround and take soviet-held territory. Communist demands for men and materiel to resist this encirclement deeply damaged the soviet economy, bringing hardship to the entire population.[37] The Communists were outnumbered, outmaneuvered, and weakened by disagreements in the top Party leadership. Their forces included about seventy thousand regular troops and perhaps fifty thousand guerrillas. In October 1934, about eighty-six thousand of them, including twenty to thirty thousand noncombatant Party officials, porters, teachers, medical personnel, and skilled workers, left in search of a safer base in which to establish a new soviet.[38]

As the troops assembled prior to setting out, Gregor Benton writes,

> women threaded their way through the crowds of soldiers, handing out straw sandals, conical sun-rain hats, oil-paper umbrellas, food, tea, peppers, dried vegetables, and cloth shoes with rope soles tipped and heeled with metal and twice as thick as usual (few knew why). By the river, another group of women sang songs praising the Red Army.

But these women did not know where the troops were headed; most in the soviet thought that their relatives in the Red Army were leaving for a short-term expedition.[39]

This expedition, which became known as the Long March, lasted a year and involved several different armies from different soviet areas marching thousands of miles across China. The heroism and determination of its soldiers became a core legend of subsequent CCP history, with tales of crossing fourteen rivers, eighteen mountain ranges, and grasslands full of quicksand. Nevertheless, the Long March was less a triumphal procession than a retreat, with Nationalist forces in pursuit.[40] In the midst of the Long March, a Party meeting at Zunyi in January 1935 validated Mao Zedong's approach to military strategy and appointed him to the Standing Committee of the Politburo. The year of headlong flight was harrowing for most of the marchers; only an estimated one-tenth of the initial group arrived in northern Shaanxi in late 1935, leaving many dead, wounded, and exhausted soldiers along the way.

Only about thirty women marched with Mao's First Front Army. Half were spouses of CCP leaders who also were activists in their own right; one additional woman from each province was selected to do support work, after passing a stringent medical examination.[41] Other sections of the army had more women: in the three main army columns that made up different strands of the march, between two thousand and eight thousand women worked as nurses, administrative workers, or members of the propaganda corps. They often marched at night, and even during the day they had to concentrate on keeping up a rapid pace while carrying heavy loads on uneven mountain paths, often without enough to eat.[42]

Male soldiers had decidedly mixed attitudes about the women marchers, who were seen as hindering men's ability to fight because they needed protection, and causing jealousy among men, even as men recognized their nursing and propaganda work as useful.[43] Some women were injured or could not maintain the brutal pace of the march—or so the male leadership decided—and were ordered to drop out. Anyone left behind along the way risked arrest or worse if captured by the pursuing Nationalists.[44] Women marchers kept close track of one another, finding in the Party and the army a network of support unavailable to them in their home communities.[45]

Among them was Mao Zedong's wife, He Zizhen. The couple's son was left behind, like all the children of those in Mao's army contingent, and He Zizhen gave away another child she bore during the march.[46] Women in other contingents of the army gave birth on the march and kept their children, contending with pregnancy, postpartum difficulties, infant fevers, and hunger en route.[47]

When conditions eased and the marchers stayed in one place for a time, many women did propaganda work. They could approach women directly in situations where it was not acceptable for a man to do so. They convinced peasant women to let their family members join the army, found out which landlords had excess grain that could be requisitioned, and performed street dramas about local land relations.[48]

Of the thirty or so women who had left the Jiangxi Soviet with the First Front Army, nineteen reached Shaanxi.[49] After their arrival in Yan'an, some of the women attended classes at the Resistance University or the Party School, training to be cadres—Party members with administrative responsibilities. Others went directly into organizing work.[50] Many of the women Long Marchers went on to post-1949 careers in Party or state organizations.[51]

The history of the revolution tends to follow Mao. When the Long Marchers abandoned the Jiangxi Soviet, the attention of subsequent historians went with them, and the Jiangxi Soviet dropped out of sight. For the two to three million inhabitants of the Jiangxi Soviet left behind, however—including all of the women except those few who had joined the troops—the aftermath of the soviet's collapse was catastrophic.

Four-fifths of the people in the core area of the soviet were dependents of Red Army men, who lost both their military protection and their labor power when the men departed.[52] Left behind also were about fifteen thousand soldiers and another ten thousand sick and injured ones, as well as many local male fighters who knew the terrain well and could mount resistance.[53] Irregular left-behind Communist troops fought the Nationalists, in fourteen regions scattered across eight provinces. Small bands of fighters took to the mountains to blend in with local inhabitants and to engage in guerrilla warfare when possible. Small groups of women who had been revolutionary activists, some left behind because they were pregnant, roamed the mountains looking for guerrilla groups.[54] Some women who remained in what had been the soviet were raped by Nationalist or warlord soldiers or sold off as prostitutes.[55]

Xie Peilan and Wan Xiang, both of whom had been activists in the Jiangxi Soviet, were imprisoned by Nationalist forces. Xie recalled that

> a Nationalist official wanted to bail me out of prison to force me to be his concubine. I didn't want to, but he threatened me, saying, "If you won't, we'll put a firecracker in your vagina and light it. Aren't you afraid?" Sitting or standing, I was just as tall as anyone else. Why should I be someone's concubine? I didn't want to, but what could I do?

Wan Xiang, a Party member, was pierced through the leg with red-hot wires, strung up by the arms, and then told that if she did not reveal the names of Party members,

> "Tomorrow we'll send a platoon of soldiers and rape you to death." That really frightened me. I wasn't afraid of being killed, but how could I stand being raped? Though they were just threatening me, they really made it look real. When I was taken out the next morning, there really was a platoon of soldiers waiting. The officer said, "Just look at those men. If you don't confess, you'll be raped to death right here." I said, "I don't know who is a Communist. And I'm not a Communist leader. I'm just a laundrywoman." I didn't tell them a thing, and in the end, they sent me to the concentration camp at Zhejiang. They never got anything out of my mouth.[56]

The terrible circumstances of those left behind to fight brought women into newly important roles. Some women fought with guerrilla bands, because the improvisational aspect of military operations in this period allowed them more scope for activity.[57] Women revolutionaries attracted less suspicion than men and could move around the landscape more freely. Women agents reported on enemy troop movements and traitors among the local population, sometimes by leaving notes among the religious messages in local Buddhist temples. They also performed the kind of logistical and support work that was conventionally assigned to women: laundry, cooking, mending, even running a secret factory in the mountains to produce clothing and shoes for fighters. They smuggled food and other supplies to the guerrillas, escaping detection by hiding the goods in hollow bamboo carrying poles and leaving them where they could be retrieved. In the plains, women ran liaison stations that helped scattered guerrilla groups to communicate and protected the families of Red Army guerrillas from Nationalist reprisals. They mimeographed propaganda and smuggled and distributed it into the towns. When local activists were arrested, groups of old women were mobilized to wail at local government offices to demand their release.[58]

PAN-ASIAN COLONIALISM: WOMEN IN MANZHOUGUO

In September 1931, Japanese troops invaded China's three northeastern provinces, consolidating their control in a region where they had long been economically and politically active.[59] The Nationalist government, preoccupied with encircling the Communist soviet areas in central China, offered little support to Chinese troops that put up resistance. In 1932 the Japanese authorities established Manzhouguo, a nominally independent "nation of the Manchus" held in place by the Japanese military presence. They placed on the throne the Manchu Emperor Puyi, who had been deposed in 1911 while still a toddler.[60] In Japan's vision of what was called the "Greater East Asia Co-Prosperity Sphere," Manzhouguo was to provide grain, minerals, and labor to meet the needs of the Japanese empire. It was also to be a destination for resettlement of Japanese farmers from impoverished regions, although far more Chinese than Japanese immigrated to the new state.[61]

For the inhabitants of Manzhouguo, unlike those in the rest of China, the wartime years after 1931 were not marked by open military conflict or widespread guerrilla warfare and peasant organizing. Construction and manufacturing flourished, and Manzhouguo became highly industrialized, although workers were paid less than a third of what their Japanese counterparts earned.[62] Public health facilities grew, modeled on those in Japan.[63] Expressions of resistance to Japan were efficiently repressed by the Japanese and their collaborationist government, as were Communist sympathies, and at least one famous woman guerrilla leader, Zhao Yiman, was captured and executed in 1937. But government control remained spotty beyond the major cities and railway lines.[64]

The ideal figure of Woman in Manzhouguo looked quite similar to that of the Nationalists during the Nanjing Decade. Girls were to be educated

to become good wives and wise mothers, full of modern scientific knowledge to be applied inside the home. Articles in the Japanese-owned,
Chinese-language press promoted model housewives, while cartoons
derided the New Woman/Modern Girl as frivolous and self-destructive.[65]

Few women could remain in school for higher education, which required fluency in Japanese and the means to study in Japan.[66] One young
woman who was trained as a nurse in Manzhouguo's only nursing school
recalled in 1946 that Chinese students were never allowed to forget their
place in an ethnic hierarchy with Japanese at the top:

> The vast majority of the students were Japanese women. They ate rice, while
> we ate sorghum, and we didn't even get enough of that to fill ourselves. But
> the leftover rice from the Japanese women was fed to the dogs, and when
> the Japanese women complained that their rice wasn't any good, it was just
> simply given to the draft animals. . . . Those Japanese women were telling
> us all the time that this came from Japan and that came from Japan, that if
> it hadn't been for the Japanese we wouldn't have rice or apples. One time I
> got into a quarrel with a Japanese woman over eating an apple. I said, "That
> apple was grown in China." They reported me to the head of the school for
> harboring dangerous thoughts.[67]

Yet in spite of limited opportunities and ethnic prejudice, Chinese women
were active outside the home in many domains of Manzhouguo life.

Women were among the most prominent regional writers. Their
portrayals of local life often departed from the roseate official vision of
pan-ethnic harmony and women serving the family and the state. The
region's most famous woman writer, Xiao Hong, portrayed in her autobiographical fiction the brutal treatment of poor rural women by both
Japanese occupiers and Chinese men.[68] In early 1941 the state forbade
writing about topics that could be understood as undermining the ideals of Manzhouguo. These included "recreational love that denigrates
chastity, lust, abnormal sexual desire" and "use of matchmakers and
domestics as the main topic, and especially exaggerated descriptions of
the customs and human relationships of the entertainment districts." But
women writers were not censored as consistently as men, perhaps because cultural authorities did not take their writing as seriously.[69] Women
including Zhu Ti, Dan Di, Yang Xu, and Mei Niang published regularly
in literary journals. They criticized gender segregation and outmoded
gender ideals taught in the schools, the social expectation that women
would exhibit patience and endure mistreatment, women's subjugation
to men, arranged marriages, unwed mothers, difficult childbirth, poverty,
community violence, oppressive parental authority, widow chastity, and
rape. They celebrated romantic love, free-choice marriage, and women's

sexual pleasure. As an ensemble, the writings of these women offered pointed commentaries on patriarchy in Manzhouguo society.[70]

But not all women were critics of Manzhouguo. One source of popular support for the regime was the redemptive societies, religious groups that combined tenets of Confucianism, Buddhism, and Daoism. One of them, the Morality Society, claimed one-fifth of the Manzhouguo population as members, with women as prominent and enthusiastic participants. Their activities, often segregated by gender, were encouraged by the state. Women gave public lectures on topics ranging from women's education to breast-feeding, preaching the importance of service to society, self-sacrifice, and the ability to support oneself. In Manzhouguo the figure of Woman blended modernity with tradition, and educated women were called upon to guard treasured cultural values while expertly managing small families that contributed to a strong nation.[71]

Widespread opium addiction among the Chinese population of Manzhouguo was a source of tension and public debate in which women figured prominently as victims and social miscreants. In 1932, a new Opium Law established state control over production and distribution, with a stated aim of reforming addicts and reducing consumption, but the main effect was to strengthen Japanese control over a constantly expanding trade.[72] Women addicts, although not in the majority, were addressed in starkly gendered terms. Newspaper reports and popular fiction in the 1930s offered lurid details of addicts selling their wives to support their drug and alcohol habits, and Puyi's wife, the Empress, was debilitated by addiction. Sometimes misogyny and discrimination were blamed for women's addiction, but women also were excoriated for neglecting their domestic duties, wasting household resources, decking themselves out to mingle inappropriately with men in opium dens, and funding their habits through sex work. Depending upon the political sympathies of the writer, women were blamed either for contributing to the fall of the northeast to Japan, or for preventing Manzhouguo from becoming the "paradise land" envisioned by the Japanese.[73]

During the 1930s, a debate about women's role as hostesses in opium retail outlets roiled the popular press.[74] Women workers in Manzhouguo bars and coffeehouses, and opium hostesses who prepared and served the pipes, came in for special scrutiny as seductive, duplicitous, and eager to promote addiction and relieve men of their money. Because opium hostesses were paid only in tips after 1932 and purportedly sold sex to augment their income, they also were portrayed as threats to the licensed prostitution industry. Some popular writings highlighted their need to support themselves and their families, and it appears that opium hostessing was far from the worst option available. In 1936, hostesses in the

Photo 6.1. Opium poppy harvest in northern Manzhouguo
Source: *Wei Manzhouguo jiu ying* (Old pictures of puppet Manzhouguo), edited by the museum of Manchukuo Palace, 2001.

Manzhouguo city of Harbin made as much money as bank tellers, civil servants, and teachers. Some opium outlets festooned their storefronts with banners naming and describing the attractiveness of their hostesses. But hostesses also were described as victims, prone to addiction themselves. In the 1930s, various cities experimented with bans on hostesses, which were no more successful than prostitution bans had been.[75]

The state also established an alcohol monopoly in 1938. Initially, alcohol was advertised as beneficial for women's health, and serving alcohol to one's husband was portrayed as the sign of a modern wife's loving care. But by the 1940s, the press occasionally reported on the unfavorable eugenic, physical, and psychological effects of alcohol. Here, too, women were singled out as both perpetrators (drunken mothers) and victims (wives battered by drunken husbands, alcoholic wives who committed suicide). In 1935, a group called the Married Women's Rectify Customs Society began an unsuccessful campaign to prohibit alcohol use, providing an occasion for women's organized social activism.[76]

Ultimately, Manzhouguo, a node in the Greater East Asia Co-Prosperity Sphere, was overwhelmed by the needs of the Japanese military. In 1937 the region provided supplies for the Japanese invasion of China. After

1941, many resources were channeled toward war production, leading to inflation, an increase in taxes, persistent shortages, and a black market, as well as increasing political repression.[77] Access to goods was ethnically determined, with Japanese having priority.[78] We still know far too little about how these events affected the daily lives of women in the northeast, their survival strategies, and their understanding of the global forces that constrained them during those years.

INVASION, RETREAT, AND WOMEN REFUGEES

On July 7, 1937, Japanese forces tried to occupy a key railroad bridge near Beijing. When Chinese troops resisted, the Japanese sent reinforcements, plunging Japan and China into a full-scale war that would last eight years and cost fourteen million lives.[79] Rape, coerced prostitution, unwanted pregnancy, abandonment, widowhood, and the disappearance of men who had been conscripted all contributed to the trauma and life-threatening poverty women experienced during the invasion and retreat.[80]

Beijing and Tianjin fell by late July. In the early months of the invasion, Song Qingling, Sun Yat-sen's widow and a well-known leftist figure, and other prominent women in Shanghai joined forces to organize wall newspapers conveying war news in simple language and raise funds for the war effort. Leaders of women's organizations formed a Shanghai branch of the Women's Consolation Society, which sent toiletries and other supplies to soldiers, coordinated nursing care for wounded soldiers, and worked on refugee relief. Communists, some of whom were now working aboveground in the wartime context, participated in these activities.[81]

Beginning in August 1937, Chinese-controlled sectors of Shanghai were heavily damaged during three months of fighting, and civilian casualties were extremely high. A young woman Girl Scout named Yang Huimin emerged as a national figure during this battle for delivering supplies and a Chinese flag to soldiers defending a warehouse.[82] Much of the city was occupied by Japanese forces, but the International Settlement and the French Concession remained under foreign control until 1941, when Pearl Harbor made the war global. The Japanese army pushed on toward the Nationalist capital of Nanjing, as government officials evacuated. In December 1937, hundreds of thousands of civilians who remained in Nanjing were murdered by Japanese forces.[83]

Rape was a standard practice of war during the period of rapid Japanese military advance and a terrible feature of women's wartime suffering (see box 6.1). The Nanjing Massacre also was known as the Rape of Nanjing, a name that should be understood literally. This campaign of terror included the rape of an estimated tens of thousands of girls and

Photo 6.2.   Girl Scout Yang Huimin, 1937

women in Nanjing and surrounding communities, often followed by
their murder.[84] One typical incident report, submitted by foreign Nanjing
residents to the Japanese military authorities, read:

> January 3, 1938. A woman who was taken with five others . . . ostensibly
> for washing clothes for Japanese officers, came to the University Hospital.
> They were taken by Japanese soldiers to a place in the west central portion
> of the city . . . The women washed clothes during the day and were raped

---

BOX 6.1.
Rape and Military Invasion

The following account by a young woman student at Associated University in Kunming was collected by Robert Payne in late 1944 while he was teaching English there. It recounts the arrival of Japanese forces at her native village about seven years earlier.

> I was fourteen—they came very early in the morning. I was sleeping, and suddenly my grandfather came to where I was sleeping and whispered: "Don't say anything, don't speak," and he put a handkerchief over my face and carried me quickly to the tunnel. There was an escape tunnel near the wall. He dropped me down—about ten feet, and I remember I groaned, and at that moment there was a tremendous hammering on the door. I thought my sisters were in the tunnel, but there was no one else except me. I could hear everything that was going on.
>
> I could hear things, but I couldn't understand them. The Japanese talked such bad Chinese. I heard the sound of wood breaking, and then screams—they were my elder sister's screams. I knew they were hers because she had once cut herself with a chopper. And then she was begging for life. There was no sound from the other sister. I thought she was safe. . . . But the screams went on. She was fifteen, and at fifteen you know how to scream loudest. . . . I wanted to get out of the tunnel. I could hear the floorboards creaking rhythmically . . . and sometimes laughter, and once I heard a bottle being broken. . . .
>
> When I woke up it was night. I climbed up the tunnel. My grandfather was dead, shot through the temple. My sister was lying naked on the floor with blood all over her legs; she was alive and shaking her head from side to side like a madwoman, and there was no sign of my other sister. . . . We never found my other sister. What was strange was that even when the Japanese were defeated, the girls would hardly ever go out of their houses; they had all been raped and they did not want to see each other. They preferred only to speak to old men.

Source: Robert Payne, *China Awake* (New York: Dodd, Mead, 1947), 13–14.

---

throughout the night. The older ones were being raped from 10 to 20 times, the younger and good looking ones as many as 40 times a night. On January 2, two soldiers took our patient with them to a deserted school house and struck her ten times with a bayonet knife. . . . The soldiers left her for dead.[85]

Rape was also an important symbolic weapon deployed by the Chinese government in the anti-Japanese propaganda war. Chinese war cartoons graphically depicted Japanese soldiers raping and then murdering Chinese women. These cartoons were widely distributed on posters and pamphlets aimed at mobilizing a minimally literate population. The raped and often mutilated Woman embodied not only the suffering of actual women, but also China's dismemberment by Japan. Cartoonists felt that depictions of Japanese soldiers sexually abusing women would inspire patriotism and resistance, whereas depictions of Chinese men wounded or killed in combat would damage morale. The more explicit the depiction of sexual violence, cartoonists believed, the more effective it would be at inciting the desire for national revenge. For these cartoons to be maximally effective, the rape victims had to die. This avoided imagining the possibility that Chinese women would be forced to bear the babies of their conquerors, further undermining the integrity of the nation.[86]

Civilians suffered not only from Japanese war crimes, but also from Nationalist military strategy. In June 1938, Chiang Kai-shek blew up dikes on the Yellow River in a vain attempt to slow the Japanese advance, flooding parts of three provinces without warning. At least eight hundred thousand people died, and almost four million were displaced from their flooded villages.[87] Tens of thousands more died later that year when Nationalist forces burned down the city of Changsha to prevent its capture.[88] By late 1938, the Japanese had much of east China, as well as Guangzhou, gaining control over parts of twenty-one provinces.

An estimated one hundred million refugees—urban and rural, rich and poor—fled the war zones, converging on any city offering a modicum of safety in what one historian has called "the greatest forced migration in Chinese history."[89] For much of 1938, the Nationalist government made its capital in the central Chinese city of Wuhan, where some 430,000 refugees gathered.[90] In January 1938, U.S. war reporter Agnes Smedley described a train station platform crowded with refugees from Hebei, mainly women and children, carrying everything they owned in wheelbarrows, some with no quilts to shield them from the frigid winter air. The women had no food and no money.[91]

Photo 6.3.   Women's Defense Corps training in Canton, 1938

Public and private groups worked to provide refugee assistance in the city, particularly to women and children. Shi Liang, a woman lawyer, took a leading role in this effort. Prior to the outbreak of war, Shi had been imprisoned for half a year by the Nationalist government for advocating resistance to Japan. But under the United Front policies of the early wartime years, women with a range of political allegiances, including many Communists, became publicly active.[92]

During the initial years of invasion and retreat, nurses were in short supply. The Nationalist government mobilized women students to learn battlefield nursing skills, and members of women's organizations also flocked to field hospitals to help care for the wounded.[93] Xie Bingying, whose experiences in the Northern Expedition were discussed in chapter 4, organized a Hunan Women's War Zone Service Corps in Changsha. Setting off with sixteen young women she had recruited, she recalled,

> I was overwhelmed with happiness. It had been a full ten years since I had taken off my uniform, and during all that time not a day had passed that I did not remember the meaningful and satisfying life I had lived in those army days, and not a day had passed that I did not long for that life. . . . This would be a day for me to feel honored, glorious.

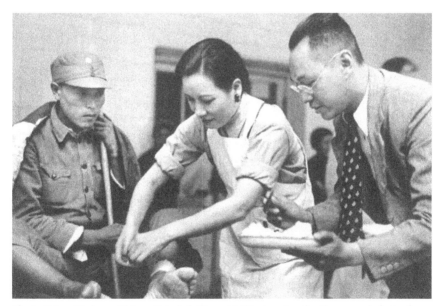

Photo 6.4.   Madame Chiang Kai-shek (Song Meiling) caring for the wounded, Hankow, 1938

Source: Cornell Capa, ed., *Behind the Great Wall of China: Photographs from 1870 to the Present* (Greenwich, CT: Metropolitan Museum of Art, 1972).

Her Service Corps nursed seriously wounded soldiers and organized logistical support from the community just outside of Shanghai, until they were forced inland with the Nationalist army's retreat. As they traveled, the women explained the war and the importance of resistance to people in the rural areas they passed through.[94] It was not until 1943 that a formal system of military nursing was established, with women as the majority of the recruits. By the end of the war, nursing was firmly established as a women's profession.[95]

The Nationalists abandoned Wuhan in late 1938 and fled further inland to Chongqing. Hundreds of thousands of refugees followed the Nationalist government to Sichuan, many of them women and children who were vulnerable to sexual violence and robbery along the way (see box 6.2).

BOX 6.2.
The Price of Passage

Among the refugees who made their way to Chongqing after the fall of Wuhan was a seventeen-year-old named Li Qunying. After she was injured and a neighbor was killed when Li's house was bombed, she fled with her widowed mother and younger brother. They were heading to Enshi, a town in Sichuan where her night school was being relocated:

In early September 1938, we joined the refugee movement toward Sichuan. By then, hundreds of thousands of refugees had swamped all the major roads. . . . A sea of people with their belongings congested the roads and made the movement very slow and chaotic. . . . We . . . were easy targets for robbers and sex offenders in that chaotic situation. We had to stay with the crowd on the major roads for bandits often attacked straying refugees, especially women and children. . . . On the way to Shashi, we met two brothers in their twenties who were refugees from Anhui Province. When they saw our difficulty in carrying our luggage and my brother, they offered us help. . . . We walked for weeks. . . . Without the two brothers' help in carrying my mother and being with us, the three of us could not have reached Enshi safely.

However, I soon realized that the two brothers did not offer us help for free. The older brother had his eye on me and wanted me to have sex with him. Since the three of us could not survive the chaotic refugee journey without them, my mother silently allowed his sexual advances toward me.

When they reached Enshi, they discovered that Li's high school had not succeeded in reestablishing itself there. Their small refugee group of five eventually decided to move on to Chongqing, where the men had a relative who was a Nationalist official.

Going to Chongqing with them was our only choice at that moment. . . . We did not have any control over our lives, and we lived in great fear. . . . For our safety, we had to stay with the two brothers. To me, it meant that I had to satisfy the older brother's sexual needs against my will, to endure a painful existence for the sake of my mother and my young brother. I was a seventeen-year-old high school student. I had my dreams of love, marriage, and family. I never envisioned that my life would go this way.

For Li, the refugee journey to Chongqing culminated in an unwanted pregnancy, the baby's death en route, and a disastrous marriage to the older brother that disintegrated before the end of the war.

My mother felt guilty that she had let my husband take sexual advantage of me during our journey to Chongqing, which had forced me into the terrible marriage. However, I did not blame her for my own misfortune. What could we do? Without the two brothers' help, we would have been robbed and raped by the bandits anyway.

Source: Danke Li, *Echoes of Chongqing: Women in Wartime China* (Urbana: University of Illinois Press, 2010), 55–60.

OCCUPIED CHINA

The Japanese exercised uneven control over the areas they had occupied, establishing a patchwork of puppet regimes in Manzhouguo, north China, and the Yangzi Delta. Effectively, there was not one occupation, but many, varying in intrusiveness and brutality. By 1940, Nationalist official Wang Jingwei had left Chongqing and helped to found a collaborationist Nanjing government. Many collaborators saw themselves as nationalist patriots cooperating with an unavoidable force that in any case was less objectionable than Western imperialism. The term they preferred to use was *hezuo*, "to work together."[96]

When the Battle of Shanghai was over, the Japanese sponsored a local collaborationist regime known as the Great Way Government, staffed by local bureaucrats.[97] The International Settlement and the French Concession, still under foreign control through 1941, created what was popularly known as a "lone island" in the midst of occupied territory. Although Shanghai under occupation saw considerable intrigue, assassinations, espionage, and gang activities, many features of urban life went on as before.[98]

Economic pressures pushed more married women into the workforce during this period and caused single women to delay marriage in order to continue working.[99] The Chinese Career Women's Club, founded in Shanghai in 1938, had close to a thousand members, mainly unmarried white-collar businesswomen, educators, civil servants, and medical workers. The club provided networking opportunities, store discounts, and sewing classes, engaged in volunteer social welfare work, and sponsored leisure-time activities such as political discussion groups, job-related classes, singing, biking, swimming, basketball, volleyball, and drama groups. The club provided a place for women to discuss gender discrimination at work, while celebrating the career woman as a new social identity organized around work and group leisure. It also raised funds for the CCP New Fourth Army, which was active in central China, although many club members were probably unaware that the club's founder, a woman named Mao Liying, was a CCP member. But the veneer of normality was fragile. The club dissolved after Mao Liying, who had received death threats, was murdered on a Shanghai street in 1939, possibly by agents of the collaborationist regime.[100]

The war propelled people from around the region into the International Settlement, which housed hundreds of thousands of war refugees in hundreds of camps. The camps also became venues for CCP organizing.[101] War refugees from other areas were shocked at public displays of affection between courting couples in the parks; one 1939 refugee described "a gorgeously dressed new woman with hanging long hair, a powdered face, red lips, in stockings and high-heeled leather shoes," walking and laughing with an equally fashionable young man in a manner that "in the hinterland . . . would surely cause gossip and be considered shameless."[102] Large department stores such as Wing On did a brisk business during the lone island years, employing women to sell cosmetics, stationery, and candy, and to model clothing.[103]

Nightlife in wartime Shanghai flourished. The theaters were full. Overt expressions of nationalism were dangerous, but most writers wanted to avoid the Japanese rhetoric of the Greater East Asia Co-Prosperity Sphere. They wrote instead about love, family, and daily life in the city.[104] Yue opera performances of love stories, performed by all-women troupes and closely followed by middle-class women fans, some of whom were also well-off war refugees, became one of the city's predominant cultural forms. Struggling to distinguish their social status from that of prostitutes, women opera stars sought to avoid gossip or any hint of sexual scandal. Some committed suicide under circumstances similar to those of Ruan Lingyu described in chapter 5.[105]

Prostitutes in wartime Shanghai continued to be licensed by the municipal government.[106] Cabarets hired increasing numbers of Chinese dance hostesses, and many young people flocked to the dance halls at night. The city's collaborationist government depended on the revenue stream from cabarets and casinos to fund its operations, and gangsters were active investors, managers, and operators of protection rackets. Numerous periodicals were devoted to cabaret culture, publishing elaborate accounts of the careers of dance hostesses. In the latter years of the war, the municipal police undertook to count dance hostesses with the aim of issuing licenses to them, a project that continued into the postwar period.[107]

The Shanghai cotton mills in the International Settlement also flourished in the early years of the war. The changed political environment gave underground CCP members new opportunities to organize workers on nationalist grounds. Rather than attempting to form clandestine unions, they shifted their organizing strategy and began to work through native-place associations and other groups to which workers belonged.[108] Among these were the sisterhoods described in chapter 5, as well as night schools run by the YWCA. After developing relationships and swearing sisterhood with groups of women workers in the mills, CCP organizers recruited some of them into the Party. Under their leadership, many women engaged in low-visibility subversion of production in Japanese-run mills through stealing, industrial sabotage, and slowdowns.

It is difficult to reconstruct whether the women saw a larger political significance in their activities. But it is clear that their daily needs for subsistence and protection overlapped with the anti-Japanese organizing agenda, and certainly engendered an awareness of the power of acting as a group.[109] After the bombing of Pearl Harbor in December 1941, the Japanese assumed control of British and American mills, and as the war progressed some mills shifted to the production of military uniforms, while the machinery in others was melted down for ammunition. By 1943 only a few thousand workers remained in the cotton mills, and former mill hands sought casual labor, peddling, and smuggling jobs to survive.[110]

In the cities of occupied China, lawsuits involving marriage and divorce, and criminal cases involving women, continued to be adjudicated under the laws passed during the Nanjing Decade.[111] Men frequently disappeared and no longer contributed to the support of the family. Women in 1942 Beijing brought 77 percent of all divorce suits, and of those suits, more than half were on grounds of desertion.[112] In court, women told of husbands who had left home to seek work and had either disappeared or not been able to send any funds home, leaving wives struggling to support themselves and dependent children. Women married to Nationalist soldiers were separated for years from husbands who could rarely communicate across Japanese lines and had no means of sending remittances, even if they had been able to do so. (Given the low pay of enlisted men in the Nationalist army, this would have been difficult in any case.) In such cases, courts were inclined to grant the wife a divorce.[113]

Equally striking was the phenomenon of runaway wives. Women who were not satisfied with their economic circumstances, living arrangements, or treatment by spouses frequently just disappeared. For women to run away from a marriage was not in itself a criminal act, as it had been during the Qing. An unhappy wife's most common recourse—with or without a formal divorce—was to find another man to marry. If a husband could not locate his wife through police searches, newspaper ads, or contact with her relatives, he could seek divorce after she had been missing for three years, or sooner if he could prove "malicious intent to abandon."[114] Men also pressed charges of abduction, bigamy, or adultery against other men when their wives ran away.

The Civil Code of 1930 remained in force during the Japanese occupation. As chapter 5 detailed, the code sought to make men and women equal within marriage.[115] But for poor women trying to survive in the tenements and alleyways of occupied Beijing, the problem that preoccupied them on a daily basis was not that they were subordinated in the family. It was that their husbands were indigent or absent, they themselves could not find regular work, food prices were rising at an alarming rate, and starvation was a real possibility. Faced with dire circumstances, women looked for casual labor including handicrafts, domestic service, sex work, human trafficking, and opium and grain smuggling. And they ran away, effectively dissolving their own marriages.[116] The Civil Code might have been speaking the language of May Fourth, but on the streets of Beijing, popular ideology held that a man needed to provide for his wife, or she could go elsewhere.[117]

In occupied areas outside the major cities, many men were also absent, having been conscripted into the Nationalist army or press-ganged into labor crews for the Japanese. Moving about in public space was risky, and many women stayed home. Tens of thousands were recruited under false pretenses or abducted outright and sent as "comfort women" to provide sexual services under conditions of virtual slavery to Japanese soldiers in military brothels.[118] Others who had to be out and about took care to disguise themselves. Chen Huiqin, who grew up in a village not far from Shanghai, recalls:

> The Japanese were always looking for "flower girls." When I became a teenager, I had to pretend that I was an ugly . . . old lady when I worked in the fields. I smeared ashes from the back of the kitchen wok on my face, wore Mother's old clothes, which were too big for me, added a worn-out work skirt at my waist, and put on my grandmother's old headcloth. When Grandmother, Mother and I worked in the fields, I stood between them. Wherever possible, I stood in ditches or hunched over . . . when Japanese soldiers passed by.[119]

Under wartime conditions, it was dangerous for women to be publicly visible. And yet, as the experience of Jiangxi Soviet women, wartime nurses, and countless women workers and farmers suggests, women's labor was more necessary than ever.

7

Wartime Women, 1935–49

During the years when China was consumed by war, women's labor fueled efforts at resistance, reconstruction, and revolution in the disparate zones controlled by the Japanese, the Nationalists, and the Communists. Woman as symbol, meanwhile, was recast to embody endurance and fortitude rather than modernity or social transformation.

Beginning in 1937, the Nationalists and Communists were formally allied again in a second United Front against the Japanese. But the cooperation between the two supposed allies remained tense, and after Nationalist forces destroyed the headquarters of the Communist New Fourth Army in 1941, relations erupted periodically into open conflict.

By 1939, much of the Nationalist government apparatus, as well as universities and urban professionals displaced from occupied China, settled in southwest China. They brought their various reform agendas, including the education of women, to areas where Nationalist government control had hitherto been weak. But the overwhelming imperative was war, not gender reform, and the Nationalist state made concerted efforts to mobilize both urban and rural women for wartime support.

In the Communist base area centered on Yan'an, and in other base areas the Communists established behind Japanese lines in north China, organizers mobilized rural women's labor to support military expansion. The Japanese occupation and a Nationalist blockade kept many goods from the Communist areas. The base area governments called upon women to take over much of the farming while the men joined the army. Women were organized to produce clothing, shoes, and other goods in a bid to make the base areas as self-sufficient as possible. At the same time, the

CCP adopted more conservative positions on family and marriage than those of the May Fourth era or the Jiangxi Soviet, mindful of entrenched peasant resistance to marriage reform.

Soon after the conclusion of World War II in 1945, civil war between the Nationalists and the Communists consumed much of China. Some areas endured sieges and pitched battles, while others shifted to Communist control with no combat. The chapter concludes with a brief look at the last years of the 1940s and the gendered contours of a society emerging from decades of war.

CHONGQING AND BEYOND: DOWNRIVER WOMEN IN UPRIVER COUNTRY

Wartime displacement brought thousands of educated girls and women from the Japanese-occupied eastern seaboard to Sichuan, Yunnan, and other inland provinces. After the Japanese military advance drove the Nationalists out of Wuhan, Chiang Kai-shek established his wartime capital in the Sichuan city of Chongqing. The city's population more than doubled in the early years of the war. The government sponsored a massive relocation of middle-school and university students and teachers from occupied areas to the interior. Among the middle schools that relocated were both girls' schools and coeducational schools.[1] In Kunming, Yunnan, faculty and students from major universities in occupied territory regrouped to found National Southwest Associated University (abbreviated in Chinese as Lianda). Male students arrived on foot, and the faculty and women students came by train via a roundabout route through Vietnam.[2]

Women students were an unusual sight in this region. Some were housed temporarily in a small town south of Kunming, where one wing of a tin merchant's family compound had been converted to a women's dormitory. A historian writes that whenever they left the compound,

> they had to pass the curiosity seekers who came from miles around to see the newly arrived aliens. . . . If a Lianda woman ventured into a crowded shop or restaurant dressed in her high-slit cheongsam and flesh-colored stockings, she risked finding a hand creeping up her leg—not the lewd hand of a dirty old man but the small hand of a woman or child who simply wanted to know whether these shockingly liberated young women wore anything underneath their provocative outer garments.

The coed socializing of these displaced urban youth was new to the region. Local people were unaccustomed to the sight of young men and women walking together, and couples who did so were sometimes struck by local police. Undeterred, male engineering students frequently made the long hike (which they called *malasong*, or "marathon") to visit their girlfriends, who were housed at a middle school.[3]

In Chongqing, "downriver" women from eastern and central China entered "upriver" Sichuan society, which had been insulated from many of the urban changes of the previous decades. Downriver women teachers began to teach at Sichuan schools. Celebrity actresses from eastern cities became part of the local cultural scene. Social dancing, skirts, qipaos with high side slits, and permed hair all made an appearance in the beleaguered city, which suffered wartime inflation, shortages of essential goods, rationing, and repeated deadly bombings.[4] Women joined Air Raid Service Teams, ushering people to shelters built into the cliff sides and tending to thousands of wounded.[5]

To mobilize the population for wartime activity, the Nationalists reinvigorated the New Life Movement, with women as its main organizers.[6] The prewar New Life Movement had emphasized women's roles as wives and mothers, but the official vision of their role expanded in wartime.[7] The wives of top nationalist officials, from Song Meiling on down, became members of the New Life Movement Women's Advisory Committee. In the early years of the war, before the United Front with the CCP disintegrated, Communist organizers also participated.[8]

In Chongqing, women civil servants were organized into New Life Women's Work Teams to raise funds, prepare care packages for the soldiers, and post propaganda slogans and wall newspapers. They also helped manage relief programs for the refugees who poured into the city during the early war years, establishing a small handicraft factory to employ refugee women.[9] Their efforts included the Songji Experimental Zone, a special project of Song Meiling. It featured a textile mill that employed hundreds of women, a farm, attractive landscaping (because, one woman recalled, "Madame Jiang [Song Meiling] liked flowers"), health facilities, a library, social services, and schools for the women workers and community children.[10]

Women cadres in the movement's rural service division fanned out to rural areas to run literacy classes, train rural women in modern hygiene and homemaking skills, and promote cooperatives. Through this organizing, relatively privileged urban women mobilized less educated women, with two aims: to improve daily life and to strengthen the war effort. In doing so, educated women also laid the basis to claim expanded political participation for themselves after the war.[11]

In Chongqing and Kunming, wartime industries hired young women workers, employing both downriver refugees and local rural women.[12] By 1945, an estimated three-quarters of Chongqing's four hundred thousand women were working outside the home in industry, commerce, and service.[13] Among the new factories in Chongqing were four large cotton mills that had been disassembled in Shanghai and moved upriver.[14] Women formed 70 percent of the labor force in Chongqing's mills, and some became skilled laborers and managers. But the work conditions for these thirteen thousand women were similar to those in Shanghai several decades earlier: twelve-hour days, impossibly brief meal breaks, constant speedup, inadequate safety equipment, gruesome accidents, humiliating body searches to make sure that no one was stealing cotton yarn, crowded and fetid dormitory rooms, rampant tuberculosis, and rules prohibiting workers from marrying.[15] Turnover was high, but women tended to change jobs rather than leaving the labor force altogether. They were not eager to return to poor families, arranged marriages, or a life lived entirely in the family.[16]

Photo 7.1.   Woman cotton mill worker, Chongqing, 1940
Source: Photo by Harrison Forman. From the American Geographical Society Library, University of Wisconsin–Milwaukee Libraries.

The Women's Advisory Committee and its Work Teams were active among women industrial workers. They resettled women factory workers from Wuhan who had evacuated to Chongqing. They ran literacy classes for women workers with a curriculum emphasizing women's responsibility to save the nation by raising production.[17] As one textbook put it, "Big Brother goes to the battleground, Big Sister joins the factory; Big Brother kills the enemy on the battle front, Big Sister works hard producing on the home front."[18]

The Work Teams found that women workers were discontented with their long hours, low wages, and abusive managers.[19] The education they were receiving gave them a new political vocabulary to express their dissatisfaction and a habit of activism that extended into the postwar period. In 1947, women cotton mill workers at the Yu Feng Mill wrote petitions to Chiang Kai-shek. They pointed out that they had "fulfilled to the best of our abilities our responsibilities for the country's economic reconstruction." But in the course of rendering this important national service, they had encountered a union leader who sexually harassed women and threatened those who resisted. The women demanded compensation for themselves and punishment for the perpetrator.[20] In learning about their duties as citizens, they also had become conscious of their collective rights.

During the wartime period, the Nationalist government continued its work on maternal and child health, linking it to eugenics and national strength. The Bureau of Public Health in Chongqing constructed a new maternity hospital and eight clinics that provided free prenatal and postnatal care, as well as professionally trained midwives. The clinics continued to operate even when forced to relocate because of frequent bombing raids. Nationalist authorities emphasized that China's strength depended on women "bearing strong children and remaining healthy enough to raise them."[21]

During the war, social scientists and service organizations who came to Sichuan from downriver undertook surveys of the rural population. Rural women in upriver China, whose lives might otherwise have gone unrecorded, emerge into partial visibility in their reports.[22] Isabel Crook and Yu Xiji, for instance, lived for a year in Prosperity Township, west of Chongqing, conducting a needs assessment survey for a rural reconstruction project sponsored by the National Christian Council. Prosperity was a bustling market town, but land in its surrounding villages was scarce, and farming plots were too small to support many families. More than half of the households surveyed were classified as poor. Farmers grew rice to sell but could not afford to eat it themselves, subsisting on cheaper goods such as maize, beans, and sweet potatoes.

In these rural households, women's labor ensured survival. Women hoed and weeded and helped with the rice harvest, cultivated staples in the less fertile upland fields, grew vegetables, raised pigs and chickens, prepared the meals, made and washed the clothing, cared for the children, and hired out as day laborers. Women were the majority of the area's casual labor force.[23] They also produced home handicrafts for the market: washing pig bristles for brushes, drying herbs and preparing ash paste for incense sticks, making rain hats from palm leaves, and spinning and weaving cotton.[24] Women took their goods to market in wicker baskets carried on their backs, widows owned one-fifth of the businesses on the market street, and poorer women operated most of the market stalls. One middle-aged woman diviner conducted séances on market days, mainly for women clients seeking an explanation for family members' illnesses. Unmarried women, however, did not attend the market. It was important in the Sichuan countryside for a potential bride to stay out of public places full of strangers.[25]

Marriages in Prosperity continued to be arranged by parents, and weddings were sometimes more extravagant than the family could afford.[26] Crook and Yu noted some cases of runaway wives, a phenomenon found in villages as well as in large, more anonymous cities. A wife dissatisfied with her household's poverty, her mother-in-law's abuse, or her husband's beatings or absence might simply walk out of her house, head for a nearby market town, and offer herself as a potential daughter-in-law to a new family. Should her first husband succeed in tracking her down, the most common outcome was a cash payment from the second marital family to the first. No legal adjudication was involved. Here, as in most of rural China, the Nationalist legal reforms of marriage and divorce had not yet supplanted older informal practices.[27]

Women's labor was particularly crucial to rural families because men could be conscripted into the Nationalist army at any time. Conscripts were usually taken by force from poor families that could not bribe their way out. They were marched off in chains; insufficiently fed, clothed, and paid; deprived of rations and medicines sold by their corrupt officers on the black market; and plagued by "dysentery, scabies, suppurating skin ulcers, typhus and trachoma." An American relief agency reported in 1943 that 78 percent of one group of conscripts headed for the front had died of dysentery.[28] Left behind when their men were conscripted, women managed their family farms and sought other work to support themselves and their children.[29]

Like the CCP authorities, whose marriage policy is discussed later in this chapter, the Nationalists were most concerned about preserving the marriages of soldiers. A government directive in 1943 forbade the granting of a divorce to a soldier's wife.[30] Nonetheless, when a man was press-ganged into the army and disappeared, his wife, hard-pressed to survive, might well cohabit with another man. Should the soldier eventually return, the second husband would pay him enough to enable him to remarry.[31]

Even away from the front lines, rural people remained vulnerable to calamity during the war years. In the province of Henan, the eastern half was occupied by Japan, and the western half was under Nationalist control. As men disappeared into the army, or went into hiding to avoid conscription, or left to find work, women and children were left with sole responsibility for farming. Women came to outnumber men in some areas, reversing the usual pattern produced by infanticide and preferential treatment of sons. Some left-behind women, a 1941 government survey reported, "sell salt in the occupied areas or dry saline soil in the marshes to make saltpeter for a living. Wading barefoot and half-naked through the floodwaters, their condition is as terrible as has ever been heard of."[32]

Conditions in Henan worsened when a drought and locust infestation led to food shortages in 1942. The Nationalists did not provide effective government relief, instead demanding that local farmers provide grain for the troops stationed in the area. The resulting famine in 1942–43 killed more than three million people and put an equal number on the road as refugees. As in the north China famine of the 1870s described in chapter 2, a large market for the sale of girls and women appeared by the end of 1942. U.S. foreign service officer John Service reported from the famine area that "the price of a woman (common index in China of hard times) has fallen from about $3000 to one tenth of that."[33]

By 1944, many sources reported low morale in the Nationalist areas. The discontent expressed itself in gossip. Rumors flew that Chiang had

Photo 7.2. Women stripping bark from tree for food, Henan, 1942–43

Source: Photo by Harrison Forman. From the American Geographical Society Library, University of Wisconsin–Milwaukee Libraries.

taken a mistress, or possibly two, while his wife, Song Meiling, was in the United States appealing to the U.S. Congress for war support; that the woman was pregnant with his child; and that Song Meiling was complaining that Chiang wore his false teeth only when he was going to visit said mistress.[34] The New Life program for reforming society, promoted both by Chiang and Song, likewise became the subject of jokes.[35]

YAN'AN: LABOR, MARRIAGE, AND THE DING LING CONTROVERSY

Meanwhile, women's labor was increasingly important to Communist survival and expansion in rural base areas, many of which were in areas occupied by the Japanese army.

In 1935, a year after they had departed from Jiangxi on the Long March, the remnants of Mao's military force entered a Communist base area centered in northern Shaanxi Province. In 1936 Yan'an became the capital of the Shaan-Gan-Ning border region, an area where one million people lived, and the wartime quarters of the central CCP leadership.[36] Although this area was remote, poor, and blockaded by the Nationalist government from late 1941 on, it was more militarily secure than the other base areas that the CCP carved out in north and central China. Here the Party worked out a wartime program that downplayed land confiscation, class struggle, and women's emancipation in favor of uniting as much of the population as possible in support of the war effort.

Women were central to this program in three respects. First, the Party mobilized them for economic production. Women took over responsibility for farming and produced uniforms and shoes, and some won acclaim as labor heroines. Second, Party officials sought to reconcile their commitment to marriage reform with their desire to avoid conflict in rural communities where they needed to muster popular support. Third, the CCP welcomed—but struggled to incorporate—educated urban men and women who were drawn to Yan'an to support the anti-Japanese effort. These urban emigrés were attracted to Yan'an by patriotism. Many also hoped to restart the revolutionary processes that had been foreclosed by the Nationalists in the 1927 coup. But urban intellectuals sometimes found themselves in conflict with the Communist leadership, who had already survived a decade of conflict in highly militarized rural environments and who had little patience for intellectual critiques of Yan'an's many inequities, including those of gender. As the case of the famous woman writer Ding Ling suggests, the process of incorporation was not always a smooth one.

Economic Production and Labor Heroines

In the base areas, the Communists controlled political life and the Eighth Route and New Fourth Armies, but the Party continually adjusted its social policies to gain the support of as much of the population as possible. Rather than confiscating landlord land, for instance, it moved to a moderate policy of limiting the rents that landlords could collect. It capped the interest peasants could be charged on the short-term loans that many relied upon to get through the year. It organized elections for local leadership at the village and county levels, allowing landlords and merchants to participate, and restricting Party members to only one-third of the seats.[37]

Women in CCP-controlled areas had the same right to vote as men, but other activities were differentiated by gender.[38] When women participated in military activity, it was most often as members of people's militias who were primarily engaged in production, not fighting.[39] This was especially true in Yan'an, an area far from the front lines. Local women's associations provided a venue for the border region government to mobilize women, and women over the age of fifteen were encouraged to join.[40] But even within the border region of Yan'an, many peasants regarded government-organized groups as a waste of their time.[41]

The CCP leadership in Yan'an relied heavily on the labor of peasant women to support the military effort: directly, by making goods for the troops; and indirectly, by replacing male soldiers at farming. Mobilizing women to perform these tasks was called "woman-work." In a report to senior cadres in December 1942, Mao said that some women could take part in regular daily field work, while others could do more short-term tasks: plant vegetables, hoe, weed, dig up roots to feed the livestock, send food to the fields, and help with the harvest. In fact, he said, many women already were performing these tasks, and woman-work cadres should be encouraging even more women to help increase the output of the border region. Part of woman-work, he added, was to convince or compel women with bound feet to unbind them, a goal toward which the border region government made only limited headway during the war.[42]

Mao's plans for women's labor extended to textile production as well, for the border region had a serious cloth shortage and could not rely on importing yarn and cloth. He called for the expansion of home spinning and weaving, noting with approval that the government had begun lending funds to cooperatives. The co-ops, in turn, provided spinning machines and raw cotton to several thousand women to use at home, paying them according to the weight of spun yarn.[43]

Beginning in 1943, the Party mounted a massive production drive to make the border region as self-sufficient as possible in the face of the

Nationalist blockade.[44] The base area newspaper, *Liberation Daily*, publicized news of production contests and labor awards.[45] Named as labor heroines in daily half-page newspaper articles were women such as Han Fengling, a young married woman barely out of her teens who organized a women's spinning co-op in her village. Women reportedly gathered to spin at her house after a full day of work in the fields. She subsequently encouraged them to raise pigs and chickens as well. Han's husband, the village head, was lauded for treating his wife as an equal and asking her advice. The notion that productive activity could improve the family's economic standing and contribute to equal treatment in a happy marriage was embodied in the figure of Han.[46] But the spinning and weaving campaign brought discord to households, too, as older women who had already retired from daily household labor were obliged to prepare meals and care for grandchildren while their daughters-in-law worked for the co-ops. Party documents reported that elders grumbled about an upended family hierarchy: "Everything is upside down since the Communist Party came. Mothers-in-law have become daughters-in-law."[47]

By the end of 1943, 41,540 women in the Yan'an region were weaving at home.[48] Fewer than half of the border region's women spun or wove, however, partly because of their other domestic responsibilities and partly because of logistical problems in supplying the co-ops.[49] In general, women living close to Yan'an city or county seats experienced more intensive mobilization than women in more remote communities.[50] But despite the limited reach of mobilization, cloth production increased eightfold in the Communist areas in the early 1940s, enhancing household incomes.[51]

Classical Marxist writings linked women's emancipation to the project of bringing women into production. Friedrich Engels had posited that as long as women were confined to domestic labor they could not achieve equality, and that only participation in social production would make their emancipation possible. The Chinese Communists, too, drew an explicit link between production and an end to women's oppression, stating in 1932 that

> if women produce a lot and are thrifty, their families will have a higher standard of living. This will not only play a big role in developing the economy of the base areas, it will also provide women with the material conditions they need to overthrow feudal oppression.[52]

When farming women joined spinning cooperatives, their social worlds expanded to encompass neighbors in labor exchanges, fellow co-op members, and even men who were not kin—although this latter type of contact was still controversial.[53] But the CCP's primary impetus for making pro-

duction a centerpiece of its program for women was not social transformation. The Party hoped to meet the border region's pressing economic
needs while avoiding community conflict about women's roles.[54]

Two other initiatives affected the daily lives of farming women in
the Yan'an base area. In the first, local midwives were taught sterile
childbirth techniques, reducing infant mortality and prefiguring a nationwide campaign undertaken by the People's Republic government
in the 1950s. Pregnant women and nursing mothers received extra food
rations.[55] The second initiative established "winter schools" during the
slack season, where many women learned to read several hundred characters in literacy classes.[56]

Marriage Policy

By far the most contentious policy involving women in the Communist
base areas was marriage reform. The 1939 Marriage Regulations issued
in the Shaan-Gan-Ning base area hewed to the principles expressed by
the earlier regulations in the Jiangxi Soviet. They affirmed that marriage
should be based on love and free choice, and banned concubinage, child
daughters-in-law, arranged marriage, marriage by purchase, and forced
marriage.[57] Either husband or wife could obtain a divorce on grounds of
bigamy, abuse, incurable disease, and incompatibility. Divorced women
were entitled to child custody and child support.[58] The minimum marriage age initially was set at twenty for men and eighteen for women. It
was lowered in 1944 to eighteen for men and sixteen for women.[59]

The marriage regulations departed from local practice in almost every
respect. Marriage in rural China had never been based on an agreement
between individuals. Betrothals were made between family elders, often
when members of the future couple were still infants, with an eye to
family security and connections. Women routinely married before they
reached legal age. Every family needed a daughter-in-law: the children
she bore would carry on the family line in a patrilineal society, her labor
would help sustain the household, and she would care for her husband's
parents in their old age. Among the very poor it was common practice to
buy a child daughter-in-law for a small sum and raise her to marry one's
son.[60] Families saved for years to acquire a fiancée or a bride. The mothers of poor men looked forward to the entry of a daughter-in-law into
the family as a moment when their own domestic burden might begin to
ease. Many families used the bride price brought in by the marriage of a
daughter to bring in a wife for a son. Acquiring a daughter-in-law was
particularly difficult in a poor area such as Yan'an, where men reportedly
outnumbered women 135 to 100.[61] Rural men and their families feared

that they could never afford to replace a woman who broke off an engagement or ended a marriage.

The border region government quickly realized that the Marriage Regulations were causing conflicts within local society, causing poor men and
their parents to turn against the Communists. The Party needed the support of poor peasants, but it was the wives of poor men who were most
likely to seek divorce. Families worried that any outside contact might
lead young wives to leave, so they were reluctant to send the women
to CCP literacy classes or meetings. Quickly, local officials modified
their approach. Party cadres acted as matchmakers for single men and
discouraged women from pursuing divorces.[62] They urged unhappily
married women cadres to stay with their husbands in order not to jeop-
ardize Party organizing efforts.[63] Wives of soldiers were not permitted
to divorce.[64] From 1942 on, articles in the Yan'an base area's newspaper
Liberation Daily stopped targeting mothers-in-law as obstacles to women's
freedom, and instead began promoting family harmony.[65] The problem
of wife-beating, common even among Party members, was largely ignored.[66] So was a woman's right to inherit property.[67]

Nevertheless, conflicts over marriage persisted in the base area courts,
where the cases were often more complicated than they appeared at first
glance. In the Shaan-Gan-Ning base area, wartime conditions exacerbated
panic among poor farming families that they would be unable to acquire
wives for their sons. Bride price, or *caili*, had been rising gradually during
the 1930s, propelled by the financial distress of farmers. With the influx
of many unmarried Communist soldiers into the base area, the relative
shortage of brides became even more acute than previously. At the same
time, inflation in the region during the 1940s meant that the price of a
bride—payable in betrothal presents, as well as marriage presents and
cash—went up considerably.

Suddenly, families that had betrothed their daughters at birth found
that they could command much higher sums if they broke off that
engagement and made a new one. Some would unilaterally break off
earlier marriage agreements, leading to protests by the family of the
abandoned young man. Families with daughters made strategic use of
the Marriage Regulations to achieve their own purposes. Many cases
appeared before local courts in which a young woman protested that
the childhood betrothal had been arranged by parents in violation of the
current Communist law—and then promptly went off to contract a more
lucrative match, also arranged by her family. So common were lawsuits
over such cases that they had their own legal category: "one woman,
two betrothals" (*yinü liangxu*).[68]

The interests of fathers and daughters often converged in such cases.
The father wanted more money for his family. For the daughter, this

might be her only chance to acquire some cash or jewelry of her own, or
to marry up into a more prosperous situation than that of her original
fiancé. A young woman was not necessarily a powerless pawn in these
negotiations, but her agency might consist of appearing at the township
government office to invoke the proscription on arranged marriage so
that she and her family could make a more advantageous match.[69] It was
impossible to disentangle the "freedom of marriage" guaranteed by the
law from the desires of parents and their marriageable daughters to improve their financial situation. In such cases poor men would always lose
out, while "freedom of marriage" remained very far from the ideal first
envisioned by May Fourth activists.

Judges were well aware that poor men and their families could be
disadvantaged by the dissolution of engagements and marriages. Court
rulings in 1943 stipulated that if a woman's parents initiated a divorce
request, it should be rejected. So should divorces requested on the basis
that a man's family was poor. Family violence, on the other hand, should
be grounds for a divorce, but only if the husband and his family ignored
repeated warnings and violated court orders to change their behavior.[70]
New 1944 regulations required that if an engagement was broken, then
the bride price needed to be returned to the groom's family, even though
this called into question whether the government was really prohibiting
marriage by purchase.[71]

The revised Marriage Regulations issued in 1944 and 1946 moved away
from the language of "freedom of marriage." Instead, the state began to
use the language of "self-determination" (*zizhu*) or "self-will" (*ziyuan*),
a formulation that put the desires of the woman front and center.[72] In
cases heard by the courts, judges would interview the woman privately
to ascertain what she wanted, attempting to disentangle her desires from
those of, say, a father looking for a higher bride price.[73] A popular 1945
performance titled *The Reunion of Liu Qiao* presented just such a case. In
the story, Liu Qiao's greedy father first arranged her engagement to a
poor peasant, then broke it off to marry her to a rich shopkeeper instead.
Liu Qiao preferred her original fiancé, Zhao, a labor hero. She sought help
to avoid the new match. Meanwhile, the labor hero's father carried out
an old-style kidnapping of the bride so that his son would not lose out.
Ultimately, a wise judge, modeled on an actual official in the base area,
confirmed the match between Liu and Zhao. The judge punished Liu's
greedy father, fined the shopkeeper, and mildly reprimanded the father-
in-law for the kidnapping. The young couple expressed their happiness
at the outcome.[74] This story did not criticize the fact that Liu's father had
arranged her engagement to Zhao in the first place, only his greediness
in trying to break it off. Parental authority over betrothals was not challenged directly. In its judicial decisions and its propaganda, the Party

recognized that instilling new forms of marriage choice in the base areas was going to be a long-term project.[75]

Ding Ling and the Feminism Question

For women who came to Yan'an from the urban areas, the adjustment to rural life and wartime communism was challenging. Many young women arrived in Yan'an fresh from the urban student movement, eager to take up arms against Japan, and quickly encountered a gendered division of labor within the Communist movement. At Yan'an's premier educational institution, Resistance University (Kangda), women in 1937 numbered only about fifty in a student body of fourteen hundred and were organized in a women-only squad.[76] But women increasingly were sent to Yan'an Women's University, where they were given some military training and coursework in political economy and Marxism and then sent off to mobilize rural women for production. The school offered one course on the women's movement.[77] As the war progressed, women were moved almost exclusively into economic activity.[78] Educated urban women were given the work of organizing rural women, even though many were reluctant to undertake woman-work, which they regarded as a humdrum assignment.[79]

Nevertheless, for women students who had come from China's eastern urban areas, engaging in production and living in Spartan circumstances changed their sense of who they were and what they could accomplish. Visiting Yan'an as part of the U.S. military Dixie Mission in summer 1944, John Service wrote:

> Women not only wear practically the same clothes [as men] (trousers, sandals or cloth shoes, and often a Russian-type smock), they act and are treated as friendly equals. Their openness and complete lack of self-consciousness is at first almost disconcerting. . . . The program to make every person a producer has a real meaning. Those who do not grow crops work at something like spinning. Each morning we see our co-ed neighbors at the university at their spinning wheels outside their caves.[80]

Ding Ling, already a famous woman writer by the time she came to Yan'an, was older than the students described by Service.[81] Born in 1904 to a mother who was a friend of the late Qing radical martyr Qiu Jin, Ding Ling spent her early years at a women's school that her widowed mother was attending. Active in the May Fourth Movement, Ding Ling fled Changsha to avoid a marriage her uncles had arranged for her. In 1920 she enrolled in school in Shanghai, and later lived in Beijing, where she married the poet Hu Yepin.

Photo 7.3.   Ding Ling, ca. 1937

In the late 1920s, Ding Ling had written "Miss Sophia's Diary," a story that candidly explored the emotional world and sexual desires of a young woman who left home and struggled with poor health and emotional malaise. Later her work became more explicitly political, and she joined the CCP in 1932, the year after her husband was executed by the Nationalists.

Arrested by the Nationalists in 1933, Ding Ling spent three years under house arrest and then escaped to Yan'an.

The CCP leadership welcomed the arrival of this prominent literary figure. After the outbreak of war, she led a drama troupe in Yan'an that wrote and presented themes of anti-Japanese resistance. Initially, she was enthusiastic about the ideals and plain living of the Communists. Already in her thirties, she found common purpose and friendship with the young women who worked with her. But as she spent more time in Yan'an, Ding Ling became dismayed by the hierarchy, hypocrisy, and sexism she saw among Party cadres. By 1941, now editor of the literary page of *Liberation Daily*, she encouraged open discussion of local social problems. Invoking the writer Lu Xun, who had died in 1936, she wrote,

> Lu Xun is dead. Customarily we say to ourselves that we should do this or that in order to live up to him. But we have not sufficiently acquired his courage in sparing no details. I think it will do us most good if we emulate his steadfastness in facing the truth, and his fearlessness.[82]

In her fiction and essays, Ding Ling spares no details in portraying women in a revolutionary movement that had promised them full personhood but delivered a host of new problems. Her short story "When I Was in Xia Village" explores the fate of Zhenzhen, a young peasant woman who had been abducted and raped by the Japanese. Confined in enemy territory, Zhenzhen collected intelligence to transmit to the Communist guerrillas. But when she finally was taken back home for treatment of a sexually transmitted disease, she encountered villagers unaware of her heroic actions and contemptuous of her for having sexual relations with Japanese soldiers. Ding Ling offers an unsparing description of village women who "became extremely self-righteous, perceiving themselves as saintly and pure. They were proud about never having been raped." The story conveys the desolate atmosphere of the village, the vicious gossip that trails Zhenzhen, her own coolness and indifference to village judgment, and a small sense of progress represented by young local activists. The story ends hopefully as Zhenzhen leaves for medical treatment in Yan'an.[83]

But another Ding Ling story, "In the Hospital," suggests that happy endings, medical or otherwise, were unlikely to be found in a clinic in Yan'an. The hospital is underequipped and dirty, the Party officials are overbearing and patronizing, and the staff, here as in Zhenzhen's village, is prone to vicious gossip about women's personal lives. The protagonist, an idealistic young nurse assigned to work there, begins to have doubts about the Party. Eventually she transfers out.[84]

On International Women's Day in 1942, Ding Ling voiced her criticisms of Yan'an attitudes toward women more directly in her essay "Thoughts on March 8," published in the *Liberation Daily*. It opened with a plaintive question, "When will it no longer be necessary to attach special weight to the word 'woman' and raise it specially?" (see box 7.1). Ding Ling described a situation in which the obstacles to women's full personhood were not so different from those in the Nationalist areas: profoundly gendered notions about women's sexual virtue, duties as a wife and

---

BOX 7.1.
Ding Ling, "Thoughts on March 8," 1942

When will it no longer be necessary to attach special weight to the word "woman" and raise it specially? . . . Women invariably want to get married. (It's even more of a sin not to be married, and single women are even more of a target for rumors and slanderous gossip.) . . . They inevitably have children. . . . Whoever they marry, the fact is that those women who are compelled to bear children will probably be publicly derided as "Noras who have returned home." . . .

The pretext for divorce is invariably the wife's political backwardness. . . . But let us consider to what degree they are backward. Before marrying, they were inspired by the desire to soar in the heavenly heights and lead a life of bitter struggle. They got married partly because of physiological necessity and partly as a response to sweet talk about "mutual help." Thereupon they are forced to toil away and become "Noras returned home." . . . When women capable of working sacrifice their careers for the joys of motherhood, people always sing their praises. But after ten years or so, they have no way of escaping the tragedy of "backwardness."

If married women sought child care or abortions, Ding Ling wrote, they were derided for avoiding work and child-rearing responsibility. After awhile, they grew less attractive and became less interesting to their husbands, who then divorced them on grounds of political backwardness.

I myself am a woman, and I therefore understand the failings of women better than others. But I also have a deeper understanding of what they suffer. Women are incapable of transcending the age they live in, of being perfect, or of being hard as steel. They are incapable of resisting all the temptations of society or all the silent oppression they suffer here in Yan'an. They each have their own past written in blood and tears. . . .

If women want equality, they must first strengthen themselves. . . . Aware, modern women should identify and cast off all their rosy illusions. Happiness is to take up the struggle in the midst of the raging storm and not to pluck the lute in the moonlight or recite poetry among the blossoms. . . .

On rereading this article, it seems to me that there is much room for improvement in the passage on what we should expect from women. . . . But I also feel that there are some things that, if said by a leader before a big audience, would probably evoke satisfaction. But when they are written by a woman, they are more than likely to be demolished.

Source: Ding Ling, Tani E. Barlow, and Gary J. Bjorge. *I Myself Am a Woman: Selected Writings of Ding Ling* (Boston: Beacon Press, 1989), 317–21.

mother, and lack of personal resolve. She observed that under current social arrangements, trying to act on a commitment to the revolution was more difficult for a woman than for a man, and that the revolution was not naming or addressing this gender disparity. She did not say how the revolution might change the collective attitudes that limited women's possibilities. But she did establish that a gendered division of labor and normative expectations about women's sexual virtue and homemaking role were at the heart of the problem.

Ding Ling's writings attracted the unhappy attention of Mao Zedong. Party priorities were to expand the war effort and consolidate the base areas. For Mao, Ding Ling's critique and those made by other intellectuals were a form of privileged class blindness, naming issues of concern only to urban intellectuals who did not understand the requirements of Party discipline in a war zone.[85] This required winning peasant support and mobilizing women's labor, not criticizing gendered limits on political activism or analyzing marital dynamics in cadre families.

Perhaps the description of Yan'an cadres casting off their wives hit a nerve. Mao had a reputation for womanizing. He was estranged from his wife, He Zizhen, who had accompanied him on the Long March and who had borne five children. She left for medical treatment in the Soviet Union, where she spent the rest of the wartime years. Mao soon divorced her and married Jiang Qing, a former Shanghai film actress who had moved to Yan'an, in spite of objections from other Party leaders.[86]

The month after "Thoughts on March 8" was published, Ding Ling was removed from her editorial position at the *Liberation Daily*. In May, at the Yan'an Forum on Literature and Art, Mao delivered a broad rebuke to intellectuals, instructing them to set aside their petty-bourgeois preoccupations and produce literature and art that could be used by workers, peasants, and soldiers.[87] Lu Xun, he said in a pointed response to Ding Ling's earlier invocation, "never ridiculed or attacked revolutionary people or parties." Her story "In the Hospital" was denounced in the *Liberation Daily* for its criticism of CCP members. Admitting that "Thoughts on March 8" expressed a type of feminism inappropriate to the circumstances in Yan'an, Ding Ling was sent off in June to learn from the peasants for what turned out to be a two-year stay. When she returned, she apparently was reformed. Her subsequent work stayed away from gender conflicts within the Party, instead describing the process of peasant mobilization and offering many finely drawn portraits of village women.[88]

Although many writers were criticized during this period, Ding Ling stands out for making gender central to her writings.[89] She highlighted the specific ways in which women continued to suffer: not only from leftover "feudal" attitudes that led villagers to doubt the virtue of a patriotic spy such as Zhenzhen, but also from male Communist cadres who were growing accustomed to privilege, even in the relatively egalitarian circumstances of Yan'an. "Thoughts on March 8" argued that "Woman" was a socially meaningful category that elicited particular kinds of treatment—generally unequal to that accorded to men—and that this problem could not be addressed without specific attention to gender.[90] In dismissing this critique, Mao disregarded the effects of gender inequality, from salacious gossip to the gendered division of labor, and their role in shaping the lives of base area women.

BEYOND YAN'AN

Life in Communist base areas elsewhere in China generally was more dangerous than in Yan'an. Women played important roles supporting the Communist army in guerrilla warfare with the Japanese. In north China, many villages were nominally Japanese-occupied territory, but by night, groups of rural partisans would blow up railway lines or otherwise disrupt Japanese military operations. Some women participated directly in combat with the Eighth Route and New Fourth Armies, but more commonly, army commanders believed that women's strength and stamina could not match those of men and advised women soldiers to cooperate with men in an appropriate division of tasks.[91]

In the early days of the war, the Eighth Route Army set up a base area in the Taihang Mountains of southeast Shanxi, engaging the Japanese with guerrilla tactics.[92] In Wuxiang County, a woman named Bao Lianzi later was nicknamed "Mother of the Eighth Route Army" for the work she did as head of a support group for soldiers. Women also formed a small guerrilla battalion that was later absorbed into the local militia and participated in women's mutual aid teams, one of which became a regional model. Nonetheless, virtually no women served in county leadership positions, and Wuxiang remained conservative in its suspicion of marriage reform. In 1943, after a Japanese mop-up campaign, a drought, and a locust plague, divorce was temporarily banned in the area, for fear that it would generate more households needing to be fed. The remarriage of widows was forbidden until 1944, in spite of agitation by the Women's Federation.[93]

Women did not always give their allegiance to the Communists. In Licheng County, many young women from relatively wealthy families were excluded from CCP activity because of their class background. In 1941 some joined a local revolt against the Communists called the Sixth Trigram Movement. Half of the participants in this religious sect turned rebel group were women—more than fifteen hundred—although few of them actually took up arms. Women held senior leadership posts among

Photo 7.4.   Xu Xiaobing, women's self-defense forces in the Taihang Mountains liberated areas, 1940
Source: Used by permission of family of Xu Xiaobing.

the rebels. Questioned about their motivations after the revolt was suppressed, Sixth Trigram women mentioned demands for marriage freedom and the ability to attend meetings—the very goals that the CCP was promoting for women. The local CCP response, which could be understood as canny cooptation, was to recruit more women into the Party and pay more attention to marriage reform and women's political participation.[94]

Mobilizing women for agricultural labor was not always a smooth process. When the Taihang Border Region government launched a cooperative movement in 1943, peasants formed mutual aid teams of families who knew and often were related to one another. But when cadres from outside the villages tried to enlarge these teams into full-scale cooperatives in the spring of 1944, in which peasants would pool their resources and farm together, many resisted incorporating non-kin into their groups. Women, who were assigned to help with farm work, produce textiles, and perform other tasks, reportedly were dissatisfied with the additional demands on their labor, in part because their husbands and in-laws were apt to retaliate against them for spending time outside the home.

Among the measures that organizers took to win women's support was to increase the work points they could earn from half those of men to an equal share, but family resistance continued to be a problem. Only when the work teams assigned women to work with their relatives at farming tasks did the objections abate somewhat.[95] The fear that women would leave their marital families if given the opportunity was pervasive, supported by what many peasants could see for themselves: across all of the north China base areas, the vast majority of divorce cases heard by the local courts during the war of resistance and the civil war of the late 1940s were initiated by wives.[96]

The Communists established another major north China base area, Jin-Cha-Ji, in 1938. Thousands of fighters and civilians died in this region during the wartime years, both in combat and as a result of Japanese repression directed at civilians, including extermination campaigns.[97] Communists launched the Hundred Regiments Offensive in north China against the Japanese in 1940, and the reprisals visited upon the rural population over the next two years were savage, summarized in the directive to "kill all, burn all, loot all." Close to half of the base area population and a quarter of the Eighth Route Army were affected.[98] "Rape all" was also a piece of this mopping-up strategy, confirmed by many peasant accounts.[99]

Wounded guerrilla soldiers often were left to be nursed by local women. When Japanese search patrols arrived, a woman might pretend that a wounded soldier was her own son, suffering from a highly contagious disease.[100] One former colonel in the Eighth Route Army described how old women were incorporated into guarding elaborate tunnel networks where civilians and wounded soldiers could be concealed (see box 7.2). Stories of women's sacrifice and martyrdom were meant to inspire and encourage a peasantry that was understandably terrorized by the repeated assaults.[101]

Among all of the Communist troops, the New Fourth Army had the youngest soldiers and the most women.[102] It drew from Shanghai and other communities along the Yangzi River.[103] Some couples joined the New Fourth Army together in order to avoid arranged marriages at home. Like the women in other CCP armies, the New Fourth women seldom participated in combat. Instead they served as teachers, administrators, clerical staff, accountants, technicians, writers, and propaganda workers. Those with less education sewed for the troops.[104]

The CCP relationship with the Nationalists broke down almost completely in early 1941 when Nationalist forces attacked and destroyed a New Fourth Army column of four thousand armed soldiers and six thousand dependents, wounded soldiers, and medical personnel in Anhui. Many women were among the marchers, who had been on the move

BOX 7.2.
Tunnel Warfare

This passage is excerpted from an account by one Colonel Ma, an Eighth Route Army fighter, as told to Robert Payne in 1946.

> The entrance to the tunnel would be beneath the *kang*, and when the Japanese entered the house they would find an old lady sitting on the *kang*. She could communicate with the people in the tunnel below by pulling on a string concealed in the bed-covers. She could tell them when the Japanese had come, and when they were gone, and many other things about them. . . .
>
> They usually arranged that their annual annihilation campaigns would take place in the autumn, when we were harvesting. They could destroy some of the crops, but they could not destroy all of it, and they could always kill a few people. They killed a lot of old women, who could not run fast enough. . . .

During a Japanese raid on a village in central Hebei, Communist soldiers clambered into a tunnel and barely escaped.

> The house where we were staying belonged to an old woman. They went to her, and asked her who we were. She said there were no soldiers there. They answered by hacking off one of the fingers of her left hand with a meat-axe, and then asked her again. She gave the same answer five times, and they cut off all five fingers. What made things so difficult was that we were accompanying a general who was bringing with him his wife and a six-months-old girl-child. . . . When [the Japanese] came to a tunnel they poured in poison gas. The general and his wife were slightly poisoned, and the baby began crying. This was dangerous. You couldn't ordinarily hear the sounds of a baby crying six or seven feet underground, but the sound might be heard near an air-let. . . . And then suddenly the baby stopped crying. . . . We stayed in the tunnel thirteen hours, always moving about. Then we heard them go away, and climbed out. It was night. We discovered then, not before, that the general's wife had smothered the baby to death for fear that the Japanese would hear her cries. She said nothing about the killing to the general. It was just there—the dead child, covered with mud, the face blue, and the woman was weeping.

Source: Robert Payne, *China Awake* (New York: Dodd, Mead, 1947), 403–6.

for days in rain and snow, wading across one frigid river when their pontoon bridge collapsed. Several thousand marchers escaped the final encirclement, and several hundred were captured and imprisoned; thousands were killed, though estimates vary widely.[105] War reporter Agnes Smedley heard accounts that "women nurses and political workers had hanged themselves from the trees," and other reports said that women had "thrown themselves off cliffs shouting patriotic slogans."[106]

But the size of the New Fourth Army, and the number and size of Communist base areas, continued to expand. By 1945, most of rural north

China was part of a base area. Nationally, nineteen Communist base areas contained a population of more than one hundred million, and the CCP itself numbered close to a million members.[107] Late in the war, John Service reported that in north and central China, "all evidence verifies Communist claims of controlling substantially all of the countryside of 'occupied' China."[108] Women contributed substantially to this Communist expansion—and the base areas became the crucible for rural policies toward women that would be enacted nationally after 1949.

CIVIL WAR

The Nationalists received considerable aid from the United States after it entered the war. Chiang Kai-shek, alarmed by the Communists' expansion, hoarded some of the war materiel coming his way for use in what he understood to be a coming civil war. When the Japanese suddenly surrendered after the atomic bombings of Hiroshima and Nagasaki, the Nationalists were not ready. Communist forces, which in 1945 numbered one million regular troops and perhaps twice that many militia members, moved swiftly to occupy parts of the former Manzhouguo, even as the United States facilitated the airlift of Nationalist troops into other parts of China. Talks between the Nationalists and Communists, begun in 1945, broke down quickly, and by 1946 China was in a state of civil war.[109]

By the later years of the war against Japan, discontent with the Nationalist government had become widespread well outside of the Communist base areas. Conscription and taxation had earned it the fear and contempt of many rural people. Maltreatment of soldiers was widespread. Inflation had brought hardship to everyone. Corruption was endemic, and the postwar rush to take over Japanese war materiel generated a constant stream of news reports about stripped vehicles, black market transactions, and Nationalist officials lining their own pockets.

Back in control of the formerly occupied cities, the Nationalist government reorganized the urban press and radio stations, seeking control over the media in an attempt to win hearts and minds.[110] Several high-profile women were brought to trial as Japanese collaborators, and many more women were attacked in the popular press, mainly for being wives or mistresses of Japanese men or famous male collaborators.[111] Among them was Aisin Gioro Xianyu. A Manchu princess raised in Japan, she had returned to China to conduct espionage work for the Japanese, became the mistress of several high-ranking Japanese military men, and briefly commanded her own troops in Manzhouguo. She was executed in 1948 as a spy for the Japanese.[112] But collaborators were not the only targets of a resurgent government. In Shanghai, where the underground

CCP had expanded its organizing efforts during the occupation years, the Nationalists resumed arrests and executions of underground operatives in a largely unsuccessful attempt to curtail Communist presence in factories, teacher and student organizations, women's organizations, and the media.[113]

Intellectuals and university students became increasingly alienated from the Nationalist government.[114] In early December 1945, after a student strike and protest march against civil war, government soldiers in Kunming attacked the universities on grounds of suspected Communist activity, ripping down pro-democracy posters and throwing hand grenades into several campuses. Four students died, including one young woman from central China named Pan Yan, a twenty-eight-year-old at the teacher training school attached to the Associated University. Fearing more unrest, local authorities would not permit a funeral procession for the four slain students until mid-March. When the funeral finally was held, twelve thousand mourners joined the cortege.[115]

These events presaged the antigovernment activities of students all over China once universities resumed normal operations. A 1946 incident in which a Beijing University student was sexually assaulted by two American marines led to anti-American demonstrations across Beijing and in other major cities as well.[116] Students who demonstrated for an end to the civil war between the Communists and the Nationalists were met with violent Nationalist suppression.[117]

During the late 1940s the Nationalist authorities resumed some of the projects they had begun during the Nanjing Decade. They sponsored frugal group weddings, conducted under the national flag and Sun Yat-sen's portrait. A marriage license now required a family health history and a thorough physical examination, "in order to allow the race to progress along the road of eugenics."[118] The enforcement of this provision, like so many others in the Nationalist repertoire, is unclear.

In Shanghai, the Nationalist government also returned to its prewar agenda of regulating prostitution, with the aim of eliminating it sometime in the indefinite future. The police chief accused the wartime collaborationist government of having spread "poison and rot" by encouraging opium, gambling, and prostitution, but he admitted that in the immediate postwar era it was not easy to ban prostitution outright. Instead, the city government decided to permit licensed sex workers to work in licensed brothels in designated red-light districts under police supervision. Police regulations stipulated everything from age restrictions to condom use and the type of lamp that would adorn each brothel door. Implementation proved difficult, and residents wrote letters of complaint to the police about the noise and disruption caused by prostitutes and their clients, especially in the vicinity of brothels that serviced American military men.

The health department estimated that more than 60 percent of Shanghai prostitutes were afflicted with syphilis, but most women could not afford to stop working long enough to complete a course of treatment. An effective regime of inspections to screen prostitutes for disease eluded government agencies, in spite of elaborate plans on paper.[119] The Nationalist ambition to impose order on Shanghai's sex workers remained unfulfilled.

Women activists resumed their prewar projects too. Suffrage for woman had been deferred repeatedly since the 1912 meeting that had caused Tang Qunying to slap Song Jiaoren. In 1936, a draft constitution had promised universal suffrage and the right of women to run for office. With the outbreak of war, full elections were postponed. But during the war years, educated middle-class women activists affiliated with the Nationalists, the CCP, and other parties campaigned for a minimum 10 percent quota of women to hold office at the national level. This effort drew a younger generation of feminist activists from the Women's National Salvation Society into the ongoing struggle for political participation. They invoked women's active role in the war effort as further justification for guaranteeing them a place in government while also arguing that women had their own gender-specific interests that needed representation. In 1947 suffrage activists won a significant victory: the establishment of minimum quotas for women in national government.[120] But this achievement was soon overshadowed by the intensifying civil war.

The last years of Nationalist rule were grim in both city and countryside. Inflation wracked the cities, provoking runs on banks and making it necessary to haul a sack of cash to the market to buy rice. Those on fixed salaries suffered uncertainty and hardship. Millions of people in central and southern China suffered famine conditions in 1947, and it is estimated that almost fifty million people were displaced by war in 1948. Refugees from fighting in north China streamed into Beijing, and heavy fighting in north Jiangsu sent a million people fleeing to Shanghai. Relief measures were nowhere near adequate. Relief agencies and the press reported desperately hungry peasants eating roots and tree bark, as well as piles of corpses showing up on city streets.[121] The government's corruption and ineffectual response to these problems estranged much of the urban populace.[122]

Postwar strikes roiled not only the old industrial centers of China's east coast, but also the newer centers such as Chongqing that had emerged during the war. In the Chongqing strikes, women were active in pushing for higher wages, larger year-end bonuses, and better treatment, sometimes destroying factory equipment and physically assaulting managers when their demands were not met.[123] In Shanghai, cotton mills reopened under the auspices of the China Textile Reconstruction Corporation. As inflation grew more extreme, workers struck for wage hikes, a shorter

Photo 7.5. A family in flight, Shanghai, April 1949

Source: Assignment, Shanghai: Photographs on the Eve of Revolution, photographs by Jack Birns, edited by Carolyn Wakeman and Ken Light (Berkeley: University of California Press, published in association with the Graduate School of Journalism, Center for Photography, University of California, Berkeley, 2003), 130.

work day, and in-kind payments of rice and cloth.[124] Strike preparations drew upon the organizing techniques that had emerged during the Japanese occupation. Underground CCP organizers pledged sisterhood with groups of women workers, and some sisterhoods grew to encompass several hundred, becoming sources of Party recruitment.[125]

Photo 7.6.   Police frisk a lineup of striking women workers after a textile mill riot, Shanghai, February 1948

Source: *Assignment, Shanghai: Photographs on the Eve of Revolution*, photographs by Jack Birns, edited by Carolyn Wakeman and Ken Light (Berkeley: University of California Press, published in association with the Graduate School of Journalism, Center for Photography, University of California, Berkeley, 2003), 73.

Photo 7.7. Dance hall hostesses mob the Bureau of Social Affairs to protest an increase in license fees. Shanghai, 1948

Source: *Assignment, Shanghai: Photographs on the Eve of Revolution*, photographs by Jack Birns, edited by Carolyn Wakeman and Ken Light (Berkeley: University of California Press, published in association with the Graduate School of Journalism, Center for Photography, University of California, Berkeley, 2003), 4.

In a series of strikes in 1946, women workers won eight weeks of maternity leave, ending a long-standing practice of firing mill hands when they became pregnant.[126] But the provision was not enforced. A January 1948 sit-down strike by six thousand women and one thousand men at the Shen Xin Number Nine Mill included among its demands the enforcement of paid maternity leave and on-site child care. The most pressing issue, however, was that inflation had reduced real wages by two-thirds from their 1946 level. The CCP presence was strongest among male machinists, but women also were active in this strike. The sit-down protest ended only when more than a thousand military police forced their way into the factory and violently ejected the strikers, killing three women and injuring several hundred. More than a hundred women were arrested and briefly held, but in the end workers won some of their demands, for coal and rice supplies.[127]

In January 1948, a day after the Shen Xin strike began, thousands of dance hall hostesses and other cabaret employees, provoked by a government plan to shut down Shanghai's dance halls, marched to the Bureau of Social Affairs. They destroyed offices, throwing furniture and files out the windows and attacking the police in what became known as the Dancers' Uprising. Hundreds of cabaret workers were arrested. A few dozen, including seven dancers, spent several months in jail awaiting a trial, although ultimately only several men were sentenced to prison. Government investigators were unable to confirm their suspicions that the CCP had organized this strike. Months later the national government, partly in response to the uprising, rescinded its order that all cabarets should close.[128]

In rural areas during the Civil War, mainly in north China, Party organizers worked to mobilize women to support the continuing war effort by the newly reorganized and renamed People's Liberation Army. Women's congresses, women's associations, and women's participation in newly established peasant associations were some of the forms that organizers used, depending partly upon whether women in their particular locale had had previous experience working together with men.[129] A 1948 Party report noted that it was a good idea for women to participate in peasant association meetings but that it was also helpful, indeed necessary, for them to meet separately in women's associations. Unused to speaking in front of men, one commented that "if we're speaking with men present, those who ought to say a lot say very little."[130]

Communists now shifted to a policy of land reform, aimed at big landlords and those who had collaborated with Japan. Small landlords or rich peasants were to donate or sell surplus landholdings to the poor; middle peasants were to be left alone; peasant associations established by the CCP were to redistribute confiscated land to the poor. By 1947 many areas had

moved toward radical redistribution, including the seizing of middle peasant holdings.[131] Convening women's meetings to help them practice public
speaking became an important part of land reform efforts. With practice,
women became comfortable expressing emotion and moving their audiences by recounting their suffering at the hands of local landlords.[132]
In some areas, women's associations also provided public support for
women whose husbands and in-laws refused to let them attend meetings,
or who beat them.[133] Divorces, which the CCP had discouraged among
poor peasants during the war against Japan, became easier to get.[134]

In areas under Communist control, women were mobilized to do the
same kinds of tasks that had become wartime women's work in the
Jiangxi Soviet and the "old liberated areas." They took over major responsibility for agriculture; nursed wounded soldiers; supplied the army with
shoes, bedding, food, and clothing; and collected intelligence. In some areas women's militia groups acted as sentries, escorted prisoners, and laid
land mines. Women had little direct role in combat, which increasingly
centered on positional rather than guerrilla warfare.[135]

By the end of 1948, the Communists controlled most of the former
Manzhouguo and parts of north China.[136] In January 1949, Communist
forces entered Beijing. Underground CCP members worked in the cities
to protect factories and prepare for a transfer of power to the approaching
troops of the People's Liberation Army. In early 1949 Communist forces
crossed the Huai River and then the Yangzi, taking Nanjing in April and
Shanghai in May. On October 1, 1949, Mao declared the establishment of
the People's Republic of China. By the end of the year Chiang Kai-shek
left for the province of Taiwan, which had been returned to Chinese
control in 1945 after fifty years as a Japanese colony. It now became the
site of the Republic of China government, with aspirations to retake the
mainland at some future point.

As the CCP moved toward victory in the civil war, a Central Committee document summed up the key lessons the Party had learned during
the war years about "woman-work." Women's labor, the document declared, was central to their liberation and to the socialist society the Communists hoped to build:

> Only by going to work with a will, so that they gradually become economically
> independent, can women gain the respect of their parents-in-law, their hus-
> bands and society at large, and increase the harmony and unity of the family;
> only thus can the economic, social and political position of women be easily
> consolidated and only thus can all the laws concerning sex equality acquire
> a strong base on which to be implemented. . . . And it must be recognized
> that women's participation in labor is not simply the key to their liberation:
> whether for the present war effort or New Democratic economic construction
> or the future victory of socialism, women's labor is absolutely indispensable.[137]

8

The Socialist Construction of Women, 1949–78

When the Chinese Communist Party established the People's Republic of China in 1949, its members brought with them almost three decades of experience in mobilizing women, mainly under circumstances of political suppression and war. After 1949, women's labor and Woman as symbol were central to the Party-state vision of socialist modernization. The period of socialist development ran from the establishment of the PRC in 1949 through Mao's death in 1976 and the beginning of economic reforms in 1978. Many accounts of this period have focused on internecine Party struggles, the sidelining and persecution of intellectuals, the lifelong stigmatizing of adults whose class backgrounds were suspect, the terrible human cost of misguided state economic initiatives, and the upheaval entailed in major political campaigns.[1] Without minimizing the importance of those aspects of Chinese socialism, this chapter explores a different set of questions: Did women have a socialist revolution? If so, which women, and when? How did the revolutionary process shape women's daily lives, and how did women's labor shape the revolutionary process?

Although the Chinese Communist Party guided national policy and the state apparatus throughout this period, it had no unified theory of socialism on which to draw, much less one already tailored to the particular circumstances of China. Socialism was improvised, in part based on the experience of the Soviet Union, but always with attention to local circumstances. The Party itself was riven by frequent arguments about what socialism should look like and how it should be constructed. Most of these arguments were not directly about women's labor—everyone agreed it was necessary. Nor were they about Woman as symbol—everyone agreed, prematurely, that the basic conditions for women's liberation had been established successfully by the official recognition that women had equal political rights with men.

The All-China Women's Federation was established as a national mass organization led by the Party. Building on organizational forms developed in the base areas, it had branches attached to every level of government. It was meant to ensure that women's interests were represented and that women were informed about their part in national reconstruction. A state-published magazine devoted to women, *Women of China* (Zhongguo funü), kept women's contributions and issues visible to a national audience.[2] But schisms within the Party about how to develop the economy, and debates after the Sino-Soviet split of 1960 about the role China should take in opening a new road to socialism, affected the lives of women even when gender equality was not explicitly on the agenda.

This chapter begins with three campaigns intended to stabilize families: the Marriage Law campaign, which was conducted in the context of land reform; the campaign to introduce scientific midwifery in rural areas; and the urban campaign against prostitution. The chapter then turns to the mobilization of women and the changing gendered division of labor during urban and rural drives for economic development. It concludes with two iconic campaigns of the Mao years, neither explicitly about gender, which had profound effects on different groups of women. The Great Leap Forward and its ensuing famine reshaped the lives of rural women, and the Cultural Revolution and its movement to send urban youth to the countryside changed the lives of a generation of urban women.

Two major themes underlie this chapter. The first is that "women" in the period of socialist construction, as in all previous periods, were not a homogeneous group. Generation, region, ethnicity, and level of education all helped determine which events of Big History most touched women's lives. But perhaps the most profound divide during the socialist period was that between city and countryside, a gap exacerbated by state socialist policies. In the process of socialist construction, resources flowed out of the countryside to fund the cities—but people moved much less, as an increasingly restrictive household registration (*hukou*) system kept farmers closely bound to their communities. Farmers worked in collectives, where income fluctuated with the harvest but generally remained low, and their only access to food was in their home communities. Social services, including education and access to health care, improved somewhat in rural areas but remained limited. So did access to manufactured goods such as cloth. Most urban dwellers were paid salaries, had easier access to schools and hospitals, and enjoyed a relatively stable supply of food, cloth, and other daily goods. The urban-rural divide meant that the daily activities and sense of possibilities were different for farming women and city women. This chapter pays attention to those differences.

The second theme is that women's labor undergirded socialist construction in ways that were not completely recognized. The socialist discourse on labor had little to say about domestic labor, which women and their families saw as women's responsibility. Even as women took on new tasks outside the home, the constant demands of household tasks structured their days before, during, and after their labor for urban work units or the rural collective. The tasks required of rural women were different and more demanding than those urban women had to perform. But for both, the incessant requirement that they maintain their households was not regarded as an urgent problem to be solved in the socialist present. It was deferred to the communist future, when material abundance and socialized housework would lighten women's burden. In the meantime, domestic labor performed thriftily and with diligence was visible in public discourse as a sign of women's accomplishment, but not as an essential—and unremunerated—contribution to the building of socialism. The Party-state's symbol of Woman—emancipated, with full political rights, striding forward into the socialist future—had only a distant, if inspiring, relationship to the daily lives and labor of women.

MARRIAGE REFORM AND LAND REFORM

The Marriage Law of 1950 was written with input from women in the Party leadership.[3] The law was not substantially different from earlier versions enacted in the Communist base areas and had elements in common with the Nationalist Civil Code of 1930 as well. It announced the end of the "feudal marriage system" and of the "supremacy of man over woman."[4] It outlawed bigamy, concubinage, child betrothal, interference in widow remarriage, the exaction of money or gifts in conjunction with a marriage agreement, and compelling someone to marry against their will. It established a minimum marriage age of twenty for men and eighteen for women and required registration of marriages with the local government. It permitted divorce when both parties desired it, required mediation and a court decision in contested divorces, forbade a husband to divorce his wife during or immediately after pregnancy, and stipulated that a soldier's spouse could not obtain a divorce without the soldier's consent.

By issuing this law, the new national leadership signaled its desire to end marriage practices that had been criticized at least since the May Fourth Movement, as well as its intention to insert the state into marriage, formerly the domain of the family, by issuing marriage certificates. Together with the campaign to redistribute land to poor households, the Marriage Law expressed the Party-state's determination to end a situation in which richer families monopolized land, wives, and concubines, while <u>poor women were trafficked</u> and poor men hired themselves out as landless laborers who could not afford to marry.

The Marriage Law, national in scope, encountered particular difficulties in the complex rural situation of the early 1950s. Inexperienced local village leaders, assisted by Party work teams sent from outside, were preoccupied with the land reform campaign. This involved determining the landholdings and class status of every household in every village and redistributing land and property from landlords and rich peasants to poor peasants.[5] The land reform process already involved considerable social conflict and violence, and there is little evidence that local leaders had the capacity or the desire to mount an aggressive campaign to implement the Marriage Law. Existing cases of concubinage, for instance, were left in place unless one of the parties asked for a divorce, although new ones were regarded as bigamy, and prohibited.[6]

Photo 8.1.   Women at Ten Mile Inn village political meeting, late 1940s
Source: Photograph by David Crook, courtesy of Isabel Crook.

However, in some ways the new political environment introduced by the land reform was conducive to marriage reform as well. Young women from the cities attached to land reform work teams spent a great deal of time visiting the women of each household, mobilizing them to attend political meetings and explaining current government policies to them. Under the Agrarian Law, women received an allotment of land just like men, even though in practice all family land was held in common and its use was controlled by the household head.[7] Older women were encouraged to "speak bitterness" at meetings accusing the landlords and rich peasants of exploitation.[8] Younger women learned to speak and sing in public in support of government policies. These activities enlarged their sense of community and social possibility, and many young women found themselves unwilling to go through with betrothals arranged by their families. Some persuaded their families to break off these engagements (see box 8.1). Girls who had been sold to families as foster daughters-in-law, to be raised by their future in-laws and then married to one of the sons, now often returned to their natal families. In short, the new Marriage Law and the new political environment did prevent some "feudal" marriages from taking place.

BOX 8.1.
Feng Gaixia Breaks Off Her Engagement

Feng Gaixia, who grew up in southern Shaanxi province, was betrothed by her parents in 1949 at the age of fourteen.

> My mother cut out a paper pattern for a pair of red cloth shoes for me to wear when I got on the wedding sedan chair. She left it there for me for several days, but I wouldn't make the shoes. I felt, I hadn't even seen him and I didn't know what he was like. Once I said to my mother, I'd rather die than accept him. If you marry me off when I am so young, I am not going to leave even if I have to die. So I threw it back at her and didn't make the shoes. The old lady matchmaker came to us and I would curse her and tell her to get out.

After Liberation, Gaixia became a land reform activist, and by the time she was eighteen she was the head of the township Women's Association. What she heard about the Party-state's marriage policy from the land reform team emboldened her to break off her own engagement.

> In the past, there was nothing to give you backbone, right? After listening to the work team, you came to understand these things. These ideas were like a mirror held up to you, and you looked and compared.
>
> The thinking of the parents was that the daughter is already a member of someone else's family. If you call off the engagement, they are going to lose face. They were doing things for the benefit of their children. They would say that that family is rich and has a better situation.

Fortunately for Gaixia, her grandfather sided with her and helped to bring her father around.

So my mother was the only one left. There was nothing she could do now.

Gaixia decided to confront her intended husband directly.

One day, that matchmaker, that blind old lady, called me to their house. At that time, people liked to write down the eight characters of the year in which you were born. There is a coin and you have a red string tied to it. And then you tell the fortuneteller your age, your birth date and the year you were born and also the [animal zodiac] sign that you have. All these are tied up to that coin and that is the ceremony for the engagement. I wanted her to take that coin back for me. I went to her house and she also called the man over.

Aiya, it really felt extremely awkward. The man was asking, why do you want to call off the marriage? I said, because it is arranged. I've never seen you before today. This is just like "buying a cat in the bag." We are strangers to each other, right? We do not communicate with each other.

In the end, he even threatened me. But I was not afraid because I was already the director of the Women's Association. So I educated him. I told him that now I understand the Marriage Law. Now women are free, and I myself am going to choose the one I love, someone that I can communicate with, share my life with, have a common language with. And in the end, I was successful. We returned all the things that he had given me: a long piece of red cloth, two pairs of socks, a big bottle of facial cream, one bar of soap. Anyway, we were kids. I didn't care much about this. But he kept the eight characters of my birth for more than a year.

Sometimes, when I had meetings in Zhoujiaping, I bumped into him. He was always there as if deliberately, wanting to make things difficult for me. He was really narrow-minded. Well, if you don't like it, you don't like it. You can't force me. I had already made up my mind. That kind of person, how could I marry him? We had already called off the marriage. So what are you doing here? Acting like a hoodlum? I didn't want to speak to him. I just glared at him and then I left. And I didn't tell my mother. Otherwise she would say, look what shame you have brought us.

Source: Interview with Feng Gaixia (pseudonym), conducted by Gao Xiaoxian and Gail Hershatter, 1997, excerpted in Gail Hershatter, *The Gender of Memory: Rural Women and China's Collective Past* (Berkeley: University of California Press, 2011), 96–98.

But the stakes were much higher in families that already had paid a bride price and acquired a daughter-in-law to contribute her labor and help carry on the family line. Many young women were not happy in such marriages, and undoubtedly some of them hoped that they could escape conditions of poverty and make a better match. Here was a contradiction: a law intended to stabilize families by improving the chances that poor rural men could make a match was now destabilizing communities by threatening to disrupt such marriages. In rural communities, the Marriage Law was popularly known as the divorce law. In-laws and husbands were arrayed against it, directing violent coercion at women who attempted to exercise their new legal rights.[9] In each year from 1950 to 1953, the Ministry of Justice said, seventy to eighty thousand people, most of them women, killed themselves or were killed by family members because of family conflicts.[10]

The Party-state criticized violence against wives who wanted to divorce. But the top leadership had differences of opinion about how forcefully to push marriage reform, and the Law was not publicized consistently on a national level until a one-month campaign in 1953.[11] After an initial period in which divorces were granted if the marriages had been made under one of the categories now forbidden by law, authorities concentrated on mediating, with the aim of maintaining household stability and community harmony. They often talked to village leaders, family members, and neighbors as well as to the unhappy couple, trying to solve marital problems while insisting that couples stay together.[12] These attempts sometimes bordered on the absurd. One provincial cadre reported in 1953 that a township head had encouraged a quarrelling couple to improve their relationship by engaging in sexual intercourse. The local official insisted that the woman throw her trousers out the window while he stood outside, but his attempt to foster marital harmony failed. The couple continued quarrelling loudly, and the township head ultimately had to throw the trousers back through the window. In cases like this, the provincial cadre argued, the couple should be permitted to divorce.[13] Rural and suburban women who were determined to divorce proved adept at finding sympathetic local officials or judges, sometimes traveling in groups to a location far from their own villages to seek redress. In 1953 alone, more than 1.17 million divorces reached the courts.[14]

Over the course of the Mao years, marriage practices changed, but on a much slower time line than that demanded by the brief and intense temporality of a state campaign. The establishment of rural schools and the collectivization of agriculture provided spaces in which youths could get to know and develop an interest in one another. It remained customary for matchmakers to have a role in formalizing a match, and for parents to have a decisive say, but it grew less common for women to be married off without their consent. By the 1970s, it was becoming common for newly married couples to separate their households from those of their parents. Companionate marriage gradually became a hope and expectation that many rural young people shared.[15]

One important feature of rural marriage was not addressed by the Marriage Law: patrilocality, in which daughters moved out of their natal homes at marriage and into the homes of their husbands, usually in a different village. This change at marriage continued to mark the lives of women, who left communities where they were known and socially embedded and entered ones where they were strangers and had to establish themselves.[16] The change was not as drastic as suggested by the marriage ritual described in chapter 1, in which water was spilled when a bride departed to indicate that she could never return. In practice, young married women often married close by and returned often to their natal families, maintaining close emotional ties, and in some areas they continued to reside more than half of the time with their parents until they became pregnant.[17] It is difficult to imagine how the new PRC state, beleaguered as it was, could possibly have challenged patrilocality as a feature of "feudal" marriage, so embedded was it in rural life. But the failure to take it up had consequences: the persistence of patrilocal marriage has continued to limit women's access to political power and has generated widespread preference for sons well into the contemporary era, as chapter 9 will explore.

MIDWIFERY

Even as the new state was moving to redistribute land and reconfigure marriage, it began to address a pervasive public health problem: the high number of women and infants who died in childbirth.[18] Not since the efforts of the Nanjing Decade had the national government been in a position to address this problem. The campaign to do so, unlike those for land reform and marriage reform, was designed to minimize conflict. In most rural areas, as chapter 5 described, babies were delivered by rural midwives who had no formal training. Some midwives had years of experience and considerable expertise in dealing with breech and other difficult births. But their general use of unsterilized implements to cut the umbilical cord led to high rates of puerperal fever in mothers and tetanus neonatorum in infants. In 1952, the Ministry of Health estimated the infant death rate nationally at 20 percent.[19]

As early as 1950, the newly constituted Women's Federation, along with the Ministry of Public Health and the very small number of trained new-style midwives, conducted surveys of childbirth practices in the countryside. This was followed by short-course retraining for older midwives and the recruitment of younger women from the villages to train as new-style midwives. Both were trained in sterile technique. The mortality rate declined considerably because of these measures. Older midwives were not vilified as a remnant of the "old society"—they were valued for the rudimentary health-care delivery network they made possible. Across the years of collectivization, except for some short-lived experiments with birth centers, it remained common for rural women to give birth at home.

Midwives, usually local farmers who had received training and were paid by the collectives, attended home births.

The midwifery campaign can be seen as part of a larger state project to introduce the latest in scientific knowledge at the grassroots level and to strengthen families by improving women's and children's health. The science behind sterile technique became broadly accepted, although rural women were skeptical about the belief current in the 1950s that it was more scientific for women to give birth lying down rather than squatting. Other scientific knowledge about women and reproduction that circulated in 1950s urban China also looks somewhat dated more than half a century later. State-published books and articles promoted the belief that sexual activity was healthy and normal mainly in the context of marriage and reproduction, and that men's sexual desire was invariably stronger than women's, which was seen as mainly responsive in nature.[20]

PROSTITUTION

When Communist forces moved into Shanghai and other big cities in 1949, they had little experience as urban administrators. The challenges facing them included rampant inflation, refugees and beggars living and dying on the streets, unemployment, and opium trafficking.[21] For newly minted CCP urban cadres, the cities' large number of madams and prostitutes was a sign of this disorder, indicative both of corrupt urban morals and the exploitation of poor women. Eliminating prostitution, like ending opium addiction, was for them intrinsic to establishing a strong modern nation, free of the taint of imperialism and the name that had often been applied to China: "sick man of East Asia." They announced their intention to eliminate prostitution at the earliest possible opportunity, but in Shanghai and other cities they first had to establish basic political control and urban services. By the time the municipal administration moved to round up madams and prostitutes in late 1951, many women had left the trade to find other urban employment or return to their home villages, which were no longer caught up in civil war.

Still, it was a matter of considerable symbolic import for the new government to round up 501 prostitutes and 324 brothel owners. The owners were sent to prison or labor reform, but the prostitutes were remanded to a Women's Labor Training Institute where they were confined for medical care, job training, and ideological remolding. Like many other urban dwellers who suddenly found themselves under Communist administration, the women were not convinced that the new authorities were there to liberate them. They feared being deprived of their source of livelihood and uprooted from their social networks. Many had close ties to their madams, whom they addressed as "mother." Some had heard rumors that they would be distributed to Communist troops, used as minesweepers in the anticipated military campaign to take Taiwan, or drained of blood to supply wounded soldiers. The arrival of health-care workers to draw their blood and test them for syphilis and other sexually transmitted infections did nothing to allay their fears. When the head of the Shanghai civil administration showed up at the Institute to give them a welcoming speech and proclaim their liberation, they greeted him with a chorus of wails and overturned their food trays onto the floor.

Ultimately, however, most of the women resigned themselves to the new order, and some eventually welcomed it. The staff of the Institute spared no effort in treating their sexually transmitted infections with scarce penicillin. They talked to the women about how they had been oppressed and why they should embrace new lives as productive citizens, taught them how to weave towels and produce socks, and attempted to reestablish links with their families in Shanghai or the surrounding countryside. Within several years, all of the incarcerated Shanghai prostitutes were released to families and jobs. Those who were not already married were provided with matchmaking services that paired them with poor urban men seeking wives, or sent them off to state farms in the far northwest to marry current or former army men working there.[22] Those who returned to Shanghai neighborhoods were under the supervision of newly established Residents' Committees, staffed by neighborhood women alert to any sign of recidivism.

Wherever women were sent, the intention was to reinsert them into a functioning household, part of a larger effort to stabilize society after many decades of war. Of course, this process was not as easy as the upbeat stories published in the state-controlled press suggested. When the Shanghai city government reviewed the membership of its Residents' Committees in 1954–55, for instance, it discovered at least one committee in which women's mobilization work was being staffed by a madam and a prostitute who was supposedly undergoing reform through labor.[23] In Beijing and other cities as well as Shanghai, authorities alternated between treating former prostitutes as victims in need of rescue from the exploitation of the "old society" (the umbrella term for the era before 1949) and suspecting them as disruptive elements who might return to their old ways or otherwise derail the project of revolutionary transformation.[24] Nevertheless, in a relatively short time the sex trade, an important economic sector in pre-revolutionary Shanghai and a prominent feature of urban social life in many other cities as well, had become invisible. Here was a clear demonstration that commercial sexual services, and the trafficking, gang ties, courtesan celebrities, and aggressive streetwalkers associated with them, were all signs of exploitation to be discarded with the rest of the semicolonial past.

The attempts to reform marriage, the midwifery campaign, and the campaign to end prostitution all aimed to stabilize family formation and reproduction. The goal was a new society in which men would be able to afford to marry, and husbands and wives would have a say in choosing their partners in order to enhance the potential of a happy, long-lasting marriage. Mothers would be able to give birth to healthy children who survived and enhanced the prosperity of the family and the collective. Women would not be sold by their families and would not sell sex in order to survive. Although acceptance of these measures, particularly the Marriage Law, was far from uniform, the idea of stability was deeply appealing to broad segments of the populace after years of war, banditry, and displacement. A woman's place in the early years of socialism was in the family—from which she could be called forth and mobilized for socialist production.

MOBILIZING URBAN WOMEN

Party-state authorities devoted much attention in the first few years of the PRC to establishing an effective presence in workplaces and neighborhoods, and women were crucial participants in both projects.

Party committees were installed in every municipal organization and workplace to guide urban administration and economic production, acting as a sort of shadow government. By 1953, the central government had launched its First Five-Year Plan, a blueprint for economic growth modeled on the Soviet example. Old factories were expanded, and new ones were established.

Most state investment went to heavy industry, a sector that historically had employed few women, and the entry of women into traditionally male jobs—drivers, miners, technicians, engineers—was celebrated in the press.[25] Industries where women had predominated before 1949, such as cotton spinning and weaving, expanded as well. Many women were drawn into manufacturing, teaching, cultural production, health care, and urban administration. The national campaign to build a modern socialist economy, and the rising numbers of women in the paid labor force, dovetailed with the theory derived from Friedrich Engels that had become dominant in the Party during the wartime years: participation in paid labor was essential to women's emancipation.

Until 1958, when it became more difficult to obtain an urban household registration, many men who had worked in cities before 1949 brought their wives from the countryside to join them. The birth rate and the number of surviving children both increased, swelling the urban population. Urban social life was increasingly organized around the <u>*danwei,*</u> or <u>work unit</u>. Large work units provided housing in apartment blocks, sometimes with communally shared cooking space, and the children of workers often went to schools affiliated with the danwei. Some danwei had canteens, clinics, and child-care facilities. Many goods and services were distributed through the danwei: health care, ration tickets for the purchase of staple goods and bicycles, and tickets for films or other entertainment. Weekly political study sessions also took place in the work unit, and political campaigns were publicized there.[26]

Not all women lived where they worked, because it was common for housing to be distributed through the husband's work unit. Many women did piece work or handicraft production in small collective workshops, which paid less than the larger state-owned enterprises and did not supply the full range of welfare benefits.[27] Even in state-owned enterprises, although men and women were paid equally when they did the same work, women tended to be tracked into lower-paying job assignments and industries.[28] And not all women worked—many middle-aged women, or those with many children at home, did not seek regular paid employment. Some took intermittent odd jobs or were mobilized periodically in hygiene campaigns to pick up trash, dredge canals, and kill insects and vermin.[29] The Women's Federation and its local branches were responsible for mobilizing unemployed women, making them aware of national priorities and incorporating them into <u>state-building projects</u>.

Photo 8.2. Spinning thread, Hangzhou silk mill, 1978
Source: Inge Morath and Arthur Miller, *Chinese Encounters* (New York: Farrar, Straus & Giroux, 1979), 214.

In older neighborhoods outside the larger danwei, the Federation and local governments recruited unemployed or retired women to run the Residents' Committees, which had their own offices and were responsible for transmitting policy, mediating local disputes, staffing a neighborhood watch, and in general being the eyes and ears of the state. Some officials felt that women who had not circulated much outside the home before 1949 would have fewer problematic social connections and would be politically less complicated to manage than other urban dwellers.[30]

Government publicity often featured urban women in socially productive roles in industry, science, engineering, administration, and the arts.[31] But these were not the only images of women that circulated widely. Women wearing brightly colored dresses, or examining some of the consumer goods newly available to urban working people, also adorned the covers of the Women's Federation magazine *Women of China* and other urban publications. Whenever industrial growth slowed, as it did in the mid-1950s, state publications emphasized that the domestic role of women, and their personal attractiveness, were crucial to the health of socialist society.[32] Ideal wives were portrayed as interested in political affairs and equal to their husbands, but also willing to sacrifice for them if the men were out contributing to the construction of socialism. No comparable literature was directed at husbands. Marital harmony, when it appeared at all in the press, was primarily a woman's duty to nurture and maintain.[33]

Many women enthusiastically embraced what they saw as a new society, free of daily threats to life and safety, in which they were recognized and valued for their work. For one woman, who had been a childhood refugee from the 1942 Henan famine, running a day-care center in the west China city of Xi'an meant providing the next generation of children with the stability she had not experienced as a child. She was willing to work around the clock on that project, even if it meant that several of her own children had to be sent to live for several years with their grandmother because she could not care for them.[34] Urban women born in the 1950s recall mothers who put in long hours at their publishing houses or theater companies or factories, sometimes returning home only once or twice a week. When women were sent out to other danwei or to the countryside on the work teams that intermittently were dispatched to do political work throughout the Mao years, they saw their families even less. They spent little time with their children, who were cared for by grandparents or sent to boarding schools at a young age.[35]

As communities were reconfigured around a common workplace or newly reorganized neighborhood, social life opened well beyond the family, creating new connections as well as irritations. Campaigns to increase production were accompanied by fines for infractions and mistakes in the work. In political meetings, numerous campaigns targeted those who came from suspect class backgrounds or who expressed criticism of the Party leadership. Some women who had been trailblazing lawyers, teachers, and journalists in the 1930s and 1940s, but who were not Communists, found themselves sidelined, their talents unwanted and their motivations put under scrutiny.[36] Other women, including the prominent Communist writer Ding Ling, found themselves the casualties of intra-Party struggles and were labeled Rightists in a 1957 campaign and removed from political life except as targets of criticism.[37] Many sources of social tension simmered, some of which would manifest themselves during the Cultural Revolution.

Juggling the demands of work, political study, and growing families was a standard feature of urban women's life in the 1950s and early 1960s, but the double (or triple) day for women was not generally conceptualized as a problem. Even as women's obligations to engage in socialist construction outside the home were radically reconfigured, government publications continued to promote the importance of a well-run household. The assumption that home was primarily a woman's responsibility was generally unquestioned.[38] A fully committed shift at the workplace followed by a second unremunerated shift at home was a standard feature of urban life for women.[39] Domestic tasks—cooking, shopping, cleaning, child rearing—remained time-consuming and expanded with the growing numbers of children. Housing stock did not keep up with the growth in population, and by the 1960s, families were crammed into small living spaces. No longer the underpinning of a dynastic empire or the proving ground of a New Life, the home was now conceptualized as an ancillary enterprise supporting socialist construction—but not appropriate as a woman's exclusive focus, because such an attitude could be construed as narrow, selfish, and bourgeois.

In spite of these material constraints and the lack of recognition of their unrelenting domestic work, for many urban women the years of early socialism remained a time of expanded horizons and optimism. Those who were workers enjoyed new social recognition as members of the leading class of socialist transformation. And for all urban dwellers, the rising standard of living and improved access to education and health care offered the prospect of an enticing future.

MOBILIZING RURAL WOMEN

In the countryside, women's labor was at the heart of the Party's drive to raise agricultural production. In the early years of the PRC, much of the rural population still had difficulty getting through the growing season with enough to eat. In some areas, the Party-state encouraged and funded projects such as women's spinning and weaving co-ops. Women pooled their labor, produced cotton yarn and cloth, and sold it on the market to help their families make ends meet. But this support did not last long. Party leaders envisioned socialism as a rapid move in the direction of collective and then state ownership and control of production and marketing. As the state increased control of the purchase and sale of all kinds of goods in 1954, local rural markets shrank, and households lost the ability to generate income by selling the products of women's labor.[40]

Soon after the land reform campaign concluded in the early 1950s, Party-state leaders began to promote mutual aid teams in which neighbors shared labor and farming equipment, particularly during the busy seasons.[41] Mutual aid was not a significant departure from customary practice before 1949. Many villages comprised networks of male kin and their married-in wives, and it was common for relatives to pool labor in times of need. But this change was not enough to spur a dramatic increase in farm production. The national strategy for industrialization relied on cheap and plentiful farm products to feed the cities, generate some foreign exchange, and provide the factories with raw material. The mutual-aid teams were soon supplanted by new ways of organizing labor that began to change women's daily lives.

First, beginning in 1953, village neighborhoods were organized into lower producers' cooperatives, where several dozen village households pooled their labor and equipment on a regular basis. The state tightened its control over the purchase of farm products, buying from farmers at relatively low prices so that, in effect, the countryside was subsidizing the food supply and production campaigns of the cities. At the end of the year, after the harvest was sold, rural households were compensated. Most of the proceeds were distributed according to the land, equipment, and livestock they had provided. About 20 percent was distributed according to their labor.

Beginning in late 1955, this arrangement was replaced by advanced producers' cooperatives. These were bigger groups, sometimes the size of an entire village, divided into work teams. Private ownership of land, so recently distributed to households, was abolished. Each farmer earned a certain number of work points per day for labor. Proceeds were distributed, as before, after the harvest was sold. The collective guaranteed that each household would receive enough grain to support its members, but if the household's members did not earn enough work points to cover even this basic subsistence, they could borrow from the collective and clear the debt later.[42]

Mobilizing women was an important piece of this state initiative. Women had long been active in the fields during the sowing and harvest

seasons, with regional variations. Now they were encouraged to participate year-round in collective agriculture, where their labor could help to
raise productivity in the fields and free up the labor of some male farmers
to work in other collective enterprises such as machine repair, flour milling, and irrigation works.

Some women already were skilled farmers, usually because the men
in their families had died or worked elsewhere before 1949. For these
women, laboring in the fields was not new, but its meaning changed: now
they were valued for their knowledge, rather than being shamed for their
poverty and their public visibility. Some became women's team leaders,
and the most skilled among them were selected as labor models.

Women labor models attended regional and even national meetings,
where they were introduced to the nation's top leaders. At home, they

Photo 8.3.   Labor model Cao Zhuxiang growing cotton, 1950s
Source: Photo courtesy of Cao Zhuxiang.

acted as a live embodiment of agricultural extension techniques, modeling for other women how to grow cotton, ward off insect pests, fertilize the fields, and participate in political campaigns. Often the women themselves were minimally literate and unaccustomed to public speaking, but teams sent by the Women's Federation helped to identify them, taught them how to sum up what they knew, answered their correspondence, and wrote accounts of their daily activity to publicize beyond their immediate community. Women labor models provided a direct link between policies generated by a faraway state and ordinary village woman.

Women labor models were meant to model mobilization, not women's emancipation. Nevertheless, being a woman labor model was a gendered experience. Both men and women labor models were expected to work hard and create new production techniques, but only women labor models were routinely praised for doing a good job of raising their children, treating the collective's livestock with maternal concern, and maintaining domestic peace and harmony with their husbands and in-laws. Women labor models had to be above reproach and controversy in their personal lives, not subjects of community gossip. They had to complete domestic tasks and manage the family's emotional life in a way that enhanced rather than interfered with collective production.[43]

For all women who came out to work in the fields, mobilization created a profound change in their social lives. Already, the land reform and marriage reform campaigns, as well as winter schools aimed at teaching villagers basic literacy, had drawn women out of their homes to meetings and classes. Initially, the senior members of a household often opposed the efforts to involve younger women because they feared that their daughters might be sexually compromised or their daughters-in-law might be tempted to seek a divorce. In the early 1950s, stories abounded of angry parents and in-laws who had locked up their young women, or barred the door and refused to feed them on their return, or abused them verbally and physically.

Patient persuasion by the work teams overcame some of this resistance. Now, with collectivization, it became absolutely necessary for every able-bodied member of a household to labor in the collective fields and earn work points.[44] Under these circumstances, the residual reluctance to let young women out unsupervised quickly evaporated. Unmarried adolescent daughters and young married women spent much of their days working and socializing in the company of their peers—and within range of groups of young men. Across the collective period, village mores about social mixing changed, and the social worlds of village women broadened.

Life in the collectives was far from idyllic for women, however. For one thing, women routinely were paid less than men for their labor, even

Photo 8.4. Two women farmers, Sichuan, 1957
Source: Marc Riboud, *The Three Banners of China* (New York: Macmillan, 1966), 25.

when they outperformed men at tasks such as topping cotton plants or picking tea. Men generally earned ten work points a day, whereas women earned seven or eight. Each person's daily working allocation was decided by his or her production team, and the decisions reflected shared assumptions that a woman's labor was worth less than that of a man, although some reports surfaced about local arguments around this issue. Even as the gendered division of labor changed rapidly, and women took on new tasks, the notion persisted that whatever women did was worth less than what men did.[45]

In addition, women routinely worked shorter hours than men in the collective fields, but they put in longer days. They came late to the fields after caring for children and preparing the morning meal, and left early to cook at noontime and before dinner. Often they labored in the fields with small children on their backs. This was the rural version of the double day, and because the only labor that was publicly visible and remunerated was labor for work points, women's earnings were lower than men's—although still absolutely essential for the welfare of families in rural collectives.

Perhaps the most taxing feature of married women farmers' lives was the hidden night shift of labor they performed.[46] After dinnertime or when evening production planning meetings concluded, women settled down at home to spin thread, weave cloth, and sew clothing and shoes for their ever-increasing numbers of children. Many villages were not electrified until the early 1970s, so this work was conducted well into the night under the light of oil lamps.[47]

Several factors converged to increase women's workload in the collective era. First, many of their daytime hours were now spent in the fields, rather than tending directly to household labor. Second, partly because of the end to war and the improvement of midwifery, along with other public-health initiatives, more children now survived infancy. Birth control was not easily accessible or accepted in rural areas, although women sometimes resorted to herbal concoctions and violent physical activities to prevent or end pregnancies.[48] These methods of family planning were not reliable, and increasing numbers of children had to be clothed and shod.

Third, machine-made cloth, clothing, and shoes were not widely available in rural areas, and they were expensive enough that even farmers who were issued ration tickets preferred to sell them on the black market and make their clothes at home. At times when state demand for cotton was high and most of the crop was requisitioned for purchase, some of the raw cotton that women used to clothe their families had to be gleaned from second pickings through the cotton bolls.[49] Their labor time, too, was scavenged from sleeping hours and from the demands of the workday, as

Photo 8.5.   Woman takes child to the fields, 1960s
Source: Marc Riboud, *The Three Banners of China* (New York: Macmillan, 1966), 60.

women brought their needlework to nighttime political meetings and to the fields to take up during breaks.

Older women, already past their childbearing years, also faced new labor demands during the collective era. Those whose physical strength no longer allowed them to earn substantial work points in the field took over child-care tasks from daughters-in-law who went out each day to farm. This household division of labor made it possible for the daughters-in-law to earn work points, but the child care performed by the older women was not remunerated if it was performed within the household. And older women felt the economic burden of grandchildren in another way as well: a multigenerational household with many children who were too young to earn work points had to stretch its resources to avoid borrowing from the collective. Strained by the demands of these growing families, some grandparents formally separated out their households as accounting units from those of their married sons, even if they continued to live in the same dwelling, so that the younger couple was primarily responsible for providing food for their own children. This gradual weakening of intergenerational co-residence eventually helped to change the nature of rural marriage and perhaps weakened the sense of obligation that grown children felt to their aging parents.

Essential as they were, the clothing women produced and the double day they worked in the collective era did not count as labor. It was neither remunerated nor publicly recognized because it appeared to take place in a separate domain from that of the collective. Focused on the need to mobilize women's agricultural labor, and supported by the Engelsian belief that in doing so they were contributing to women's emancipation, Party-state authorities never fully confronted the degree to which women's invisible labor was underwriting the entire enterprise of rural socialist construction.

CAMPAIGN TIME AND DOMESTIC TIME: THE GREAT LEAP FORWARD AND THE FAMINE

"Woman-work"—mobilizing women for fieldwork and other collective tasks—was a routine duty carried out at the village level by a local woman who was often the only woman in village leadership, intermittently aided by work teams sent by the Women's Federation.[50] But woman-work burst out of its usual routines with the heightened demand for rural labor during the Great Leap Forward from 1958 to 1960, a time of disruption, experimentation, and ultimately national disaster that left tens of millions dead and the economy badly damaged. The short and frantic period of the Great Leap was also the beginning—and the end—of the Party-state's only serious attempt to socialize some aspects of women's household labor in the countryside. With the collapse of the Leap and the devastating famine from 1959 to 1961, that project was abandoned, and domestic labor was returned to the household and social invisibility. Women's invisible labor, however, was crucial to household survival in the famine years.

Mao launched the Great Leap Forward in 1958, frustrated with China's pace of development and convinced that social reorganization would unleash the energy of farmers and power an economic breakthrough. Although many in the Party had grave reservations about his strategy, farmers initially were enthusiastic about its promise of multistory houses, electrification, and abundant food. They accepted the vision Mao articulated that several years of unstinting effort would be followed by "a thousand years of Communist happiness."[51]

In both city and countryside, production units were amalgamated into large communes that were supposed to provide economies of scale, combining the functions of both production and government. The pace of work in urban factories increased, but the reorganization did not alter most aspects of urban life. The change in the countryside, however, was fundamental. The newly created rural communes could cover an area as big as a county and incorporate as many as several hundred thousand people. Communes were subdivided into <u>production brigade</u>s with five thousand or more households, and production teams that might encompass an entire natural village.[52]

Photo 8.6. Woman worker in Yumen oil fields, 1958
Source: Henri Cartier-Bresson, in Cornell Capa, ed., *Behind the Great Wall of China: Photographs from 1870 to the Present* (Greenwich, CT: Metropolitan Museum of Art, 1972).

Suddenly, under the administration of the commune, rural people were required to coordinate their daily labor with people dozens of miles away. Many men, and some women, left their home villages for weeks on end to work on ambitious infrastructure projects in irrigation and road building.[53] As the men moved out to do this work and took on the project of smelting steel in backyard furnaces—part of the Great Leap effort to expand and decentralize industrial production—villages began to suffer an acute labor shortage. The 1958 harvest season arrived, bringing a bumper crop, but in many areas the possibility that grain would rot in the fields was very real.

In response, women farmers were mobilized to go to the fields in unprecedented numbers, working long days and nights to complete the harvest.[54] Beginning in early 1957, the national Women's Federation had promoted the "three transfers" policy, in which menstruating, pregnant, or lactating women were supposed to be assigned light tasks in nearby locations working in dry fields.[55] During the Great Leap, however, the need for women's labor overrode such precautions. Often women suffered from exhaustion and health problems, including miscarriages and many cases of uterine prolapse from returning to work too quickly after childbirth.[56] These were not always taken seriously by local leaders, including many women in charge of woman-work who felt it was important to put production first.[57]

Photo 8.7.   Farmers working in the fields at night, Xinyang, Henan, 1959
Source: https://commons.wikimedia.org/wiki/File:Xinyang_working_at_night.jpg

With women's labor so badly needed in the fields, Party-state authorities paid an unusual amount of attention to lightening women's domestic burden. The "Five Changes" policy aimed to collectivize meal preparation, clothing production, midwife services, child care, and flour milling. Some of these initiatives, had they been implemented consistently or lasted longer, might have altered rural women's lives profoundly. For instance, production brigades and teams were encouraged to organize older women to provide child care for women working in the fields and to pay the child minders in work points. But women had to go to the fields regardless of whether child care was available, and tales from this period abound of children who were left tethered to the bed, wandered off and drowned, or were bitten by animals while their mothers worked.

The most ambitious of the Five Changes was the establishment of rural collective dining halls in many production teams, beginning in the hectic summer of 1958. Farmers turned over their food supplies to the production brigade, smashed their kitchen stoves, and handed in their woks and other metal goods to be smelted down for steel. A day's work was supposed to guarantee all men and women laborers a day's food in the dining halls, with special provisions for the elderly and children. One of the Great Leap's most popular pieces of fiction, "Li Shuangshuang," which was made into a film and rendered as a comic book, centered on the efforts of a voluble and quick-tempered woman to upgrade the food in a dining hall in her village.[58]

For several months, farmers ate their fill, many for the first time in their lives. Glowing output reports coming in from around the country reassured everyone that the hoped-for Communist prosperity was imminent. But the dining halls soon foundered on the larger problems engendered by the Leap: widespread false reporting of massively inflated productivity by local leaders afraid of being characterized as laggards; excessive government requisitions of grain, in part based on these false reports and in part the result of callous decisions at the top; administrative chaos in huge new structures run by inexperienced cadres; the state decision to repay all debts to the Soviet Union, which in 1960 broke off fraternal relations with China partly over the unorthodox strategy of the Great Leap; and bad weather.

As the food supply in dining halls dwindled, daily meals began to feature thin gruel made of carrot tops, tree leaves, and other marginal sources of nutrition. Women quarreled with the cooks about fair distribution or whether portions could be taken home for sick family members. Villagers hoarded and stole food, fought with one another, and in some areas ate the raw crops directly from the fields before the state could claim them.[59] As malnutrition spread and starvation gripped parts of China, the dining halls were disbanded. The project of socializing domestic work receded into the indefinite Communist future. Even if the Party-state had remained committed to the Five Changes and had been able to fund necessary investments in rural areas, so deep was their association with discord and hunger that it is doubtful households ever again would relinquish control over the family food supply.

The famine years from 1959 to 1961 remain one of the most terrible legacies of the attempt to build rural socialism, as well as one of the most catastrophic famines worldwide, still politically controversial more than half a century later.[60] The national state, reluctant to admit the scope of the disaster and unable to mount a massive aid effort, left each province to devise its own solutions. In the most severely affected provinces, some farmers—mainly young men—took to the road, looking for itinerant work elsewhere. Older people, married women, and children were less free to move, and control of migration through the household registration system kept most people in place. (The household registration system, along with state controls on the press, meant that many farmers were unaware of the scale of the disaster outside their own locality, and many urban people remained ignorant of the suffering in the countryside.) Human trafficking, particularly a trade in brides from the most severely affected places, was not unknown. But markets for sex workers, concubines, and foster daughters-in-law no longer existed, so one potential option for saving the lives of young women and children, traumatic as it had been in earlier periods, was no longer available.[61] Malnourished women suffered high rates of amenorrhea and uterine prolapse in famine-afflicted areas across China. Births plummeted.[62] Estimates of the number of deaths across China during this period in excess of what might normally have been expected range from an official estimate of fifteen million to a high of forty-five million.[63]

Amid this chaos and devastation, women took what measures they could to keep their members alive. They scavenged for food. Those skilled at weaving cloth, embroidering pillows, or making shoes sent their men to carry these products to trade for grain in more remote mountain areas. Mountain villages were poorer than settlements in the plains, but mountainous land had been less intensively collectivized and sometimes still had stores of food. The effective unit of production in many villages shrank to the household, an unauthorized decollectivization that persisted in some areas for several years after the famine abated. The state once again permitted households to cultivate private plots and raise pigs and chickens for their own use, all tasks in which women took the lead.

As harvests began to return to normal levels and cultivation was recollectivized in the early 1960s, the expanded role of women in daily fieldwork was further consolidated. Many men moved to supervisory and technical functions in agriculture, worked in small-scale industries to support agriculture, or became contract factory laborers in towns and cities.[64] The labor force in basic-level agriculture was increasingly feminized, while women's second shift remained untouched.

THE CULTURAL REVOLUTION AND
THE SENT-DOWN YOUTH CAMPAIGN

In 1966 Mao Zedong, who had been in partial political eclipse since the failure of the Great Leap, staged a political comeback. He sidestepped the Party-state apparatus and called upon the nation's youth to "bombard the headquarters" and help him combat revisionism, which he characterized as the Party's turn away from class struggle and the original goals of a Marxist-Leninist revolution. He warned that the Party was now led by "people in authority who were taking the capitalist road" and called for criticism of both the Party leadership and possibly counterrevolutionary attitudes on the part of intellectuals and former elites. His exhortations fell on receptive ears: student activists committed to Maoist ideals, moved by Mao's call for youth to take the lead in effecting cultural transformation, and also worried about their own future prospects; factory workers dissatisfied with autocratic management backed up by Party authorities; farmers still enraged at how local leadership had permitted their communities to suffer hunger during the Great Leap; and a host of others.

Like the Great Leap Forward, the Cultural Revolution had little directly to say about women's status. Most of the period's polemics and theorizing had to do with class, centering on questions such as these: could counterrevolutionary class attitudes be passed down from adults to children born after the revolution? Was an old bourgeoisie secretly wielding power in China, or was a new bourgeoisie emerging? The Three Great Differences that Mao said he wanted to narrow were those between mental and manual labor, workers and farmers, and city and countryside. No fourth great difference between men and women existed. Problems of gender inequity were widely regarded as minor, residual, and destined to disappear with time and further economic development.

Gender was downplayed in Party-state directives of the period as well. The Women's Federation, like many other organizations, was dissolved in 1966, on the grounds that it was permeated with bourgeois ideas and that women's interests were not distinct from those of men of the same class.[65] It was not reconstituted until 1972, and even thereafter it was regarded by many urban women as having nothing to do with them because of its close association with housewives, not working women.[66] But like the Great Leap Forward, the Cultural Revolution did affect the lives of men and women in gender-differentiated ways, particularly those who were adolescents and young adults at the time. This was the case even when young men and women were involved in similar activities and nothing about gender was explicitly articulated.

The activist phase of the Cultural Revolution ran from 1966 to 1969. During this period, urban middle-school girls and university students joined their male classmates in forming groups of Red Guards. They wrote big-character posters criticizing the leadership of the nation and their own schools. In one notorious and controversial case in the summer of 1966, at a time when the top Party leadership was encouraging teenaged activists to create "great chaos" and local leadership had completely collapsed, Beijing middle-school girls beat the woman vice principal of their school and forced her and other school leaders to carry heavy loads of dirt until she collapsed and died.[67] Red Guards, including girls and young women, ransacked the homes of suspected "bad elements," a group that included intellectuals and former capitalists as well as the Party revisionists who were supposed to be under criticism.[68] Students traveled to Beijing, some from great distances, to attend one of the massive rallies in Tian'anmen Square where Chairman Mao appeared to encourage as many as a million students at a time.

Students increasingly became embroiled in the conflicts over which Red Guard faction was more accurately reflecting the intentions of Chairman Mao. By 1967, these disputes had spread to the factories and been fueled by workplace grievances there, resulting in armed conflict and many deaths among the militants, including young women.[69] By 1968, the People's Liberation Army had been sent in to restore order, and the central government inaugurated a vast campaign to "send down" urban youth to the countryside "to learn from the poor and lower-middle peas-

Photo 8.8.   Red Guards, 1966
Source: Jean Vincent/AFP/Getty, published in the *Guardian*, August 25, 1966, reprinted August 25, 2016.

ants." Shipping young people out of the city also served to quell urban violence and solve a problem of unemployment among urban youths. In 1969, the Party declared that the Cultural Revolution was over, but many of its associated policies, including the sent-down youth program, continued until Mao's death in 1976 and even beyond. The official Party-state periodization of history now dates the Cultural Revolution from 1966 to 1976, characterizing it as "ten years of chaos."

In Cultural Revolution factional warfare, particularly in the schools, young people formed alliances based mainly on their families' class labels. The sons and daughters of high cadres stuck together, both before and after their parents came under attack. So did the sons and daughters of intellectuals and bad-class elements, who were not permitted to be Red Guards, and the working-class sons and daughters who had found themselves disadvantaged with respect to the other two groups, in spite of their proletarian background.

Gender was a far less visible organizing axis. Still, it was not absent. Women's mode of dress signified their class allegiance. Red Guard girl students dressed like male soldiers, with cropped hair, armbands, and wide belts.[70] There was a missionizing zeal in their adoption of this military aesthetic: groups of Red Guards seized women pedestrians on city streets in the fall of 1966, cutting their braids, slicing up skirts and form-fitting pants, and warning violators of this new dress code not to mimic the fashion habits of the bourgeoisie. When Wang Guangmei, the wife of China's president, was hauled before a huge political rally to be criticized for her revisionist politics, Red Guards humiliated her by dressing her in a satirically exaggerated version of bourgeois women's attire: a form-fitting dress and a necklace of ping-pong balls.[71]

The model for political behavior in the early Cultural Revolution was an imagined version of the working-class male. Some young women Red Guards expressed their political enthusiasm by engaging in behavior that was more commonly associated with young men: hectoring, swearing at, and physically abusing suspected class enemies. In later years, when former Red Guards tried to make sense of the atmosphere of those years, one of the main questions they puzzled over was why girls, in particular, had behaved in that way. This puzzlement suggests that in their own assessment, girls and young women had departed more thoroughly from gendered norms of behavior than their male classmates—even though, in fact, beating teachers and abusing neighbors was a departure for young men, too.

Looking back on those years from the vantage point of the post-Mao period, women also recall their sense of adventure, excitement, and sometimes trepidation as they took to the rails and the roads to see Chairman Mao or emulated the CCP's Long March in treks across China. These travels gave both young men and young women a sense of China's vastness and provided a degree of autonomy from adult supervision that they would not have encountered in a more normal time. For young women in particular, this period of political activism and travel meant freedom from family and school constraints that young women of previous generations seldom had experienced.

The sense of being unmoored from previous expectations also characterizes women's memories of being sent down to the countryside. Assigned to state farms or rural production teams, urban young men and women learned new skills, many of them physically taxing. They experienced firsthand the enormous gap in education and living standards between the city and the countryside. Because even the middle-school students among them were better educated than most rural people, many "educated youth," as they were officially known, were quickly transferred out of fieldwork to accounting and teaching jobs. In young women's stories, several themes recur: the drudgery of rural life, their exhilaration at learning to ride horses or master agricultural tasks, their sense that rural women of their age operated under much stronger "feudal" constraints than they did, their periodic campaigns against the gendered division of labor and work-point discrepancies, their discovery that farmers often were not at all motivated by revolutionary ideals or class loyalty, their attempts to combat boredom by circulating hoarded copies of novels and language textbooks, and their growing sense of capability and self-reliance. Some also mention the difficulties of navigating adolescence, sexual attraction, sex, and unwanted pregnancy with little guidance from adults or peers, and some talk about instances of sexual assault.[72]

As young women of urban origin sought to establish themselves in these unfamiliar rural environments, they could draw upon a few propaganda slogans that were addressed to women in particular. One was an enthusiastic endorsement that had first appeared in the *People's Daily* in 1956, to the effect that "women can hold up half the sky."[73] (It is usually translated into English as "women hold up half the sky," making it an accomplished fact rather than a statement of potential. It also has been pointed out by many observers in China and beyond that Chinese women who work a double day may have been holding up more than half of the sky.) Another was an offhand statement Mao apparently made while swimming past a group of young women swimmers in 1964: "The times have changed; men and women are the same. Whatever men comrades can do, women comrades can do too." His casual observation was reproduced nationally, becoming a standard pronouncement on the state of women's emancipation: mission accomplished. Here the standard of achievement was male—no one was suggesting that men comrades take equal responsibility for housework or children—but this statement did circulate widely in the Chinese press as an encouragement that women could, and should, contribute to the revolution equally with men.[74]

A third way in which the state recognized the potential of women was in the approving coverage given to the Iron Girls[75] (see box 8.2). They were a group of young rural women in the Dazhai production brigade in north China's Shanxi Province who worked tirelessly alongside men to rescue the crops from a 1963 flood. Dazhai later became a national model for agriculture, and across the country Iron Girl Brigades were formed. They performed heroic tasks—including repair of high-voltage wires— that women had not attempted previously. Iron Girl Brigades were comprised largely of unmarried women, thus sidestepping the problem of the multiplying demands on women's time after marriage. In the late 1970s, as China entered the post-Mao reform era, the Iron Girls would become a target for satire and proof that in expecting women to perform the same work as men, the Mao era had violated a "natural" gendered division of labor (see chapter 9).

Finally, women of the Cultural Revolution era could see heroic behavior modeled for them in the eight model operas (and several ballets) created under the sponsorship of Mao's wife, Jiang Qing, whose political power reached a zenith during the Cultural Revolution.[76] These productions were almost invariably set in the pre-1949 era, and in most of them one or more of the main characters were women. The plots usually centered on struggle against cartoonishly cruel Japanese invaders or Chinese class enemies. The heroine of *The White-Haired Girl*, for instance, got her

---

BOX 8.2.
A Sent-Down Youth in the Great Northern Wilderness: Two Vignettes

Most of us did not feel inferior to men in any way at all. Whatever job they could do, we could do too. In fact, we always did it better.

Cutting soybean was probably the most physically demanding work on the farm. We did it only when the fields were drenched with rain and the machines had to stay out. Trudging through mud up to a foot deep, small sickles in our hands, we cut soybeans on ridges that were over a mile long. . . . By the day's end, those who carried off the palm were always some "iron girls."

At first, the men tried to compete with us. After a while they gave up the attempt and pretended that they did not care. Nobody could beat Old Feng, a student from Shanghai. The men nicknamed her "rubber back," because she never stopped to stretch her back no matter how long the ridge was. Her willpower was incredible! After her, there were Huar [a local young woman] and several other formidable "iron girls." Who ever heard of "iron boys" in those years anywhere? In China only "iron girls" created miracles and were admired by all.

A "gigantic counterrevolutionary incident" broke out in Hulin county. Overnight, almost every house in the region was searched and who knows how many poor peasants were implicated. In our village, some fifteen were arrested. My friend Huar and her mother, Ji Daniang, were among them. Their crime was sticking needles into Chairman Mao's face and body. In fact, they did this unintentionally, for in those days Chairman Mao's pictures were all over the newspaper the villagers had always used for wallpaper. So after the women sewed, if they stuck the needles in the wall at the wrong place, poor peasants became active counterrevolutionaries and were shut up in the cow shed for months.

After Huar's arrest, occasionally I saw her from a distance. Neither of us dared to speak to the other. . . . Her face, hands, and clothes were extremely dirty and her hair was a big pancake, filled with lice. As a punishment, the "criminals" were not allowed to wash themselves or comb their hair when they were detained.

Source: Rae Yang, *Spider Eaters: A Memoir* (Berkeley: University of California Press, 1997), 178, 242–43.

---

white hair when she retreated to a cave after she was seized from her family and sexually assaulted by a landlord, emerging later under the protection of the Eighth Route Army to denounce her tormentor. *Red Detachment of Women* was based on the experiences of a unit of women soldiers organized by the Red Army in the early 1930s.

In many of these productions, the awakening political consciousness of the women was guided by male Party secretaries. They modeled correct behavior and offered gentle but stern guidance on what the revolution required, discouraging the women from sudden outbursts and quests for personal vengeance.[77] The message was that women, too, could be revolutionaries—if they could control their emotions and properly channel their energies under the guidance of a politically experienced man. No cultural productions during the Cultural Revolution were set in the present or addressed inequalities that persisted under socialism. The main message they imparted to women was not a new one: class divisions are fundamental, the roots of women's oppression are found in <u>class oppression</u>, the road to emancipation is to work alongside men to make revolution and build socialism.

Even in a situation where the state paid little attention to analyzing or ameliorating gender inequality, however, the lives of rural women improved during the 1970s. Cultural Revolution initiatives to improve education in the countryside, and to deploy minimally trained "barefoot doctors" to broaden the scope of health-care delivery, benefited women. So did the slow spread of rural electrification and the absence of further catastrophic experiments such as the Great Leap Forward. Collective agriculture and small-scale industry managed to keep pace with population growth during this period, a significant achievement. Women earned incomes in the fields and small rural factories. Courtship practices continued to evolve in directions that gave <u>young women more say in pick</u>ing a mate. It continued to become more common for young couples to establish their own households at marriage, with young married women less constrained by their husbands' parents. The most profound improvements in rural women's lives were not produced by the utopianism of the Great Leap vision or the heightened politicization of the Cultural Revolution, but rather by the incremental improvement in productivity and stability at the grassroots level in rural communities.

In 1974, as Mao Zedong's health deteriorated and factions in the top Party leadership jockeyed for control, Mao's wife, Jiang Qing, sponsored a campaign to "criticize Lin Biao and Confucius."[78] Lin Biao was a former close comrade of Mao's, once designated as his successor, who had died in a mysterious plane crash in 1971. Confucius, the sage of antiquity who had already come under serious criticism in the May Fourth Movement of 1919, was widely seen as a proxy figure for Premier Zhou Enlai, who was regarded by Jiang Qing as an enemy and an impediment to her ambition for more political power.

This campaign rooted in intra-Party struggle did more to highlight persistent gender inequality than any other political initiative of the "ten years of chaos." In the course of criticizing Confucius, Party commentators devoted substantial time to the age and gender hierarchies that were embedded in classical Chinese political thought and that persisted in much daily social practice. The campaign raised issues about equal work points, bride prices, the need for collectivized child care and sewing groups, the duty of men to participate in domestic work, and even the possibility of matrilocal marriage.

But this campaign, so closely associated with Jiang Qing, soon foundered. In 1976, Jiang was arrested after Mao's death and put on trial for, among other things, promoting the Cultural Revolution and seizing the opportunity to take revenge on old colleagues in the film industry and the Party whom she felt had opposed her in the past. She was eventually tried, convicted, and held in confinement until her death by suicide in 1991.

The criticisms leveled at Jiang Qing in popular commentary were profoundly gendered, often invoking a saying from imperial times that when a woman seized political power, chaos would result. She was sometimes depicted wearing an imperial crown, or else as a woman's body divided down the middle—one side portrayed in revolutionary army uniform, a style she helped make popular, and the other side garbed in frilly dresses and high heels. The division was meant to signify hypocrisy, discrediting both halves—the woman who tried to seize power like a military man, and the woman who secretly fancied the life of the bourgeoisie while carrying on a violent campaign against people she castigated as bourgeois. Her political concerns were denounced as purely personal, and her assertion at trial that she had acted as "Chairman Mao's dog. I bit whomever he asked me to bite" was widely derided.

The downfall of Jiang Qing was accompanied by a popular rejection of Cultural Revolution models for womanly behavior—militant, active, striving to be as good as a man in a man's domain. An ensemble of mobilizations, slogans, and cultural expressions had been directed at women during the Mao years, encouraging them to be active outside the domestic realm and to understand themselves as equal to men. This discourse was state-initiated, instrumental in its approach to women, and insufficient in its recognition of women's labor and of newly generated inequalities. It was, however, a powerful formulation that shaped the self-perceptions and sense of possibility of many women who were born and came of age in the Mao years. As girls and young women, they did not see gender as an axis of fundamental inequality, difference, or social concern.[79]

The repudiation of the Maoist approach to social transformation intensified during the late 1970s. As the economic reforms began to take shape, the heroic women figures that graced Cultural Revolution posters were replaced by a more complicated, multi-vocal, and contradictory approach to gender.

9

Capitalized Women, 1978–

In the more than four decades since Mao Zedong's death in 1976, China has become a world power and economic powerhouse. The economic reforms initiated by Deng Xiaoping improved material life for virtually all Chinese, even as old forms of inequality deepened and new ones emerged. The reforms set in motion massive changes for women, including but not limited to family size and family relations, work opportunities and workplace discrimination, marriage law and property rights, social expectations and sense of self, and feminism.[1] These changes were shaped by generation, class, and location as well as gender. ⟋ oh!

Reforms began in the late 1970s in the countryside, as the Party-state disbanded collective agriculture and contracted out land to households. Farmers were still officially designated as rural people on their household registration forms (*hukou*), but with the expansion of markets they could now buy grain anywhere and therefore could seek work outside their rural communities. With state encouragement, millions left the countryside in what eventually became "the largest internal migration in human history."[2] Left behind in many villages were middle-aged women and the elderly, who performed farm labor while caring for grandchildren whose parents had migrated out. The press eventually began to refer to rural dwellers as the "386199 work team," referring to the dates for International Women's Day (March 8), Children's Day (June 1), and Seniors' Day (September 9).[3] Some migrants found factory work in newly opened Special Economic Zones that the government set up to attract manufacturing investment in south China. Others filled service and construction jobs in the cities.[4] Women's paid labor was essential to powering the new globally competitive economy emerging along the coast.

Initially, the urban economy changed more slowly, as attempts to reform state-owned industry and enlarge the role of the market were slow to take hold. Literary work and film production flourished, as did discussion of social problems, personal life, and gender roles in a newly expanded press. Inflation and corruption helped spur widespread urban protests in the late 1980s, culminating in violent government suppression of demonstrators in Beijing and other cities on June 4, 1989.

A period of economic stasis followed, but when the reforms resumed with Deng Xiaoping's blessing in 1992, the urban pace of change accelerated. The state retained control over key industries, but thousands of state-owned enterprises were dismantled and reorganized, and large numbers of workers were laid off. Many urban women, still in early middle age, were ejected from the shrinking state sector and found work in small commercial ventures.

Throughout the reform period, the Communist Party has retained control of political life, even as its goals and governing ethos diverged radically from those of the Mao years. The differentiated effects of rapid economic development and state-sponsored capitalist globalization were not evenly distributed. State officials made fortunes participating in new enterprises funded by both domestic and foreign capital. New class groupings proliferated, even as the language of class deployed by the Party-state during the Mao years fell into disuse. By 2010 China's index of income inequality was among the highest in the world,[5] with real estate, investment income, and other forms of new wealth widening the gaps between rich and poor, urban and rural, and men and women.

Beginning in the late 1970s, gender differences that had been minimized or ignored under Mao were named by state authorities and the press as "natural." During the Mao years women had been exhorted to contribute to socialist construction and told, as discussed in the previous chapter, that they could "do everything that men comrades can do." Now they were urged to make themselves attractive, support their men and children at work and school, and help ensure stability in an era of dizzying social change. The gendered effects of the economic reforms were topics of public concern. So was sexuality, within and beyond marriage. And as in every previous era, the proper role of women and the symbolic use of Woman—now as instantiations of China's globalized modernity—engendered comment and contention.

Women's experiences across this period are far too complex for one brief chapter to cover, and so this chapter is limited to exploring four important changes.[6] It begins with the rise and fall of the single-child policy, a state family planning initiative from 1979 to 2015 that had unanticipated and often deleterious consequences for women and children. Over the course of more than three decades, the policy altered China's demographic structure, contributed to major changes in gendered child rearing and notions of the ideal family, and left China with a looming labor, marriage, and elder-care crisis. The chapter then describes the working lives of migrant women who became factory workers, salesclerks, sex workers, and domestic servants. Migration and employment away from home have profoundly affected women's sense of self, desires, and experiences of family life. The chapter turns next to changes in marriage and divorce, particularly in urban areas, exploring changing expectations about women's sexual attractiveness and men's sexual prerogatives. As divorce rates rise, women's relatively weak social claim to joint property has opened a new gendered wealth gap even as urban wealth has grown. The chapter concludes by introducing feminist voices from several generations of women who have identified domains of gender inequality during the reform era.

THE DEMOGRAPHICS OF CHILD REARING

In the early 1970s, before the reform era began, the state introduced a family planning policy known as "later, longer, fewer." Couples were encouraged to start having children later in life, wait longer between births, and reduce the total number of children. In 1979, the state replaced this approach with the much more stringent single-child family policy.[7] In part, the single-child policy reflected the belated recognition that the Chinese population had grown substantially in the Mao years, from almost 542 million in 1949 to more than 975 million by the late 1970s. Officials feared that continued population growth would doom efforts to develop the national economy and raise the standard of living. The policy took total population size as its only relevant datum and was rushed into place without much consideration of overall population structure, acceptability to the public, women's reproductive health, or gender.[8]

Urban people generally accepted the policy and signed single-child pledges. In cities, work units could offer preferred access to housing and day care to compliant families, while docking the salaries and slowing the careers of parents who exceeded the limit. The fact that urban housing stock had not increased appreciably during the Mao years and that urban families with many children were living in extremely crowded conditions reinforced acceptance of the policy.

Over the course of more than three decades after 1979, urban families grew accustomed to the single-child policy, and new child-rearing practices emerged. Families who did well in the reform economy lavished resources on their single children, from piano and martial arts lessons to special tutors. In families where the only child was a girl, parents invested more heavily in her education than they might have if brothers also had had a claim on limited resources. Social commentators worried that with two parents and four grandparents doting on a single child, China was producing a generation of spoiled "little emperors." But single children were also the "only hope" for a family's future financial security and upward mobility. The pressures on such urban children were intense, leading to a reported spike in psychological disorders and rebellious behavior.[9]

In the countryside, in contrast, the new birth-planning policy was resented and sometimes strenuously resisted. Intended to complement the economic reforms, the policy worked at cross-purposes with them instead. As agriculture was decollectivized and households began to contract out land to farm, children took on new economic value. The disintegration of rural collective welfare, minimal as it had been, left aging parents more dependent than ever on their children—and particularly on their sons. Marriage remained patrilocal and exogamous: daughters left home at marriage and contributed their labor to their husbands' families. The economic reforms thus created incentives to strengthen the family as a unit of production by adding sons.

The single-child policy was enforced unevenly in the rural areas, and almost always it was interpreted to allow for a second child if the first one was a girl. In many areas, farmers had a second child even if the first was a son.[10] Nevertheless, local cadres were given birth-planning quotas that they had to meet, just as they had been called upon to meet crop production quotas during the Mao years. The result was social conflict and tragedy.

Birth-planning cadres hectored and coerced women into terminating over-quota pregnancies, often quite late in the process.[11] Conflicts over abortion and sterilization proliferated, and enraged families and communities insulted and sometimes physically attacked birth-planning cadres. The cadres responsible for enforcing birth-planning targets in rural areas often were middle-aged rural women. They had suffered from repeated childbearing and the economic burden of child rearing during the collective era. Many were enthusiastic proponents of the single-child policy. Now they were confronting younger women of childbearing age and their families, who were facing new pressures to strengthen their families as units of agricultural production. Campaigns to implant intrauterine devices in rural women with children resulted in equally determined efforts by women to remove them, at some risk to women's health.[12] Desperate to produce the sons they felt they needed, some families abused women who gave birth to daughters, engaged in female infanticide, or abandoned or gave away their infant girls.[13]

These were unintended consequences of a state campaign to limit births. Planners had not paused to consider how a putatively gender-neutral policy limiting children could result in gender discrimination when it collided with rural economic pressures. Shocked by rural responses, the Women's Federation launched a campaign to protect the legal rights of women and children, and to educate the general public on the fact that the sex of a baby at birth was in fact determined by whether the father's sperm bore an X or a Y chromosome.[14] In 2003, a "Care for Girls" campaign attempted to raise the status of rural girls, sometimes by characterizing them as more gentle and loving than sons. But government propaganda did not address the connection between patrilocal marriage, economic reforms, and son preference.[15]

As medical care grew increasingly sophisticated, instances of infanticide and abandonment gradually decreased. They were replaced by ultrasound screening for the sex of the fetus, which was illegal but widely practiced, and sex-selective abortion. Gender ratios became increasingly lopsided. Normally at about 105 males to 100 females at birth, in China the national ratio of male to female children under fifteen was 108.5:100 in 1990, 113.6:100 in 2000, and 118:100 in 2010.[16]

The widely shared agreement that a son was necessary in rural households, multiplied over millions of individual and family decisions taken against a background of state pressure, resulted in two linked phenomena: "missing girls" and "bare sticks." The "missing girls" were the estimated total shortfall of the female births that could have been expected,

Photo 9.1. Slogan forbidding sex-selection ultrasounds, 2012
Source: Photo by Gail Hershatter.

numbering about forty million in the mid-1990s and forecasted to rise rapidly.[17] The "bare sticks," an echo of the hardships of late imperial and Republican times, were the estimated twenty-four million surplus men who would never be able to marry, given their relative poverty and the shortage of women.[18] But wives remained essential to rural families not only for childbearing, but also for the labor power they provided in agriculture, small family enterprises, and elder care. In the 1980s and 1990s, the press reported on women who were kidnapped and trafficked to other regions of China to be sold as cut-rate brides to men who could otherwise not afford to marry.[19]

The increasing mobility and prosperity of rural people made it more difficult for the state to enforce birth-planning quotas. Many women were away from home working in cities, often for years on end, marrying people from other provinces and evading the inquiries of family planning cadres, in spite of attempts to track them down in the cities. Rural people who stayed at home and made enough money simply paid the fines for having over-quota children.

State writings sometimes referred to the desire for sons as a feudal remnant that somehow had endured in the more "backward" segments of the population. This formulation ignored the ways that household farming and the disintegration of the collective social safety net, both new in the reform era, reinforced the need for sons. Even under these circumstances, rural desires for children did not appear to be unlimited. Rural women spoke of wanting two children: a son to support them in their old age and a daughter for emotional and some financial support. In their view, a daughter would remain attached to her mother even after marrying out, whereas a son would inevitably divide his loyalties and his resources between his mother and his wife.[20]

Their fears were not unfounded. By the 2000s, reports proliferated of rural elder neglect and elder abuse. Even families with many sons often disagreed about how much each person should contribute to the care of aged parents. The Chinese Constitution continued to require that grown children support their parents. But the new economic pressures of the reform era, as well as the trend for couples to form new households rather than co-residing with the husband's parents, meant that this requirement often was ignored or only partially fulfilled, particularly among poorer families. Elderly women and men both needed elder care, but the problem was most acute in the case of poor rural women, who tended to outlive their husbands and had no access to the pensions available to some urban residents.[21]

By the turn of the century, the birth-planning policy was questioned and then vociferously debated in state policy circles as well as in the wider society. Most of the criticisms did not center on the gender discrimination that the policy had provoked. Rather, the prevailing worry was that as the birth rate fell, a decreasing number of people of working age would have to support an increasing number of aged citizens. In the aggregate, an inverted demographic pyramid did not bode well for economic development. In 2013, the government decreed that if one spouse was an only child, a couple should be permitted to have two children. In fall 2015, the policy was modified further, to allow every family to have two children.[22]

It is telling that the immediate urban response to the end of the single-child policy ranged from indifference to dismay. Upwardly mobile couples commented that it was not easy or inexpensive to raise children, and that one child might be all they could afford to provide with child care, safe food (often imported and expensive), extracurricular lessons, and tutoring.[23] Women in particular feared that their in-laws would pressure them to have a second child, adding years to their double-day burden, or else postponing their return to paid employment and consigning them to an existence shaped by domestic demands.[24] A questionnaire about women's fertility desires circulated in 2017 outlined the calculations clearly. Among the reasons men and women respondents could choose for wanting a second child were

> [I] like children, want a boy/girl, spouse's request, relieve the pressure of eldercare on one's children, possess the economic conditions to support a second child, [a sibling] will benefit the children's physical and mental health and development, and benefit for the household's stability.

The reasons arrayed against having a second child included

> [I] don't like too many children, birthing a child is painful and don't want to suffer again, fear I will be partial [to one child over another] and that will not be beneficial to the child's health and development, raising children is too much trouble and I don't have time, economic conditions don't permit it and the burden is too heavy, will influence the woman's work and professional development, colleagues and friends all don't want a second child.[25]

The questions, like much of the press coverage about the policy, suggest that within a generation, the single-child policy, combined with other changes in Chinese society, had altered desires about family size in economically advantaged households.

Whether because of rural outmigration, or because desires in the countryside were changing as well, rural families also were not rushing to take on the economic burden of additional children. By early 2018, billboards urged rural families to have second children, and instructed local officials to encourage them to do so. One declared, "Letting everyone in the village have a second child is the unshirkable duty of the village Party branch secretary" (see photo 9.2).

Photo 9.2.   Everyone must have two children, 2018
Source: Photo courtesy of Rebecca Karl and Qian Zhu.

OUT OF THE VILLAGE: FACTORY WORKERS, SALESCLERKS, SEX WORKERS, AND DOMESTIC SERVANTS

In April 2017, a forty-four-year-old woman became an overnight literary celebrity for her autobiographical web essay "I am Fan Yusu."[26] The youngest of five children in a poor rural Hubei family, Fan Yusu grew up reading novels. She longed to "walk barefoot to the end of the world."

Her indomitable mother, for four decades the local village women's chair, struggled to secure her children's health and future with little success. Fan's two sisters had serious physical disabilities. One brother became a bitter failed writer, the other a small-time official and gambling addict. Fan's essay describes her decision to leave the village to seek work in Beijing, her life there as a waitress and domestic worker, her brief marriage to another migrant, her struggles as a single mother of two, and the many forms of injustice she observed in her travels.

Fan Yusu left the countryside twice, and each time she was reminded that girls had less status in her home village than boys. The first time, at age twelve, she ran away to explore Hainan Island for three months. On her return she discovered that the villagers regarded her absence as scandalous; she learned that she had "hurt my virtue and shamed my family." To stop the gossip, her family hastily bundled her off to a teaching job in another village. A few years later, Fan left rural Hubei again, this time for Beijing, where she found work, married, and had two daughters. But when she subsequently left her violent alcoholic husband and went back to her village with her children in tow, she found that if a girl was not free to wander, a married woman was not free to return. Her oldest brother regarded her as a potential threat to his claim on the family's land and resources. Her mother's political convictions and years of experience as a women's chair were of no help in the face of local assumptions about patrilocality and property. Fan Yusu realized that she was now "merely a passer-by in the village where I was raised." She took her two children back to Beijing, rented them a room where she could visit them periodically, and found work as a live-in nanny.

Fan Yusu was part of the great migration of rural people to China's cities that began in the early 1980s and intensified in the 1990s. By the turn of the millennium, one hundred million people were working as migrants away from their places of origin. By 2015, the number had grown to an estimated 282 million, comprising more than one-third of China's workforce.[27] Migrants became the backbone of manufacturing in both foreign- and Chinese-controlled enterprises, as well as the construction workers, vendors, street sweepers, and domestic servants who made the urban economy run.[28] About 40 percent of rural migrants were women, often referred to as *dagongmei*, or "working younger sisters."[29]

Rural migrant workers generally found low-skilled jobs that paid little, required long hours, offered no job security, and lacked adequate safety conditions. Without urban household registration, they remained second-class citizens in the cities, with limited access to housing, health care, and schools. Municipal governments could, and did, expel them periodically. Nevertheless, new migrant neighborhoods grew in many Chinese cities.

Photo 9.3. Migrant women at Shanghai railroad station, ca. 2017
Source: Reuters/Aly Song

Women migrants regarded the village life they had left as narrow and constraining. As Fan Yusu put it, "I couldn't bear to stay in the countryside and view the sky from the bottom of a well."[30] Some chafed at the marriage plans their parents had for them; many dreamed of becoming entrepreneurs or white-collar workers and leaving rural life behind permanently.[31] In the Special Economic Zones, women mainly found employment in apparel, electronics, and toy manufacture, industries where they were more than 70 percent of the workforce.[32] They also predominated in retail and hotel work, sex work, and domestic service. Women migrants earned only 72 percent of what men migrants did, and all migrants were paid less than full-time urban employees, but women nonetheless continued to migrate.[33]

The manufacturing zones such as those in the Pearl River Delta cities of Shenzhen and Dongguan resembled many other areas of the world where capital sought low-cost labor. "Factory girls" worked long hours at repetitive tasks. Manufacturing work could be dangerous. Workers who produced electronic good or batteries were exposed to toxic chemicals. Companies fiercely resisted workers' demands that they be compensated for damage to their health.[34] Women often were required to work compulsory—and illegal—overtime, fined for infractions of dress codes and behavior rules, sexually harassed, and restricted in how often they could go to the toilet.[35] Women workers at Foxconn, a major producer of Apple electronics and China's largest industrial employer with about one million workers, reported frequent rituals of humiliation:

A girl is forced to stand at attention to read aloud a statement of self-criticism. She must be loud enough to be heard. Our line leader would ask if the worker at the far end of the workshop could hear clearly the mistake she has made. Oftentimes girls feel they are losing face. It's very embarrassing. Her tears drop. Her voice becomes very small.[36]

The only housing option for women in the larger factories was to live six or twelve people to a room in dormitories that kept women workers under employer control even after their shifts ended. The factory dormitories also fostered information networks about alternative job opportunities and occasionally became sites of labor protest.[37]

If they left their jobs without permission, workers forfeited a substantial deposit required by the factory. Nevertheless, young women changed jobs and cell phone numbers frequently, seeking new skills, upward mobility, and the chance to shed their rural appearance and remake themselves as respected urban dwellers.[38] Larger factories generally hired women in their late teens and early twenties, with the expectation that they would leave the factory workforce by their late twenties. Many, however, did not return to the villages but took jobs in smaller-scale enterprises that

Photo 9.4.   Women factory workers, 2005
Source: © Edward Burtynsky, courtesy Metivier Gallery, Toronto/Weinstein Gallery, Minneapolis

subcontracted work from larger factories or directly from marketers. Migrants often married other migrants, sometimes from faraway provinces. Gradually, these new families became urbanized, although they were not eligible for many urban benefits and suffered intermittent abuse from the authorities. Sometimes their children were sent home to be raised by grandparents, and sometimes they grew up in the cities, with no farming skills and no experience of village life. When these second-generation migrants came of working age and entered factories in the late 1990s and 2000s, they objected to their continued exclusion from full urban residence and the consequent sense of being neither farmer nor worker.[39]

Factory work was not the only employment niche in the urban labor market. Women service workers in retail establishments, hotels, and restaurants were often referred to as "eating from the rice bowl of youth" or "eating spring rice"—that is, trading on their youthful attractiveness. At work they were taught how to look like city girls, eagerly adopting an aesthetic that concealed their rural origins.[40] Women service workers conveyed class distinctions through their mode of dress. In one study of Harbin, the middle-aged saleswomen in a state-owned department store that catered to working-class customers were not required to be attractive or attentive. The small-scale clothing vendors in a bargain basement wore layers of makeup and a come-hither look, drawing caustic comments about their supposed lack of virtue. The shop attendants in an upscale cashmere sweater boutique were invariably young and attractive. Fellow workers instructed them on how to select the correct bra, tone their buttock muscles, express deference, and appear stylish but not excessively seductive, the better to attract upscale customers.[41]

High-end hotels enforced similar protocols. In daily employee gatherings, managers exhorted women hotel workers to present themselves as paragons of feminine attentiveness, utterly attuned to the habits and needs of each guest.[42] For these women, careful cultivation of youthful beauty and appropriate comportment became a job requirement, a form of labor discipline, an entry point to urban modernity, and a means of self-expression.[43]

Another way to eat from the rice bowl of youth was to work as a bar girl, escort, masseuse, or streetwalker.[44] Each of these jobs involved some combination of companionship and services (massage, drinks, dancing) and often entailed the exchange of sex for money, although remuneration and working conditions varied widely. It appears that rural migrant women predominated in the sexual service sector, many finding it preferable to the exhausting, tedious, and potentially dangerous demands of factory labor.[45] Some women were trafficked from villages into prostitution with the promise of waitressing or other jobs, whereas others chose to sell sexual services; some worked as independent agents and others were

Photo 9.5. Bar hostesses at a nightclub in Jishou, Hunan, 2005
Source: Photograph by Rian Dundon. Used by permission of photographer.

controlled and coerced by madams and pimps who took a substantial cut of their earnings. All were vulnerable to violent treatment by customers and police, and to sexually transmitted diseases.[46]

National law decreed that prostitutes could be fined or detained for up to fifteen days, sentenced to reform through education for six months to two years, and in cases of recidivism sent for labor reeducation for up to three years.[47] And yet, in spite of periodic arrests of prostitutes and their customers in the course of campaigns to "strike hard" at crime, the 1990s and 2000s saw a steady persistence of sex work. One estimate, almost certainly a serious undercount, placed the number of sex workers nationwide at six million in 2000.[48] Women solicited long-distance haulers at truck stops, systematically phoned hotel rooms each night propositioning guests, worked at hair salons and massage parlors where no haircuts or massages were offered, accompanied foreign and Chinese businessmen to sing at karaoke bars and dance at nightclubs, and staffed elite escort services.[49] In Sipsongpanna, a minority ethnic area in the southwest where domestic tourism was developing, migrant Han women dressed in local minority costumes to give male Han customers an authentic-looking exotic experience.[50] High-end sexual service providers, some with college degrees and the means to pay for cosmetic surgery, sought extended intimate relationships with elite men and expats working in industrial investment zones. Some developed online subscription services so that customers could converse with them or view strip shows on WeChat, Skype, and other apps.[51]

Police had considerable leeway in enforcing antiprostitution laws, a situation that easily could lead to extortion.[52] An extensive national crackdown in 2010 drove sexual service providers to stay out of sight, letting only known customers into the karaoke halls or hair salons where they operated, switching venues and working hours frequently. This made it more difficult for HIV/STI prevention workers to contact them. Many women avoided using condoms during police campaigns, fearful that possession could be used as evidence against them. This also increased their health risks.[53]

Adopting terminology from a global debate, some scholars proposed that those who sold sexual services should be regarded as sex workers (*xing gongzuozhe*). But this term did not seem quite right to the women that sociologist Ding Yu interviewed in the Pearl River Delta in the first decade of the twenty-first century. The term "sex workers," they said, failed to convey that what they were providing was a complicated mix of sex, companionship, and emotional support. And if what they did was "work," they demanded to know, why was it not legal, with guaranteed hours and wages and benefits?

The women told Ding Yu that they preferred to be called *xiaojie*, a term sometimes translated as "Miss." Before 1949, xiaojie had been used as a polite form of address for unmarried women from well-off families, but it was regarded as bourgeois in the Mao years and then was revivified in the reform era as a derogatory term for prostitutes. To these women, however, xiaojie was a term of respect. They saw themselves as engaged in the pursuit of a modern identity that could bring autonomy, personal transformation, and in some cases erotic and emotional fulfillment.[54]

Nonetheless, women who provided commercialized sexual services also expressed some ambivalence about their situation. They observed that they had no other good choices for supporting themselves and avoided telling their families what they did.[55] They felt that they should be entitled to legal protection. Some asserted that they were contributing to the stability of their clients' marriages by fulfilling sexual needs that were not being met at home.[56] Sexologist and social theorist Li Yinhe echoed their arguments that consensual adult prostitution should be decriminalized, adding that prostitution would only decrease when women had access to adequate job training and social services.[57]

Another employment option, available to middle-aged as well as younger women, was domestic work in a private household.[58] In 2015 domestic workers comprised 11 percent of the migrant workforce. Women predominated in this sector, working for upper- and middle-class families as nannies, cleaners, cooks, elder-care providers, and all-round assistants.

Frequently they lived in the homes of their employers. In return for free housing, they were required to be on call virtually all of the time.

For some, the attraction of living in close proximity to urban families was that they could observe and adopt urban life practices. Domestic workers moved as quickly as they could to buy fashionable clothes and lighten their skin by shielding it from the sun. They avoided speaking their local dialects in public, so as not to betray their rural origins. In training classes for domestic workers, and through direct instruction from their employers, maids learned to dress neatly but not too provocatively.[59]

The desire of rural migrants to look, act, and become urban was reinforced by a government-initiated effort in the 1990s and 2000s to raise the "quality" (*suzhi*) of the Chinese population. Suzhi encompassed everything from educational level and economic self-reliance to personal bodily comportment. Urban Chinese were generally thought to have higher suzhi than rural people.[60] Raising one's suzhi was a personal responsibility as well as a shared social goal, and those who failed to attend to the process of self-improvement were commonly decried as a drag on national progress.

But work as a nanny or maid also enabled rural women to take an intimate look at urban families, giving rise to critical commentary. Was it really necessary, one maid wondered, for her employer to search her luggage as she left for another job, implying that she must be a thief?[61] And was it really desirable, Fan Yusu asked, to become the mistress of a wealthy man, like the beautiful young woman whose child Fan cared for? Fan watched her employer sitting on the sofa late at night, fully made up "like an imperial concubine from a Palace drama," waiting for her patron to come home. Was this, she wondered, a stable situation?[62] In such shrewd observations, domestic workers provided trenchant, if indirect, commentary on the suzhi question.[63]

By the mid-2010s, not all women migrants were eating from the rice bowl of youth. The number of migrant workers over forty years of age rose steadily.[64] Some migrant women sought to remain in cities indefinitely, opening small businesses of their own.[65] Other women encountered conflict with their husbands or in-laws when they did return to their home villages.[66]

In any case, those villages were beginning to disappear. As cities and county towns expanded into the surrounding countryside and expropriated village land, the remaining rural residents typically were relocated into high-rise apartments in return for a one-time cash payment. Often the terms were not satisfactory, and farmers who still lived on the land resisted. Fan Yusu's octogenarian mother suffered a dislocated shoulder when security guards handled her roughly at a protest about the expropriation of village land.

Increasingly rural migrants had no home to return to, and the limited safety net provided by their small rural plots no longer sustained
them when urban employers defaulted on their wages or laid them off.
But their rural household registration, and the pervasive discourse that
categorized rural people as inferior in suzhi, continued to render them
contingent and vulnerable dwellers in the cities.

Migrant women with children faced difficult choices. Many migrants
took their children back to their home villages to be raised by grandparents, returning to see them once or twice a year. In 2013, a national
Women's Federation survey based on the 2010 census estimated that
sixty-one million children had been left behind in the countryside—more
than 20 percent of China's children and 38 percent of all village children.[67]
The long-term separation of migrant parents and left-behind children has
engendered literature and films about parental heartache and problems
with left-behind children ranging from alienation to cognitive delays.[68]

Migrant children who stayed with their parents in the cities, however,
were subject to the vagaries of local policies that determined what services they were permitted to access. Their number in 2010 was estimated
at 35.8 million.[69] In some places they could attend local schools only if
there was space and their parents paid steep tuition. In other places they
had the option of attending makeshift private schools of widely varying
quality that were organized specifically for migrant children by migrant
communities or social welfare agencies.[70] When Fan Yusu began work as
a live-in nanny, she rented a room for her two daughters in Beijing, even
though her work only permitted her to visit them once a week. Her older
daughter apparently did not attend school at all but taught herself to read
by looking at the subtitles on television shows. Fan Yusu then provided
her with a steady supply of novels picked up at flea markets and paper-
recycling stations. The daughter went to work at fourteen, and by twenty
she had secured a white-collar position. Fan's younger daughter did manage to attend school episodically. In Beijing, neither child was able to live
consistently with Fan.

COURTSHIP, MARRIAGE, DIVORCE, AND REAL ESTATE

Public discussion in the early reform years turned energetically to
personal life. Portrayals of feminine adornment and sexually enticing
images filled the pages of popular magazines and dominated the re-
emergent sector of advertising.[71] Personal life and individual desires—
particularly with respect to dating, marriage, and aspirational patterns
of consumption—engendered enthusiastic discussion in the press and
on television.[72] Parental control of marriage choice was no longer a tar-

get of criticism: if not completely a thing of the past, it had been weakened considerably during the Mao years. In both city and countryside, younger women—as daughters and daughters-in-law—gradually had gained more leverage over matters that used to be left to the older generation, including mate choice. New imperatives entered into the public discussion of marriage, including sex appeal, mutual compatibility, emotional support, material aspirations, and property ownership.[73] As the reforms began to commodify social life, public discussion shifted to the question of what sort of spouse was desirable and how a woman should choose—and keep—a man.

The beauty industry grew exponentially to become the fifth largest consumer goods sector by the early 2000s. It was aimed at young unmarried women who competed in beauty pageants and modeling contests, as well as married women who became eager consumers of cosmetics, beauty salon services, and cosmetic surgery, sometimes with the explicitly stated aim of retaining the loyalty of their husbands. The Miss Plastic Surgery Pageant of 2004 named finalists aged seventeen to sixty-two, promoting the message that it was natural to pursue beauty, here understood as freedom from wrinkles and body fat, regardless of one's age.[74]

Not all of the public discussion of sexuality was about maintaining attractiveness to potential or current husbands. Some discussions began to focus on women's active desires and sexual pleasure, departing from the Mao-era characterization of women as primarily passive and responsive to men's sexual initiatives.[75] Same-sex desire was acknowledged in sexological discourse, and communities of lesbians became visible (though somewhat less visible than gay men) on internet sites, in activist groups, and in bars and other social venues. Lively discussions circulated about whether global categories of gay identity were appropriate to the local situation, and how they might be reconfigured or discarded.[76]

But in a society where premarital and nonmarital sex were becoming increasingly common, state authorities in the reform era opted to promote heterosexual marriage and household formation energetically.[77] Government officials were apparently concerned that the quality (suzhi) of the population would decline if educated and affluent women decided to postpone or opt out of childbearing, and that social stability depended in part on men being able to afford to marry. Marriage and childbearing were portrayed as essential components of the "harmonious society" that state authorities began to promote in 2004.[78]

One result was a state campaign beginning in 2007 directed at "leftover women"—a disdainful term that was particularly odd in light of the numerical predominance of men in the aftermath of the birth-planning policy.[79] China's rate of marriage for women was about 98 percent, high by world standards.[80] But women were warned—on the Women's Federation website as well as in popular media—that if they postponed marriage past the age of twenty-seven, they would become like "yellowed pearls."[81] News coverage stigmatized single women for their unmarried status, emphasizing conflicts with their families as well as their failure to fulfill societal and state expectations.[82] Professional matchmaking agencies, many of which operated online dating sites, ceaselessly promoted the idea that marriage was a required feature of adulthood and a particularly urgent matter for women in their late twenties.[83] The 2015 TV New Year's Gala, perhaps the most-watched show in China, featured a skit in which a "goddess" (pretty woman) was contrasted with a "manly lady" who was having trouble attracting suitors.[84] And the message apparently found a receptive audience among many women: a national survey in 2010 found almost half of women respondents agreed that "a good marriage is better than a career," up ten percentage points from ten years earlier.[85]

Anxious middle-class parents in Shanghai frequented a weekend matchmaking corner in People's Park, advertising the virtues of their grown children, most of whom were educated women.[86] Advice columnists on the online messaging service Weibo and the social media platform WeChat addressed themselves to large followings of unmarried women looking for the right man.[87] Women were chided in the press for being so demanding and materialistic that they failed to recognize men with excellent character, high ideals, and the capacity for hard work. Often criticized was the line delivered by a woman on the televised dating show *If You Are the One* that she would "rather cry in the back of a BMW than smile on the back of a bicycle."[88]

On the show, women were required to answer certain questions about their romantic history, family background, housework abilities, and ideal marital relationship. Male contestants were invited to describe the sort of woman they wanted, producing monologues such as this one from June 2013:

> My favorite woman resembles a Z4 model, having the best functions with the most reasonable price. Like the surface of my car, my woman is fashionable yet without being overbearing. . . . That means it is of great importance that she does housework well . . . Dating a girlfriend feels like driving a car. . . . I expect that in our future life, the woman will make decisions over trivial matters while I control the steering wheel and decide which main direction to go.

In the end, *If You Are the One* did not emphasize a woman's ability to choose her likely suitor. A male contestant who garnered a certain level of approval from the show's panel of women won an international trip and could choose which of the women he wanted to date.[89]

Even as the popular press criticized women's purported greed, it also promoted the expectation that a "real man" should be wealthier, more

makes no sense

educated, and more accomplished than his spouse—leading to many jokes about the unmarriageability of precisely the educated women that state authorities were most eager to see marry. One persistent joke named three genders: men, women, and women with a graduate degree. Only the first two were conventionally regarded as marriageable.[90]

As criteria for marriage choice shifted in the reform era, so did the practices surrounding divorce. In 1980, a new Marriage Law was issued for the first time since 1950. It reiterated most of the principles of the earlier law and raised the minimum marriage age to twenty-two for men and twenty for women, in line with the campaign to limit births. But perhaps the most noteworthy change in the law was a new criterion for divorce: alienation of affection. During the Mao years, petitions for divorce frequently had resulted in years of mediation and even official pressure to remain married. The new law stated that if mediation failed, the courts should grant a divorce.[91]

Whether the law changed social practice or merely reflected it, the incidence of divorce began to rise. Beginning in 2003, couples no longer needed permission of their employers or village leadership to divorce, and the majority of divorces were registered with the local Civil Affairs Bureau rather than going through the courts.[92] The number of divorces nationally soared to 4.8 million in 2016, a tenfold increase over the 1980 total. In the 2010s, in large cities, the ratio of divorces to new marriages was more than one to three.[93]

Behind these statistics were a host of social changes that tended to disadvantage women. From the late 1970s official sources, the popular press, and even comedy routines opined that gender differences were rooted in biology and that assigning gender-inappropriate work to women would be injurious to their health.[94] At several points during the 1980s, economists and sociologists recommended that women should exit the paid labor force and return home, freeing up jobs for men and providing much-needed (but unremunerated) domestic support.[95] During the reform era, many jobs specified that only men need apply; gender discrimination in hiring, promotion, and layoffs was not regarded as a problem.[96] Commenting on the small proportion of women on corporate boards and in senior executive positions at both private and state-owned companies, one Chinese feminist commented, "There is a glass ceiling here too, but most women never even get off the sticky floor."[97]

The situation was similar in Party leadership positions. More than a quarter of the almost ninety million CCP members nationwide were women in 2017, and women were almost a quarter of the representatives to the National People's Congress, not all of whom were in the Party.[98] But women's representation was scarcer at top Party levels. No woman has ever sat on the seven-person Politburo Standing Committee; the twenty-five-person Politburo in 2017 included two women before the nineteenth Party Congress, reduced to one woman after the Congress; 4.9 percent of the Party's Central Committee members in 2017 were women (a total of ten), down from 6.4 percent five years earlier. Women were only two of sixty-two top provincial leaders (party secretaries and governors), the ranks from which most top central officials were drawn.[99]

Across the reform era, women's labor force participation fell, propelled by layoffs in state enterprises, the falling prestige of state enterprise factory jobs, the rise of the urban rich, and changing portrayals of women's role. In 1990 more than three-quarters of women were employed; by 2010, the rate had fallen to just above 60 percent.[100] In urban families, it became more common for women to stay home after they married, or to change jobs based on whether their labor was needed at home rather than to advance their careers, as men did.[101] Raising children and managing the household—including, in many families, supervising household servants—remained chiefly a woman's responsibility.[102]

In an uncanny echo of Ding Ling's 1942 essay "Thoughts on March 8," advice literature in women's magazines, as well as radio shows, call-in hotlines, and the 2004 hit television show *Chinese-Style Divorce*, all cautioned wives that they needed to work on remaining interesting and attractive to their husbands. The middle-aged woman protagonist of *Chinese-Style Divorce*, a woman who resigns from her job in order to care full-time for her son, is portrayed as an unattractive, hectoring spouse. She attempts to rely on public shaming rather than self-development in order to prevent her husband from divorcing her.[103]

Much discussion in advice columns and television shows centered on perilous situations in which wives might lose the interest of their husbands. Entertainment venues expanded in the reform era, and it became common for men in the course of after-work socializing to consort with karaoke girls and sexual service workers. As married men earned more money, wives were warned, they might attract the attention of younger women and become vulnerable to their wiles.[104] Debates about divorce often focused on the question of infidelity, reportedly a factor in about one-third of cases. Younger women were excoriated as the "third parties" or "Little Third" who broke up otherwise stable marriages.[105]

By the 2010s a new profession had emerged: the "mistress dispeller," a private investigator hired by wives whose husbands were having affairs. The dispeller's assignment was to persuade, threaten, or discredit the mistress in a way that would leave the marriage intact. Mistress-dispeller companies also offered counseling services to economically well-off wives, advising them on how to modify their behavior so that they would remain attractive to their husbands, or at least retain their loyalty.[106]

The Republican Civil Code of 1930 and the Marriage Law of 1950 had been controversial in part because they made it easier for women to divorce. But by the early twenty-first century, wives were well aware that they would suffer disproportionately if their marriages broke up. The gender wage gap continued to grow with privatization, with the ratio of women's to men's wages dropping from 84 percent to 74 percent between 1995 and 2007, and to 67.3 percent in 2010.[107] Women were more likely to be laid off first as unprofitable state enterprises shed employees and privatized. Many women then entered the informal labor market and worked part-time.[108] Even women who retained their state jobs were expected to retire at fifty, while men worked until sixty, and so women's savings and pension payments tended to be lower than those of men.[109] Women's prospects of remarriage, at any age, were more unlikely. As one mistress dispeller put it, "In today's world, a secondhand woman is like a secondhand car. Once it's been driven, it's not worth a fraction of its original selling price." A divorced man on the marriage market, in contrast, was like a choice piece of real estate: "The value only appreciates."[110]

Divorcing women were economically vulnerable in new ways because of the changing importance of real estate.[111] During the Mao years, most urban housing had been a welfare benefit provided through the work unit in exchange for a nominal rent. Even then, divorce had created housing problems: because housing usually was assigned through the husband's work unit, a divorced wife often found herself without a place to live, or staying with her former spouse in a tiny living space divided by a makeshift partition. The problem sharpened considerably with reform-era changes in the urban real estate market. Beginning in the late 1990s, work unit housing was sold off to its residents at relatively low prices. By 2005 China had become the world's largest society of homeowners.[112] Then the value of urban real estate rose sharply in the mid-2000s, as urban development projects razed old housing and replaced it with new high-rises of expensive apartments.[113]

In a booming economy with very few lucrative outlets for investment, buying a home became one of the major ways that a family could increase its assets, and many did so repeatedly, trading up to ever grander homes. An estimated 60–85 percent of urban residents owned their own homes, and by 2013 the aggregate value of residential real estate was estimated at more than $30 trillion. Real estate became the main form of personal wealth. With soaring prices, an urban home could cost fifteen to twenty-two times a buyer's annual income.[114] Because few young people could afford to buy homes, parents made substantial contributions to their children's purchases of real estate.[115]

But here women were at a disadvantage. In buying a home for a new couple it was customary, following long-standing marriage practices, for a man's family to finance part or all of the purchase of the structure, whereas a woman and her family took responsibility for internal walls, fixtures, paint, and appliances.[116] In popular understanding, the man was buying the house, even when the internal construction was extremely expensive. In most cases only the man's name appeared on the deed. This was true even when the wife and her parents contributed to the down payment—which could happen if they had more available capital. It remained the case even if the woman contributed to the mortgage and residential upkeep after marriage.[117]

The assumption that housing was a man's responsibility—and his possession—was widely shared. In some instances, urban parents of a daughter preferred to contribute their resources to the purchase of a house by a male cousin or other more distant relative, even when the daughter was their only child.[118] Few young women insisted that their name be on the property deed, particularly if their own parents did not support the idea. Further, because joint bank accounts were not common in China, a woman's contributions to ongoing housing expenses, if they were funneled first into her husband's account, were not likely to be well documented.

Why did urban women, many highly educated and lucratively employed, find it acceptable that their husbands should appear as the sole owner on property deeds? Many believed that marriage required a house—and that women should decline to marry a man who could not provide one. People who got married without acquiring a house were referred to as entering a "naked marriage." Real estate developers and brokers supported the idea that homeownership was necessary to family formation.[119]

A woman's lack of formal claim to the main form of household wealth soon became a problem. In 2001, amendments to the 1980 Marriage Law clarified which sorts of property should be regarded as jointly owned and which individually owned.[120] In 2003, the Supreme People's Court interpreted the law to mean that gifts made to a child before a marriage—for instance, funds for a house—were the property of that child alone, rather than becoming joint marital property.[121] In 2011, the court issued a further interpretation of the law, holding that property purchased by parents for a child even after marriage and registered in that child's name would be considered as that child's separate property.[122]

As with the family planning policy, a law that on its face was gender neutral had profoundly gendered effects. The interpretation contained a number of ameliorating phrases, but its net effect was to buttress the man's claim to real estate and put the burden of proving joint contributions—

often not well documented within households—on the woman.[123] In a contested divorce, a wife could find herself without access to the marital household's main share of wealth. This produced a growing gender gap in wealth accumulation, even among the most privileged women residents.[124]

In rural areas, a separate property crisis for women was unfolding.[125] At the beginning of the reform period, land-use rights were redistributed from the collective to households, who contracted to farm the land for a given number of years. In an effort to induce farmers to make long-term investments in cultivation, over time the state lengthened the duration of the contracts, from three to thirty and then fifty years, and limited the number of adjustments that could be made in ownership when a household added or lost members.

In theory, rural women had land rights, but in practice the head of the household, usually the father, controlled those rights. When a daughter married and moved to her husband's village, her land share remained with her natal family. Selling her individual share at marriage in order to buy land elsewhere would have meant shrinking her natal family's landholdings. For a newly married woman, acquiring a land share in her marital village was a long and uncertain process, because it meant further dividing the shares of that village. This problem became most acute for women who divorced and were then left without land in either village. Land rights did not reflect the fact that women continued to perform a substantial proportion of agricultural labor.[126]

The problem of rural women's property claims persisted even as the property itself began to disappear. During the reform era, cities and county towns expropriated property in surrounding villages in order to expand and develop. Payments for such property generally went to heads of household, who were overwhelmingly male. The assumption that men had primary claims on family assets left unmarried daughters and divorced women at a disadvantage but was not generally disputed in rural communities. Even as these communities became urbanized, gendered disparities in property ownership persisted and even widened.[127]

It was common in state publications to criticize gender discrimination as a "feudal remnant"—a vestige of older thinking and practices held by rural people who stubbornly refused to modernize. But in the case of rural access to land and payouts for land, this was not entirely accurate. Women were not always regarded as citizens of a particular village at least in part because the state itself had never challenged the practice of patrilocality, either during the marriage reforms of the Mao years or in the reform period.[128] Most rural communities still were organized around networks of male kin, with men as permanent community members and women marrying in and out. This made it likely that control of rural assets would remain in male hands and that new forms of gender inequality would appear, even as the property regime underwent major changes and the villagers themselves were relocated to apartment blocks.

FEMINIST VOICES

As we have seen, previously unaddressed forms of gender inequality persisted during the reform era and new ones emerged. Nevertheless, gender became a prominent feature of a number of social controversies and critiques, even while class as an analytical category was downplayed or repudiated.[129] In the process, the Women's Federation became less of a transmission belt for government policy than it had been in the Mao years, and periodically assumed a somewhat more activist role as an advocate for women's interests. At the same time, new feminist voices began to emerge outside the Party-state apparatus.

Women who were critical of the changes in women's situation under the reforms usually did not call themselves feminists, for at least three reasons. First, "feminism" had long been modified by the adjective "bourgeois," a legacy of CCP theorizing during the Republican era. Party organizers held that to focus on gender equality was to neglect the more fundamental class inequality that structured society, and this approach shaped the policies of the Mao years as well. In the early years of the post-Mao reforms, the term "feminism" retained a suspect quality, tainted by the implication of bad class politics and subservience to cultural imperialism. Second, the standard statements about women during the Mao years asserted that men and women already had achieved equality as political subjects and laborers, implying that no further agitation was required and rendering some forms of gender inequity invisible. And third, by the early years of the reform era, the Women's Federation was widely regarded as a bureaucratic, unresponsive, and generally ineffectual organization.[130] Nevertheless, beginning in the 1980s and accelerating during the 1990s, Federation officials, women intellectuals, legal scholars, and activists began to use the terms "women's studies," "research on women," and "feminism," rendered in several different ways.

During the reform years, the Women's Federation attempted to address emergent problems concerning the status of women. Federation writers developed a concept they called the "Marxist theory of women." Its content was not at all fixed, but it allowed them to remind the Party of its historical commitment to women's liberation.[131] Federation officials agreed that women's work assignments should be adjusted to conform to their physiological needs, but also vigorously opposed proposals that women leave the workforce. They continued to support free-choice marriage but opposed easing controls on divorce for fear that this would reward men who had affairs and would economically disadvantage their discarded wives.[132] They sought to limit government sponsorship of beauty contests but also promoted beauty salons as sites of re-employment for women who were laid off from state-owned enterprises.[133]

Federation voices, long the only authorized source of pronouncements about women, soon were joined by voices outside the Party-state. In 1985, literary scholar Li Xiaojiang formed the Association for Women's Studies in Henan, which was followed by the creation of similar groups at many universities and the opening of a women's hotline.[134] Li argued that in the Mao years the standard of achievement had remained male, and that the form women's liberation had taken—mobilization for paid productive labor—had left women with a double burden. Woman, she argued, had to be treated as a gendered subject, different in nature from man. Women's problems could not be described completely by referring to class categories. In Li's view, because women's liberation had been formulated and bestowed by the Party-state, and implemented by the Women's Federation, women never had considered what their own interests might be or how best to achieve them. The urgent task facing women, she said, was to develop their own consciousness.[135] Li and other scholars—as well as many researchers working within the Women's Federation—went on to develop the nascent field of women's studies in China in the 1980s, addressing history, literature, and the emergence of new forms of gender inequality under the reforms.[136]

In summer 1995, China hosted the UN Fourth World Conference on Women and its associated forum for nongovernmental organizations (NGOs). The suppression of the 1989 Tian'anmen demonstrations had drawn condemnation worldwide, and hosting the Women's Conference was an important move back onto the transnational stage. More than forty thousand feminist activists arrived in China. Although state authorities moved the nongovernmental forum to a distant suburb of Beijing amid rumors that lesbians were planning a naked parade through the city center, they also actively promoted the participation of Chinese women from the Women's Federation and new nongovernmental organizations in the meetings. They also encouraged the development of research on women within the Federation, universities, and nongovernmental organizations.[137]

For Chinese women activists, preparing for the forum created a political space in which to develop national networks, introduce new topics such as domestic violence, participate in meetings abroad, and engage in exchanges with feminists outside of China.[138] This process was legitimized under the slogan *jiegui*—to connect the tracks, joining China to the rest of the world, in this case explicitly along feminist lines.[139]

Soon after the forum's conclusion, the Chinese government announced a comprehensive program aimed at improving women's political participation, economic conditions, educational opportunities, and general welfare. Subsequent action programs also pledged to incorporate consideration of gender into the state policy-making process.[140] Feminism, detached from the negative connotations of "bourgeois feminism," became a recognized national discourse with substantial global connections. The term "gender," translated as *shehui xingbie* or "social sex difference," called attention to the social production of "natural" difference and inequality.[141]

By the 2000s, Chinese feminists were exploring how they might participate in a transnational feminist network without ceding all powers of definition to Western theories. They discussed how feminism could be "indigenized," or made most responsive to local circumstances, taking account of the ongoing involvement of the Women's Federation and the Party-state, while also maintaining a critical edge about the causes of gender inequality.[142] Such debates took place mainly in academic settings. A recurrent subject of discussion was how to address the problems faced by women workers, former workers, farmers, prostitutes, and others whose lives had been deeply shaped by globalizing processes and Chinese state policies during the reform era.[143]

One important effect of the 1995 conference and the discussions that followed was the slow codification of domestic violence as a social and legal category. The 1992 Law on Protection of Women's Rights and Interests had criticized ill treatment of women, but without providing legal penalties, and was regarded as irrelevant by many women activists.[144] Domestic violence was shrugged off as "smacking the wife around" (*da laopo*) throughout the Mao years and into the reform period.[145] In 2007, the Women's Federation estimated that it affected one-third of families.[146] But domestic violence increasingly was named as an unacceptable practice and a violation of the rights of women. In the 2001 amendment to the Marriage Law, family violence was cited as a legitimate ground for divorce (along with bigamy, abandonment, gambling, and drug addiction). Local government organs were instructed to mediate, the Public Security Bureau was told to stop the violence, and victims were empowered to lodge a criminal complaint, although the parameters of such violence were not outlined.[147] Years of Women's Federation advocacy, police training sessions, and public service announcements followed, some of them guided by nongovernmental organizations devoted to women's issues.[148]

In March 2016, a new Domestic Violence Law took effect in China. Among its provisions were that police should issue written warnings to wife abusers and that courts should provide protective orders to victims, with police and local government following up to make sure that the violence ceased. Nevertheless, the law treated domestic violence as a civil offense rather than a crime, unless the harm inflicted was grave enough to invoke other articles of Chinese penal law. Courts were empowered mainly to enforce fines and minor administrative penalties, and the police largely were limited to an administrative and mediating role. Absent a strong criminal provision, the law provided only a limited challenge to older ideas that family affairs should be resolved in-house. Reflecting state fears of any social unrest engendered by the rapid and destabilizing changes of the reform era, the law also supported the state idea that family harmony—understood as stability—was an absolute social good, more important than the well-being of those who suffered domestic abuse.[149]

This pervasive state fear of any potential threat to social stability carried over into controls on public demonstrations, even when they were not directed at the state. In March 2015, police detained five young feminist activists in their twenties and early thirties as they were planning a demonstration for the eve of International Women's Day in which they would hand out stickers on public transportation, denouncing sexual harassment.[150] Beginning in 2012, these young women and others already had staged several highly visible actions denouncing domestic violence, including one on Valentine's Day that year in which three of them marched along a public street in bloodstained wedding gowns. They also had agitated for an end to gender discrimination in hiring as well as for more public toilets for women, initiating an "Occupy the Men's Toilets" movement in several cities. The latter initiative eventually garnered a favorable response from national government officials.[151]

Authorities detained the "Feminist Five" for thirty-seven days, interrogating them repeatedly about who was funding their activities. Several worked for a feminist nongovernmental organization. In the years after the 1995 UN conference on women, the Party-state had encouraged nongovernmental organizations—including ones concerned with women's welfare—to take on social welfare projects previously dominated (or neglected) by state authorities.[152] But by the mid-2010s, the state suppression reflected a growing concern that such organizations, funded in part by foreign foundations, might engage in activities beyond the state agenda and outside direct state control.[153]

After considerable international attention, the Feminist Five were released on bail. But the charge against them—gathering a crowd to disturb public order—was not dismissed, leaving them in a legal limbo where they could easily be detained again if they continued to engage in public protest. State measures suggest suspicion about the women's commitment to theatrical direct action, their sophisticated deployment of social media, and their lack of connection to the Women's Federation. It is possible as well that state authorities were concerned by the activists' expressed lack of interest in taking up the gendered roles of heterosexual marriage and childbearing.[154] For the first time in more than a century, Chinese feminism was added to the list of government-proscribed activities.[155] Nonetheless, periodic feminist agitation has continued to surface. In late 2017 and early 2018, petitions and online accounts appeared by women protesting pervasive sexual harassment and assault in universities, state agencies, private companies, and public spaces.[156]

The past few decades of capitalist globalization in China, in combination with the continued control of the Party-state, have left no sector of society untouched. New ideas, practices, and goods circulate across Chinese territory, producing differentiated effects, many of them profoundly gendered.[157] For women—a heterogeneous group fractured along lines of class, region, ethnicity, and generation that nonetheless face some common challenges—the reform era has meant new forms of labor and commodification, new inequalities and social struggles, and a new prominence of gender and sexuality as categories of analysis. It also has stimulated new critical discussions about how women, and Woman, should feature in the latest iteration of Chinese modernity.[158] Much discussion of women's role has emphasized the individual subject and her "quality" (suzhi), rather than the collective subject of women as laborers. At the same time new forms of interaction, often enabled by online connections, have begun to generate new collectivities and modes of feminist action.

It would be a mistake to regard the emphasis on social stability as exclusively a state concern pertaining to demonstrations and other overt political activity. Many sectors of society have been unnerved by the rapid social changes of the reform period and by the new vulnerabilities brought by China's engagement in a global economy, increasingly visible as rates of high growth are now slowing. The idea that stability is crucial garners wide support, and one often-cited locus of stability is the home, a domain that remains primarily a woman's responsibility to manage. One can see this emphasis on the larger significance of family in the statements by mistress dispellers that their work entailed protecting the home and thus protecting the country.[159] This belief is not so far from the late imperial statecraft dictum that "well-run families were the foundation of a flourishing state" (see chapter 1). In the new and unsettling circumstances of increasing wealth, rising inequality, and an uncertain future, yearning for stability is widely expressed in popular discourse as well. The social glue here is to be provided by women, who are expected—and often expect themselves—to sacrifice their own desires and aspirations for the greater familial and social good. And the labor women are called upon to perform—not only new forms of paid work and domestic tasks, but now also the emotional work of maintaining marriages—can be understood as the reconfiguration of a gendered division of labor under new and challenging circumstances.

This book began with a series of questions, including how our understanding of China's modern history might change if women were at the center of our analysis, and whether women had a Chinese revolution or revolutions. The answers are not simple. Women's labor within and beyond domestic space enabled the survival of households in the difficult circumstances and upheaval of the late Qing empire. It underwrote revolutionary organizing and socialist construction, and it has powered important sectors of China's recent economic rise. Yet that labor has remained inadequately compensated and often unseen. Meanwhile, the powerful symbolic language of gender has been deployed across the more than two centuries examined here to create a figure of Woman with constantly changing and contradictory characteristics: guardian of chastity, paragon of industriousness, footbound impediment to China's progress, good wife and wise mother, citizen and mother of citizens, abject victim and courageous challenger of Confucian family values, virtuous New Woman, salacious Modern Girl, wartime target and resistance fighter, patriotic Nationalist, patriotic Communist, labor model, socialist constructor, hardworking migrant, enthusiastic consumer, feminist critic. In short, Woman is a figure critical to tracking the full complexity of China's recent past.

The question of whether women had a revolution is similarly tangled. The signal moments we call revolutions—1911, 1949, as well as the recent era of capitalist globalization—have not produced the same effects for all women in China, but each has produced effects that are differentiated by gender. Put more simply, women had revolutions—they were not outside of history as we conventionally organize it—but they did not have exactly the same revolutions as men. Complete exploration of what a revolution meant—where it succeeded, where it missed the mark, where it was less important than other modalities of historical change—has to look at those gendered differences. It also must look at how women worked with the circumstances in which they found themselves: sometimes as rebels or revolutionaries, but often as participants in less dramatic temporalities of change. Through their daily activities, women enlarged their own spaces of possibility during and between the events of Big History.

Glossary

Aiguo nüxiao	爱国女校
Aisin Gioro Xianyu	爱新觉罗·显玗
Ban Zhao	班昭
Bingru	冰如
Cai Chang	蔡畅
Cai Hesen	蔡和森
Cai Yuanpei	蔡元培
caili	彩礼
Cao Zhuxiang	曹竹香
Chen Biyun	陈碧云
Chen Duxiu	陳獨秀
Chen Hengzhe	陈衡哲
Chen Jitong	陈季同
Chen Shoupeng	陈寿彭
Chen Xuezhao	陈学昭
Chen Yongsheng	陈泳声
Chiang Kai-shek (Jiang Jieshi)	蒋介石
Cixi	慈禧
da laopo	打老婆
Dagong bao	大公报
danwei	单位
Datong shu	大同书
Deng Xiaoping	邓小平

Deng Yingchao	邓颖超
Ding Ling	丁玲
Dong Baohong	董宝鸿
Dongfang zazhi	东方杂志
Duan Qirui	段祺瑞
Fan Yusu	范雨素
Feng Gaixia	冯改霞
funü	妇女
Funü shenghuo	妇女生活
Funü shibao	妇女时报
Funü zazhi	妇女杂志
Gao Junman	高君曼
Guangren tang	广仁堂
Guangxu	光绪
He Xiangning	何香凝
He Zizhen	贺子珍
He-Yin Zhen	何殷震
hezuo	合作
Hong Xiuquan	洪秀全
Hu Binxia	胡彬夏
Hu Shi	胡適
Huang Shuhua	黃淑華
hukou	户口
Jiang Qing	江青
Jiangbei	江北
jiegui	接轨
Jissen	实践
juanshi	卷葹
Kang Cheng, Kang Aide	康成，康爱德
Kang Youwei	康有為
Kangda	抗大
Li Da	李達
Li Dazhao	李大釗
Li Hongzhang	李鸿章
Li Ruzhen	李汝珍
Li Shuangshuang	李双双
Li Xiaojiang	李小江
Li Yinhe	李银河
Lianda	联大
Liang Qichao	梁啟超

Lin Biao	林彪
Lin Zexu	林则徐
Linglong	玲珑
Liu Hezhen	刘和珍
Liu Shipei	刘师培
Liu Surong	刘漱容
Lu Cui	陆璀
Lu Lihua	陆礼华
Lu Xun	鲁迅
Lü Bicheng	吕碧城
malasong	马拉松
Manzhouguo	满洲国
Mao Liying	茅丽瑛
Mao Zedong	毛泽东
Mei Niang	梅娘
Meng Lijun	孟丽君
modeng	摩登
modeng nülang	摩登女郎
modeng nüzi	摩登女子
nei	内
Nian	捻
Nie Er	聂耳
Nü xuebao	女学报
Nü xuetang	女学堂
nü zhaodai	女招待
nügong	女工
nüling	女伶
nüquan zhuyi	女权主义
Nüsheng	女声
Nüzi shijie	女子世界
Nüzi yuekan	女子月刊
Pan Guangdan	潘光旦
Peng Shuzhi	彭述之
Puyi	溥仪
Qing	清
qipao	旗袍
Qiu Jin	秋瑾
Ruan Lingyu	阮玲玉
shehui xingbie	社会性别
Shen Peizhen	沈佩贞

Shen Shanbao	沈善宝
Shenbao	申報
Shi Liang	史良
Shi Meiyu	石美玉
Shimoda Utako	下田 歌子
Shuntian	顺天
Song Jiaoren	宋教仁
Song Meiling	宋美龄
Song Qingling	宋庆龄
Subei	苏北
Sun Yat-sen (Sun Zhongshan)	孫中山
suzhi	素质
taijiao	胎教
Taiping	太平
tanci	弹词
Tang Jiezhi	汤茆之
Tang Qunying	唐群英
Tao Yi	陶毅
Tianyi	天义
wai	外
Wang Changguo	王昌国
Wang Guangmei	王光美
Wang Huiwu	王会悟
Wang Jingwei	汪精卫
Wang Yiwei	王伊蔚
Wu Zhiying	吴芝瑛
Wuben nüshu	务本女塾
Xi Shangzhen	席上珍
Xiang Jingyu	向警予
Xiao Hong	萧红
xiaojie	小姐
Xie Bingying	谢冰莹
Xin nüxing	新女性
Xin qingnian	新青年
xing gongzuozhe	性工作者
Xu Zihua	徐自华
Xue Shaohui	薛绍徽
Xunwu (County)	寻乌 (县)
Yang Chongrui	杨崇瑞
Yang Huimin	杨惠敏

Yang Kaihui	杨开慧
Yang Shuhui	杨书蕙
Yang Xu	杨 絮
Yang Yinyu	杨荫榆
Yesu jiao	耶稣教
yinü liangxu	一女两许
You Huaigao	尤懷高
Yu Zhi	余治
yuan	元
Yuan Mei	袁枚
Yuan Shikai	袁世凯
Zeng Guofan	曾国藩
Zeng Yong	曾咏藩
Zhang Ji	張繼
Zhang Xuecheng	章学诚
Zhang Zhidong	张之洞
Zhang Zhujun	张竹君
Zhao Wuzhen	赵五贞
Zhao Yiman	赵一曼
Zhao Zhiqian	赵志千
Zhongguo funü	中国妇女
Zhongguo nübao	中国女报
Zhonghua funü jie	中华妇女界
Zhou Enlai	周恩来
Zhu Su'e	朱素萼
Zhu Ti	朱娣
ziyou	自由
ziyuan	自愿
zizhu	自主
Zuo Xijia	左锡嘉

Notes

INTRODUCTION

1. Gates (2001, 131–32) offers several reasons why women's labor in prerevolutionary China is little known: elites who knew little about manual work kept the records, labor was conducted and its value subsumed within the family, and much of it was construed as "helping" older kinswomen or men. A separate question, outside the scope of her study but taken up in the present book, is why much of women's labor remained so invisible even as post-1949 mobilization of women for social production became a publicly articulated goal.

CHAPTER 1: THE GENDERED LABOR OF EMPIRE, 1800–1840

1. Some of the illustrations in this chapter date from the latter half of the nineteenth century rather than its early years; they have been chosen for the detail they convey rather than complete chronological exactitude.

2. Watson 1986.

3. For accounts of what legal and police records can tell us about such women, see Sommer 2015 and Ransmeier 2017.

4. Mann 2007 and Mann 1997 are the inspiration and source for much of this section.

5. Furth 1999, 6.

6. On domestic architecture and gender segregation, see Bray 1997, 130–33.

7. Elman 2000, 236–37.

8. Unless otherwise specified, the account of the examination system is based on Elman 2000 (esp. 294–302 on changing content) and Miyazaki 1976.

9. Rawski 1979, 6–8, 23, 140. Rawski estimates the comparable rate among men as 30–45 percent. Reed 2010, 14–15, suggests that 100 million people in China were functionally literate during this period. See also Brokaw 2007, 527. If the population, which was rising steadily from 1700 to 1850, was 450 million during this period, and 220 million were women, this could have meant anywhere from nine million to twenty-two million functionally literate women, with some smaller percentage possessing classical literacy.

10. Brokaw 2007; Brokaw 2010.

11. Mann 1997, 83–94.

12. For examples of such practices, see Widmer 2006, 4, 9.

13. Widmer 2006, 21, 28.

14. On *tanci* about or by women, see Widmer 2006, 72–85; and Siao-chen Hu 2010, 250–52.

15. Elman 2000, 263.

16. With 200,000 military licentiates and 350,000 purchased degrees, the total number of degree holders across the empire was 1.1 million. Elman 2000, 236.

17. On the increase in purchased degrees from 1764 to 1871, see Elman 2000, 227–28. He reports that 315,000 degrees were sold from 1820 to 1850 alone.

18. Perdue 2005, 367–68.

19. Mann 2007; Mann 2008. This task could fall to daughters in elite families where the father had died as well; see Fong 2000.

20. Mann 2008, 64.

21. On widows, virtue, generational transitions, and women's religious practice, see Mann 1997. On local charitable institutions for widows intended to support them so that they could remain chaste and care for their children, see Leung 1993.

22. See Ransmeier 2017, 2 and passim on the transactional features of Chinese families.

23. On the importance of affinal relations in late imperial China in both elite and commoner families, see Bossler 2000.

24. Mann 1997, 94–108, 112–17; Widmer 2006, 25, 127–31; Widmer 2010, 81, 87–92.

25. Bray 1997, 260, 265; Mann 2007. Fong 2004 discusses the Qing association of embroidery with poetry and the role of embroidery in shaping women's self-perceptions.

26. On the history of footbinding, see Ko 2001; Ko 2005. For a recent article demonstrating that the Manchu rulers of the Qing dynasty did not ban the practice after their conquest of China, as many scholars have assumed, see Shepherd 2016.

27. When a family had no male heir, parents would sometimes arrange to "call in a son-in-law" in a uxorilocal marriage. A young married woman in such cases continued to live with her parents, and perhaps with her sisters and their husbands as well. For life in such a family, see Mann 2007; for uxorilocal marriage among Qing literati, see Lu 1998. On a regionally specific form of marriage in late Qing and Republican south China, in which a woman delayed or permanently deferred transfer to her husband's family, see Topley 1975; Stockard 1989; Siu 1990.

28. Bernhardt 1994, 189; on resale of wives, see Sommer 2015, 117–274.

29. Finnane 2004, 213–35.

30. Bray 1997, 346–53.

31. On medical knowledge about women's reproductive health and its relationship to women's status, see Bray 1997 (Ming and Qing dynasties), Furth 1999 (Song through Ming dynasties), Wu 2000 (Qing dynasty), and Wu 2010 (late Ming and Qing dynasties).

32. For descriptions of women's work in Yangzi Delta communities see Huang 1990, 49–57; Pomeranz 2000, 91–99, 290–92; Pomeranz 2005. Scholars agree that women's labor in the late imperial Yangzi Delta was increasingly oriented toward production for the market. They disagree on whether this was an "involutionary" development in which more and more household labor yielded less and less return, or an "industrious revolution" similar to that which occurred before the industrial revolution in early modern Europe, in which an increase in labor by every member of the household led to an increase in the standard of living.

33. Ko 2001, 16 and 112, shows straw sandals and other work shoes for bound feet.

34. For an argument mainly centering on the early twentieth century that footbinding was closely connected to women's textile production and could be regarded as a form of labor control, see Gates 2001; Bossen 2002, 42–45; Bossen et al. 2011; Brown et al. 2012; Gates 2014; Bossen and Gates 2017.

35. Mann 1992, 243; Pomeranz 2005, 241.

36. Bray 1997, 242–46; Mann 1997, 148–65.

37. Pomeranz 2005, 239–47.

38. On the rise of the putting-out system in the lower Yangzi, including an argument that men ultimately replaced women at the looms, see Bray 1997, 222, 225–26, 235–36.

39. Mann 1992, 249.

40. Bossen 2002, 61, 100.

41. Pomeranz 2005, 251; Gardella 1994, 103–5, 172–73; Lu 2004, 20, 25.

42. Lu 2004.

43. Friedman 2006, 35–36. On indigenous women in Taiwan performing the majority of agricultural work during the Qing, and on the discourse of indigenous gender as fashioned by Han Chinese settlers, see Teng 1998 and Teng 2004, 173–93.

44. Pomeranz 2000, 87.

45. Bossen 2002, 66.

46. Pomeranz 2005, 250.

47. Reardon-Anderson 2005, 15, 17–70. By the late nineteenth century, the dynasty was actively promoting Han settlement in the region, leading to a rapid increase in population. Ibid., 16, 71–93, 98.

48. Reardon-Anderson 2005, 123, 137–40, 145. On the continuation of this pattern into the early twentieth century, see Reardon-Anderson 2005, 151–52; Gottschang and Lary 2000, 73–78, 83–87.

49. Isett 2007, 220. Isett (2007, 215–16) finds that women in Manchuria generally did not weave cotton because it was too cold to grow the crop locally.

50. Perdue 2005, 333–56; Millward 1998, 50–52. Millward (51, 229) notes that by the beginning of the nineteenth century, about 155,000 Han and Tungan (north-

west China Muslim) homesteaders had settled in northern Xinjiang, whereas southern Xinjiang became a destination for Han farming families by the 1840s.

51. Pomeranz 2005, 250.

52. For estimates of Jiangnan women weavers' earnings for a slightly earlier period, the mid-eighteenth century, see Pomeranz 2000, 100–102; and Pomeranz 2005, 243–47.

53. Bray 1997, 132. In north China, where women often still wash clothes in a basin, Xiujie Wu (2008: 225) writes that "in the sacrificial rituals for a deceased woman, a daughter is obliged to burn a paper cow in offering to her dead mother. The folk interpretation is: because during her life a woman has polluted so much water through washing and cleaning, she would need a cow to help her drink all the dirty water in her after life."

54. Goldman 2012, 64, 87–97; Brokaw 2007, 527–28; Cheng 2011, 103–6, 108–11, 122.

55. Brokaw 2007, 2.

56. Brokaw 2007, 14–17, 99, 101–2, 105, 109–11, 132–33.

57. Finnane 2004, 221–22.

58. Huntington 2005, 19–20. A common theme (1) was the ghost of a hanged woman convincing another woman to hang herself after a quarrel, replacing the ghost so that she could be reborn. Ghosts (21) might also return after death to take revenge on mothers-in-law or others who had wronged them.

59. Sommer 2005, 29–54; Sommer 2015.

60. Bray 1997, 326–34.

61. King 2014, 21; Bray 1997, 341.

62. Reliable information on infanticide rates is scant. For a demographic analysis of a community in eighteenth- and nineteenth-century Liaoning, in northeast China, see Lee and Campbell 1997, 65–70. Lee and Wang (1999) also discuss abortion and contraception in the Qing era. Sommer (2010) provides a critique of their work and other recent scholarship suggesting that abortion was commonplace in the late imperial era, pointing out that abortifacient drugs were "dangerous and unreliable, and that access to them and their use required specialized knowledge and often a fair amount of money" (99). They were used only in the event of a medical or a social crisis. On how the practice of infanticide became understood as a uniquely Chinese phenomenon under conditions of imperialism in the nineteenth century, see King 2014.

CHAPTER 2: DISTURBANCES, 1840–1900

1. Biographical details on Zuo Xijia in this account are drawn from Ho 1998, 324–25; Meyer-Fong 2013, 112, 243n50, 243n51; "Zuo Xijia"(左锡嘉), Baidu.com; "Zeng Yong" (曾咏), Baidu.com; Zuo 2008; Shan Shili 1911, 44b–51b.

2. Zuo 2008, 52–53.

3. Zuo 2008, 54, 57.

4. Zuo 2008, 57.

5. Zuo 2008, 49.

6. Her second daughter, Zeng Yi, went on to become a renowned embroiderer, calligrapher, and medical writer. Zeng Yi's younger sister Zeng Yan was also a poet, painter, and embroiderer. Ho 1998, 325, 288–89, 287–88.

7. Zheng 2005, 11–14, 20, 22.

8. Zheng 2005, 56–57, 7, 71–86, 91.

9. On the opium trade and its economic effects from 1839 to 1952, see Brook and Wakabayashi 2000, 1–27.

10. James Hevia has called this entire process, encompassing both military action and nonmilitary encounters, "the pedagogy of imperialism." Hevia 2003.

11. For a succinct listing of problems, see Meyer-Fong 2013, 7–8.

12. Bickers 2011, 83–84.

13. Mann 2010, 283, 293–96. For the circumstances under which this poem was written, see Mann 2007, 103–6.

14. Brook and Wakabayashi 2000, 7.

15. Zheng 2005, 117; McMahon 2002, 132; Brook and Wakabayashi 2000, 8. Estimates of the number of addicts in the late nineteenth century ranged from one million to forty million. Lodwick 1996, 19.

16. Zheng 2005, 101–5. By 1904 Sichuan alone produced four times more opium than the total amount imported from India, though 90 percent of it stayed in the province. Wyman 2000, 214. Bello (2000, 128–29) traces the cultivation of opium in the southwest and northwest (Yunnan, Guizhou, Sichuan, Gansu, Shaanxi, Xinjiang) back before the 1830s. See also Bello 2005.

17. Brook and Wakabayashi 2000, 9, 13. British imports were halted in 1913; see Blue 2000. On domestic cultivation, see also Bello 2005.

18. Blue 2000, 40. Baumler 2007, 1–2, 56, characterizes the campaign as similar to those against footbinding and for modern schools: "an attempt by a social and political elite to discipline the masses, with all the implications of coercion that implies" (2). The imperial edict aimed to gradually ban opium cultivation, sales, and consumption.

19. Opium was taxed and could then circulate. Baumler 2007, 74–75.

20. Brook and Wakabayashi 2000, 14.

21. McMahon 2002, 149; Zheng 2005, 125; Des Forges 2000.

22. McMahon 2002, 2, 10, 33, 114, 130; Des Forges 2000. On opium and courtesans in the eighteenth and early nineteenth century, see Zheng 2005, 7–8, 50–52, 119–22; on fictional portrayals of addicted prostitutes in the late Qing, see McMahon 2002, 132, 162–67.

23. McMahon 2002, 157, 180; Zheng 2005, 129.

24. Zheng 2005, 6, 172–74; Des Forges 2000.

25. Little 1899, 178–79.

26. Wyman 2000, 214.

27. On the gender imbalance among registered opium users in Fujian, with statistics drawn from the late 1930s, see Baumler 2000, 290n42. On a national estimate from 1906 that 12 percent of men and 2 percent of women used opium regularly, see Baumler 2007, 29.

28. Actually, because she was born just before the lunar New Year and children are considered a year old at birth and another year older at each New Year's, Ning was only thirteen at her marriage. Pruitt 1967, 33.

29. Pruitt 1967, 46–47, 56, 62, 72, 83, 111, 142–43, 153–62, 168, 170. On household functions of the *kang*, see Flitsch 2008.

30. Cao Zhuxiang 1996. On Alexander Hosie's 1907 trip up the Wei River valley in Shaanxi (where Cao later harvested opium), he observed hundreds of fields of poppies being cultivated illegally in violation of the 1906 ban and was told by a local Chinese that opium produced seven times the income of wheat. Lodwick 1996, 153–56. For descriptions of young girls harvesting opium in late nineteenth-century Fujian, see Gates 2001, 138.

31. On the Nian rebellion, see Perry 1980, 96–151.

32. Meyer-Fong 2013, 89–91.

33. On rules of separation and their eventual abandonment, see Spence 1996, 146–51, 234; Michael 1966, vol. 1: 45–46, 82; vol. 2: 364–65, 387, 390, 580. On Taiping marriage licenses, see Michael 1966, vol. 3: 1563–64.

34. On the number of permissible wives for Taiping officials of various ranks, see Michael 1966, vol. 3: 984–85. On unmanageable consorts, see Michael 1966, vol. 2: 585–666; quotation from 620.

35. On Chinese Communist characterizations of the Taiping as a revolution or a "peasant utopia," see Platt 2012, xxviii.

36. On the unlikelihood that these examinations were actually held, see Elman 2000, 574–75. On the woman official Fu Shanxiang, see Michael 1966, vol. 2: 507–9.

37. Michael 1966, vol. 2: 309–14.

38. Michael 1966, vol. 2: 182. Platt 2012, 156, notes that one decree declared that a woman who continued to bind her feet should be punished by amputation of the feet, but that the ban was completely unenforceable.

39. For a doctrine threatening to decapitate soldiers who hired women to wash or sew their clothing, and banning relations with prostitutes, see Michael 1966, vol. 2: 457–58.

40. Michael 1966, vol. 2: 162–66.

41. Michael 1966, vol. 2: 458.

42. Stephen Platt points out that because the Taiping Rebellion and the U.S. Civil War overlapped, and the United States and China were Britain's largest markets, Britain was concerned with losing both of these markets at the same time. The British decided to intervene in China to keep those markets open while maintaining neutrality in the U.S. Civil War. Platt 2012, xxiv.

43. The following account of wartime devastation is drawn largely from Meyer-Fong 2013 and Platt 2012.

44. Platt 2012, 21–22.

45. Platt 2012, 286–88.

46. Platt 2012, 304.

47. Arthur Evans Moule, *Personal Recollections of the T'ai-p'ing Rebellion, 1861–63* (Shanghai: Shanghai Mercury Offices, 1898), 24, cited in Meyer-Fong 2013, 119. See also Platt 2012, 66–67. On the deaths of thousands of virtuous women martyrs in Yangzhou, see Finnane 2004, 309, and Yang 2012, 257; on women's suicides in Suzhou, see Leung 1993, 10.

48. Meyer-Fong 2013, 142–43.
49. Meyer-Fong 2013, 51–57.
50. Meyer-Fong 2011, 10.
51. Meyer-Fong 2013, 172.
52. Meyer-Fong 2013, 110.
53. Platt 2012, 351–52; Meyer-Fong 2013, 150–51.
54. Judge 2012 (471) also notes that from the 1850s to the 1880s, awards for widows who lived and preserved their chastity increased so quickly that erecting individual arches to honor them became impossible. Instead women were honored with communal arches, one per province per year.
55. On the Panthay Rebellion, see Atwill 2006. On memories of women regenerating the community, see Armijo 2001, 302–5. On the Northwest Rebellion, see Liu and Smith 1980; Kim 2004; Millward 2007. On Xinjiang in particular and the rule of Xinjiang leader Ya'qub Beg, see Millward 2007, especially 116–35; Kim 2004; Boulger 1878. Ya'qub Beg briefly enforced an Islamic law ban on prostitution and ordered the flogging of women who did not wear the veil.
56. Leung 1993, 9; Rogaski 1997, 55–57.
57. This discussion of infanticide is largely based upon King 2014; see also Mungello 2008.
58. On Yu Zhi's work against infanticide as part of his post-Taiping philanthropic activities, see King 2014, 46–76.
59. King 2014, 34–37.
60. Musee des Families: Lectures du Soir 16 (1848–49): 213–14, cited in Harrison 2008, 73.
61. King 2014, 77–96, 111–43; Harrison 2008. Harrison (76) points out that the success of the association was due in part to the fact that abandonment of unwanted children was a common practice in European cities at the time.
62. King 2014, 81–98; Fielde 1887, 20, 23. Swatow is now romanized as Shantou.
63. Perry 1980, 51, 277.
64. Ransmeier 2017, 29; Lee and Wang 1999, 69–74.
65. King 2014, 149–78.
66. Bickers 2011, 153; Cordier 1913: http://en.wikisource.org/wiki/Catholic_Encyclopedia_%281913%29/China.
67. Shanghai's Bund got electric power in 1882. Bickers 2011, 316–17.
68. Bickers 2011, 108, 174.
69. Cordier 1913: http://en.wikisource.org/wiki/Catholic_Encyclopedia_%281913%29/China.
70. Goodman 2000, 890 n1; this figure is from 1893. Cordier 1913 gives the number in the early twentieth century as 651,000. Shanghai had 569 foreign residents in 1859. The number had grown to 2,800 by 1865, nine-tenths of them male. Bickers 2011, 172. In 1870 foreign men outnumbered foreign women six to one, but by 1895, the ratio had fallen to 1.7 to 1, and almost 1,400 foreign children had been added. Bickers 2011, 311.
71. Bailey 2007, 12–13.
72. Honig 1986, 15; Luo 2011, 15–16.
73. Bickers 2011, 312.

74. Bickers 2011, 225–27, 315–16, 321–22; census figures from 352. See Teng 2013 for discourses about Eurasians on both sides of the Pacific.

75. Rogaski 1997, 57–59.

76. Bickers 2011, 223.

77. Bickers 2011, 319. See also Henriot 2001; Hershatter 1997.

78. Yip 2012, from whom the description of images in this section is drawn, gives a thorough account of prostitute images and thematics in the pictorial *Dianshizhai huabao*. On the pictorial itself, and its targeting of women as part of a potential reading audience, see Mittler 2004, 251, 302–3.

79. Yeh 2006.

80. Liang 2010, especially 8–9, 53–112, 121–43.

81. Liang 2010, 56–57; Hershatter 1997, 119–26; Henriot 2001, 59–61.

82. For the figure of the courtesan in this transition, see Liang 2010; Yeh 1998; Yeh 2006; Henriot 2001. On sympathetic and critical portrayals of courtesans in turn-of-the-century novels, see McMahon 2002; Yeh 2006; Des Forges 2007; Starr 2007; Zamperini 2010; Liang 2010.

83. Hershatter 1997; Yip 2012.

84. Fielde added, however, that Chinese women were nevertheless better off than in India, Turkey, Burma, Tibet, or Siam. Fielde 1887, 1.

85. On individual women missionaries, see Hyatt 1976, 63–136; Hunter 1984. Hunter offers a compelling account of the missionary ideology of domesticity and the society women missionaries created.

86. Hyatt 1976, 67; Ebrey 1999, 8–9; Hunter 1984, xv.

87. Ebrey 1999, 8–9.

88. Dunch 2010, 77–78; Lutz 2010, 16.

89. Bays 2012, 57.

90. Bays 2012, 21–36, 48, 52–53, 60; Bickers 2011, 237; Lutz 2010, 395.

91. Harrison 2008, 83–84, 87.

92. Dunch 2009, 78.

93. Hyatt 1976, 68.

94. Hyatt 1976, 68. He observes that by 1907, there were 2,481 women, 1,038 of them single. Drucker 1979, 425, notes that in 1914 women comprised close to 60 percent of Protestant missionaries in China, increasing in the 1920s to more than two-thirds.

95. Dunch 2009, 76–77.

96. Fielde 1887, 2.

97. Lottie Moon, cited in Hyatt 1976, 100.

98. Helen Nevius, cited in Hyatt 1976, 73.

99. For an argument that footbinding did not generally help rural women to marry up the social scale, see Brown, Bossen, Gates, and Satterthwaite-Phillips 2012, 1035–36, 1039, 1052, 1057.

100. Ko 1997; Ko 2005; Ko 2012.

101. A 2012 study based on questionnaires given to 4,180 ever-bound women found that 86 percent had had their feet bound by their mothers. Brown, Bossen, Gates, and Satterthwaite-Phillips 2012, 1037n2.

102. Ko 2005, 1–106. Ko warns against the assumption that "footbinding is a uniform and timeless practice motivated by a single cause" (3).

103. Drucker 1981 provides an early account of how Western women influenced the Chinese anti-footbinding movement. On the missionary category of "natural feet," see Ko 2005, 14–18.

104. See, for instance, the 1836 writings of John Francis Davis, quoted in Ebrey 1999, 7.

105. Burton 1918, 23; see also chapter 3.

106. Ebrey 1999, 18–19, 22.

107. Later, in his 1913 book *How England Saved China*, Macgowan asserted that England had saved the Chinese from footbinding, female infanticide, and disease. Zito 2007, 5–8.

108. Zito 2006, 27.

109. Ko 2005, 41–42; Heinrich 2008, 85.

110. Fielde 1887, 31.

111. Little 1899, 145; Zito 2006, 21. On mission schools' footbinding and physical education for girls in the late nineteenth and early twentieth centuries, see Graham 1994.

112. Gewurtz 2010, 207; Little 1899, 147; Drucker 1981, 187.

113. Ebrey 1999, 15.

114. Dunch 2009, 67.

115. Lutz 2010, 404.

116. Hyatt 1976, 76.

117. Lutz 2010, 404.

118. Dunch 2010, 334–35.

119. Lutz 2010, 394–95; Chin 2003, 331–40.

120. Hyatt 1976, 82–83.

121. Fielde 1887, 206.

122. Lutz 2010, 401–2; Chin 2003, 336.

123. Dunch 2010, 338–39.

124. Dunch 2009, 78; Gewurtz 2010, 204.

125. Lutz 2010, 399, 404–5.

126. Dunch 2010, 333 and 345n39.

127. Widmer 2006, 271; Dunch 2009, 65, 82.

128. Dunch 2009, 83–95.

129. "Foreword" (no author given) to Fielde 1887, x.

130. Fielde 1887, 93–99; Lutz 2010, 217–19, 398; Hyatt 1976, 70–72; Dunch 2010, 335.

131. Bays 2012, 79–80; Lutz 2010, 398; Dunch 2010, 332; Chin 2003, 332, 338.

132. Bays 2012, 69.

133. Hyatt 1976, 84; Stanley 2010, 275.

134. Stanley 2010, 9, 276, and 278–79, finds programs to offer hands-on medical training to women in 1879 and the early 1890s. On Chinese women physicians, see also Pripas-Kapit 2015.

135. Shemo 2010, 294; see also Shemo 2011.

136. Dunch 2010, 327; Chin 2003, 342–44; Shemo 2010, 294–95; Ye 2001, 114–29. The most detailed study of the lives of Kang and Shi is Shemo 2011.

137. Shemo 2010, 295–301; Shemo 2011, 71–100, 123–39. On nurse training from this period through the 1920s, see Stanley 2010.

138. Dunch 2010, 342; Shemo 2011, 2, 51–56; for an extended discussion of Kang Aide's life and Liang Qichao's interpretation of it, see Hu Ying 2002.

139. Bickers 2011, 245–50.

140. Harrison 2008, 81–82, 85, 89; King 2014, 155–58; Cohen 1963, 229–61; Bickers 2011, 231–36, 250; Ransmeier 2017, 70–75.

141. It was the worst famine until that time. The Great Leap Famine, discussed in chapter 8, was larger in scope and more lethal. Except where otherwise specified, this account of the famine and its gendered effects is drawn from Edgerton-Tarpley 2008. See also Ransmeier 2017, 80–89.

142. Cited in Pietz 2015, 74–75.

143. Rogaski 1997, 62, 66.

144. Rogaski 1997, 73–77. Shue 2006 provides further details of the Hall's operation and analysis of its development and complex economic investments, its matchmaking for its residents, and its vocational training for women until the late 1920s.

145. Rogaski 1997, 71–72; Ransmeier 2017.

146. Bickers 2011, 349 reports that 40 Catholics and 135 Protestants lost their lives at the hands of the Boxers.

147. Cohen 1997, 125.

148. Cited in Cohen 1997, 139.

149. For accounts of the fantastical deeds later attributed to the Red Lanterns, as well as alleged parallel organizations of Blue Lanterns (middle-aged women) and Black Lanterns (elderly women), see Ono 1989, 49–52.

150. Cohen 1997, 138–45; quotation from 141.

151. Cohen 1997, 134–38.

152. Former courtesan Sai Jinhua is said to have spared Beijing from even worse violence by intervening with a former lover then in command of occupying forces. Hu Ying 2000, 21–66; Zamperini 2010, 125, 181; Wu 2009, 35–62.

153. See, for example, Lynch 1901, 137, 140–41.

154. Lynch 1901, 140.

155. Lynch 1901, 39.

156. Lynch 1901, 141.

157. Judge 2012, 472–74. For a contemporary comment on Tongzhou by a General Wilson of the U.S. Army, in which he says "some of the foreign troops gave unbridled license to their passion for rapine, robbery and destruction," see Lynch 1901, 304–5.

CHAPTER 3: REVOLUTIONARY CURRENTS, 1895–1912

1. On the co-emergence of feminism and nationalism in this period see, inter alia, Judge 2001, 766; Karl 2002a.

2. Schwartz 1964; Pusey 1983; Qian 2008, 286.

3. The Empress Dowager Cixi, Joan Judge points out, "demonstrates what certain willful women could do within apparently restrictive conditions of historical possibility." Personal communication. See, inter alia, Conger 1909; Sergeant 1911; Chung 1979.

4. Chinese students in Tokyo numbered eight thousand in 1905, twelve thousand in 1906, and dropped to four thousand in 1910. Elman 2004, 323.

5. On late Qing opium policies, see Baumler 2007, 1–2, 56, 74–77.

6. Liu, Karl, and Ko 2013, 189–90; Borthwick 1985.

7. Liu, Karl, and Ko 2013, 194. Eighteenth-century thinkers such as Chen Hongmou had also asserted that educated mothers would raise filial children and thus enhance the stability of the Qing empire. Rowe 2001, 426–29; Mann 1997, 28–29; Barlow 2004, 45.

8. Liu, Karl, and Ko 2013; quotations are from 192 and 191, respectively. See also Hu Ying 2002, passim; Judge 2002; Judge 2008b, 87–106; Orliski 2003, 57.

9. Orliski 2003, 57.

10. Liu, Karl, and Ko 2013, 193.

11. Kang 1958, 149–55. On the eugenic and racialized aspects of Kang Youwei's thought, and its Japanese antecedents, see Dikötter 1998, 61–63; Sakamoto 2004, 337.

12. On the link Liang and others made between enslavement in an era of global imperialism and the need to mobilize a citizenry that included women, see Karl 2002a.

13. Bailey 2007, 57.

14. Barlow 2004, 92.

15. Barlow 2004, 60.

16. Zito 2006, 26, 31. On the lifelong ongoing effort required to maintain bound feet, see Ko 2005, 1–2, 223.

17. Little 1899, 1; Zito 2006, 27.

18. Little 1899, 38.

19. Little 1899, 45, 134. On the economic productivity of footbound women who produced textiles at home, see Brown et al. 2012, 1044; Gates 2014; Bossen and Gates 2017.

20. Little 1899, 137; Little 1909, 280.

21. Little 1909, 256.

22. Little 1899, 137–43, quotation 139–40; Little 1909, 276–77.

23. Zito 2006, 28.

24. Little 1899, 150. See also Zito 2006, 27, 29; Drucker 1981, 189–90.

25. Drucker 1981, 189.

26. In Amoy (Xiamen), Little discovered that Christian women converts had all unbound their feet. Little 1909, 282. John Macgowan and his wife convened sixty Chinese Christian women in Amoy to discuss footbinding in 1874. Zito 2007, 4.

27. Little 1899, 149–53; Drucker 1981, 190.

28. Little 1909, 253–54, 273; Zito 2007, 12–14.

29. Little 1909, 257.

30. Little 1899, 162; Little 1909, 281–82; on unbinding, see also Brown et al. 2012, 1037; Ko 2001, 138; Ko 2005, 11, 43–49.

31. Kang 1958, 13; Shepherd 2016, 298. Rong 1986, 144, gives the date as 1884; Little 1899, 155, gives the date as 1896, but she may be talking about the South China Anti-Footbinding Society that Kang's younger brother and Liang Qichao founded in 1896–97, or about an 1896 essay by Liang Qichao. See Drucker 1981, 194; Shepherd 2016, 298.

32. Borthwick 1985, 70–71.
33. Little 1909, 255.
34. Little 1909, 266–67.
35. Little 1899, 160–62; see also Drucker 1981, 190.
36. Quoted in Cheng 2000, 127–28.
37. Drucker 1981, 193–97; Ko 2005, 9–37; Yang Xingmei 2010.
38. Ko 2005; Zito 2006.
39. Drucker 1981, 197; Beahan 1981, 231–32.
40. Ko 2005, 13.
41. Stapleton 2000, 227.
42. Hinton and Gordon 1984. On unbinding campaigns, see also Ko 2005, 11, 13, 38–68; on the continuing aesthetic appeal of the bound foot as a guarantee of marriage during the Republican period, see Yang Xingmei 2000.
43. For an argument that footbinding was a means of labor control, see Bossen et al. 2011; Gates 2014; Bossen and Gates 2017.
44. Ko 2001, 133; Bossen 2002, 37–83.
45. The number of periodicals in China rose from fifteen in 1890 to sixty in 1898 to 487 in 1913. Britton 1966, 127, cited in Beahan 1975, 379. On late Qing women's journals, and the many men (and some women) who wrote for them, see Zhang Yun 2015, 251–67.
46. Mittler 2004, 248. On novels that put forward a reformist agenda for women, see Widmer 2006 and Widmer 2007.
47. Mittler 2004, 284–85.
48. Judge 2012, 461–68.
49. Mittler 2004, 255–57, 303–11.
50. Mittler 2004, 253n32, 260–68.
51. Mittler 2004, 269; Beahan 1981, 223–24.
52. Mittler 2004, 252–53, 270–75, 286–93.
53. On Chengdu, see Stapleton 2016, 146–47; on Beijing, see Goldman 2012, 82–83; Cheng 2011, 111–13.
54. Judge 1997; Judge 2008b, 107–38. On the importance of mothers of citizens, see also Zhang Yun 2015.
55. Qian 2008, 271–72.
56. Except where otherwise noted, details about Xue's activities are from Qian 2015.
57. Xue was a member of the all-women editorial board; thirty women moved on and off the board over the eight issues of the journal, which was published for four months in summer and fall of 1898. Qian 2010, 340; Qian 2008, 266; Qian 2004, 66, 72.
58. Qian 2010, 341–51.
59. Xue, "Nü xuebao xu," *Nü xuebao* 1 (24 July 1898): 2b–3a, translated in Qian 2008, 265. During the same period she helped begin China's first women's association, the Women's Study Society. Qian 2010, 340.
60. Qian 2015; Qian 2004, 63–79, 85–86, 91; see also Judge 2008b, 63.
61. Judge 2004; Judge 2008a, 158. Other writers often based their work on Japanese translations of Western sources. Judge 2008a, 148–50.

62. Beahan 1981, 219; Judge 2008b, 144–86; Judge 2008a, 154–55. On literary portrayals of some of these figures, see Hu Ying 2000.

63. Judge 2008a, 160–61. Chinese heroines such as Hua Mulan were also prominently featured in many publications; see Judge 2008b.

64. Judge 2009, 60, 63.

65. Judge 2009, 59; Qian 2015.

66. Judge 2009, 75.

67. Huters 2005.

68. Qian 2004, 65. McTyeire Home and School for Girls had been founded by missionaries in Shanghai in 1892, aimed at upper-class families. Cong 2008, 122.

69. Others included her husband, brother-in-law, and French sister-in-law, as well as Liang Qichao and his wife, and some foreigners. Qian 2004, 66; Qian 2010, 340; Bailey 2007, 19. For a drawing depicting one of their meetings in the *Dianshizhai huabao*, see Liang 2010, 179.

70. Qian 2004, 68–71.

71. Qian 2010, 339–40, 352; Qian 2004, 65, 72; Cong 2008, 126; Bailey 2007, 21.

72. Beahan 1981, 232–35, and Borthwick 1983, 114–18, provide an overview of developments in girls' education during this period.

73. Cheng 2000, 117; Cong 2008, 127–28; P. Chen 2008, 336; Bailey 2004, 225; Bailey 2007, 28. The first sentence of the translation is found in the pieces by Cong and Chen, and the second sentence is in Cheng's essay. These statements are attributed to Zhang Zhidong, governor-general of Hunan and Hubei and a prime mover behind the educational reforms.

74. Cong 2008, 115, 136–39; Cong 2007, 52–60; Beahan 1975, 381; Cheng 2000, 117.

75. Mittler 2004, 283, citing *Shenbao*, March 8, 1907; see also Cheng 2000, 118.

76. Cong 2008, 140.

77. Bailey 2004, 228.

78. Cheng 2000, 118.

79. Cheng 2000, 118; Cong 2008, 141.

80. Cong 2008, 141; see also Bailey 2004, 225–26.

81. On the Aiguo nüxiao, see Beahan 1981, 217; Mittler 2004, 277; Cong 2008, 133; Zhang Shiying 2012, 47; quotation is from Bailey 2007, 25.

82. Xia Xiaohong 2008, 294.

83. On Wuben, see Cong 2008, 132, 135; Bailey 2007, 1–2, 24–25; Bailey 2004, 224–25.

84. Judge 2008b, 31–32, 73–83.

85. Bailey 2004, 224–25.

86. P. Chen 2008, 332; Cheng 2000, 129.

87. *Funü huabao*, July 9, 1907, cited in Cheng 2000, 130.

88. P. Chen 2008, 334, 338–39; Cheng 2011, 124–23.

89. On household schedules and budgets, see Bailey 2007, 56.

90. On late Qing discourse on women's education, see Bailey 2004, 239; on Shimoda Utako (1854–1936) and her girls' school in Japan, which many Chinese students attended, and on conflicts about the role of women between Shimoda and the young Chinese women she educated, see Judge 2001, 772–801. See also

Judge 2008b, 111–17; Bailey 2007, 35, 46–47. On "good wives, wise mothers" see also Judge 2001, 771; Judge 2008b, 109–15.

91. Ye 2001, 115, 129–33.

92. Paul Bailey has dubbed this approach to women's public education in the late Qing and early Republic "modernizing conservatism," in which "public education for girls was seen primarily in terms of the reconfiguration of traditional skills and virtues in the service of family harmony, social order and national wealth and strength." Bailey 2007, 45 and passim. On home economics in China, see Schneider 2011.

93. On eugenics in China, see Dikötter 1998; Sakamoto 2004. On physical education for girls and its links to national strength, strengthening the race, and women's rights, see Bailey 2007, 41, 72; Yu Chien Ming 1996; Yu Chien Ming 2009; Cheng 2011, 120–21.

94. Zheng 1997, 96–97.

95. Gimpel 2006, 338–43; quotation from 340.

96. *Shuntian shibao* (hereafter, STSB), July 19, 1905, quoted in Cheng 2000, 111. This newspaper was Japanese-owned but staffed by Chinese.

97. Zhang Yun 2015, 258–67.

98. *Shuntian shibao*, May 10, 1906, quoted in Cheng 2000, 115.

99. Cong 2008, 131. Luo Suwen suggests that Beijing textbooks emphasized women's domestic role, and Shanghai textbooks, women's role as citizens. Luo 1996, 145–52, cited in Cheng 2000, 125.

100. On Jiang Shaoquan, an educator who expressed this view, see Cheng 2000, 112.

101. *Zhongguo xin nüjie zazhi*, Tokyo, February 1907, cited in Beahan 1975, 383–84. For a similar argument by the editor of Tianjin's *Dagong bao*, attributing the weakness and strength of nations (China, Korea, India, Persia, and Turkey vs. the United States and Japan) to their degree of education for girls, see Cheng 2000, 111–12.

102. Mittler 2004, 277; Bailey 2007, 24. The *North China Herald* reported on July 19, 1907, that "a thousand girls were pupils in foreign and Chinese schools in Shanghai's Foreign Concession area as of 1907." Beahan 1975, 381.

103. Cong 2008, 136–37.

104. Leung 2006, 73. A women's medical school had been founded in Guangzhou by Mary Fulton in 1901. Ibid., 75. The Shanghai school was cofounded by a doctor of traditional Chinese medicine and a woman doctor who had been trained by missionaries in Canton, and it aimed to train women aged fourteen to twenty-three in gynecology. Ibid., 76. On medicine portrayed as an appropriate career for women in the press, see Orliski 2003, 49–50.

105. Cong 2008, 133; on state-sponsored vocational training for women in the late Qing and early Republic, see also Bailey 2007, 54–55; Cheng 2000, 126; Orliski 2003, 50–55, 63.

106. Bailey 2007, 26–27, 34–35, says that in 1907, there were 434 girls' schools and 15,324 students nationwide, compared to 33,513 boys' schools with 928,775 students. In 1908, the number of girls' schools rose to 512 and the number of students to 20,557. In 1909, there were 722 girls' schools and 26,465 students. In

addition, in 1910, 16,190 girls attended Protestant schools, and in 1912, there were 49,987 in Catholic schools. Bailey 2004, 221, adds that by 1912–13 the number of girl students nationwide was 141,130, and that by 1922–23 it had grown to 417,820, with the vast majority of these (403,742) in primary school. Elman 2000, 606, notes that in 1910, out of a population of 406 million, fewer than 1 percent were enrolled in schools. The overwhelming majority of these students would have been male. See also Borthwick 1985, 79.

107. On the term *nüjie*, which can be understood as "the collectivity of women," and its relationship to emergent nationalism and feminism, see Zhang Yun 2015.

108. Unless otherwise specified, biographical information on Qiu Jin is drawn from Borthwick 1985; Rankin 1971; Rankin 1974; Rankin 1975; Spence 1981, 83–94; Wang Lingzhen 2004; Judge 2008b, 216–23; Hu Ying 2009, 258; Hu Ying 2016, especially 96–183; Hieronymus 2005; Edwards 2016b, 40–65.

109. Hu Ying (2007; 2016, 182–333) counts nine distinct burials of Qiu Jin: one by a local charity, after which her brother retrieved her body and laid it out at a shed in a mortuary; a second in 1908 by two women friends, discussed below; a third next to her recently deceased husband in 1909; a fourth in Changsha in 1912, after she became a national heroine in the wake of the 1911 revolution; a fifth near West Lake in 1913; and four burials in the vicinity of West Lake after 1949.

110. Elman 2004, 323; Rankin 1975, 50, puts the total number of students at more than fifteen hundred. On the number of women students enrolled in Japanese schools from 1901 to 1911, with annual figures ranging from just under 100 to 149, see Judge 2009, 190; Beahan 1975 (381) also cites a 1907 estimate of about one hundred women formally registered and a larger number in Tokyo studying language or learning informally.

111. On women's role in Tokyo-based Chinese publications and political organizations, see Judge 2001; Judge 2002; Judge 2005; Judge 2008b, 190–200, 203–9; Edwards 2008a, 42–45.

112. Judge 2009.

113. Hu Ying 2009, 265.

114. Rankin 1971, 41; Beahan 1981, 216, 222–23. Russian troops stayed in Manchuria even after the Western nations and Japan suppressed the Boxer movement.

115. Strand 2011, 95.

116. Judge 2008b, 217.

117. For the growth of this sentiment and the global analysis of imperialism it partially displaced, see Karl 2002b.

118. Hu Ying 2012, 441; Hu Ying 2008, 58. The comparison to Liang is mine.

119. Qiu Jin 1998 (1905–07); Wang Lingzhen 2004, 53–59; on the *tanci*, see Widmer 2006, 272.

120. Wang Lingzhen 2004, 58.

121. Judge 2008b, 222; Wang Lingzhen 2004, 59.

122. Beahan 1975, 399–401.

123. Bailey 2007, 59. On a related formulation linking women and the nation, in which women were referred to as the slaves of slaves, see Karl 2002a; Zhang Yun 2015.

124. Beahan 1975, 382.

125. Hu Ying 2007, 143.

126. On the various modalities in which she was memorialized, including as a female martyr, see Hu Ying 2011.

127. Spence 1981, 94.

128. Rankin 1975, 62.

129. Hu Ying 2009, 259.

130. Hu Ying 2009, 261.

131. Judge 2008b, 217.

132. Hu Ying 2000, 142; Spence 1981, 87.

133. Rankin 1971, 172.

134. Judge 2008b, 219.

135. Hu Ying 2009, 260; Hu Ying 2004, 132–33.

136. Hu Ying 2004, 133; see also Widmer 2006, 272–73.

137. Hu Ying 2000, especially 106–96.

138. Hu Ying 2009, 263.

139. Hu Ying 2009, 236. Hu Ying 2016 is, in the author's words, a "linked biography" (5) of Qiu Jin, Wu Zhiying, and Xu Zihua.

140. Hu Ying 2004, 121–32.

141. Hu Ying 2007, 145–53; Hu Ying 2016, 184–254.

142. Rankin 1975, 40.

143. Karl 2012 offers an account of the broader late Qing and Tokyo intellectual context in which He-Yin Zhen wrote. Liu, Karl, and Ko 2013 provide a discussion and translation of He-Yin's works and those of several of her contemporaries. See also Zarrow 1988; Zarrow 1990; Dirlik 1991, 103–4; Sudo 2006, 483–85; Zhang Yun 2015, 267–73.

144. Xia Xiaohong 2008, 294.

145. Liu, Karl, and Ko 2013, 2–3.

146. Liu, Karl, and Ko 2013, 51; Beahan 1975, 410.

147. Liu, Karl, and Ko 2013, 106–68.

148. Xia Xiaohong 2008, 297.

149. This criticism was aimed, among others, at male feminist Jin Tianhe's arguments in *The Women's Bell* in 1903 that if women had education, employment, the vote, and human dignity, this would help to strengthen the nation. Liu, Karl, and Ko 2013, 60; for a discussion of Jin and a full translation of *The Women's Bell*, see ibid., 6, 204–85; other discussions of Jin include Edwards 2008a, 38–40; Sudo 2006, 476–77; Zhang Yun 2015, 245–46.

150. Liu, Karl, and Ko 2013, 57–61. For her critique of capitalist exploitation in Euro-America and in China, see her 1907 essay "On the Question of Women's Labor" in ibid., 72–91. For anarchist views of the family beyond He-Yin Zhen, see Dirlik 1991, 98–99, 139–40.

151. Liu, Karl, and Ko 2013, 64–70.

152. Liu, Karl, and Ko 2013, 70, 87, 91, 103.

153. Liu, Karl, and Ko 2013, 184.

154. Prazniak 1999, 17, 8, 131–37, 213–56, especially 213–16, 220–44. See also Prazniak 1986. On the role of housewives in rice riots preceding the 1911 revolution, see Ono 1989, 70–72.

155. On women's military and support action just before and during the 1911 revolution, see Lin 1975; Beahan 1981, 228–30; Ono 1989, 82–80; Edwards 2008a, 47–52. On visual representations in lithographs and woodblock prints of women soldiers, see Laing 2013.

156. Cited in Strand 2011, 106.

157. Bailey 2007, 74.

158. Edwards and Zhou 2011, 493–94, provide a brief list of women's military groups. They observe (493) that historically, in times of crisis, "women's participation in formal military action was encouraged, applauded and invited," as long as they returned to their domestic roles when hostilities concluded.

159. Leung 2006, 87–88; Ho 1998, 310–12; Burton 1918; Edwards and Zhou 2011. On Zhang's activities promoting women's education, see Drucker 1981, 217–18.

160. Ho 1998, 313; see also Sudo 2006, 481–83.

161. Bailey 2007, 74; Bailey 2004, 182; Rong 1986, 158–60.

162. Strand 2011, 22.

163. Except where otherwise noted, the account of the slap that follows is based upon Strand 2011, 13–21, 38–51, 97–145. Also see Beahan 1981, 236–38; Ono 1989, 80–89. On suffrage politics in this period and its broader political context, see Witke 1973b, 38–41; Edwards 2008a, 66–102; Ma Yuxin 2005b, 60–61; Ma Yuxin 2007.

164. Strand 2011, 17–18.

165. Strand 2011, 109–10; Edwards and Zhou 2011, 494.

166. Edwards and Zhou 2011, 495.

167. Edwards 2008a, 69–70, 74–77.

168. Edwards and Zhou 2011.

169. Strand 2011, 115; Bailey 2007, 196, 75–78; Hu Ying 2004, 140.

170. Strand 2011, 121; Edwards 2008a, 70–83; Edwards and Zhou 2011, 496–97.

171. Strand 2011, 45.

172. Bailey 2007, 68; Bailey 2006, 186–88.

173. Beahan 1981, 237.

174. Beahan 1981, 237; Strand 2011, 144.

175. Borthwick 1985, 82; Bailey 2006, 178–79.

176. Strand 2011, 143.

177. Strand 2011, 13. For an upsurge in the movement for women's constitutional rights during the early 1920s, see Wang 1999, 99–100; Edwards 2008a, 103–38.

178. Edwards and Zhou 2011, 497.

179. Virtue for women, now as earlier, meant no sexual liaisons outside of marriage. For men on both sides of the revolutionary divide, this restriction did not apply. Kang Youwei, for example, had six concubines, and Liang Qichao took one concubine. It was said that Liang initially resisted the idea on the grounds that it made his feminism look hypocritical, but his wife urged him to make her maid his concubine. Sun Yat-sen was rumored to have had numerous affairs. Yuan Shikai had at least nine concubines, and probably more, but he never proclaimed the equality of the sexes. My thanks to Peter Zarrow for highlighting this issue and tallying the numbers.

180. Strand 2011, 129–39; see also C. Chin 2006, 510–11; Edwards 2008a, 20, 66, 88.

181. Strand 2011, 14.

CHAPTER 4: IMAGINED FUTURES, 1912–27

1. Gilmartin 1995, 26–27. On a similar case in 1925 Beijing, see Cheng 2011, 92.

2. A brief biography of Tao Yi is at http://baike.baidu.com/subview/877 383/8356148.htm.

3. Tao Yi 1999 [1919], 83–84.

4. Mao 1999 [1919], 79–83, 85–88, quotation about rape from 79; Witke 1973a, quotation about family revolution from 19.

5. Young 1977.

6. Gillin 1967, 34–35.

7. Stapleton 2000, 244.

8. Glosser 2003, 9–12, 27–80.

9. Chen Duxiu, 1999 [1916], 5–6.

10. On the terms used to render "feminism," see Wang 1999, 7–9; on the "woman question," see, inter alia, Barlow 2004.

11. Schwarcz 1986, 114.

12. Lu Xun 1999 [1923]; Lu Xun 2017; Spence 1981, 254–55. The essay also was published in the *Ladies' Journal* in August 1924. Ma 2003, 24. On Lu Xun's criticism of the "Nora Phenomenon," see also Cheng 2013, 12, 83, 88–91, 94, 107.

13. On *Women's Eastern Times*, which published twenty-one issues between 1911 and 1917, see Judge 2015, 17 and passim. She gives a circulation figure for the *Women's Eastern Times* as six to seven thousand issues and, considering the practice of passing one copy from one reader to another, a possible total readership of 140,000 (18). The *Ladies' Journal*, published from 1915 to 1931, had an estimated circulation of ten thousand in the early 1920s, more if multiple readers are considered. Nivard 1984, 37–38. It was edited first by Mao Dun and then by Zhang Xichen from 1921 to 1925, with Zhou Jianren (Lu Xun's younger brother) as assistant editor. In late 1925 Zhang was fired and went on to edit *New Woman* from 1926 to 1929. On Zhang's editorship, see Link 1981, 251; Nivard 1984, 40–42, 45–46; Wang 1999, 84–89; Ma 2003, 3–8; Chiang 2006, 531–40. On the *Ladies' Journal*, see Nivard 1984; Wang 1999, 67–116; C. Chin 2006; S. Hu 2008; Hubbard 2014. *New Youth* magazine also had a column on women's issues beginning in 1917, to which women contributed essays on footbinding, motherhood, education, family reform, and suffrage. Ma 2005b, 59–60. On *Fiction Monthly* [Xiaoshuo yuebao], a journal that dealt with similar content in popular fiction, see Gimpel 2001.

14. Judge 2015, 42.

15. Judge 2015, 13, 33, 52–61.

16. According to *Women's Eastern Times* editor Bao Tianxiao, fewer than 10 percent of his readers were women. Link 1981, 250, 195. Nivard, 1984, 47, estimates that 90 percent of the *Ladies' Journal* readers were men.

17. Link 1981, 171; Widmer 2006, 254; Hu Ying 2008, 65; Widmer 2007, 40.

18. On visual portrayals of women on magazine covers, illustrating desired attire and approved household and professional activities, see Judge 2015, 81–89, and Laing 2003, 83–86.

19. Judge 2015, 62; C. Chin 2006, 497, 500–502; on Western examples in the *Ladies' Journal*, see Wang 1999, 68; Chiang 2006, 523.

20. Gimpel 2001, 88–89.

21. Judge 2015, 109–11.

22. Judge 2015, 20, 23–27; Chiang 2006, 521–22.

23. Bailey 2007, 96; Schneider 2011, who also surveys a number of other journals; Wang 1999, 73.

24. Nivard 1984, 39; Orliski 2003, 56.

25. Judge 2015, 167–69, 131, 102–3; Chiang 2006, 522.

26. Schneider 2011, 22.

27. Schneider 2011, 21–22; on the relationship of this thinking to eugenics in May Fourth writings, see Sakamoto 2004, 351–54.

28. Bailey 2004, 232.

29. Judge 2015, 141, 144–45, 132; Lin 2013, 303.

30. Zhu 2014, 154.

31. Wang 1999, 71.

32. Nivard 1984, 40–41.

33. Wang 1999, 79–84, 87.

34. Borthwick 1985, 84; Wang 1999, 101. On the localization of a global discourse on sex in China during the 1920s, see Rocha 2010.

35. Wang 1999, 101.

36. Chiang 2006, 536. On Key's influence in China at this time, see Witke 1970, 140–43; Nivard 1984, 41; Chiang 2006, 531–40.

37. Ma 2003, 5–6; quotation on 5. See also Hubbard 2014, 352–53. Controversy over this special issue contributed to Zhang Xichen's removal as editor. Wang 1999, 111.

38. On eugenics in late Qing and May Fourth discourse, see Dikötter 1992, 169–77; Dikötter 2015, 108–14; Sakamoto 2004; Barlow 2004, especially 78–87. Dikötter 1998, 105–11, observes that the term "eugenics" (*youshengxue*) became popular in the 1920s and 1930s. He also points out (1992, 175–77; and 2015, 112–14) that eugenics and feminism were not always compatible. Pan Guangdan, China's preeminent eugenicist, was not in favor of birth control, late marriage, or women's independence, preferring China's older marriage practices as eugenically beneficial.

39. Barlow 2004; Chiang 2006.

40. Chiang 2006, 537; Stapleton 2016, 169; Sakamoto 2004, 345–50; Barkey 2000.

41. Barlow 2004, 100; see also Dikötter 1995; Dikötter 1998, 103–4; Sakamoto 2004.

42. "Gei nanxing" [To men], *New Woman* 1.12 (December, 1926): 897–901, first quotation cited in Ma 2003, 17–18; Dooling and Torgeson 1998, 165–73, second quotation from 171. On the short stories, see Ma 2003, 16–17; see also Zurndorfer 2005.

43. Wang 1999, 16, 23. On the emergence of the modern woman as a concept developed by intellectual reformers during the New Culture/May Fourth Movement, see Edwards 2000, 116; on literary portrayals, see Feng 2004. On women's white-collar and professional employment, see also Cheng 2011, 65–67; Stapleton 2016, 180.

44. Goodman 2005b, 265.

45. The account that follows, except where otherwise specified, is based on Goodman 2005a, Goodman 2005b, Goodman 2005c.

46. Goodman 2005a, 83; Goodman 2005c. On press commentary, see Lan and Fong 1999, 102–10.

47. Goodman 2005a, 71.

48. Goodman 2005a, 86–88; Goodman 2005b, 275, 278–79.

49. Judge 2015, 61.

50. Stapleton 2016, 17–47; Topley 1975, 77; Stockard 1989, 27–28; Jaschok 1989; Chin 2012, 11, 37–51, 61–63, 73–77. Jaschok and Chin include substantial discussion on the practice in Hong Kong.

51. Mann 1992, 255–56.

52. Cheng 2011, 53–54; Ma 2015, 64–65, 169–70.

53. Pruitt 1967, 73.

54. Pruitt 1967, 76, 114, 141, 107–8.

55. Except where otherwise noted, all information about Xie Bingying is drawn from her autobiography, Xie 2001. See also Edwards 2016b, 66–90; Dooling 2005, 32, 118–21.

56. Xie 2001; Stapleton 2008, 157–64.

57. Bailey 2006, 179. In 1917, an estimated 172,000 girls were attending Chinese-run schools, still less than 5 percent of the total number of students nationwide. Borthwick 1985, 82. Bailey 2007, 85–86, adds that in 1912, there were 10,146 girl students in secondary schools, 9.77 percent of the total. By 1922, the number had grown only slightly to 11,824 girl secondary students, and the percentage had declined to 6.46 percent of the total. In 1910–12, perhaps an additional sixty to seventy thousand girls attended mission schools, and into the early 1920s, Christian colleges enrolled about half the number of women students as non-mission schools. Bailey 2007, 34–35; Dunch 2009, 69. Christian schools at all levels thus were educating about one-third of the girls and young women attending school in the early years of the Republic.

58. Bailey 2007, 109.

59. Bailey 2007, 88.

60. Cong 2007, especially 87–94. Cong notes (91) that in 1923 China had twenty-five women's middle schools and sixty-seven women's teacher training schools. See also McElroy 2001; Orliski 2003, 49.

61. Ye 2001, 146–49; Gimpel 2015. Chen published a best-selling history of the Western world and a history of the European Renaissance.

62. Culp 2007, 33–36.

63. Culp 2007, 140–43, 308–9.

64. Judge 2015, 159.

65. Culp 2007, 213; McElroy 2001, 359–61.

66. Culp 2007, 132–39.

67. Bailey 2004, 238; Bailey 2006, 177–78; Bailey 2007, 95–96, 103, 106. Cong 2007, 93–94, argues that such courses expanded women's career possibilities in teaching. On the debate over the content of women's education, which continued into the 1940s, see also Schneider 2011, 57–80.

68. Judge 2015, 178, 187–88, 182; Bailey 2007, 83–84; Bailey 2006, 190; Xie 2001, 40–44. On discussions in the *Ladies' Journal* on the possibility of same-sex desire, see Hubbard 2014, 351, 353–55. On same-sex love among women in 1920s essays and fiction, see Sang 2003, 99–160; Dooling and Torgeson 1998, 177, 184–95; on

same-sex love in the tabloid press, see Kang 2009, 90–96. Wang 2011 discusses critical and pathologizing portrayals of same-sex love in the magazine *Linglong* during the 1930s.

69. Bailey 2004, 235–36, 227; Bailey 2006, 180, 190; Bailey 2007, 100–101; Bailey 2001; Chiang 2006, 524; Finnane 1996, 108.

70. Ma 2005b, 78; Deng 1999 [1921].

71. Xie 2001, 25–28.

72. Judge 2015, 161; Bailey 2004, 237.

73. Gilmartin 1995, 124–25; and Cong 2007, 104–105. On the history of this college, see Cong 2007, 16, 81, 91–93, 103–5.

74. Cong 2007, 105.

75. Culp 2007, 254–55.

76. Chow 1960, 151; Cheng 2011, 29.

77. Xie 2001, 35.

78. Lu Xun 1980b, 272.

79. Borthwick 1985, 83.

80. Bailey 2007, 90, cites government statistics counting 245,076 women factory workers in 1915, but elsewhere quotes a 1915 survey as finding "230,000 female industrial workers (mainly in the provinces of Jiangsu, Guangdong, Zhejiang, Jiangxi and Anhui)." Bailey 2006, 194–95.

81. Judge 2015, 105.

82. Burton 1918, 50, says two thousand women were in this factory; Ma 2015, 55, says three to five thousand.

83. Burton 1927, 27–29; Perry 1993, 170.

84. Tong Lam 2011.

85. On leftist writings about women factory workers in the 1920s and 1930s, see Laughlin 2002, 118–48; Ma 2005b, 61–62.

86. Honig 1986, 28.

87. Burton 1918, 51.

88. Honig 1986, 24. The statistics are drawn from a report by the Shanghai Bureau of Social Affairs. See also Smith 1994, 143; Smith 2002, 18. On the Shanghai tobacco industry and the role of women in it, see Perry 1993, 135–66. Howard 2011, 514, adds that in the mid-1930s, cigarette and tobacco factories in Shanghai employed more than eleven thousand women.

89. In Tianjin, large numbers of women did not enter the factories until the late 1930s. Hershatter 1986, 48, 54–57. Beijing had very few women employed in manufacturing well into the 1940s. Ma 2015, 53–54. He notes (56) that even in 1949, Beijing factories employed only 3,138 women. There, proportionally more women found employment in small handicraft workshops, pulled rickshaws, ran streetside stalls, or collected paper, boxes, and rags to exchange for household goods for their own use or for resale. Ma 2015, 55–56; Cheng 2011, 61–63.

90. Honig 1986, 62.

91. See, for example, Perry 1993, 55.

92. Honig 1986, 80–84; Honig 1992.

93. On the trafficking of indigent girls to Tianjin in 1921, see Shue 2006, 434–36; on Beijing in the mid-1920s, see Cheng 2011, 86–87.

94. Honig 1986, 94–114.

95. Honig 1986, 96, 121–24.

96. On the working-class geography of Shanghai, see Honig 1986, 22.

97. Burton 1918, 51. On child labor and attempts to regulate it, see also Howard 2011; Drucker 1979, especially 432–33; Littell-Lamb 2011.

98. Honig 1986, 23.

99. Burton 1927, 30.

100. Honig 1986, 155, 43–49, 142–48.

101. Honig 1986, 134, 145–46.

102. Burton 1918, 51–53; Judge 2015, 104–5.

103. Burton 1927, 33.

104. Judge 2015, 105; Honig 1986, 144, 148–49; Chen 2015, 14.

105. Honig 1986, 70–75; Honig 1992.

106. Honig 1986, 76–78.

107. Honig 1986, 50.

108. Honig 1986, 205.

109. Honig 1986, 50–51; on their relative quiescence, see also Perry 1993, 60–61; for accounts of militant actions by striking women cotton, silk, and tobacco workers, however, see Smith 1994; Smith 2002, 54–59, 141–44.

110. Honig 1986, 203–9.

111. On Subei origins of the silk filature workers, see Eng 1990, 80. Steamed-powered filatures where silk thread was reeled for export had been founded in Shanghai in the 1880s, and by 1927 the city had ninety-one filatures. Eng 1990, 66; for strike statistics for 1922–32 (for a total of seventy strikes), idem, 85. On militance relative to the cotton mills, see Perry 1993, 167–68.

112. Gilmartin 1995, 90, 94, 143–44; Eng 1990, 86–92; Perry 1993, 168–80; Ma 2005b, 63.

113. Yang Zhihua, cited in Perry 1993, 177.

114. Ma 2015, 58–59.

115. Honig 1986, 185–88.

116. Cheng 2011, 40.

117. Ma 2015, 55; Cheng 2011, 62.

118. Ma 2015, 71–72; Mann 1992, 260.

119. In 1930 Shanghai, men outnumbered women 135:100 in the Chinese governed sector, 156:100 in the International Settlement, and 164:100 in the French Concession. Hershatter 1997, 40. The two urban counties that encompassed Chengdu city recorded 800,000 males and 410,000 females in a 1916 census. Stapleton 2016, 124.

120. On Shanghai prostitution see Hershatter 1997; Henriot 2001; Yeh 2006; Pang 2005, 60–63. On Beijing, see Cheng 2011, 168–86; Ma 2015, 77–82.

121. Terminology and categories differed by location. Beijing had four classes of licensed brothels, as well as unregistered houses and some featuring foreign prostitutes. Courtesans often were linked in the press to specific politicians. Cheng 2011, 168–69, 172.

122. On geographical hierarchies, see Hershatter 1997, 53–56; on Beijing, see Cheng 2011, 172–73.

123. Cheng 2011, 86–87, 210–13. On trafficking in the Beijing-Tianjin area during this period, see Ransmeier 2017, 170–238.

124. On the influence of courtesan album aesthetics on portraits of Republican women in the *Women's Eastern Times*, see Judge 2015, 178–200.

125. Hershatter 1997, 250.

126. Chin 2012, 86.

127. Chin 2012, 86–87.

128. On an unsuccessful 1906 campaign in Chengdu to register and move all brothels to a special licensed zone, see Stapleton 2000, 128–33.

129. Ma 2015, 77; on Beijing discussions about abolishing prostitution, see Cheng 2011, 186–95, 218–23, 226–29.

130. Hershatter 1997, 19, 275–87, quotation on 285.

131. Hershatter 1997, 283.

132. On taxation and the proliferation of unlicensed prostitutes, in addition to the sources mentioned above, see Remick 2014; Chin 2012, 88–89.

133. Hershatter 1997, 19, 39; Ma 2015, 81; Chin 2012, 88–89.

134. Chow 1960, 258–59; Witke 1973b, 38–39; Edwards 2008a, 103–38.

135. Gilmartin 1995, 81; Edwards 2008a, 135–38.

136. Gilmartin 1995, 48.

137. Gilmartin 1995, 97, 249n1, 107.

138. Edwards 2008a, 143.

139. Edwards 2008a, 143–45.

140. Gilmartin 1995, 39.

141. Edwards 2008a, 146–54; see also Evans 2003.

142. Gilmartin 1995, 91.

143. Gilmartin 1995, 59–66.

144. Gilmartin 1995, 65, 94.

145. Unless otherwise noted, the account in this section is drawn from Gilmartin 1995, especially 96–114, 141–45.

146. Ip 2003, 334.

147. Gilmartin 1995, 104–14.

148. Gilmartin 1995, 57–58.

149. Gilmartin 1995, 108, 48.

150. Gilmartin 1995, 108–9.

151. Gilmartin 1995, 110; on separations from children, see Beahan 1984, 29–30.

152. The account that follows draws primarily upon Gilmartin 1995, 71–95, 104–8, 112–13, 122–25, 141–45, 231; also see Edwards 2008a, 149–54; Witke 1973b, 41–43; Leith 1973; Gipoulon 1984; McElderry 1986.

153. McElderry 1986, 106–7.

154. Gilmartin 1995, 130–31.

155. Gilmartin 1995, 112.

156. Edwards 2008a, 154–61; Gilmartin 1995, 128–29.

157. Such affairs were not uncommon. See Beahan 1984, 27–28.

158. Gilmartin 1995, 157–62; Leith 1973, 51–52.

159. Gilmartin 1995, 157–62; Leith 1973, 52. Deng Yingchao headed the Guangdong Women's Emancipation Association. Fitzgerald 1996, 285.

160. Later, when women engaged in armed combat during the Northern Expedition, some did so in Rosa Luxemburg battalions. Gilmartin 1995, 153–55; on

leaflets, see Fitzgerald 1996, 392n70. On International Women's Day in the United Front period, see Edwards 2016a, 91–95.

161. Gilmartin 1995, 133–35, 139. On women in the May Thirtieth Movement, see also Honig 1986, 27, 203–9; Edwards 2008a, 161–63.

162. Gilmartin 1995, 97, 249n1.

163. Gilmartin 1995, 138, 141.

164. Fitzgerald 1996, 284.

165. Gilmartin 1995, 163–64.

166. Fitzgerald 1996, 285.

167. Gilmartin 1995, 163–67.

168. Chin 2012, 23.

169. Gilmartin 1995, 175–81; Edwards 2016b, 67–69; on the role of women students, also see Culp 2007, 114, 251.

170. Xie 2001, 49.

171. Xie 2001, 51–52, 57–58.

172. Xie 2001, 53, 65–67. On Xie's *Army Diary*, published in 1928, see Laughlin 2002, 200–205.

173. Gilmartin 1995, 189–93.

174. Gilmartin 1995, 185–87.

175. Gilmartin 1995, 198–99.

176. Gilmartin 1995, 212; on the politics of short hair, see also Sun 1997; Yao Fei 2009; Edwards 2016b, 87–88.

177. Lu 1980a [1927], 353–54. See also Smedley 1976, 22; Edwards 2000, 129.

178. Xie 2001, 87–91; quotation from 88–89.

179. Xie 2001, 97–98.

180. Spence 1969, 200.

181. Gilmartin 1995, 211.

182. Wang 1999, 80–81.

183. Barlow 2004, 2–3.

CHAPTER 5: REGULATORY REGIMES, 1928–37

1. Zanasi 2006; Clinton 2017; Tsui 2018.

2. On Nationalist Party reconfiguration of International Women's Day to accord with its own agenda, see Edwards 2016a.

3. Rogaski 2004, 240–45; on eugenics and Pan Guangdan see Dikötter 1992, 174–85; Dikötter 2015, 112–19; Dikötter 1998, 104–18; Dikötter 1995, 109–21; Culp 2007, 147.

4. Kuo 2012b, 302.

5. Glosser 2003, 25, 81–133; Ma 2015, 184, 202, 206–13.

6. Kuo 2012a, 40–43; Bernhardt 1999; Huang 2001; Glosser 2003, 90–99; Edwards 2008a, 182–85. Li 2010 provides a summary of women's property rights under the Civil Code. On ways that widows were deprived of some custodial and inheritance rights by the Civil Code, see Bernhardt 1999, 117–32. On limitations on daughters' inheritance rights because of conflicts between the code and prevailing custom, see Bernhardt 1999, 133–60.

7. Kuo 2012a, 4; Bernhardt 1994; Bernhardt 1999; Huang 2001; Kuo 2012b, 305; Watson 1984, 2.

8. Kuo 2012a, 112.

9. Kuo 2012a, 17, 48n33.

10. Kuo 2012a, 6–7, 115–16, 198.

11. Bernhardt 1994, 200–205; Kuo 2012a, 109–13.

12. Bernhardt 1994, 194.

13. Ma 2015, 101, 107; Kuo 2012a, 6–7, 109–54.

14. Tran 2015, 14; Bernhardt 1999, 188–89.

15. Bernhardt 1994, 209–14; Bernhardt 1999, 188–95; Tran 2015, 48–53, 66–68, 73–75, 83–85, 88–94, 202–4.

16. Tran 2015, 15, 120–26, 205.

17. Kuo, 2012a, 156; Tran 2015, 3.

18. Kuo 2012a, 155; Tran 2015, 204.

19. Tran 2015, 41–48; on women's critiques of the legal code, see also Ma 2010, 273–80.

20. Watson 1984, 2; Kuo 2012b.

21. Rogaski 2004, 234–40.

22. Merkel-Hess 2016b, passim.

23. Richardson 2012; quotation from 6. The quotation about cubic meters of blood (a very large unit) is on 17.

24. Dikötter 1998, 99–104; Dikötter 1995, 9, 22–23, 25, 93–101.

25. Johnson 2011, 150–51; Hershatter 2011, 161.

26. Hershatter 2011, 154–63; Chen 2015, 12–13, 16.

27. Merkel-Hess 2016b, 8. Noting that rural women in their teens and twenties had higher death rates than men in that age group, Nanjing University economist John Lossing Buck surmised in 1930 that tetanus contracted during childbirth was the chief cause. Buck 1982, 323; see also Johnson 2011, 83.

28. Johnson 2011, xxv–xxvi; Hershatter 2011, 161.

29. Johnson 2011, xxvii, xxix, xxxi, xxxv, 52, 93–102, 113, 133–66.

30. Merkel-Hess 2016b, 11–12; see also Johnson 2011, 139–40.

31. Hershatter 2011, 349n41.

32. Johnson 2011, 156.

33. Merkel-Hess 2016b, 12–13; on urban birth control methods, see also Dikötter 1995, 119.

34. Han 2007. Such methods remained in use until the 1970s; see chapter 8.

35. Sommer 2010, 140–43; Johnson 2011, 148.

36. This account of Nanjing, except where otherwise noted, is based upon Lipkin 2006.

37. Lipkin 2006, 51–52. Nanjing was not an industrial city; women worked as farm laborers, sewed, made shoe soles, wove mats, hired out as servants, or worked as prostitutes. Lipkin 2006, 86.

38. Lipkin 2006, 217.

39. Lipkin 2006, 216.

40. Chen 2012, 11, 94, 87.

41. Chen 2012, 97–100, 106.

42. Dryburgh 2016.

43. Hershatter 1997, 58–65; Henriot 2001, 99–103.

44. Coercing a woman into prostitution remained illegal. Huang 2001, 183; Hershatter 1997, 187.

45. Remick 2014, 44.

46. Except where otherwise specified, the following account comes from Lipkin 2006, 167–99; tax information is from 169.

47. Hershatter 1997, 263–64.

48. Lipkin 2006, 53.

49. Remick 2014, especially 52–53, 13–14, 18–20, xi.

50. Remick 2014, 98–100, 121–49; Chin 2012, 138–40, 147.

51. Henriot 2001, 314–15.

52. Hershatter 1997, 272–87; Henriot 2001, 291–311.

53. Hershatter 1997, 204, 207–13; Henriot 2001, 314–16.

54. Henriot 2001, 316.

55. Rogaski 2004, 268–69.

56. Hershatter 1997, 235–41.

57. Remick 2014, 46–47.

58. Hershatter 1997, 264.

59. Chin 2012, 72–73, 78–80; Finnane 2008, 161–67; Lu 1980a [1927], 354. On indentured servitude, see also Jaschok and Miers 1994; White 2014.

60. Chin 2012, 99–127; on waitresses in Beijing, see Ma 2015, 50–51, 67–70; on similar dynamics in Chengdu teahouses during the late 1930s and early 1940s, see D. Wang 2004.

61. Chin 2012, 143–44.

62. Cowden 2012; Finnane 2013; Ma 2015, 191.

63. Ma 2015, 194–95; Cowden 2012; on Nationalist guidance for wedding rituals, see also Glosser 2003, 84–90, 128–33.

64. Except where otherwise noted, this section is based upon Duara 1995, 95–110; Ownby 2015, 687–88; Nedostup 2009, 23–23, 39, 52, 68–108, 180–81, 222–24; Kang 2014.

65. On Muslim women's religious practice and the emergence of women's mosques and religious schools, see Jaschok and Shui 2000, 94–99, 307–14, and passim; Jaschok and Shui 2011, 78–101.

66. This account is drawn from Nedostup 2009, 111–15; quotation is from 113.

67. Edwards 2000 provides a cogent account of social and political anxieties surrounding the new woman. Stevens 2003 maps the differences, and the common anxieties, between the New Woman and the Modern Girl. For an argument that the two figures were not fully distinct from one another, see Barlow 2006, 30n16; Gao 2013, 10, 114–26, and passim.

68. Mittler 2007b; see also Gao 2006; Gao 2013, 58–80; Yen 2005. On approving portrayals of opposite-sex love and stigmatization of same-sex love in *Linglong*, see Wang 2011. On sexualized American women in *Linglong* as a foil to more restrained Chinese women, see Edwards 2012.

69. On career women in Shanghai, see Lien 2001; on women journalists, see Ma 2010, 203–313.

70. Edwards (2000, 117) argues that "the new woman was a creature of the progressive, intellectual class's political aspirations, and as a result, her utility for the feminist movement was limited."

71. The account that follows, except where otherwise noted, is based on Wang Zheng 1999. Wang's fifth interviewee, Huang Dinghui, was the only interviewee who was a Communist Party member, and her story (286–356), which is quite different from the others, is not discussed here.

72. On Lu Lihua, see also Gao 2013, 81–126.

73. Yu 2005; Yu 2009; Gao 2006; Gao 2013; Finnane 1996; Wang 2011, 314–25. Gao 2013, 17–57, provides a biography of another educator active in women's physical education, Zhang Huilan.

74. Gao 2013, 122.

75. On literary uses of the New Woman trope by both men and women authors, see also Dooling 2005, 7, 19–20, 113–14; Larson 1998; Cheng 2007; Welland 2006; Lee 2007. On women's magazines during the Nanjing Decade, see Ma 2010, 255–313.

76. Wang Zheng 1999, 231.

77. Lien 2001 (25–26, 29–30) finds perhaps sixteen thousand career women in the entire city of Shanghai in 1935, plus 3,746 teachers.

78. Wang Zheng 1999, 183.

79. The following account is based on Harris 1995; Harris 1997; Meyer 2005; Hong 2007; Foliot 2010; Ma 2010, 288–90; Jiang 2009, 60–61, 65–69, 171–72.

80. Zheng 1997.

81. Jiang 2009, 66.

82. Lien 2001, 81–87.

83. Glosser 2003, 72–73, 78, 159–65; Yeh 2007, 116–17; Lien 2001, 106–7; Hubbard 2014. Some career women did continue to work outside the home after marriage; for an account of the hectic double day this produced, even with a household servant, see Lien 2001, 40.

84. Lien 2001, 83–84.

85. On newspaper advertising featuring women cleaning and caring for children, see Mittler 2007a; on savings, see Sheehan 2006, 137–39.

86. For the controversy surrounding this formulation see Lien 2001, 110–22; Ma 2010, 264–71.

87. Glosser 2003, 3–4, 23–24, and passim.

88. Glosser 2003, 135.

89. Glosser 2003, 25, 134–66; Yeh 2007, 69–70; on interior decoration, see Lee 1999, 68–71. On debates over women's education in home economics during this period, see also Schneider 2011, 93–110, 126–28.

90. Glosser 2003, 162.

91. On the qipao and the question of modern national fashion, see Finnane 1996; Finnane 2008, 139–75; Edwards 2000, 130–31; Laing 2003, 72, 91, 70, 97, 99, 101–8. On women who dressed in men's clothing and the anxieties that engendered in commentators, see Finnane 2008, 193–98.

92. See, for example, Laing 2004, 143.

93. Lin 2013; quotation from 307.

94. Rogaski 2004, 230–32. "In Tianjin," she writes, "Lysol was advertised to clean vaginas, not kitchen counters."

95. Lin 2013, 310.

96. Gerth 2003, 158–200.

97. Yeh 2007, 71–73.

98. Glosser 2003, 159–65; Gerth 2003, 285–332; quotation from 296.

99. Yeh 2007, 67–68; see also Lee 1999, 76–80; Laing 2004; dal Lago 2012; Mittler 2007a, 21–23; Tsai 2006, 136–43.

100. On intellectual critiques of the "commercial modern woman," see Edwards 2000, 124, 130, 133, 136–38.

101. The contemporaneous Japanese term was *moga*. The discussion of the Modern Girl in the next two paragraphs draws on Lien 2001, 121–28; Barlow 2005; Dong 2008; Modern Girl around the World Research Group 2008; Finnane 2008, 167–68; Stevens 2003. On the Modern Girl in literature, see also Larson 1998; Shih 2001; L. Wang 2004, 112.

102. Gerth 2003, 288–89.

103. Benedict 2011, 222–32, 235–36; on the resignification of women's smoking from a common late imperial practice to a stigmatized sign of sexual availability, see Benedict 2011, passim.

104. Dong 2008, 208–11.

105. Gerth 2003, 297, 300–308; Edwards 2000, 134–35.

106. Dong 2008, 196–201.

107. Field 2010, 119–75; see also Field 2010, 4, 53–55, 63–82, 119–75; Farrer and Field 2015, 16–38, 154–59; Zheng 1997, 109–13; Lee 1999, 23–29.

108. Field 2010, 119–75; Hershatter 1997, 59–60; Henriot 2001, 99, 103–14.

109. These numbers are derived from the 1929 figures in Honig 1986, 24.

110. Shiroyama 2008, 114–39.

111. Perry 1993, 92–103.

112. Honig 1986, 94–131.

113. This discussion is limited to factory workers. For labor activism among women teahouse workers in Guangzhou, see Chin 2012, 219–34.

114. Honig 1986, 209–17.

115. Honig 1986, 217–24.

116. Eng 1990, 90–91.

117. On underground CCP operations in Shanghai during the Nanjing Decade, see Stranahan 1998; Young 2001, 68–70. For an account of a Nationalist raid on underground Communists, and the broader repression of labor activists and intellectuals in the late 1920s and early 1930s, see Smedley 1945, 70–86.

118. Perry 1993, 186–201; quotation from 194; Perry 2002, 134–55.

119. Place mattered: in a 1930 study covering seven provinces, economist John Lossing Buck found women performing from 1.2 percent to almost half of the field labor. A larger survey he directed of more than thirty-eight thousand farm families across China from 1929 to 1933 found that women were an average of 24 percent of the workforce, comprising more than one-third in some rice-growing regions, and 42 percent in households that relied only on subsidiary production such as handicrafts or raising livestock. Nevertheless, Buck estimated that women performed only 13 percent of all farm labor and 16 percent of sideline production

nationwide, numbers that later scholars consider to be too low. Buck 1956, 291–93, 297; Hershatter 2007, 56–57. For a comprehensive critique of Buck's work, see Stross 1986, 161–87. In Wuxi, James Kung and Daniel Lee have found, women's economic contribution to the household was similar to that of men: they worked in agriculture (rice, wheat, mulberry) and silkworm raising, and some migrated to work in Shanghai factories. Kung and Lee 2010.

120. Burton 1918, 22–25; Huang 1990, 50–57; Buck 1982, 237, 254; Chen 2015, 24–25; McLaren 2008, 54–55.

121. See, for instance, Chen 2015, 15.

122. Huang 1990, 52.

123. On agricultural commercialization see, inter alia, Huang 1985, 121–37; Bell 1999; Walker 1999.

124. Topley 1975; Stockard 1989, especially 134–66.

125. Bell 1994; Bell 1999; Bell 2000; Shiroyama 2008, 92–105, 114–24.

126. Huang 1990, 140–41; Shiroyama 2008, 122–24.

127. Stockard 1989, 169.

128. Walker 1993; Walker 1999, 178–82, 188, 192–95; McLaren 2008, 54–55.

129. Mann 1992, 253; Gilmartin 1995, 149.

130. Bossen 2002, 100–101; Friedman 2006.

131. Pomeranz 2005, 251; Xie 2001, 12–13.

132. Hershatter 2011, 69, 63, 70.

133. Ma 2015, 136; Kapp 1973; Crook and Gilmartin 2014; Hershatter 2011, 54–55.

134. Stross 1986, 174–75.

135. Li 1991, 489n51.

136. Shiroyama 2008, 125; Pietz 2002, 61–75; Pietz 2015, 88–89.

137. Pietz 2015, 104.

138. Li 1991, 478, 487–95; on lopsided sex ratios in 1934 Anhui, see Perry 1980, 51.

139. Chen 1984, 62–67.

140. Finnane 2008, 169. For the social and economic logics underlying the continued practice of footbinding in some rural areas, see Bossen 2002, 37–83; Bossen et al. 2011; Brown et al. 2012; Gates 2001; Gates 2014; Brown 2016; Bossen and Gates 2017.

141. Zanasi 2006, 26–78, 133–73.

142. Merkel-Hess 2016a, 49; Stross 1986, 206.

143. Zanasi 2006, 173.

144. Lien 2001, 72–78, 98.

145. On women activists' continuing struggle for suffrage and women's rights during the Nanjing Decade, see Edwards 2008a, 168–94; Ma 2010, 272–73.

146. Rogaski 2004, 238–39; Johnson 2011, xxxi, 130, 155–56; Lipkin 2006, 53–54; Gerth 2003, 292–98.

147. X. Sun 2008.

148. Lien 2001, 83–84; Culp 2007, 172–73.

149. X. Sun 2008.

150. Laing 2003, 108; Finnane 1996, 118; Chin 2012, 144, 140–48; Johnson 2011, 155; Benedict 2011, 234–35; Edwards 2000, 133; Edwards 2008a, 185–88; Finnane 2008, 170–75; Gao 2013, 72–78, 182–89; Yen 2005.

151. Ma 2010, 255.

152. Yen 2005; Gao 2013, 78–80. On the role of the Girl Scouts organization in promoting young women's physical activities, see Tillman 2014.

153. Cong 2007, 152–58, 17.

154. Culp 2007, 117–20.

155. Culp 2007, 209, 221, 224, 228–30.

156. Culp 2007, 189–90, 196–97, 202–4.

157. Culp 2010, 265; Culp 2007, 258.

158. Smedley 1945, 109.

159. Israel 1966, 120; Israel and Klein 1976, 1.

160. On Lu Cui, see Pan 1997, 119; Israel and Klein 1976, 55–57, quotation from 56–57.

161. Translated in Pan 1997, 119.

CHAPTER 6: WARTIME WOMEN, 1928–41

1. In addition to the sources cited in this chapter, Chinese-speaking readers may be interested in the oral histories of women in wartime collected in Li 2003 and Yu et al. 2004.

2. This period was characterized by much intra-Party struggle, and Mao Zedong's approach to organizing and military strategy was much contested and generally not dominant from 1931 to 1934, although he was chair of the Central Executive Committee of the Jiangxi Soviet government. For a useful summary, see Mao 1997, xxvii–ci.

3. Mao 1995, 31, 36.

4. On this point see, inter alia, Benton 1992, 5.

5. Mao 1997, lxiv–lxv, 822–25. The Land Law, promulgated in December 1931, bears Mao's signature as chair of the Central Executive Committee, but it probably had been drafted in Shanghai by members of the Central Committee and should not be regarded as an expression of his own approach. See lxivn68.

6. Williams 1989.

7. Williams 1989.

8. Because Mao went on to become the CCP's longtime preeminent leader, many of his writings have been preserved, and we know far more about his thinking on the woman question than we do about that of other Party leaders.

9. Mao 1990, 216. As early as 1927, reporting on a peasant movement in Hunan during the First United Front, he had also noticed that "in the villages, triangular and multilateral relationships are almost universal among poor peasants." This sentence was not included in the later official text of his report. Hu (1974, 478) understands this comment to be a sign of Mao's view that peasants were less bound by feudal sexual norms than members of the elite, but it is also possible that he was merely noting the prevalence of polyandry among the poor. On polyandry, see Sommer 2015.

10. Mao 1990, 213–17. Quotations from 214.

11. Landlords were those whose main income came from land rent. Rich peasants produced more than they needed, much of it by exploiting hired labor.

Middle peasants could support themselves. Poor peasants rented or owned land but often did not produce enough to survive. Hired laborers owned no land and lived on their wages. For descriptions of the categories of landlords and peasants, see, inter alia, Benton 1992, xxxviii.

12. On Xingguo County's marriage statistics and the dictum to freely seek spouses, see Hu 1974, 478–80. See also Mao 1995, 625, 628, 629–30, 633; quotation on *ziyou* is from 628; quotation on farm laborers is from 630.

13. Hu 1974, 480.

14. Mao 1995, 630.

15. Mao 1990, 213–17.

16. Davin 1976, 29–30.

17. Mao 1990, 217; Hu 1974, 480.

18. Mao 1997, 791–93.

19. Mao 1997, 958–60.

20. Mao 1997, 715, 959.

21. Mao 1997, 959–60.

22. Hu 1974, 483–84.

23. Hu 1974, 486.

24. Mao 1997, 616.

25. Hu 1974, 477.

26. Mao 1997, lxxii–lxxiii. Except where otherwise noted, the following discussion of women's mobilization and women's rights draws upon Mao 1997, 225–29, 264, 271, 319–20, 340–43, 472, 476, 683, 696; Davin 1976, 22–32; Spakowski 2005, 133–35.

27. For this exclusion of women from regular Red Army ranks, see Mao 1997, 273.

28. Mao 1997, 542.

29. Spakowski 2005, 132, 137–40; Spakowski 2009.

30. Mao 1995, 217.

31. Mao 1995, 670.

32. For one account of such recruitment, see Sun 2006, 14–25.

33. Mao 1997, 597–98, 605–6.

34. Mao 1997, vol. 4: 474, 533; these targets appear in documents from August and September 1933. On the voting rights of all women from poor and middle peasant backgrounds, see Edwards 2008a, 189–90.

35. The Labor Law passed in November 1931 specified equal pay for equal work (chapter 6, Article 29). Chapter 7 of the Law also provided specific protections for women: they were not to work in mines; various types of factories processing metals, rubber, and glue; or in foundries. Nor were they to fell high trees. They were not to be required to lift weights heavier than forty kilograms. Pregnant women were not to work the night shift. Six weeks' paid maternity leave was to be provided to white-collar workers, eight weeks to manual workers. Nursing mothers were to be provided with paid nursing breaks, and factories were to provide child care. Another labor law, passed in October 1933, reiterated these provisions with minor modifications. Mao 1997, 803–4, 887.

36. For a 1934 report citing one evening school with 15,740 students, 69 percent of them female, see Mao 1997, 696.

37. Benton 1992, 9–12.

38. Benton 1992, 4.

39. For a description of the evacuation and the numbers involved, see Benton 1992, 3–6, 15, 18. Quotation is from 3.

40. On mountains, rivers, and grasslands, see Ono 1989, 155–57. The Long March was actually several marches, with varying numbers of women and children. See Spakowski 2005, 141–47. Zhang Guotao's Fourth Front Army, in contrast to Mao's First Front Army, had several thousand women, as well as children. On the experiences of women Long Marchers from the First, Second, and Fourth Armies, see Young 2001; Young 2005; Xiao Yun 2003.

41. Benton 1992, 5, gives the number of thirty-five women, as does Helen Young for the number who initially joined the First Front Army March (Young 2005, 173–74); Young 2001, 187, 199 says there were thirty. For biographies of thirty of the women, see Lee and Wiles 1999, 249–74. On criteria for selection, see Spakowski 2005 142–43, n30; Young 2001, 147; Lee and Wiles 1999, 46–47; King 2010, 24–26; Sun 2006, 22–25. On women's role in the march, in addition to the sources cited below, see also Sun 2006; King 2010.

42. Young 2001, 12, 109–15.

43. Young 2005, 172; Young 2001, 54.

44. Spakowski 2005, 145–47; Young 2005, 181, 185–86; Young 2001, 1034, 216–39; Lee and Wiles 1999, 28–29, 134–50.

45. Young 2001, 131–45, 163–75, 100–101, 243; Young 2005, 181, 183, 188–89; Lee 1994, 71.

46. Young 2005, 174n2; Young 2001, 202–3; Lee and Wiles 1999, 27, 33–34. On others who left children behind, see Young 2001, 73, 79–80, 111, 195–96, 206; Lee and Wiles 1999, 28–31, 35–36, 41.

47. Young notes (2005, 174–75) that both the Second and Fourth Front Armies had more lenient policies about carrying babies along with the marchers. On childbirth and child care during the Long March, see also Young 2001, 31–34, 36–43, 47–56, 75–76, 205–7. Many women interviewed later also talked about the difficulty of managing menstrual periods on the march without access to any supplies; reportedly, half stopped menstruating altogether, and many ended up with lifelong gynecological problems. See, inter alia, Young 2001, 12, 18, 203–4; Sun 2006, 151.

48. Young 2001, 35, 45–47, 90–92, 146–61, 191–94; Young 2005, 172, 174, 179–80, 184–85, 188.

49. Lee and Wiles 1999, 41.

50. Lee and Wiles 1999, 156–58, 170, 172.

51. Young 2005, 190–91; Young 2001, 56–58, 80–81, 161; Lee 1994, 76–88; Lee and Wiles 1999, 181–247; 249–74; Ono 1989, 158. Many were investigated and imprisoned during the Cultural Revolution, collateral damage of factional conflicts in the top Party leadership at that time.

52. Benton 1992, 24.

53. For an estimate of ten to fifteen thousand regular and local forces and other details about those left behind, see Benton 1992, 7–8, 18, 24.

54. Benton 1992, xvi, xix, xxxii–xxxiii, 10, 73–74.

55. Benton 1992, 24, 148, 341.

56. Williams 1989.

57. Spakowski 2005, 132, 142, 147–51; Spakowski 2009. On women's direct participation in combat, see Benton 1992, 363.

58. Benton 1992, 73–74, 98–99, 147–48, 164, 272, 361–62, 399, 486–87; Spakowski 2005.

59. For a useful summary of Japanese presence in Manchuria before 1931, see Duara 2009, 46–50.

60. For an autobiographical account by Li Yuqin, whom Puyi took as a consort in 1943 when she was fifteen, see Li 1992, 226–46.

61. Duara 2009, 52. On Japanese women settlers in Manzhouguo, and their representation as pioneers and mothers, see Young 1998, 368–70 and passim.

62. Smith 2012, 30; Duara 2009, 52, 57.

63. Dubois 2014, 525–29.

64. Levine 1989, 154, 160; Mitter 2013, 62; Smith 2007, 4, 24. On the activities of Zhao Yiman in rural Manzhouguo, her execution by the Japanese, and her posthumous career as a heroine in the People's Republic, see Edwards 2016b, 117–36.

65. Smith 2007, 32–35, 38–39. On state ideals and their promotion in Manzhouguo schools and state-sponsored films, see also Ma 2005a.

66. Smith 2012, 113; Smith 2007, 27.

67. Li 1992, 248–49.

68. Xiao Hong was born into a rural landlord family outside of Harbin in 1911 and attended middle school in Harbin. See, inter alia, Xiao 1979; Xiao 1986; Liu 1994. Howard Goldblatt's introductions to his translations of Xiao's books offer useful biographical information.

69. Smith 2007, 50–51, 59; quotation from 50.

70. Smith 2007, 52, 56, 60, 61, 67, 71, 85–125.

71. Duara 2009, 53, 117–18, 30–147; Duara 2003, 131–69.

72. Smith 2012, 22–32.

73. Smith 2012, 40, 45–46, 64–65, 95–97, 99, 103–4, 106–9, 139–40, 142–43. Meyer 2014 provides a vivid description of life in a Harbin slum building, based on a Japanese police report from 1941.

74. Smith 2012, 6, 111.

75. Smith 2012, 113–29.

76. Smith 2012, 32, 74, 80–83, 86–87, 62–65, 49.

77. Duara 2003, 67–70; Smith 2007, 24–25, 28.

78. Smith 2007, 4, 23.

79. Spence 1981, 309–10; Mitter 2013, 5.

80. Lary and MacKinnon 2001, 9.

81. Stranahan 1998, 221–23; Wang 1999, 199–200.

82. Yang went on to travel to the United States and Europe to raise funds for the war effort in China but was later accused of collaboration with Japanese authorities. Tillman 2014, 151–59.

83. The number of those murdered is itself a subject of historical controversy. See, inter alia, Honda 1999, xiii, 285; Brook 1999, 2; Fogel 2000, 6; Spence 1981, 312. The fact that widespread murder of civilians was a common practice during this Japanese advance is well-documented in testimony from Japanese soldiers, surviving Chinese eyewitnesses, and foreigners resident in Nanjing.

84. Ono 1989, 162; Honda 1999; Yang 2000, 142; Brook 1999, 10–11, 17, 19–20, 26, 28–38, 40–48, 54–56, 61–65, 77, 88–89, 94–95, 119–33, 135–56, 158–60, 214, 220–21, 235–36, 259 (this last page, from the postwar judgment of the International Military Tribunal, estimates twenty thousand rape cases in the first month of the occupation); Brook 2005, 127–43.

85. Brook 1999, 65.

86. Edwards 2013, 567–68, 571, 573–77, 563. Edwards (571) also notes that women's magazines during the war took a very different tack, avoiding depictions of violence and instead discussing "how to assist women victims of sexual violence and how to simultaneously advance women's rights and promote resistance to the Japanese invasion." On a similar gendered division of labor in propaganda posters, see Yao and Ma 2015.

87. Lary and MacKinnon 2001, 3, 112; Perry 1980, 15; Pietz 2015, 104–8. In 1946 a UN report estimated that 1.7 million people displaced by the Yellow River flooding had migrated to Shaanxi Province. Muscolino 2015, 79.

88. Lary 2010, 63–64.

89. Lary and MacKinnon 2001, 6, 121; on refugees and refugee relief in Wuhan, see also Zurndorfer 2013, 78–83; Chen 2012, 128–72, also discusses welfare facilities for beggars in occupied Beijing and Shanghai.

90. MacKinnon 2008, 57.

91. Smedley 1976, 85–87.

92. MacKinnon 2001, 127–31; MacKinnon 2008, 55–59; Zurndorfer 2013, 78–82. On magazines in Wuhan directed at women, see MacKinnon 2008, 67.

93. Chou 2014; Zhao 2015.

94. Xie 2001, 271–81; quotation from 271. See also Edwards 2016b, 72–73, 77; Stapleton 2008, 166–67.

95. Chou 2014.

96. Brook 2005, 9 and passim. He observes (24–25) that women's relative exclusion from political life rendered them less likely to become collaborators. For a useful summary of the scholarship on collaboration, see also Smith 2007, 3–8.

97. Brook 2005, 162–65.

98. On assassinations, crime, and terrorism in Shanghai between 1937 and 1941, see Wakeman 1996; Brook 2005, 184–85; Edwards 2016b, 137–57. For a recent overview of many aspects of gendered life in wartime Shanghai, see Chen 2014.

99. Lien 2001, 147–48.

100. Lien 2006. On gender discrimination in the civil service, see also Lien 2001, 159–68.

101. Yeh 2007, 170; on refugees in Shanghai, also see Chen 2012, 143–148; Stranahan 1998, 223–27; Zurndorfer 2013, 73–76.

102. *Shanghai shenghuo* (October 1939), cited in Jiang 2009, 17.

103. Yeh 2007, 152–63, 170, 173–74, 181–83; Lien 2001, 143.

104. Honig 1986, 35; Jiang 2009, 3–4, 18–25, 51, 58–59, 79–80, 115–32. Jiang (57) points out that many women from Zhejiang, where Yue opera originated, became performers after the collapse of the silk industry during the 1930s Depression.

105. Jiang 2009, 60–75.

106. Hershatter 1997, 206, 223–24; on various plans to regulate and inspect prostitutes, and their general lack of success in Shanghai, see Henriot 2001, 322–25. On stringent Japanese medical inspections of prostitutes in Tianjin, see Rogaski 2004, 272.

107. Field 2010, 179–99, 211–15, 225–32.

108. Perry 1993, 109–15. The CCP role among silk weavers during this period is discussed on 208–9. On the overall strategy for the underground Party in Shanghai during this period, see Stranahan 1998, 210–13, 217.

109. Honig 1986, 224–29.

110. Honig 1986, 34–36, 108, 126–28, 184, 199–200.

111. Bernhardt 1994; Kuo 2012a; Glosser 2003, 110–28.

112. Bernhardt 1994, 195–196. In Shanghai in 1940–42, the percentage was 74 percent.

113. Ma 2015, 86–119.

114. Glosser 2003, 113–21; Ma 2015, passim.

115. Ma 2015, 110.

116. Ma 2015, 3, 15–119, 125–31, 165, 223, 249, 257, 269, 272, 318.

117. Ma 2015, 4, 319–21.

118. Lary 2010, 25–26, 68, 100, 118. For a description of the military comfort women system and personal testimonies, see Qiu 2013, which offers an estimate of two hundred thousand Chinese comfort women (38).

119. Chen 2015, 37.

CHAPTER 7: WARTIME WOMEN, 1935–49

1. Liu 2013. Schneider 2011, 57–80, 96–97, 128–42 traces the continuation of debates about the purpose of women's education, the importance of family education, good-wife-wise-motherism, and adjustments in university-level home economic curricula during the wartime period.

2. Spence 1981, 314; Israel 1998.

3. Israel 1998, 64–67, 233.

4. Li 2010, 52–53, 47–49; Lary 2010, 87–88; Ferlanti 2012, 206.

5. Ferlanti 2012, 206–7. On women's New Life work in the Sichuan countryside, see X. Sun 2008, 188–230.

6. Ferlanti 2012, 191; X. Sun 2008, 125–235; Schneider 2012; Zurndorfer 2013, 86–87. For a survey of women's organizations in Chongqing, see Li 2010, 20–22.

7. Edwards 2008a, 206.

8. Ferlanti 2012, 193, 200–201; Howard 2013, 1894, 1910–11; X. Sun 2008, 136–37; Schneider 2012; Pan 1997, 121; Ma 2010, 317–18.

9. Ferlanti 2012, 188, 191, 193, 198–204; Schneider 2012; Schneider 2013; Pan 1997, 121–22; see X. Sun 2008, 178–82 on the role of housewives in these activities.

10. Li 2010, 97, 123–27. Quotation from 124.

11. Schneider 2012; Schneider 2013. Schneider 2011, 148–69 analyzes a related project, the creation of "family education experimental zones" staffed by educators, including home economists, to teach rural women and children, and to im-

prove domestic management, handicraft production, and awareness of national issues.

12. Lary 2010, 97, 99; Howard 2013, 1904.

13. Howard 2013, 1894; Zurndorfer 2013, 87. On the move of women waitresses into the teahouse service industry in Chengdu during the war, their union activity, and the harassment they faced from waiters and customers, see Wang 2004. On the wives of arsenal workers taking in laundry and working as wet nurses, see Howard 2004, 100.

14. Howard 2013, 1897.

15. Howard 2013, 1900–1901, 1913–17; Howard 2011, 523.

16. Howard 2013, 1900–1902, 1905–07.

17. Howard 2013, 1894, 1908–11; Ferlanti 2012, 204, 208; X. Sun 2008, 232–34.

18. Howard 2013, 1903. I have slightly modified the translation, which could be rendered more literally as "Big Sister works hard producing at the Rear."

19. Howard 2013, 1923.

20. Howard 2013, 1890–92, 1894–95.

21. Barnes 2012; quotation from 291.

22. On Fei Xiaotong's work in Yunnan villages in 1938, see Bossen 2002.

23. Crook and Gilmartin 2014, 45, 62, 54, 66.

24. Crook and Gilmartin 2014, 73, 75–77, 81.

25. Crook and Gilmartin 2014, 25–26, 35, 192–95.

26. Crook and Gilmartin 2014, 209–15.

27. Crook and Gilmartin 2014, 218–23. On runaway wives in the Yan'an area, see Cong 2016, 79–83.

28. Spence 1981, 339–40; Barnes 2012, 298 (quotation from 298). See also Crook and Gilmartin 2014, 240–45.

29. Lary 2010, 97.

30. Glosser 2003, 118.

31. Crook and Gilmartin 2014, 85.

32. Muscolino 2015, 74–75, 78, 142–43, 151–55, 170. Quotation from 78.

33. Lary 2010, 126–28; Service 1974, 9–19, quotation from 11.

34. Service 1974, 93–96.

35. Peck 1950, 94–98.

36. The Long March eventually brought Mao's army to Sichuan, where he reunited with another Communist force, and then to northern Shaanxi. Benton 1992, xlii–xliii. On population, see Spence 1981, 309. By 1946, the Yan'an population had grown (through in-migration as well as other means) to close to 1.6 million people, 750,704 of them women. Stranahan 1983, 74.

37. On CCP policies during the Yan'an years see, inter alia, Selden 1995; Service 1974, 228–33; Stranahan 1983, 25–86; Johnson 1983.

38. Selden 1995, 104.

39. Spakowski 2005, 151; Spakowski 2009.

40. Stranahan 1983, 33.

41. Keating 1997, 186.

42. Mao 2015, 199, 201, 204, 205, 214, 216, 224; Davin 1976, 34–35; Stranahan 1983, 103–4.

43. Mao 2015, 225–27, 233, 261, 263, 279. See also Ono 1989, 167–68. On the spinning and weaving campaign that began in 1943, see Stranahan 1983, 60–62.

44. Selden 1995, 196–208. As Yung-fa Chen has shown, they also produced and sold opium to Nationalist areas. Selden 1995, 247–49, provides a brief summary.

45. Davin 1976, 40–42; Stranahan 1983, 52–53, 63–67.

46. Stranahan 1983, 69–70; for translations of three labor model life histories, see also Sheridan and Salaff 1984, 180–96.

47. Davin 1976, 42.

48. Selden 1995, 202.

49. Stranahan 1983, 75–77; on problems with the co-ops, see also Keating 1997, 231–33.

50. Keating 1997.

51. Davin 1976, 42.

52. Davin 1976, 198–99; Stranahan 1983, 59.

53. Davin 1976, 42. On men opposed to their wives working with non-kin men, see Keating 1997, 211–12.

54. Johnson 1983, 63–89 provides a useful analysis of these issues. See also Selden 1995, 92.

55. Ono 1989, 168; Johnson 2011, 169; on hygiene initiatives, see also Selden 1995, 209; Hua 1984, 11–12.

56. Ono 1989, 168–69; Stranahan 1983, 44, 81–83.

57. Cong 2016, 43. On conditions under which presents were not to be considered bride purchase, and a discussion of how local practices differed from the Marriage Regulations, see Hua 1984, 2–4.

58. On the conditions for divorce, see Stranahan 1983, 35; Cong 2016, 43.

59. Hua 1984, 5; Cong 2016, 43. Johnson 1983, 66–71, provides a summary of Party policy on marriage reform as it developed in Yan'an.

60. Hua 1984, 5–6.

61. Stranahan 1983, 28; Hua 1984, 1. On men's resistance to divorce in north China base areas, see Jiang and Wang 2016, 73–77.

62. Keating 1997, 250; see also Hua 1984, 14–15, 18–19.

63. Hua 1984, 9–14.

64. Hua 1984, 14; for the complicated issues involved and the government's evolving approach, see Cong 2016, 88–95.

65. Stranahan 1983, 37–41, 45–48; on elections, see also 102. Davin 1976, 36 reports that women were elected to 8 percent of local government positions in 1941, much lower than rates in Jiangxi. See also Edwards 2008a, 226–27.

66. Hua 1984, 14–15.

67. Hua 1984, 16–17.

68. Cong 2013, 198; Cong 2016, 52–56; see also Hua 1984, 6–7.

69. Cong 2016, 96–99.

70. Cong 2016, 158–61; Cong 2013, 207; Hua 1984, 9.

71. Cong 2013, 202–3; Cong 2016, 163–71. In response, the 1946 regulations distinguished between caili as a local custom and sign of agreement to a marriage and caili as outright purchase.

72. Cong 2016, 9–16, 139–61.

73. Cong 2016, 107–11, 156–57; 175–206.

74. Hung 1993, 410–12.

75. Cong (2016 and 2013) argues that these adjustments were not a retreat from Party ideals, but rather a recognition that it would take time for marriage practices to change.

76. Israel and Klein 1976, 183.

77. Spakowski 2005, 155–56; Spakowski 2009; Ono 1989, 169–70; Stranahan 1983, 101. On women students sent out to organize for the 1941 elections, see Selden 1995, 127, 141n77. For largely celebratory firsthand reminiscences by women who went from the cities to Yan'an, written half a century later, see Su and Xu 1991.

78. Spakowski 2005, 151, 154; Spakowski 2009.

79. Spakowski 2005, 160; Edwards 2008a, 191.

80. Service 1974, 179–80.

81. Barlow (2004, 127–252) provides an extended and provocative analysis of Ding Ling's work. The following discussion of Ding Ling also draws upon Dooling and Torgeson 1998, 263–66; Spence 1981, 308–37; Stranahan 1983, 54–57; Selden 1995, 127.

82. Spence 1981, 327.

83. Ding Ling et al. 1989, 298–315; quotation from 309. On changing interpretations of this story and the post-1949 need to reestablish claims to sexual morality by repudiating the activities of women sex spies, see Edwards 2016b, 158–74.

84. Ding 1981.

85. On the CCP's rectification movement during this period see, inter alia, Selden 1995, 152–65.

86. For one account of the divorce and He Zizhen's subsequent years in Moscow, see Lee and Wiles 1999, 110–33. On Jiang Qing's account of her own life, see Witke 1975; Witke 1977. For her 1937 account of why she left her previous husband, Tang Na, see Li 1992, 216–25. On the phenomenon of older women revolutionary wives being displaced by attractive young arrivals from the cities, see Ip 2003, 343–45.

87. Mao 2015, 102–32. On the subsequent attempts by cultural workers to identify, collect, and help reshape folk arts such as paper cuts and folk songs, see Wu 2015a, 96–99; Wu 2015b.

88. Spence 1981, 332–35, 337, 345, 347–52; quotation from 333 and from Mao 2015, 127. See also Evans 2003. For an upbeat postwar account in Ding Ling's own words of her work collecting stories from blind peasant storytellers, see Payne 1947, 381–86. Her post-1942 writings conformed closely to the model Mao had laid out at the Yan'an Forum, including her 1948 novel *The Sun Shines over the Sanggan River*, which won the Stalin Prize in China. But in 1958 she was declared a rightist and spent much time between then and the early 1980s in internal exile or prison. Barlow 2004, 233–52.

89. Some suffered far worse consequences. On Wang Shiwei's critical writings exploring similar issues, and his eventual execution, see Benton and Hunter 1995, 10–13, 69–84; Dai 1994; Spence 1981, 331–34; Selden 1995, 157, 245–46. Ding Ling, who had published essays by Wang Shiwei, joined in the criticism of him.

90. Barlow in Ding Ling et al. 1989, 316.

91. Spakowski 2005, 157, 159–60.

92. Lee and Wiles 1999, 159–61.

93. Goodman 2000a, 915–17, 927–29; Ngo 2009, 291. Jiang and Wang 2016 (69–70), however, find 327 divorces recorded in Wuxiang County in 1944, and argue that wife-initiated divorces across north China base areas numbered in the thousands from the early 1940s into the Civil War period.

94. Goodman 1997; Goodman 2000b, 213, 240–45, 260; Goodman 2000a, 932–35.

95. Ngo 2009, 292–97, 303, 305.

96. Jiang and Wang 2016, 70–71, 78–79.

97. Hartford 1989.

98. Spence 1981, 323; Hartford 1989; Selden 1995, 144–45, 232.

99. See, for instance, Lary 2010, 145.

100. Davin 1976, 45.

101. On the question of morale and heroism, see Hartford 1989. The exigencies of wartime work in such places contributed to an autocratic and brutal work style among local Communist revolutionaries that continued to create much suffering after Communist rule was consolidated in 1949. Thaxton 2008, 51–70; see also Selden 1995, 242–52.

102. Benton 1992, xiii, 451–58.

103. Benton 1999, 50.

104. Benton 1999, 69, 78.

105. Benton 1999, 511–616; figures from 545, 570–72; weather and pontoon details from 547, 589–90.

106. Smedley 1945, 365; Benton 1999, 572.

107. Hartford 1989, 92; Levine 1989, 151; Service 1974, 221; Spence 1981, 336; Perry 1980, 211–13, 224–47; Lee and Wiles 1999, 177.

108. Service 1974, 244.

109. Spence 1981, 342–45. On the civil war, see Pepper 1999; Lary 2015; Westad 2003.

110. Jiang 2009, 140–41.

111. Xia 2013; she notes (115) that "state-authorized legal purges and popular campaigns alike considered women unable to act on their own initiative in making political decisions."

112. Edwards 2016b, 91–116.

113. Jiang 2009, 141–49.

114. On corruption, see Pepper 1999, 20–28. Payne 1947 provides an account of the political atmosphere at Southwest Associated University in Kunming from late 1944 to mid-1946.

115. Payne 1947, 63, 207–11, 224–26, 234–36; on the funeral, see Israel 1998, 372–73; also see Pepper 1999, 44–52.

116. Pepper 1999, 52–58.

117. Pepper 1999, 42–93; Honig 1986, 38.

118. Glosser 2003, 129–33; quotation from 131–32.

119. Hershatter 1997, 288–303; quotation from 289; Henriot 2001, 144–47, 325–33.

120. Edwards 2008a, 192–231.

121. Chen 2012, 173–78, 186–89, 205–12. On Beijing's Relief Home and its attempts to care for poor women, sometimes by arranging marriages for them, see 182–84.

122. Pepper 1999, 423–29.

123. Howard 2013, 1892, 1927–35.

124. Honig 1986, 36–37, 88, 230, 235.

125. Honig 1986, 229–34. Just as in the late 1920s, women were more than three-quarters of the cotton spinners, although their absolute numbers had dropped from 84,270 on 1929 to 35,306 in 1946. Honig 1986, 24–25.

126. Honig 1986, 191. On women silk weavers who became labor activists during this period, see Perry 1993, 210–11.

127. Honig 1986, 229, 234–43. On the role of skilled male machinists and numbers of military police, see Perry 1993, 125. Perry (214) finds evidence that male CCP members suspected one of the women leaders of being too close to the mill management and assaulted her. See also Pepper 1999, 114.

128. Honig 1986, 38, 239; Perry 1993, 124; Field 2010, 233–61; Hershatter 1997, 300–303; Henriot 2001, 105–7.

129. Davin 1976, 54–57.

130. Davin 1976, 44.

131. Spence 1981, 346–47; Pepper 1999, 277–330.

132. Wu 2014, 13.

133. Johnson 1983, 79.

134. Hua 1984, 12–13.

135. Davin 1976, 44–45; Ono 1989, 178; Stranahan 1983, 97; Lary 2015, 119, 160; Spakowski 2009.

136. Lary 2015, 143–45.

137. Davin 1976, 203.

CHAPTER 8: THE SOCIALIST CONSTRUCTION OF WOMEN, 1949–78

1. Many aspects of life in the PRC, including the specifics of intra-Party contention, important political campaigns, and the consolidation of state control over borderland areas with large ethnic minority populations, are dealt with glancingly or not at all in this chapter. Fortunately, a large and easily accessible body of scholarship exists on these topics. For one useful overview, see Meisner 1999. For selections of interviews with women about their lives before and during the PRC, see Cusack 1958; Davin 1989; Verschuur-Basse 1996; Xinran 2002.

2. On the conflicts that emerged between state-affiliated feminists and other Party leaders see, inter alia, Wang 2006; Wang 2010a; Wang 2017; Manning 2006b.

3. On the Marriage Law, marriage, and popular cultural portrayals of both in this period, see Ono 1989, 176–86; Davin 1976, 70–114; Johnson 1983, 115–53; Diamant 2000; Diamant 2014, 86–94; Glosser 2003, 167–95; Cong 2016, 244–83; Friedman 2006, 77–81, 89–96; Hershatter 2011, 96–128; Wang 2017, 14.

4. On the significance of labeling a practice feudal and thus attempting to consign it to the past, see Friedman 2006, 69–70; Hershatter 2011.

5. The fixing of class status in the early PRC had unforeseen effects. People were given class labels, inheritable through the patriline, which kept categories such as "landlord" in place long after the actual social phenomenon of landlordism had disappeared, influencing subsequent generations. Women could change their class labels if they married, for example, into a poor peasant family, though gossip about being a "landlord's daughter" might persist. More generally, the freezing of class labels meant that no language of class was available to express emergent relationships of inequality, for instance between city and countryside, cadre and worker, village leader and peasant. The dominance of class labels in public discourse also made the naming of other inequalities, such as those of gender, difficult to articulate. For a discussion of how class labels affected selection of marriage partners in rural areas, see Zhang 2013.

6. Tran 2015, 175–98.

7. Hinton 1997, 396–99.

8. On speaking bitterness and women's mobilization, see Hershatter 2011, 34–37, 62–64, 79; Ono 1989, 171–73, Hinton 1997, 157–60; for an urban use of the practice among factory women, see Ma 2014. On the difficulties of mobilizing women for more extended political activity, see Crook and Crook 1979, 195–203. On the persistence of speaking bitterness as a narrative practice among urban women into the post-Mao years, see also Anagnost 1997; Rofel 1999, 137–48; Huang 2014.

9. Of course, men petitioned for divorce too, including in cases where rising cadres wanted to end marriages to aging or poor wives and "trade up." See inter alia, Wang 2010a, 839–40.

10. Johnson 1983, 132; Huang 2005, 179.

11. Johnson 1983, 115–53.

12. On mediation, see Huang 2005.

13. Hershatter 2011, 111–12.

14. Cong 2016, 249.

15. Yan 2003.

16. The foundational discussion in English of the difference between men's and women's lives within this marriage pattern is Wolf 1972. On patrilocality, see also Johnson 1983.

17. See, inter alia, Judd 1989; Hershatter 2011; F. Liu 2011.

18. Except where otherwise noted, this section is based on Hershatter 2011, 154–81; Fang 2017.

19. Hershatter 2011, 351n51.

20. Evans 1997, 41–47. On attempts to introduce a Soviet method of painless childbirth in urban China in the 1950s and its entanglement with Cold War politics, see Ahn 2013.

21. Except where otherwise indicated, this account is based on Hershatter 1997, 304–24.

22. On resettlement of other women to Qinghai during this period, and the importance of women's role in establishing families and bearing children there, see Rohlf 2016. On the reform of singing girls in Qingdao and their transformation into socialist cultural workers, see Zhao 2014.

23. Zhang 2015, 65.

24. Evans 1997, 145, 160, 174; Smith 2013a; Smith 2013b, 20–21, 63, 65–67, 74–82, 102–6.

25. Davin 1976, 154–90, provides an overview of policies toward urban women. On women in the press, see also Davin 1975b, 365; Honig 2000, 100. On women who became models for being the first to do particular kinds of work, see Chen 2003. On the reconfiguration of labor for urban women and how it was recalled nostalgically in the reform era, see Rofel 1999.

26. On the difficulties of political mobilization among women factory members in the early years of CCP control in Beijing, see Ma 2014.

27. Davin 1976, 163–64; Ma 2015, 326–28.

28. Large state-owned enterprises also employed temporary and contract workers, who helped fuel labor unrest in 1956–57 and during the Cultural Revolution; see Perry 1993, 254–56; Perry 2002, 206–74.

29. Evans 2012; Rogaski 2004, 296–97; Ma 2015, 329–30.

30. Wang 2005, 197 and passim; Wang 2017, 29–53; Ma 2015, 329–34.

31. On women in industrial and agricultural production on the covers of *Women of China*, see Luo and Hao 2007, 287–88; Finnane 2008, 203; Wang 2010a; Wang 2017, 78–111. On women in mass-produced posters, see Sun 2011.

32. Davin 1975b, 365–72. On women's fashion and its political significance in the Mao years, see Chen 2001; Finnane 2008, 206–26. Harriet Evans (personal communication) points out that *Women of China* introduced the slogan "let's be pretty" (*zamen haokanqilai ba!*) during a mid-1950s production slowdown.

33. Evans 2002.

34. Personal communication. For similar situations recounted by Beijing women of that generation, see Zuo 2013, 108–11.

35. See, inter alia, Evans 2008, 44–53, 105–6.

36. Wang 1999, 285–86 and passim.

37. Barlow 2004, 194, 233–52; Spence 1981, 379–85, 394–98.

38. On women's work and family obligations during the 1950s, see, inter alia, Zuo 2013.

39. Evans 2008, 106–9; Liu 2007a, 1–86; Zuo 2016, 21–76.

40. Hershatter 2011, 70–72, 83; Eyferth 2015, 132–33.

41. Except where otherwise noted, this discussion of women's rural labor during the collective era draws upon Hershatter 2011; Davin 1975a; Davin 1976, 115–53; Johnson 1983, 157–77. Other sources that include discussion of women's role in rural life during this period are Parish and Whyte 1978; Croll 1981, 380–86; Friedman et al. 1991; Friedman et al. 2005.

42. For firsthand descriptions of women's daily lives in a rural collective, see Sheridan 1984; Chen 2015, 67–87.

43. On rural labor models and production contests, see Gao 2006; Hershatter 2011, 210–35; Chen 2003. For brief accounts of rural and urban labor models, see Sheridan 1976.

44. Huang 1990, 200–203; Hershatter 2011, 136–39.

45. For this pattern in a papermaking village, see Eyferth 2009, 130.

46. See, inter alia, Gao 2006; Gao 2008; Hershatter 2011, 182–209; Manning 2006a.

47. Wu 2008.

48. Han 2007; White 2006, 19–41. On rural women's distress about the large numbers of children, see Hershatter 2011, 206–9.

49. Eyferth 2012; Eyferth 2015.

50. Where not otherwise specified, this discussion of the Great Leap and its aftermath draws upon Hershatter 2011, 236–66. See also Chen 2015, 88–107; Guo 2007.

51. Meisner 1999, 216.

52. Pietz 2015, 207.

53. On women's work on infrastructure projects, see Friedman 2006, 43–45; Pietz 2015, 144–45, 207–9.

54. On rapidly rising rates of women's participation in production during the 1950s, reaching 80–95 percent in the Great Leap, see Thorborg 1978.

55. Manning 2006a, 359–60.

56. Gao 2006, 607–8; Manning 2006a; Manning 2006b. Yang Jisheng (2012, 220) points out that prolapse also was widespread during the ensuing famine.

57. Manning 2006a; Manning 2006b.

58. King et al. 2010; King 2013.

59. Thaxton 2008, 199–207.

60. Accounts of the Great Leap Famine not otherwise cited here, many of which include tales of starvation and cannibalism in some regions of China, include Yang 2012; Dikötter 2010; Manning and Wemheuer 2011; Wemheuer 2014.

61. For an Anhui County in which male cadres disbursed grain in return for sexual services from local women and more than a quarter of the population died during the famine, see Yang and Cao 2016.

62. Yang 2012 (67, 132, 135, 136, 217, 220, 228, 275, 348) cites interviews with former Women's Federation cadres, and Party and state committee reports, from Henan, Gansu, Sichuan, and Anhui. Yang (409) calculates the national shortfall in births from 1958 to 1961 at 31.5 million.

63. Hershatter 2011, 391n164.

64. On feminization of agriculture in the 1960s and 1970s, see Gao 2006; Hershatter 2011, 129–30, 145–49, 242–44, 264–66; Honig 2015, 194–95; Friedman 2006, 52–54. For a description of men flipping irrigation switches, a technical job, while women did the physical work of ditching and damming—at a lower work-point rate because this was ordinary day labor—see Wolf 1985, 83–84.

65. Johnson 1983, 181, 195. For the origins of this attack on the Women's Federation and *Women of China* in particular, see Wang 2017, 112–39.

66. Wang 2001; Wang 2005, 198.

67. Honig 2002; Hinton et al. 2005; Ye 2006. An ongoing controversy about responsibility for this death was rekindled when former Red Guards apologized in a 2014 ceremony for having failed to protect the principal. Yang 2016, 184–86.

68. Honig 2002.

69. Yang 2016, 1, 54–55, 57–58. On factory violence during the Cultural Revolution, see also Perry 2002, 238–74.

70. Honig 2002, 257–58. On men's and women's dress across the Mao years, see Steele and Major 1999, 55–67; on the Cultural Revolution in particular, see Wilson 1999.

71. For surveys of women's dress and its significance across the Cultural Revolution period, see Chen 2001; Chen 2011; Finnane 2008, 227–55.

72. See, inter alia, Honig 2003; Yang 1997; Honig 2000, 102–9.

73. Honig 2015, 190–91; Zhong 2011.

74. Honig 2015.

75. On the Iron Girls, see Honig and Hershatter 1988, 23–26; Honig 2000; Jin 2006; Sun 2011, 133–37; Wang 2017, 221–41. On a less well-known precursor, the Mu Guiying Brigade of the Great Leap Forward period, see Manning 2006b; Manning 2010.

76. On the suppression of the enormously popular Yue opera performed by women during the Cultural Revolution, see Jiang 2009, 194–98.

77. On gender roles in the model operas and ballets, see Chen 2002; Roberts 2010; Bai 2010; Honig 2000, 100–101; Edwards 2016b, 198–206. On similar gender hierarchy in Cultural Revolution posters, see Evans 1999.

78. On Jiang Qing in her own words, see Witke 1975; Witke 1977. On her role in the film industry just before and during the Cultural Revolution, see Wang Zheng 2017, 205–20. On the campaign to criticize Lin Biao and Confucius, see Johnson 1983, 194–207; Honig 2015, 195–96; Croll 1977.

79. Zhong 2011; see also the individual essays by women of this generation in Zhong et al. 2001; Ye and Ma 2005.

CHAPTER 9: CAPITALIZED WOMEN, 1978–

1. For a summary account of women's status across the reform era, drawing on three national surveys conducted by the Women's Federation and the Bureau of Statistics in 1990, 2000, and 2010, see Attané 2012. On urban gender inequalities in education and employment in the early reform era, see Hooper 1984; Bauer et al. 1992. Findings not otherwise discussed in this chapter include improvement in girls' access to education (though gender gaps and urban-rural gaps persist) and improvements in women's reproductive health (again with an urban-rural gap).

2. Washington 2012.

3. Judd 2010, 928; Jacka 2014, 187; Ye et al. 2016, 911.

4. See, inter alia, Woon 1999.

5. Hsu 2016.

6. A sampling of important topics not extensively discussed in this chapter: on urban educated professional women identified as "white collar beauties," see Liu 2017. On women entrepreneurs, see Osburg 2013, 143–82. On gender and urban employment, as well as women in the rural economy, see the essays in Wang et al. 2016; on changes in both urban and rural families, see the essays in Santos and Harrell 2017. On the varied experiences of women who are members of ethnic minority groups in China, see White 1997; Schein 1997; Schein 2000; Hansen 2001; Yang and Matheiu 2003; Chao 2012; Makley 2007; Chio 2014. On women and contemporary religious practice, see Jaschok and Shui 2000; Jaschok and Shui 2011; Kao 2009; Cline 2010; Kang 2014; Bryson 2016.

7. The birth rate already had declined from 34 per 1,000 in 1970 to 17.9 per 1,000 in 1979, under the "later, longer, fewer" policy. Tien 1987, 441–42.

8. In addition to the sources cited below, see also Wasserstrom 1984; Bossen 2002, 273–309; Greenhalgh 2001; Greenhalgh 2008; Greenhalgh and Li 1995; Greenhalgh and Winckler 2005; White 2006; Fong 2016.

9. On "little emperors," see Jing 2000; Fong 2016; on single children as a family's "only hope," see Fong 2004; on the pressures felt by young women high school students in 2011, see Liu 2014.

10. Tien 1987; Jacka 2012, 12.

11. On the incidence of abortion, see Tien 1987; on a range of attitudes toward abortion, see Nie 2005.

12. Government statistics indicate that 324 million Chinese women received IUDs from 1980 to 2014. Wee 2017.

13. On abandonment and adoption, see Johnson 2016.

14. Honig and Hershatter 1988, 190, 204–5, 297–98; Wang 1997.

15. Angeloff and Lieber 2012, 21; Eklund 2011; Murphy 2014.

16. See, inter alia, Jacka, Kipnis, and Sargeson 2013, 38–39; Attané 2012, 12.

17. Croll 2001, 229.

18. Osnos 2012; Attané 2012, 13. This number of "bare sticks" is projected as of 2020.

19. Honig and Hershatter 1988, 286–91; Gates 1996.

20. Greenhalgh and Li 1995; Hershatter 2011, 276–87; Jacka 2012, 15. On women's continued ties with and financial support for natal families, see also Judd 1989. On contacts between married rural women and their natal families, see Zhang 2009; for an argument that the shrinking number of siblings in rural families has led parents to invest more in the education of their daughters, see Zhang 2007. On the continuing importance of mother-daughter bonds in urban professional Chinese families, see Evans 2008; Evans 2010.

21. Hershatter 2011, 276–87. Yan (2003, 2011) describes the trend toward neo-local residence, the decline in multigenerational families, increased emphasis on conjugal bonds rather than father-son relations, and what he calls the "individualization of the family." Huang 1990, 297–301, discusses generational tensions in the early reform era. Wang Danning 2010, 961–62, describes a similar set of conflicting generational expectations about elder support among urban working-class families. On promotion of conjugal self-sufficiency among aging couples, see Shea 2005.

22. Buckley 2015. By mid-2017, thirty provinces had instructed employers to extend paid maternity leave from the previously mandated ninety-eight days to four months, six months, and in one case a year. Feng, July 10, 2017.

23. Tatlow 2015; Buckley 2015.

24. GZLSHZS 2015; Lan 2015; Tatlow 2015. It also remained unclear whether parents would still have to pay hefty fines for children born in violation of the policy before it was changed. Zhao 2016.

25. "Women's Fertility Desires" 2017.

26. Y. Fan 2017a; English translation quoted in this chapter is found in Y. Fan 2017b, translated by Koetse. See also Zhuang 2017. For other pieces of writing by and about rural women migrants, see Sun 2014.

27. Fu 2009, 528; "Migrant Workers and Their Children" 2015; Qi 2017.

28. Between 1992 and 2001 employees in urban SOEs and collective enterprises declined from 145 to 89 million, while nonpublic employees rose from 33 to 150

million. Chan and Zhu 2003, 561. On women being laid off first, see Goodman 2002, 331; Liu 2007a; Liu 2007b.

29. Pun 2007, 241, gives the figure of 40 percent, and 60 percent in Guangdong. Others say that women were one-third of the total migrants; see Fu 2009, 528; "Migrant Workers and Their Children" 2015; Qi 2017. On the experiences of rural women migrants, in addition to the sources cited below, see West et al. 1999, 69–133; Gaetano and Jacka 2004; Zhang 2007; Loyalka 2012; Gaetano 2015; Zavoretti 2017. Sheng 2012 offers a fictionalized account.

30. Fan Yusu 2017b.

31. On dissatisfaction with the villages and the draw of the cities, see Jacka 2005; Jacka 2006b; Pun 2005; Chang 2008; Spakowski 2011, 45–46.

32. Pun 2007, 240.

33. Tong 2008, 516.

34. On electronics, see Pun 2005; Litzinger 2013, 174–76; Pun and Chan 2013, 186; on batteries and cadmium poisoning, see Mak 2010; Mak 2014.

35. Chan and Zhu 2003; Zhang 2004; Pun 2005.

36. Pun et al. 2016, quotation from 173–74.

37. Pun 2007; Pun and Chan 2013; Pun et al. 2016.

38. Pun 2005; Chang 2008; see also Hessler 2006, 77–98, 149–68.

39. Pun and Lu 2010; Pun and Chan 2013.

40. Otis 2016.

41. Hanser 2005; Hanser 2008. On women clothing vendors in Beijing's Silk St. Market and the language and cultural skills required in their work, see Pang et al. 2014.

42. Otis 2012.

43. On beauty and consumer culture, and their connection to gendered subject making in the reform era, see also Yang 2011.

44. In addition to the sources cited in the next few paragraphs, see also Jeffreys 1997; Evans 1997, 174–78; Jeffreys 2004b; Jeffreys 2012; Chin 2017.

45. "Nüboshi yanjiu" 2017; Boittin 2013, 267.

46. Boittin 2013. On two high-profile cases in which women were recruited under false pretenses to sell sexual services, see Jeffreys 2006. On government policies, often coercive, aimed at testing prostitutes for HIV/AIDS, see Boittin 2013, 252–53, 259–60; Hyde 2007. On prostitution and trafficking, see M. Liu 2011. On HIV transmission with particular attention to masculinity and masculine forms of socializing, see Uretsky 2016.

47. Hershatter 1997, 343–48; Boittin 2013, 252; Jeffreys 2004a, 138–49; on regulations, see also Jeffreys 2006, 4–5, 8–9; Huang and Pan 2014, 1068.

48. Ding Yu 2016.

49. Boittin 2013, 251; Hyde 2007, 128–49; Hershatter 1997, 327, 333–43; Zheng 2008; Zheng 2009. On the emergence of dance venues and bars in the reform era, see Farrer and Field 2015.

50. Hyde 2007, 105–27; also see Chao 2003, 77–80, 83.

51. Tsang 2017.

52. Boittin 2013, 251–52, 257–59; Huang and Pan 2014, 1071, 1074–75, 1076–77.

53. Huang and Pan 2014; Branigan 2010. On a 2014 crackdown in Dongguan, see Tsang 2017, 8. On condoms, see also Hyde 2007, 150–68. On sexual activity and the HIV epidemic, see also Uretsky 2016.

54. Ding 2012; Ding 2016.

55. "Nüboshi yanjiu" 2017.

56. Boittin 2013, 262–65 and passim.

57. Jeffreys 2015, 113.

58. On regional origins of maids in Beijing and Shanghai, see W. Sun 2004.

59. Sun 2009a; Sun 2008; Sun 2009b; on training classes for domestic laborers and how they were taught to understand their labor as a commodity, see Yan 2013.

60. On *suzhi* see, inter alia, Anagnost 1997; Gao 2008, 21–22; Yan 2008; Judd 2002; Chao 2003; Jacka 2006a; Jacka 2006b; Jacka 2009; W. Sun 2009b. On middle-class fears of maids and privacy concerns about employing them, see Sun 2008; Sun 2009b.

61. Yan 2006.

62. Fan Yusu 2017a; Fan Yusu 2017b.

63. Fu 2009; Fan Yusu 2017a; Fan Yusu 2017b. Some rural migrants, including Fan, were encouraged to write in social programs aimed at raising their status. On the Beijing Migrant Women's Club, an NGO that offered classes, discussions, and other activities for migrant women, see Jacka 2005; on its parent organization, the Cultural Development Center for Rural Women, and its work on suicide prevention and training for women village leaders, see Wesoky 2011.

64. "Migrant Workers and Their Children" 2015.

65. On marriage among migrants see, inter alia, Jacka 2005.

66. Woon 1999; May 2010; Pun and Lu 2010; Jacka 2012; Pang et al. 2014.

67. "Migrant Workers and Their Children" 2015.

68. Yue et al. 2017; "Migrant Workers and Their Children" 2015; Ye et al. 2016. A related literature addresses the circumstances of women and the elderly left behind in Chinese villages, as virtually all men of working age, many single women, and increasingly young married women work away from home. Many of the left-behind wives worked before or just after marriage as migrants. See, inter alia, Ye et al. 2016; Jacka 2012; Jacka 2014. Jacka suggests that migration and the maintenance of a rural household should be seen as parts of a single social process, and that "left-behind" women, including elderly women, exercise considerable agency. She also points out (2012, 11; 2013) that middle-aged and elderly women are responsible for most of the dependent care in rural areas. On the relatively scarce leisure time of middle-aged and older rural women compared to men and younger women, see Huang 2011; Yan 2011.

69. "Migrant Workers and Their Children" 2015.

70. "Migrant Workers and Their Children" 2015; Litzinger 2013, 173.

71. Hooper 1984, 329–31; Honig and Hershatter 1988, 41–80; Evans 1997; Finnane 2008, 257–90; Wang 2017, 250–58. Liu 2014 offers an analysis of preference for "manly" and/or androgynous styles among Beijing young women high school students, coexisting with their beliefs that boys and girls were naturally different and that men should outperform women economically.

72. Hooper 1984, 331; Honig and Hershatter 1988, 81–136; Evans 1997; Rofel 1999; Rofel 2007; Yan 2011. On early twenty-first century dating within (and

occasionally across) cohorts of college students, professionals, and rural migrants in Beijing, see Wang and Nehring 2014. On ideas about womanhood among Beijing high school young women in 2011, see Liu 2014. On sexual activity among middle-aged and older women, see Shea 2005.

73. On women as emotionally attuned nurturers, see Honig and Hershatter 1988, 173–86; Evans 2010. On requirements that a reform-era wife be supportive and self-sacrificing, see Evans 2002. On change in the discourses of sexuality in reform-era China, see, inter alia, Farquhar 2002, 211–42; Uretsky 2016. On sexual attitudes among urban and rural Beijing-area women aged forty to sixty-five, see Shea 2005; on marital relationships of professional women, see Liu 2017.

74. On the beauty industry and its workers, see Hooper 1994, 74–75; Yang 2011; Liao 2016; Ip 2017. On the history of cosmetic surgery in China, see Brownell 2005. On beauty as the primary criterion for dating a woman, and financial success as the primary criterion for dating a man, see Wang and Nehring 2014.

75. Evans 2002.

76. No one should mistake these few sentences for an adequate discussion of same-sex desire, gender fluidity, or queer communities in China, all of which warrant an extended exploration. On the emergence into visibility of nonnormative sexuality, including same-sex terms, relationships, spaces, and communities in reform-era (mainly urban) China, see Evans 2002, 206–12; Sang 2003, 163–222; Rofel 2007, 85–110, 135–55; Ho 2008; Engebretsen 2014; Jeffreys 2015; Engebretsen et al. 2015; Engebretsen 2017; Jacobs 2015; Farrer and Field 2015, 167–73; "Where Are Gay Rights and Feminism Headed in China? Leading Activist Li Maizi Speaks Out" 2017.

77. On the rise in premarital sex during the reform era see, inter alia, Farrer 2002; Yan 2003; Farrer 2014; Jacobs 2015; Lake 2015.

78. On the harmonious society see, inter alia, Spakowski 2011, 41; Wesoky 2016, 62; Boittin 2013, 263–64.

79. Hong Fincher 2014; Zhang and Sun 2014; Wang and Nehring 2014; Gong et al. 2015. For public discussions in the 1980s about the urgency of finding husbands for *da guniang*, literally "big girls" but perhaps better understood as "aging young women," see Honig and Hershatter 1988, 104–10. On difficulties experienced by educated women on the marriage market, see Hooper 1984, 331–32; Hong Fincher 2014, 25–27.

80. Osnos 2012.

81. Hong Fincher 2012.

82. Gong et al. 2015.

83. For a largely positive account of the operations of one such agency, stressing its woman founder's role in promoting choice and self-confidence for women, see Osnos 2012.

84. Fu 2015.

85. Attané 2012, 9.

86. Zhang and Sun 2014.

87. Kan 2017.

88. This show and others like it were scripted, and it is unclear whether that line was a spontaneous utterance. Hong Fincher 2014, 55–56.

89. Luo and Sun 2015, 247–50; quotation from 250.

90. Osnos 2012; Chin 2016.

91. Honig and Hershatter 1988, 207; Davis 2014b, 554. Huang 2005 argues that even before 1980, state authorities also took into account whether a couple's emotional connection could be repaired.

92. Davis 2010, 465, 468. Davis (2014b) refers to the lessening of state interference in sexual relationships, marriage, and divorce as the privatization of marriage. See also Huang 2005. For an argument that (mainly male) legal workers handling divorce cases in two rural townships routinely disregarded women's rights to child custody, property, and spousal support and ignored evidence of domestic violence, see Li 2015.

93. Divorces stood at about 0.4 million in 1980, rose steadily until 1997, then almost doubled from 1.17 million in 2002 to 2.26 million in 2008. On the 1980s, see Honig and Hershatter 1988, 226; on the number of divorces through 2008, see Davis 2010, 446; and Davis 2014b, 561–62; on 2016, see Feng, June 16, 2017. On large cities in 2014, see Hong Fincher 2014, 49. On divorce as represented in fiction, film, and television dramas during the reform era, see Xiao 2014.

94. Honig and Hershatter 1988, 23–26; Honig 2015; Beaver, Hou, and Wang 1995; Wang 2017, 221–41. On the changing images of women on the cover of *Women of China* during the reform era, see Luo and Hao 2007, 288–90. For critiques of this rejection of gender configurations in the Mao era as "unnatural" and a robust defense of the possibilities opened for women in that era, see, inter alia, Lin 2001; Zhong et al. 2001.

95. Hooper 1984, 326–27; Honig and Hershatter 1988, 251–53; Wang 1997, 130; for a version of this discussion centering on the rapidly industrializing village of Daqiuzhuang, see Beaver, Hou, and Wang 1995; Evans 2002, 353–54. Rofel (1999) explores persistent reform-era criticisms of the labor system during the Mao years and women's changing attitudes about factory work. Zuo (2014) argues that denigration of labor during the reform period has contributed to women's alienation and desire to return home.

96. On gender discrimination in the reform-era workforce see Hooper 1984; Li and Zhang 1994, 139; Cao and Hu 2007; Yang 2011; Attané 2012, 8. On women being tracked into tech company jobs as "programmer motivators," where they were expected to talk to male coders and ease their work stress, see Wee 2018.

97. Tatlow and Forsythe 2015.

98. "Reality Check" 2017.

99. Tatlow 2017; Ruwitch 2017.

100. Attané 2012, 8.

101. Zuo 2003; Wang Danning 2010, 970; Cao and Hu 2007; W. Sun 2008; Kim et al. 2010; Zuo 2014; Liao 2016.

102. See, inter alia, Hooper 1984, 327–28, 334–35; Hooper 1994, 76–77, 80–82; Honig and Hershatter 1988, 255–63, 265–72; Zuo and Bian 2001; Evans 2008, 101–24; Attané 2012, 10; Zuo 2016. On the gendered division of labor in the households of wealthy women entrepreneurs, see M. Chen 2008. On wives of entrepreneurs who play crucial under-recognized roles in managing their husbands' businesses, see Goodman 2002.

103. Xiao 2014, 116–39, discusses *Chinese-Style Divorce.*

104. J. Fan 2017.

105. Honig and Hershatter 1988, 219–24; Evans 2002, 352; J. Fan 2017.

106. J. Fan 2017. This approach encapsulated an assumption that had taken hold in the early years of the reforms: that maintaining a marriage was women's work, and that they should perform it in a subtle manner so that their husbands never realized that they were the object of a concerted strategy. Honig and Hershatter 1988, 177–80.

107. Jacka, Kipnis, and Sargeson 2013, 242, 251–52; Chin 2016; see also Hong Fincher 2016, 86.

108. Tong 2008, 515. Liu (2007b) points out that women's workplace disadvantages in the Mao years—lower levels of skill and connections, greater domestic responsibilities—made them particularly vulnerable to layoffs in the reform era.

109. Davis 2010, 479.

110. J. Fan 2017. The comparison of acquiring a wife and buying a car in a May 2017 Audi ad caused considerable controversy. Feng, July 18, 2017.

111. Except where otherwise noted, the discussion of marriage, real estate, and leftover women is drawn from Hong Fincher 2014.

112. Davis 2010, 464.

113. For an account of the struggle over one such project, see Shao 2013.

114. Hong Fincher 2014, 93. The unit here is U.S. dollars.

115. Davis 2010, 477; Hong Fincher 2014.

116. Hong Fincher 2014, 60–61.

117. Davis 2010, 477–78; Hong Fincher 2014.

118. Hong Fincher 2014, 61–62, 84.

119. Hong Fincher 2014, 92–103, 31–32; Osnos 2012.

120. "Marriage Law of the People's Republic of China, amended April 28, 2001"; Davis 2010, 471, 480; Davis 2014a, 45–49; Davis 2014b, 556–57. Davis (2010) finds that in urban focus groups from 2004 to 2008, many people accepted the principle of joint ownership of the home but favored use rights by wives who had custody of the children.

121. Davis 2014b, 559; Davis 2014a, 50.

122. Tatlow 2011; "Judicial Interpretation of Marriage Law" 2011; Davis 2014b, 559–60; Davis 2014a, 50–51.

123. One analysis summarized the interpretation as follows: if parents of both spouses had contributed but the property was registered in the name of only one of them, then it might be regarded as joint property. Similarly, if one spouse took out a bank loan before marriage to purchase a piece of immovable property, and after marriage both spouses contributed to mortgage payments, in the event of a disputed divorce the Marriage Law should be interpreted to allow the purchaser title to the property, paying compensation to the other spouse for his or her contribution. Zeldin 2011.

124. Hong Fincher 2014, 104–5. A further Supreme Court interpretation on this matter issued in February 2017 held that if parents contributed to the purchase of a house for their child and his or her intended spouse before the marriage took place, then the funding they contributed should be regarded as a gift to that child unless the parents specified that it was a gift to the couple. Conversely, if

the parents made such a contribution after a couple was married, the funding would be regarded as a gift to the couple unless the parents specified that it was intended for their child only. This interpretation, which attempted to protect parental investment while also recognizing housing as the joint property of a married couple, seemed unlikely to improve the disadvantaged situation of divorcing wives whose names were not on a property deed. Supreme Court of the People's Republic of China 2017.

125. This is only one aspect of the emergence of new forms of gender inequality in the countryside. For the extremely low and falling rate of women's political participation during the reform era in Party and government organizations at the township and village levels, and one attempt to reverse the trend in Shaanxi, see Jacka 2008; Gao 2010; Jacka 2010. On the inadequacy of official discourse in describing rural women's actual economic roles, see Judd 1994; Jacka 1997. For discussions of women's land rights, in addition to the sources cited below, see Bossen 2002, 91–98; and West et al. 1999, 137–92.

126. Jacka 1997; Liaw 2008; Sargeson and Song 2011; Sargeson 2012; Jacka 2012, 17–18; Jacka 2014, 193. Jacka (1997) argued that in the 1980s and 1990s, agriculture was redefined as "inner" work appropriate for women and was devalued as the gendered division of labor shifted, with men moving out of agriculture. A national 2010 survey found that more than 82 percent of rural women, but only 64.7 percent of men, were engaged in agriculture full-time. Attané 2012, 9. Whether China has seen a feminization of agriculture is a matter of some disagreement; for various positions, see Bossen 2002, 98–121; Zuo 2004; Gao 2008; Wu 2008; Jacka, Kipnis, and Sargeson 2013, 250; Hershatter 2011, 129–30, 145–49, 264–66. Brauw et al. 2008 show that hours spent on farm work are declining across the board, and that participation in farm work is falling both among young women (who seek off-farm work) and women over fifty-five (who do housework and care for grandchildren), but that middle-aged women farm at higher rates than middle-aged men.

127. Sargeson 2012; Bossen 2011.
128. Sargeson and Song 2011.
129. Wang 2010b; Lim 2017.
130. Honig and Hershatter 1998, 317–19.
131. Wang 1997, 130–31.
132. Honig and Hershatter 1988, 251–53, 319.
133. Hooper 1984, 332–33; Hooper 1994, 82–83; Yang 2011.
134. Wang 1997, 128–30.
135. On Li Xiaojiang, see, inter alia, Wang 1997, 128, 132–34, 137–39; Barlow 1997; Hsiung and Wong 1998, 482; Li 2001; Barlow 2004, 253–301; Xu 2009, 199–201, 204–8; Spakowski 2011, 35–39, 43; Zhong 2011; Wang 2013; Wesoky 2016, 54–55, 57; Li and Zhang 1994; Li 2016.
136. See, inter alia, Hsiung 2001; the essays in West et al. 1999, 195–224; Liu 2012.
137. Wang 1997; Xu 2009, 199–200.
138. Wang 1996; Wang 1997, 139–42; Hsiung and Wong 1998, 473; Chow 1996. The Forum also became a showcase for the burgeoning commercial economy.

Each conferee received a packet of VIP passes sponsored by the "Hansun Pharma-ceuttal [*sic*] Company" to exhibits of Chinese silk, medicine, clothing, jewelry, and "exquisite products," as well as an advertisement for Women's Spring, described as a suppository "especially designed for married women whose vagina has been loose after parturition." Administrative Office of the Shopping Centers 1995.

139. Hsiung and Wong 1998, 470.

140. Angeloff and Lieber 2012, 19–21; Gao 2008.

141. Wang 1997; on different approaches to translating gender, see Spakowski 2011, 34–35.

142. Spakowski 2011; Xu 2009, 197, 207–8; Wesoky 2016.

143. Spakowski 2011, 41–42; Wesoky 2016, 64; Edwards 2008b. For discussions of the development discourse employed by the Women's Federation, see Judd 2002; Jacka 2006a. For an argument that feminism has, by and large, not appealed to younger women during the reform era, see Liu 2014.

144. Hom 1994; Hsiung and Wong 1998, 487–88; Han 2017b.

145. Honig and Hershatter 1988, 232–34, 281–98, 303–7.

146. Xinhua 2007; Hong Fincher 2014, 140–64; Han 2017a. Almost one-quarter of women questioned in the 2010 national survey reported having experienced domestic violence. Attané 2012, 10. On continued normalization of domestic violence among rural legal workers who were supposed to be assisting women with divorce claims in 2010, see Li 2015, 169–70.

147. "Marriage Law of the People's Republic of China, amended April 28, 2001."

148. See, inter alia, Wang 2010b.

149. Han 2017a; Han 2017b.

150. In addition to the sources cited below, see Wang 2015; Wang 2017, 262–64; Feng, March 8, 2017.

151. Hong Fincher 2016, 86–87; Zhao 2015; Zoe 2016; Hong Fincher 2014, 165–69. The toilet initiative continued after the women's release from detention, with notable success and publicity in December 2016.

152. Xu 2009, 201–3, 206–9; Wesoky 2016, 58; Gao 2008. Many NGOs had at-tracted funding from the Ford Foundation, Save the Children, Oxfam, and other agencies. They cooperated closely with local governments and Women's Fed-eration branches to initiate projects on gender and rural development, domestic violence, suicide prevention, and increasing women's representation among elected village leaders. For an example of one such NGO, the Shaanxi Research Association for Women and Family, and its activities in Shaanxi, see Gao 2010; westwomen.org; Jacka 2010.

153. Wesoky 2016, 60–61.

154. Several of the five detained feminists were lesbians, a fact that was re-peated as a slur by the police in the interrogation of at least one of them. Hong Fincher 2016.

155. Wang 2015.

156. Feng, October 16, 2017; McCarthy 2017; Feng, January 22, 2018; Feng, Janu-ary 26, 2018; Feng, April 9, 2018; Xiao 2018; Hernández and Mou 2018.

157. On the emergence of young women "ceremonial volunteers" whom the state deployed to embody national propriety and civilization at the 2008 Beijing Olympics and on subsequent occasions, see Wu 2018.

158. On embrace of the term "feminism" and continued ambivalence about it among various women writers, see Zhong 2006. Gender is surprisingly absent in the writings of some of China's intellectuals involved in what is loosely labeled the New Left and the rural reconstruction movement. On the New Left, see Wesoky 2015. Jacka 2013 offers a critique of new rural reconstruction, a movement to improve the situation of reform-era farmers, for its lack of attention to gender inequality. For feminist voices associated with left critique, see, inter alia, Barlow 2004, 302–54; Lin 2006, 113–28; Dai 2006; Song 2015.

159. J. Fan 2017.

Works Cited

Administrative Office of the Shopping Centers. 1995. "Shopping Voucher for the VIPs of the '95 World Conference on Women." Han Sun Pharmaceuttal [*sic*].

Ahn, Byungil. 2013. "Reinventing Scientific Medicine for the Socialist Republic: The Soviet Psycho-Prophylactic Method of Delivery in 1950s China." *Twentieth-Century China* 38, no. 2 (May): 139–55.

Anagnost, Ann. 1997. *National Past-Times: Narrative, Representation, and Power in Modern China.* Durham, NC: Duke University Press.

Angeloff, Tania, and Marylène Lieber. 2012. "Equality, Did You Say?" *China Perspectives* 2012, no. 4 (December): 17–24.

Armijo, Jacqueline. 2001. "Narratives Engendering Survival: How the Muslims of Southwest China Remember the Massacres of 1873." In *"Race" Panic and the Memory of Migration*, ed. Meaghan Morris and Brett de Bary, 293–329. Hong Kong: Hong Kong University Press.

Attané, Isabelle. 2012. "Being a Woman in China Today: A Demography of Gender." *China Perspectives* 2012, no. 4 (December): 5–15.

Atwill, David G. 2006. *The Chinese Sultanate: Islam, Ethnicity, and the Panthay Rebellion in Southwest China, 1856–1873.* Stanford, CA: Stanford University Press.

Bai, Di. 2010. "Feminism in the Revolutionary Model Ballets: The White-Haired Girl and The Red Detachment of Women." In *Art in Turmoil: The Chinese Cultural Revolution, 1966–76*, ed. Richard King, 188–202. Vancouver: UBC Press.

Bailey, Paul. 2001. "Active Citizen or Efficient Housewife? The Debate over Women's Education in Early-Twentieth-Century China." In *Education, Culture, and Identity in Twentieth-Century China*, ed. Glen Peterson, Ruth Hayhoe, and Yongling Lu, 318–47. Ann Arbor: University of Michigan Press.

———. 2004. "'Modernising Conservatism' in Early Twentieth-Century China: The Discourse and Practice of Women's Education." *European Journal of East Asian Studies* 3, no. 2 (September): 217–41.

———. 2006. "'Women Behaving Badly': Crime, Transgressive Behaviour and Gender in Early Twentieth Century China." *Nan Nü—Men, Women & Gender in Early & Imperial China* 8, no. 1 (March): 156–97.

———. 2007. *Gender and Education in China: Gender Discourses and Women's Schooling in the Early Twentieth Century.* New York: Routledge.

Barkey, Cheryl Lynn. 2000. "Gender, Medicine and Modernity: The Politics of Reproduction in Republican China." PhD diss., University of California, Davis.

Barlow, Tani E. 1997. "Woman at the Close of the Maoist Era in the Polemics of Li Xiaojiang and Her Associates." In *The Politics of Culture in the Shadow of Capital,* ed. Lisa Lowe and David Lloyd, 506–43. Durham, NC: Duke University Press.

———. 2004. *The Question of Women in Chinese Feminism.* Next Wave Series. Durham, NC: Duke University Press.

———. 2005. "Wanting Some: Commodity Desire and the Eugenic Modern Girl." In *Women in China: The Republican Period in Historical Perspective,* ed. Mechthild Leutner and Nicola Spakowski, 312–50. Berliner China-Studien 44. Münster: Lit.

———. 2006. "History and the Border." *Journal of Women's History* 18, no. 2: 8–32.

Barnes, Nicole Elizabeth. 2012. "Disease in the Capital: Nationalist Health Services and the 'Sick [Wo]man of East Asia' in Wartime Chongqing." *European Journal of East Asian Studies* 11, no. 2 (September): 283–303.

Bauer, John, Wang Feng, Nancy E. Riley, and Zhao Xiaohua. 1992. "Gender Inequality in Urban China: Education and Employment." *Modern China* 18, no. 3: 333–70.

Baumler, Alan. 2000 "Opium Control versus Opium Suppression: The Origins of the 1935 Six-Year Plan to Eliminate Opium and Drugs." In *Opium Regimes China, Britain, and Japan, 1839–1952,* ed. Timothy Brook and Bob Tadashi Wakabayashi, 270–91. Berkeley: University of California Press.

———. 2007. *The Chinese and Opium under the Republic: Worse Than Floods and Wild Beasts.* Albany: State University of New York Press.

Bays, Daniel H. 2012. *A New History of Christianity in China.* Chichester, West Sussex, and Malden, MA: Wiley-Blackwell.

Beahan, Charlotte L. 1975 "Feminism and Nationalism in the Chinese Women's Press, 1902–1911." *Modern China* 1, no. 4 (October): 379–416.

———. 1981. "In the Public Eye: Women in Early Twentieth-Century China." In *Women in China: Current Directions in Historical Scholarship,* ed. R. W. L Guisso and Stanley Johannesen, 215–38. Youngstown, NY: Philo Press.

———. 1984. "One Woman's View of the Early Chinese Communist Movement: The Autobiography of Yang Zilie." *Republican China* 10, no. 1 (November): 25–35.

Beaver, Patricia D., Hou Lihui, and Wang Xue. 1995. "Rural Chinese Women: Two Faces of Economic Reform." *Modern China* 21, no. 2 (April): 205–32.

Bell, Lynda S. 1994. "For Better, for Worse: Women and the World Market in Rural China." *Modern China* 20, no. 2: 180–210.

———. 1999. *One Industry, Two Chinas: Silk Filatures and Peasant-Family Production in Wuxi County, 1865–1937.* Stanford, CA: Stanford University Press.

———. 2000. "Of Silk, Women, and Capital: Peasant Women's Labor in Chinese and Other Third World Capitalisms." *Journal of Women's History* 11, no. 4 (Winter): 82.

Bello, David. 2000. "Opium in Xinjiang and Beyond." In *Opium Regimes: China, Britain, and Japan, 1839–1952*, ed. Timothy Brook and Bob Tadashi Wakabayashi, 127–51. Berkeley: University of California Press.

———. 2005. *Opium and the Limits of Empire: Drug Prohibition in the Chinese Interior, 1729–1850*. Cambridge, MA: Harvard University Asia Center; distributed by Harvard University Press.

Benedict, Carol. 2011. *Golden-Silk Smoke: A History of Tobacco in China, 1550–2010*. Berkeley: University of California Press.

Benton, Gregor. 1992. *Mountain Fires: The Red Army's Three-Year War in South China, 1934–1938*. Berkeley: University of California Press.

———. 1999. *New Fourth Army: Communist Resistance along the Yangtze and the Huai, 1938–1941*. Berkeley: University of California Press.

Benton, Gregor, and Alan Hunter, eds. 1995. *Wild Lily, Prairie Fire: China's Road to Democracy, Yan'an to Tian'anmen, 1942–1989*. Princeton, NJ: Princeton University Press.

Bernhardt, Kathryn. 1994. "Women and the Law: Divorce in the Republican Period." In *Civil Law in Qing and Republican China*, ed. Kathryn Bernhardt and Philip C. C. Huang, 187–214. Stanford, CA: Stanford University Press.

———. 1999. *Women and Property in China, 960–1949*. Stanford, CA: Stanford University Press.

Bickers, Robert A. 2011. *The Scramble for China: Foreign Devils in the Qing Empire, 1832–1914*. London: Allen Lane.

"The Biggest TV Show in the World." 2017. *SupChina*, February 1. http://supchina.com/2017/02/01/biggest-tv-show-world.

Blue, Gregory. 2000. "Opium for China: The British Connection." In *Opium Regimes China, Britain, and Japan, 1839–1952*, ed. Timothy Brook and Bob Tadashi Wakabayashi, 31–51. Berkeley: University of California Press.

Boittin, Margaret L. 2013. "New Perspectives from the Oldest Profession: Abuse and the Legal Consciousness of Sex Workers in China." *Law & Society Review* 47, no. 2 (June): 245–78.

Borthwick, Sally. 1983. *Education and Social Change in China: The Beginnings of the Modern Era*. Stanford, CA: Hoover Institution Press.

———. 1985. "Changing Concepts of Women from the Late Qing to the May Fourth Period." In *Ideal and Reality: Social and Political Change in Modern China, 1860–1949*, ed. David Pong and Edmund S. K. Fung, 63–91. Lanham, MD: University Press of America.

Bossen, Laurel. 2002. *Chinese Women and Rural Development: Sixty Years of Change in Lu Village, Yunnan*. Lanham, MD: Rowman & Littlefield.

———. 2011. "Reproduction and Real Property in Rural China: Three Decades of Development and Discrimination." In *Women, Gender and Rural Development in China*, ed. Tamara Jacka and Sally Sargeson, 97–124. Cheltenham: Edward Elgar.

Bossen, Laurel, and Hill Gates. 2017. *Bound Feet, Young Hands: Tracking the Demise of Footbinding in Village China*. Stanford, CA: Stanford University Press.

Bossen, Laurel, Xurui Wang, Melissa J. Brown, and Hill Gates. 2011. "Feet and Fabrication: Footbinding and Early Twentieth-Century Rural Women's Labor in Shaanxi." *Modern China* 37, no. 4 (July): 347–83.

Bossler, Beverly Jo. 2000. "'A Daughter Is a Daughter All Her Life': Affinal Relations and Women's Networks in Song and Late Imperial China." *Late Imperial China* 21, no. 1: 77–106.

Boulger, Demetrius Charles. 1878. *The Life of Yakoob Beg; Athalik Ghazi, and Badaulet; Ameer of Kashgar.* London.

Branigan, Tania. 2010. "Chinese Sex Workers Protest against Crackdown." *Guardian*, August 3, sec. World News. http://www.theguardian.com/world/2010/aug/03/china-prostitution-sex-workers-protest.

Brauw, Alan de, Qiang Li, Chengfang Liu, Scott Rozelle, and Linxiu Zhang. 2008. "Feminization of Agriculture in China? Myths Surrounding Women's Participation in Farming." *China Quarterly* 194 (June): 327–48.

Bray, Francesca. 1997. *Technology and Gender: Fabrics of Power in Late Imperial China.* Berkeley: University of California Press.

Britton, Roswell S. 1976 [1966]. *The Chinese Periodical Press, 1800–1912.* Taipei: Ch'eng-wen.

Brokaw, Cynthia. 2010. "Commercial Woodblock Publishing in the Qing (1644–1911) and the Transition to Modern Print Technology." In *From Woodblocks to the Internet: Chinese Publishing and Print Culture in Transition, circa 1800 to 2008*, ed. Cynthia Brokaw and Christopher A. Reed, 39–58. Leiden and Boston: Brill.

———. 2007. *Commerce in Culture: The Sibao Book Trade in the Qing and Republican Periods.* Cambridge, MA: Harvard University Asia Center; distributed by Harvard University Press.

Brook, Timothy, ed. 1999. *Documents on the Rape of Nanking.* Ann Arbor: University of Michigan Press.

———. 2005. *Collaboration: Japanese Agents and Local Elites in Wartime China.* Cambridge, MA: Harvard University Press.

Brook, Timothy, and Bob Tadashi Wakabayashi, eds. 2000. *Opium Regimes: China, Britain, and Japan, 1839–1952.* Berkeley: University of California Press.

Brown, Melissa J. 2016. "Footbinding, Industrialization, and Evolutionary Explanation." *Human Nature* 27, no. 4 (December): 501–32.

Brown, Melissa J., Laurel Bossen, Hill Gates, and Damian Satterthwaite-Phillips. 2012. "Marriage Mobility and Footbinding in Pre-1949 Rural China: A Reconsideration of Gender, Economics, and Meaning in Social Causation." *Journal of Asian Studies* 71, no. 4.

Brownell, Susan. 2005. "China Reconstructs: Cosmetic Surgery and Nationalism in the Reform Era." In *Asian Medicine and Globalization*, ed. Joseph S. Alter, 132–50. Philadelphia: University of Pennsylvania Press.

Bryson, Megan. 2016. *Goddess on the Frontier: Religion, Ethnicity, and Gender in Southwest China.* Stanford, CA: Stanford University Press.

Buck, John Lossing. 1956. *Land Utilization in China: A Study of 16,786 Farms in 168 Localities, and 38,256 Farm Families in Twenty-Two Provinces in China, 1929–1933.* New York: Reproduced by the Council on Economic and Cultural Affairs. Originally published 1937 by University of Nanking.

———. 1982. *Chinese Farm Economy (China during the Interregnum, 1911–1949).* New York: Garland.

Buckley, Chris. 2015. "China Ends One-Child Policy, Allowing Families Two Children." *New York Times,* October 29. http://www.nytimes.com/2015/10/30/world/asia/china-end-one-child-policy.html.

Burton, Margaret E. 1918. *Women Workers of the Orient.* West Medford, MA: Central Committee on the United Study of Foreign Missions.

———. 1927. *New Paths for Old Purposes: World Challenges to Christianity in Our Generation.* New York: Missionary Education Movement and Council of Women for Home Missions.

Cao, Yang, and Chiung-Yin Hu. 2007. "Gender and Job Mobility in Postsocialist China: A Longitudinal Study of Job Changes in Six Coastal Cities." *Social Forces* 85, no. 4 (June): 1535–60.

Cao Zhuxiang. 1996. Personal interview with Gao Xiaoxian and Gail Hershatter. August 2–4.

Chan, Anita, and Zhu Xiaoyang. 2003. "Disciplinary Labor Regimes in Chinese Factories." *Critical Asian Studies* 35, no. 4 (December): 559–84.

Chan, Kim-kwong. 2002. "A New Marriage Law in China." *ChinaSource,* June 17. http://www.chinasource.org/resource-library/articles/a-new-marriage-law-in-china.

Chang, Leslie T. 2008. *Factory Girls: From Village to City in a Changing China.* New York: Spiegel & Grau.

Chao, Emily. 2003. "Dangerous Work." *Modern China* 29, no. 1 (January): 71.

———. 2012. *Lijiang Stories: Shamans, Taxi Drivers, and Runaway Brides in Reform-Era China.* Seattle: University of Washington Press.

Chen, Biyun. 1984. "The Depression in the Countryside and Peasant Women." Translated by Susan Mann. *Republican China* 10, no. 1 (November): 62–67.

Chen, Duxiu. 1999. "What Happens after Nora Leaves Home?" In *Women in Republican China: A Sourcebook,* ed. Hua R. Lan and Vanessa L. Fong, 5–8. Armonk, NY, and London: M. E. Sharpe.

Chen, Huiqin, with Shehong Chen. 2015. *Daughter of Good Fortune: A Twentieth-Century Chinese Peasant Memoir.* Seattle and London: University of Washington Press.

Chen, Janet Y. 2012. *Guilty of Indigence: The Urban Poor in China, 1900–1953.* Princeton, NJ: Princeton University Press.

Chen, Minglu. 2008. "Entrepreneurial Women: Personal Wealth, Local Politics and Tradition." In *The New Rich in China: Future Rulers, Present Lives,* ed. David S. G. Goodman, 112–25. Abingdon and New York: Routledge.

Chen, Pingyuan. 2008. "Male Gaze/Female Students: Late Qing Education for Women as Portrayed in Beijing Pictorials, 1902–08." Translated by Anne S. Chao. In *Different Worlds of Discourse: Transformations of Gender and Genre in Late Qing and Early Republican China,* ed. Nanxiu Qian, Grace Fong, and Richard Joseph Smith, 315–48. Leiden: Brill.

Chen, Tina Mai. 2001. "Dressing for the Party: Clothing, Citizenship, and Gender-Formation in Mao's China." *Fashion Theory: The Journal of Dress, Body & Culture* 5, no. 2 (June): 143–71.

———. 2003 "Female Icons, Feminist Iconography? Socialist Rhetoric and Women's Agency in 1950s China." *Gender & History* 15, no. 2: 268–95.

———. 2011. "They Love Battle Array, Not Silks and Satins." In *Words and Their Stories: Essays on the Language of the Chinese Revolution,* ed. Ban Wang, 263–81. Leiden and Boston: Brill,.

Chen, Xiaomei. 2002. *Acting the Right Part: Political Theater and Popular Drama in Contemporary China.* Honolulu: University of Hawai'i Press.

Chen Yan 陈雁. 2014. 性别与战争：上海，1932–1945 [Gender and War: Shanghai, 1932–1945]. Beijing: Shehui kexue wenxian chuban she.

Cheng, Eileen J. 2007. "Virtue in Silence: Voice and Femininity in Ling Shuhua's Boudoir Fiction." *Nan Nü—Men, Women & Gender in Early & Imperial China* 9, no. 2 (September): 330–70.

———. 2013. *Literary Remains: Death, Trauma, and Lu Xun's Refusal to Mourn.* Honolulu: University of Hawai'i Press.

Cheng, Weikun. 2000. "Going Public through Education: Female Reformers and Girls' Schools in Late Qing Beijing." *Late Imperial China* 21, no. 1: 107–44.

———. 2011. *City of Working Women: Life, Space, and Social Control in Early Twentieth-Century Beijing.* Berkeley: Institute of East Asian Studies, University of California.

Chiang, Yung-chen. 2006. "Womanhood, Motherhood and Biology: The Early Phases of The Ladies' Journal, 1915–25." *Gender & History* 18, no. 3 (November): 519–45.

Chin, Angelina. 2012. *Bound to Emancipate: Working Women and Urban Citizenship in Early Twentieth-Century China and Hong Kong.* Lanham, MD: Rowman & Littlefield.

Chin, Carol C. 2003. "Beneficent Imperialists: American Women Missionaries in China at the Turn of the Twentieth Century." *Diplomatic History* 27, no. 3 (June): 327–52.

———. 2006. "Translating the New Woman: Chinese Feminists View the West, 1905–15." *Gender & History* 18, no. 3 (November): 490–518.

Chin, Josh. 2016. "Tips on Breaking Through the Glass Ceiling in China." *Wall Street Journal,* November 11. http://blogs.wsj.com/chinarealtime/2016/11/11/tips-on-breaking-through-the-glass-ceiling-in-china.

———. 2017. "Writing China: Faith and Love in a Shenzhen Brothel." *Wall Street Journal,* May 3. https://blogs.wsj.com/chinarealtime/2017/05/03/writing-china-faith-and-love-in-a-shenzhen-brothel.

Chio, Jenny. 2014. *A Landscape of Travel: The Work of Tourism in Rural Ethnic China.* Seattle: University of Washington Press.

Chou Chun-yen 周春燕. 2014. "妇女与抗战时期的战地救护" [Women and Battlefield First Aid during the Second Sino-Japanese War]. *Jindai Zhongguo funüshi yanjiu,* no. 24 (December): 133–220.

Chow, Esther Ngan-ling. 1996. "Making Waves, Moving Mountains: Reflections on Beijing '95 and Beyond." *Signs* 22, no. 1: 185–92.

Chow, Ts'e-tsung. 1960. *The May Fourth Movement: Intellectual Revolution in Modern China.* Cambridge: Harvard University Press.

Chung, Sue Fawn. 1979. "The Much Maligned Empress Dowager: A Revisionist Study of the Empress Dowager Tz'u-Hsi (1835–1908)." *Modern Asian Studies* 13, no. 2: 177–96.

Cline, Erin M. 2010. "Female Spirit Mediums and Religious Authority in Contemporary Southeastern China." *Modern China* 36, no. 5 (September): 520–55.

Clinton, Maggie. 2017. *Revolutionary Nativism: Fascism and Culture in China, 1925–1937*. Durham, NC: Duke University Press.

Cohen, Paul A. 1963. *China and Christianity: The Missionary Movement and the Growth of Chinese Antiforeignism, 1860–1870*. Cambridge: Harvard University Press.

———. 1997. *History in Three Keys: The Boxers as Event, Experience, and Myth*. New York: Columbia University Press.

Cong, Xiaoping. 2007. *Teachers' Schools and the Making of the Modern Chinese Nation-State, 1897–1937*. Vancouver: UBC Press.

———. 2008. "From 'Cainü' to 'Nü Jiaoxi': Female Normal Schools and the Transformation of Women's Education in the Late Qing Period, 1895–1911." In *Different Worlds of Discourse: Transformations of Gender and Genre in Late Qing and Early Republican China*, ed. Nanxiu Qian, Grace Fong, and Richard Joseph Smith, 115–44. Leiden: Brill.

———. 2013. "From 'Freedom of Marriage' to 'Self-determined Marriage': Recasting Marriage in the Shaan-Gan-Ning Border Region of the 1940s." *Twentieth-Century China* 38, no. 3 (October): 184–209.

———. 2016. *Marriage, Law and Gender in Revolutionary China*. Cambridge: Cambridge University Press.

Conger, Sarah Pike. 1909. *Letters from China, with Particular Reference to the Empress Dowager and the Women of China*. Chicago: A. C. McClurg.

Cordier, Henri. 1913. "China." *Catholic Encyclopedia (1913)*. Wikisource.

Cowden, Charlotte. 2012. "Wedding Culture in 1930s Shanghai: Consumerism, Ritual, and the Municipality." *Frontiers of History in China* 7, no. 1 (March): 61–89.

Croll, Elisabeth. 1977."The Movement to Criticize Confucius and Lin Piao: A Comment on 'The Women of China' (vol. 2, no. 1)." *Signs* 2, no. 3: 721–26.

———. 1981. "Women in Rural Production and Reproduction in the Soviet Union, China, Cuba, and Tanzania: Case Studies." *Signs* 7, no. 2: 375–99.

———. 2001. "Amartya Sen's 100 Million Missing Women." *Oxford Development Studies* 29, no. 3: 226–44.

Crook, Isabel, and David Crook. 1979. *Ten Mile Inn: Mass Movement in a Chinese Village*. New York: Pantheon Books.

Crook, Isabel, and Christina K. Gilmartin. 2014. *Prosperity's Predicament: Identity, Reform, and Resistance in Rural Wartime China*. Lanham, MD: Rowman & Littlefield.

Culp, Robert Joseph. 2007. *Articulating Citizenship: Civic Education and Student Politics in Southeastern China, 1912–1940*. Cambridge, MA: Harvard University Asia Center.

———. 2010. "Reading and Writing Zhejiang Youth: Local Textual Economies and Cultural Production in Republican Jiangnan." In *From Woodblocks to the Internet: Chinese Publishing and Print Culture in Transition, circa 1800 to 2008*, ed. Cynthia J. Brokaw and Christopher Reed, 249–74. Leiden and Boston: Brill.

Cusack, Dymphna. 1958. *Chinese Women Speak*. London: Century Hutchinson.

Dai Jinhua. 2006. *Xingbie Zhongguo*. Taibei shi: Mai tian chu ban: Chengbang wen-
hua shiye gufen youxian gongsi.

Dai, Qing. 1994. *Wang Shiwei and "Wild Lilies": Rectification and Purges in the
Chinese Communist Party, 1942–1944*, ed. David E. Apter and Timothy Cheek.
Armonk, NY: M. E. Sharpe.

Dal Lago, Francesca. 2012. "How 'Modern' Was the Modern Woman? Crossed
Legs and Modernity in 1930s Shanghai Calendar Posters, Pictorial Magazines,
and Cartoons." In *Visualizing Beauty: Gender and Ideology in Modern East Asia*, ed.
Aida Yuen Wong, 45–61. Hong Kong: Hong Kong University Press.

Davin, Delia. 1975a. "Women in the Countryside of China." In *Women in Chinese
Society*, ed. Margery Wolf and Roxane Witke, 243–73. Stanford, CA: Stanford
University Press.

———. 1975b. "The Implications of Some Aspects of C.C.P. Policy toward Urban
Women in the 1950s." *Modern China* 1, no. 4 (October): 363–78.

———. 1976. *Woman-Work: Women and the Party in Revolutionary China*. Oxford,
UK: Clarendon.

———. 1989. "How Do We Know When It's Dark? Individual Witness: Public
Policy and Private Lives in 20th Century China." *Gender & History* 1, no. 3 (September): 273–90.

Davis, Deborah. 2010. "Who Gets the House? Renegotiating Property Rights in
Post-Socialist Urban China." *Modern China* 36, no. 5 (September): 463–92.

———. 2014a. "On the Limits of Personal Autonomy: PRC Law and the Institu-
tion of Marriage." In *Wives, Husbands, and Lovers: Marriage and Sexuality in Hong
Kong, Taiwan, and Urban China*, ed. Deborah Davis and Sara Friedman, 41–61.
Stanford, CA: Stanford University Press.

———. 2014b. "Privatization of Marriage in Post-Socialist China." *Modern China*
40, no. 6 (November): 551–77.

Davis, Deborah, and Sara Friedman, eds. 2014. *Wives, Husbands, and Lovers: Marriage and Sexuality in Hong Kong, Taiwan, and Urban China*. Stanford, CA: Stanford University Press.

Deng, Enming. 1999. "The Condition of Female Education in Jinan." In *Women in
Republican China: A Sourcebook*, ed. Hua R. Lan and Vanessa L. Fong, 135–41.
Armonk, NY, and London: M. E. Sharpe.

Des Forges, Alexander Townsend. 2000. "Opium/Leisure/Shanghai: Urban
Economies of Consumption." In *Opium Regimes: China, Britain, and Japan,
1839–1952*, ed. Timothy Brook and Bob Tadashi Wakabayashi, 167–85. Berkeley:
University of California Press.

———. 2007. *Mediasphere Shanghai: The Aesthetics of Cultural Production*. Honolulu:
University of Hawai'i Press.

Diamant, Neil Jeffrey. 2000. *Revolutionizing the Family: Politics, Love, and Divorce
in Urban and Rural China, 1949–1968*. Berkeley: University of California Press.

———. 2014. "Policy Blending, Fuzzy Chronology, and Local Understandings of
National Initiatives in Early 1950s China." *Frontiers of History in China* 9, no. 1
(January): 83–101.

Dikötter, Frank. 1992. *The Discourse of Race in Modern China*. Stanford, CA: Stanford University Press.

———. 1995. *Sex, Culture and Modernity in China: Medical Science and the Construction of Sexual Identities in the Early Republican Period*. London: Hurst.

———. 1998. *Imperfect Conceptions: Medical Knowledge, Birth Defects, and Eugenics in China*. New York: Columbia University Press.

———. 2010. *Mao's Great Famine: The History of China's Most Devastating Catastrophe, 1958–62*. London: Bloomsbury.

———. 2015. *The Discourse of Race in Modern China*. Fully revised and expanded second edition. New York: Oxford University Press.

Ding, Ling. 1981. "In the Hospital." In *Modern Chinese Stories and Novellas, 1919–1949*, ed. Joseph S. M. Lau, C. T. Hsia, and Leo Ou-fan Lee. Translated by Gary J. Bjorge, 279–91. New York: Columbia University Press.

Ding, Ling, Tani E. Barlow, and Gary J. Bjorge. 1989. *I Myself Am a Woman: Selected Writings of Ding Ling*. Boston: Beacon Press.

Ding, Yu. 2012. "Negotiating Intimacies in an Eroticized Environment: Xiaojies and South China Entertainment Business—ProQuest." *International Journal of Business Anthropology* 3, no. 1: 158–75.

———. 2016. "'小姐': 一个文化符号 丨 珠三角性工作者研究" ["Misses": A Cultural Symbol; Research on Sex Workers in the Pearl River Delta]. May 30. http://www.ssap.com.cn/c/2016-05-30/1018094.shtml.

Dirlik, Arif. 1991. *Anarchism in the Chinese Revolution*. Berkeley: University of California Press.

Dong, Madeleine Y. 2008. "Who Is Afraid of the Chinese Modern Girl?" In *The Modern Girl around the World Consumption, Modernity, and Globalization*, 194–219. Durham, NC: Duke University Press.

Dooling, Amy D. 2005. *Women's Literary Feminism in Twentieth-Century China*. New York: Palgrave Macmillan.

Dooling, Amy D., and Kristina M. Torgeson, eds. 1998. *Writing Women in Modern China: An Anthology of Women's Literature from the Early Twentieth Century*. New York: Columbia University Press.

Drucker, Alison R. 1979. "The Role of the YWCA in the Development of the Chinese Women's Movement, 1890–1927." *Social Service Review* 53, no. 3: 421–40.

———. 1981. "The Influence of Western Women on the Anti-Footbinding Movement 1840–1911." In *Women in China: Current Directions in Historical Scholarship*, ed. R. W. L Guisso and Stanley Johannesen, 179–99. Youngstown, NY: Philo.

Dryburgh, Marjorie. 2016. "Living on the Edge: Welfare and the Urban Poor in 1930s Beijing." *Social History* 41, no. 1 (January): 14–33.

Duara, Prasenjit. 1995. *Rescuing History from the Nation: Questioning Narratives of Modern China*. Chicago: University of Chicago Press.

———. 2003. *Sovereignty and Authenticity: Manchukuo and the East Asian Modern*. Lanham, MD: Rowman & Littlefield.

———. 2009. *The Global and Regional in China's Nation-Formation*. Milton Park, Abingdon, Oxon; New York: Routledge.

DuBois, Thomas David. 2014. "Public Health and Private Charity in Northeast China, 1905–1945." *Frontiers of History in China* 9, no. 4 (December): 506–33.

Dunch, Ryan. 2009. "Christianizing Confucian Didacticism: Protestant Publications for Women, 1832–1911." *Nan Nü* 11, no. 1 (June): 65–101.

———. 2010. "'Mothers to Our Country': Conversion, Education, and Ideology among Chinese Protestant Women, 1870–1930." In *Pioneer Chinese Christian Women: Gender, Christianity, and Social Mobility*, ed. Jessie Gregory Lutz, 324–50. Bethlehem, PA: Lehigh University Press.

Ebrey, Patricia Buckley. 1999. "Gender and Sinology: Shifting Western Interpretations of Footbinding, 1300–1890." *Late Imperial China* 20, no. 2: 1–34.

Edgerton-Tarpley, Kathryn. 2008. *Tears from Iron: Cultural Responses to Famine in Nineteenth-Century China*. Asia-Local Studies/Global Themes 15. Berkeley: University of California Press.

Edwards, Louise. 2000. "Policing the Modern Woman in Republican China." *Modern China* 26, no. 2 (April): 115–47.

———. 2004. "Constraining Women's Political Work with 'Women's Work.'" In *Chinese Women, Living and Working*, ed. Anne E. McLaren, 109–30. London and New York: RoutledgeCurzon.

———. 2008a. *Gender, Politics, and Democracy: Women's Suffrage in China*. Stanford, CA: Stanford University Press.

———. 2008b. "Issue-Based Politics: Feminism with Chinese Characteristics or the Return of Bourgeois Feminism?" In *The New Rich in China: Future Rulers, Present Lives*, ed. David S. G. Goodman, 201–12. Abingdon and New York, NY: Routledge.

———. 2012. "The Shanghai Modern Woman's American Dreams: Imagining America's Depravity to Produce China's 'Moderate Modernity.'" *Pacific Historical Review* 81, no. 4 (November): 567–601.

———. 2013. "Drawing Sexual Violence in Wartime China: Anti-Japanese Propaganda Cartoons." *Journal of Asian Studies* 72, no. 3 (August): 563–86.

———. 2016a. "International Women's Day in China: Feminism Meets Militarised Nationalism and Competing Political Party Programs." *Asian Studies Review* 40, no. 1 (January): 89–105.

———. 2016b. *Women Warriors and Wartime Spies of China*. Cambridge: Cambridge University Press.

Edwards, Louise, and Lili Zhou. 2011. "Gender and the 'Virtue of Violence': Creating a New Vision of Political Engagement through the 1911 Revolution." *Frontiers of History in China* 6, no. 4 (January): 485–504.

Eklund, Lisa. 2011. "'Good Citizens Prefer Daughters': Gender, Rurality and the Care for Girls Campaign." In *Women, Gender and Rural Development in China*, ed. Tamara Jacka and Sally Sargeson, 124–42. Cheltenham: Edward Elgar.

Elman, Benjamin A. 2000. *A Cultural History of Civil Examinations in Late Imperial China*. Berkeley: University of California Press.

———. 2004. "Naval Warfare and the Refraction of China's Self-Strengthening Reforms into Scientific and Technological Failure, 1865–1895." *Modern Asian Studies* 38, no. 2: 283–326.

Eng, Robert Y. 1990. "Luddism and Labor Protest Among Silk Artisans and Workers in Jiangnan and Guangdong, 1860–1930." *Late Imperial China* 11, no. 2: 63–101.

Engebretsen, Elisabeth L. 2014. *Queer Women in Urban China: An Ethnography*. New York: Routledge.

———. 2017. "Under Pressure: Lesbian-Gay Contract Marriages and Their Patriarchal Bargains." In *Transforming Patriarchy: Chinese Families in the Twenty-First Century*, ed. Gonçalo D. Santos and Stevan Harrell, 163–81. Seattle: University of Washington Press.

Engebretsen, Elisabeth L., William F. Schroeder, Hongwei Bao, and Nordic Institute of Asian Studies, eds. 2015. *Queer/Tongzhi China: New Perspectives on Research, Activism and Media Cultures*. Copenhagen: NIAS Press.

Evans, Harriet. 1997. *Women and Sexuality in China: Dominant Discourses of Female Sexuality and Gender since 1949*. Cambridge, UK: Polity Press.

———. 1999. "'Comrade Sisters': Gendered Bodies and Spaces." In *Picturing Power in the People's Republic of China: Posters of the Cultural Revolution*, ed. Harriet Evans and Stephanie Donald, 63–78. Lanham, MD: Rowman & Littlefield.

———. 2002. "Past, Perfect or Imperfect: Changing Images of the Ideal Wife." In *Chinese Femininities, Chinese Masculinities: A Reader*, ed. Susan Brownell and Jeffrey N. Wasserstrom, 335–60. Berkeley: University of California Press.

———. 2003. "The Language of Liberation: Gender and Jiefang in Early Chinese Communist Party Discourse." In *Twentieth-Century China: New Approaches*, ed. Jeffrey N. Wasserstrom, 193–220. London and New York: Routledge.

———. 2008. *The Subject of Gender: Daughters and Mothers in Urban China*. Lanham, MD: Rowman & Littlefield.

———. 2010. "The Gender of Communication: Changing Expectations of Mothers and Daughters in Urban China." *China Quarterly* 204: 980–1000.

———. 2012. "Belonging to Old Beijing." In *Chinese Characters: Profiles of Fast-Changing Lives in a Fast-Changing Land*, ed. Angilee Shah and Jeffrey N. Wasserstrom, 55–66. Berkeley: University of California Press.

Eyferth, Jacob. 2009. *Eating Rice from Bamboo Roots: The Social History of a Community of Handicraft Papermakers in Rural Sichuan, 1920–2000*. Cambridge, MA: Harvard University Asia Center.

———. 2012. "Women's Work and the Politics of Homespun in Socialist China, 1949–1980." *International Review of Social History* 57, no. 3: 365–91.

———. 2015. "Liberation from the Loom?: Rural Women, Textile Work, and Revolution in North China." In *Maoism at the Grassroots: Everyday Life in China's Era of High Socialism*, ed. Jeremy Brown and Matthew D. Johnson. Cambridge, MA: Harvard University Press.

Fan, Jiayang. 2017. "China's Mistress-Dispellers." *New Yorker*, June 26. http://www.newyorker.com/magazine/2017/06/26/chinas-mistress-dispellers.

Fan Yusu 范雨素. "我是范雨素." [I am Fan Yusu]. April 29, 2017a. http://hx.cnd.org/2017/04/29/139522.

———. 2017b. "'I Am Fan Yusu' (我是范雨素) (Full Translation)." *What's on Weibo*, May 10. http://www.whatsonweibo.com/fan-yusu-%e6%88%91%e6%98%af%e8%8c%83%e9%9b%a8%e7%b4%a0-full-translation.

Fang, Xiaoping. 2017. "Bamboo Steamers and Red Flags: Building Discipline and Collegiality among China's Traditional Rural Midwives in the 1950s." *China Quarterly* (May): 1–24.

Farquhar, Judith. 2002. *Appetites: Food and Sex in Postsocialist China*. Durham, NC: Duke University Press.

Farrer, James. 2002. *Opening Up: Youth Sex Culture and Market Reform in Shanghai.* Chicago: University of Chicago Press.

———. 2014 "Love, Sex, and Commitment: Delinking Premarital Intimacy from Marriage in Urban China." In *Wives, Husbands, and Lovers: Marriage and Sexuality in Hong Kong, Taiwan, and Urban China*, ed. Deborah Davis and Sara Friedman, 62–96. Stanford, CA: Stanford University Press.

Farrer, James, and Andrew David Field. 2015. *Shanghai Nightscapes: A Nocturnal Biography of a Global City.* Chicago: University of Chicago Press.

Feng, Jiayun. 2017. "Hard Times for Feminists in China." *SupChina*, March 8. http://supchina.com/2017/03/08/hard-times-feminists-china.

———. 2017. "Marriage Rate Falls While Divorce Soars—China's Latest Society and Culture News." *SupChina*, June 16. http://supchina.com/2017/06/16/marriage-rate-falls-divorce-soars-chinas-latest-society-culture-news.

———. 2017. "Will Longer Maternity Leave Harm Women's Career Prospects in China?—China's Latest Society and Culture News." *SupChina*, July 10. http://supchina.com/2017/07/10/will-longer-maternity-leave-harm-womens-career-prospects-china-chinas-latest-society-culture-news.

———. 2017. "Outrage over Audi Ad Comparing Women to Used Cars—China's Latest Society and Culture News." *SupChina*, July 18. http://supchina.com/2017/07/18/outrage-audi-ad-comparing-women-used-cars-chinas-latest-society-culture-news.

———. 2017. "Sexual Harassment in China: Different than in the U.S.?—China's Latest Society and Culture News." October 16. https://supchina.com/2017/10/16/sexual-harassment-china-different-u-s-chinas-latest-society-culture-news.

———. 2018. "Chinese University Instructors Sign Anti-Sexual Harassment Manifesto (full translation)." *Society News*, January 22. https://supchina.com/2018/01/22/chinese-university-instructors-sign-anti-sexual-harassment-manifesto.

———. 2018. "'I Am a Woman Worker at Foxconn, and I Demand a System That Opposes Sexual Harassment': A Translated Essay." *Society News*, January 26. https://supchina.com/2018/01/26/i-am-a-woman-worker-at-foxconn-demand-system-opposes-sexual-harassment.

———. 2018. "Nanjing University Professor Suspended over Sexual Misconduct 20 Years after His Student's Suicide." April 9. https://supchina.com/2018/04/09/nanjing-university-professor-suspended-over-sexual-misconduct-20-years-after-his-students-suicide.

Feng, Jin. 2004. *The New Woman in Early Twentieth-Century Chinese Fiction.* West Lafayette, IN: Purdue University Press.

Ferlanti, Federica. 2012. "The New Life Movement at War: Wartime Mobilisation and State Control in Chongqing and Chengdu, 1938–1942." *European Journal of East Asian Studies* 11, no. 2 (September): 187–212.

Field, Andrew David. 2010. *Shanghai's Dancing World: Cabaret Culture and Urban Politics, 1919–1954.* Hong Kong: Chinese University Press.

Fielde, Adele M. (Adele Marion). 1887. *Pagoda Shadows: Studies from Life in China.* London: T. Ogilvie Smith.

Finnane, Antonia. 1996. "What Should Chinese Women Wear?: A National Problem." *Modern China* 22, no. 2 (April): 99–131.

———. 2004. *Speaking of Yangzhou: A Chinese City, 1550–1850.* Cambridge, MA: Harvard University Asia Center; distributed by Harvard University Press.

———. 2008. *Changing Clothes in China: Fashion, History, Nation.* New York: Columbia University Press.

———. 2013. "Changing Spaces and Civilizing Weddings in Republican China." In *New Narratives of Urban Space in Republican Chinese Cities: Emerging Social, Legal and Governance Orders,* ed. Billy K. L. So and Madeleine Zelin, 15–44. Leiden: Brill.

Fitzgerald, John. 1996. *Awakening China: Politics, Culture, and Class in the Nationalist Revolution.* Stanford, CA: Stanford University Press.

Flitsch, Mareile. 2008. "Knowledge, Embodiment, Skill and Risk: Anthropological Perspectives on Women's Everyday Technologies in Rural Northern China." *East Asian Science, Technology and Society* 2, no. 2 (June): 265–88.

Fogel, Joshua A., ed. 2000. *The Nanjing Massacre in History and Historiography.* Berkeley: University of California Press.

Foliot, G. 2010. "A Biography (Ruan Lingyu 1910–1935)." Accessed October 24, 2016. http://www.vcea.net/Ruan_Lingyu/Essay/Biography_en.php.

Fong, Grace S. 2000. "Writing Self and Writing Lives: Shen Shanbao's (1808–1862) Gendered Auto/Biographical Practices." *Nan Nü—Men, Women & Gender in Early & Imperial China* 2, no. 2 (April): 259–303.

———. 2004. "Female Hands: Embroidery as a Knowledge Field in Women's Everyday Life in Late Imperial and Early Republican China." *Late Imperial China* 25, no. 1: 1–58.

Fong, Mei. 2016. *One Child: The Story of China's Most Radical Experiment.* Boston: Houghton Mifflin Harcourt.

Fong, Vanessa L. 2004. *Only Hope: Coming of Age under China's One-Child Policy.* Stanford, CA: Stanford University Press.

Friedman, Edward, Paul Pickowicz, and Mark Selden. 1991. *Chinese Village, Socialist State.* New Haven, CT: Yale University Press.

———. 2005. *Revolution, Resistance, and Reform in Village China.* New Haven, CT: Yale University Press.

Friedman, Sara. 2006. *Intimate Politics: Marriage, the Market, and State Power in Southeastern China.* Cambridge, MA: Harvard University Asia Center; distributed by Harvard University Press.

Fu, Diana. 2009. "A Cage of Voices: Producing and Doing Dagongmei in Contemporary China." *Modern China* 35, no. 5 (September): 527–61.

Fu, Yiqin. 2015. "China's TV Spectacular Was Spectacularly Misogynistic." *Foreign Policy.* Accessed February 24. https://foreignpolicy.com/2015/02/20/chinas-tv-spectacular-misogyny-body-shame-sex-harassment-not-funny.

Furth, Charlotte. 1999. *A Flourishing Yin: Gender in China's Medical History, 960–1665.* Berkeley: University of California Press.

Gaetano, Arianne M. 2015. *Out to Work: Migration, Gender, and the Changing Lives of Rural Women in Contemporary China.* Honolulu: University of Hawai'i Press.

Gaetano, Arianne M., and Tamara Jacka, eds. 2004. *On the Move: Women and Rural-to-Urban Migration in Contemporary China.* New York: Columbia University Press.

Gao, Xiaoxian. 2006. "'The Silver Flower Contest': Rural Women in 1950s China and the Gendered Division of Labour." Translated by Yuanxi Ma. *Gender & History* 18, no. 3 (November): 594–612.

———. 2008. "Women and Development in China." *Chinese Sociology & Anthropology* 40, no. 4 (Summer): 13–26.

———. 2010. "From the Heyang Model to the Shaanxi Model: Action Research on Women's Participation in Village Governance." *China Quarterly* 204: 870–98.

Gao, Yunxiang. 2006. "Nationalist and Feminist Discourses on Jianmei (Robust Beauty) during China's 'National Crisis' in the 1930s." *Gender & History* 18, no. 3 (November): 546–73.

———. 2013. *Sporting Gender: Women Athletes and Celebrity-Making during China's National Crisis, 1931–45*. Vancouver: UBC Press.

Gardella, Robert. 1994. *Harvesting Mountains: Fujian and the China Tea Trade, 1757–1937*. Berkeley: University of California Press.

Gates, Hill. 1996. "Buying Brides in China—Again." *Anthropology Today* 12, no. 4 (August): 8.

———. 2001. "Footloose in Fujian: Economic Correlates of Footbinding." *Comparative Studies in Society and History* 43, no. 1 (January): 130–48.

———. 2014. *Footbinding and Women's Labor in Sichuan*. Routledge Contemporary China Series. Milton Park, Abingdon, Oxon, and New York: Routledge.

Gerth, Karl. 2003. *China Made: Consumer Culture and the Creation of the Nation*. Cambridge, MA: Harvard University Asia Center.

Gewurtz, Margo S. 2010. "Women and Christianity in Rural North Henan, 1890–1912." In *Pioneer Chinese Christian Women: Gender, Christianity, and Social Mobility*, ed. Jessie Gregory Lutz, 199–213. Bethlehem, PA: Lehigh University Press.

Gillin, Donald G. 1967. *Warlord: Yen Hsi-shan in Shansi Province, 1911–1949*. Princeton, NJ: Princeton University Press.

Gilmartin, Christina K. 1995. *Engendering the Chinese Revolution: Radical Women, Communist Politics, and Mass Movements in the 1920s*. Berkeley: University of California Press.

Gimpel, Denise. 2001. *Lost Voices of Modernity: A Chinese Popular Fiction Magazine in Context*. Honolulu: University of Hawai'i Press.

———. 2006. "Freeing the Mind through the Body: Women's Thoughts on Physical Education in Late Qing and Early Republican China." *Nan Nü—Men, Women & Gender in Early & Imperial China* 8, no. 2 (September): 316–58.

———. 2015. *Chen Hengzhe: A Life between Orthodoxies*. Lanham, MD: Lexington Books.

Gipoulon, Catherine. 1984. "Integrating the Feminist and Worker's Movement: The Case of Xiang Jingyu." *Republican China* 10, no. 1 (November): 29–41.

Glosser, Susan L. 2003. *Chinese Visions of Family and State, 1915–1953*. Berkeley: University of California Press.

Goldman, Andrea S. 2012. *Opera and the City: The Politics of Culture in Beijing, 1770–1900*. Stanford, CA: Stanford University Press.

Gong, Wanqi, Caixie Tu, and L. Crystal Jiang. 2015. "Stigmatized Portrayals of Single Women: A Content Analysis of News Coverage on Single Women and Single Men in China." *Journal of Gender Studies* 26, no. 2: 197–211.

Goodman, Bryna. 2000. "Improvisations on a Semicolonial Theme, or, How to Read a Celebration of Transnational Urban Community." *Journal of Asian Studies* 59, no. 4 (November): 889–926.

———. 2005a. "The New Woman Commits Suicide: The Press, Cultural Memory, and the New Republic." *Journal of Asian Studies* 641: 67–101.

———. 2005b. "The Vocational Woman and the Elusiveness of 'Personhood' in Early Republican China." In *Gender in Motion: Divisions of Labor and Cultural Change in Late Imperial and Modern China*, ed. Bryna Goodman and Wendy Larson, 265–86. Lanham, MD: Rowman & Littlefield.

———. 2005c. "Unvirtuous Exchanges: Women and the Corruptions of the Stock Market in Early Republican Shanghai." In *Women in China: The Republican Period in Historical Perspective*, ed. Mechthild Leutner and Nicola Spakowski. Münster: Lit.

Goodman, David S. G. 1997. "The Licheng Rebellion of 1941: Class, Gender, and Leadership in the Sino-Japanese War." *Modern China* 23, no. 2 (April): 216–45.

———. 2000a. "Revolutionary Women and Women in the Revolution: The Chinese Communist Party and Women in the War of Resistance to Japan, 1937–1945." *China Quarterly*, no. 164 (December): 915–942.

———. 2000b. *Social and Political Change in Revolutionary China: The Taihang Base Area in the War of Resistance to Japan, 1937–1945*. Lanham, MD: Rowman & Littlefield.

———. 2002. "Why Women Count: Chinese Women and the Leadership of Reform." *Asian Studies Review* 26, no. 3 (September): 331–53.

Gottschang, Thomas R., and Diana Lary. 2000. *Swallows and Settlers: The Great Migration from North China to Manchuria*. Ann Arbor: Center for Chinese Studies, University of Michigan.

Graham, Gael. 1994. "Exercising Control: Sports and Physical Education in American Protestant Mission Schools in China, 1880–1930." *Signs* 20, no. 1: 23–48.

Greenhalgh, Susan. 2001. "Fresh Winds in Beijing: Chinese Feminists Speak Out on the One-Child Policy and Women's Lives." *Signs* 26, no. 3: 847–86.

———. 2008. *Just One Child: Science and Policy in Deng's China*. Berkeley: University of California Press.

Greenhalgh, Susan, and Jiali Li. 1995. "Engendering Reproductive Policy and Practice in Peasant China: For a Feminist Demography of Reproduction." *Signs* 20, no. 3: 601–41.

Greenhalgh, Susan, and Edwin A. Winckler. 2005. *Governing China's Population: From Leninist to Neoliberal Biopolitics*. Stanford, CA: Stanford University Press.

Grove, Linda. 2006. *A Chinese Economic Revolution: Rural Entrepreneurship in the Twentieth Century*. Lanham, MD: Rowman & Littlefield.

Guo, Yuhua. 2007. "'Nous Étions Comme Un Feu Ardent': La Collectivisation Des Esprits Dans Les Récits Des Femmes Du Village de Jicun (Nord Du Shaanxi)" ["'We Were Like an Ardent Fire': Collectivism of Spirit in the Stories of the Jicun Village Women of the North Shanxi Province"]. *Civilisations* 56, no. 1/2: 43–62.

GZLSHZS. 2015. "二胎全面放开了！我为什么不生二胎" [The Way to a Second Child Is Fully Open! Why I Will Not Have a Second Child]. October 30. http://mp.weixin.qq.com/s/b4b0AI2JcNUzn5eNOivXXQ.

Han, Hua. 2007. "Under the Shadow of the Collective Good: An Ethnographic Analysis of Fertility Control in Xiaoshan, Zhejiang Province, China." *Modern China* 33, no. 3 (July): 320–48.

Han, Su Lin. 2017a. "China Has a New Domestic Violence Law. So Why Are Victims Still Often Unsafe?" *ChinaFile*, June 5. http://www.chinafile.com/reporting-opinion/viewpoint/china-has-a-new-domestic-violence-law-so-why-are-victims-still-often.

———. 2017b. "China's New Domestic Violence Law: Keeping Victims Out of Harm's Way? Working Paper." *Paul Tsai China Center* 耶鲁大学法学院蔡中曾中国中心.

Hansen, Mette Halskov. 2001. "Ethnic Minority Girls on Chinese School Benches: Gender Perspectives on Minority Education." In *Education, Culture, and Identity in Twentieth-Century China*, ed. Glen Peterson, Ruth Hayhoe, and Yongling Lu, 403–29. Ann Arbor: University of Michigan Press.

Hanser, Amy. 2005. "The Gendered Rice Bowl: The Sexual Politics of Service Work in Urban China." *Gender and Society* 19, no. 5: 581–600.

———. 2008. *Service Encounters: Class, Gender, and the Market for Social Distinction in Urban China*. Stanford, CA: Stanford University Press.

Harris, Kristine. 1995. "'The New Woman': Image, Subject, and Dissent in 1930s Shanghai Film Culture." *Republican China* 20, no. 2 (April): 55–79.

———. 1997. "The New Woman Incident: Cinema, Scandal and Spectacle in 1935 Shanghai." In *Transnational Chinese Cinemas: Identity, Nationhood, Gender*, ed. Sheldon Hsiao-peng Lu, 277–302. Honolulu: University of Hawai'i Press.

Harrison, Henrietta. 2008 "'A Penny for the Little Chinese': The French Holy Childhood Association in China, 1843–1951." *American Historical Review* 113, no. 1: 72–92.

Hartford, Kathleen. 1989. "Repression and Communist Success: The Case of Jin-Cha-Ji, 1938–1943." In *Single Sparks: China's Rural Revolutions*, ed. Kathleen Hartford and Steven M. Goldstein, 92–127. Armonk, NY: M. E. Sharpe.

Heinrich, Larissa. 2008. *The Afterlife of Images: Translating the Pathological Body between China and the West*. Durham, NC: Duke University Press.

Henriot, Christian. 2001. *Prostitution and Sexuality in Shanghai: A Social History, 1849–1949*. Cambridge and New York: Cambridge University Press.

Hernández, Javier C., and Zoe Mou. 2018. "'Me Too,' Chinese Women Say. Not So Fast, Say the Censors." *New York Times*, January 23, sec. Asia Pacific. https://www.nytimes.com/2018/01/23/world/asia/china-women-me-too-censorship.html.

Hershatter, Gail. 1986. *The Workers of Tianjin, 1900–1949*. Stanford, CA: Stanford University Press.

———. 1997. *Dangerous Pleasures: Prostitution and Modernity in Twentieth-Century Shanghai*. Berkeley: University of California Press.

———. 2007. *Women in China's Long Twentieth Century*. Berkeley: Global, Area, and International Archive: University of California Press.

———. 2011. *The Gender of Memory: Rural Women and China's Collective Past*. Berkeley: University of California Press.

Hessler, Peter. 2006. *Oracle Bones: A Journey between China's Past and Present*. New York: HarperCollins.

Hevia, James Louis. 2003. *English Lessons: The Pedagogy of Imperialism in Nineteenth-Century China*. Durham, NC: Duke University Press.

Hieronymus, Sabine. 2005. "Qiu Jin (1875–1907)—A Heroine for All Seasons." In *Women in China: The Republican Period in Historical Perspective*, ed. Mechthild Leutner and Nicola Spakowski, 194–207. Münster: Lit.

Hinton, Carma, Geremie Barmé, Richard Gordon, John Crowley, Jane Balfour, David Carnochan, and Margot Adler. 2005. *Morning Sun*. Brookline, MA: Long Bow Group.

Hinton, Carma, and Richard Gordon. 1984. *Small Happiness: Women of a Chinese Village*. Philadelphia: Long Bow Group.

Hinton, William. 1997. *Fanshen: A Documentary of Revolution in a Chinese Village*. Berkeley: University of California Press.

Ho, Clara Wing-chung, ed. 1998. *Biographical Dictionary of Chinese Women*. University of Hong Kong Libraries Publications, no. 10, 14. Armonk, NY: M. E. Sharpe.

———. 2012. *Overt and Covert Treasures: Essays on the Sources for Chinese Women's History*. Hong Kong: Chinese University Press.

Ho, Loretta Wing Wah. 2008. "Speaking of Same-Sex Subjects in China." *Asian Studies Review* 32, no. 4 (December): 491–509.

Hom, Sharon K. 1994. "Engendering Chinese Legal Studies: Gatekeeping, Master Discourses, and Other Challenges." *Signs* 19, no. 4: 1020–47.

Honda, Katsuichi. 1999. *The Nanjing Massacre: A Japanese Journalist Confronts Japan's National Shame*. Armonk, NY: M. E. Sharpe.

Hong Fincher, Leta. 2012. "China's 'Leftover' Women." Global Opinion, *New York Times*, October 11. https://www.nytimes.com/2012/10/12/opinion/global/chinas-leftover-women.html.

———. 2014. *Leftover Women: The Resurgence of Gender Inequality in China*. London: Zed Books.

———. 2015 "China's Two-Child Policy: Single Mothers Left Out." *BBC News*, November 2. http://www.bbc.com/news/world-asia-china-34695899.

———. 2016. "China's Feminist Five." *Dissent* 63, no. 4 (Fall): 84–90.

Hong, Guo-Juin. 2007. "Framing Time: New Women and the Cinematic Representation of Colonial Modernity in 1930s Shanghai." *positions: east asia cultures critique* 15, no. 3 (December): 553–79.

Honig, Emily. 1986. *Sisters and Strangers: Women in the Shanghai Cotton Mills, 1919–1949*. Stanford, CA: Stanford University Press.

———. 1992. *Creating Chinese Ethnicity: Subei People in Shanghai, 1850–1980*. New Haven, CT: Yale University Press.

———. 2000. "Iron Girls Revisited: Gender and the Politics of Work in the Cultural Revolution, 1966–1976." In *Re-Drawing Boundaries: Work, Households, and Gender in China*, ed. Barbara Entwisle and Gail Henderson, 97–110. Berkeley: University of California Press.

———. 2002. "Maoist Mappings of Gender: Reassessing the Red Guards." In *Chinese Femininities, Chinese Masculinities: A Reader*, ed. Susan Brownell and Jeffrey N. Wasserstrom, 255–68. Berkeley: University of California Press.

———. 2003. "Socialist Sex: The Cultural Revolution Revisited." *Modern China* 29, no. 2 (April): 143–75.

———. 2015. "Life of a Slogan." In *Gender and Chinese History: Transformative Encounters*, ed. Beverly Jo Bossler, 185–207. Seattle: University of Washington Press.

Honig, Emily, and Gail Hershatter. 1988. *Personal Voices: Chinese Women in the 1980's*. Stanford, CA: Stanford University Press.

Hooper, Beverley. 1984. "China's Modernization: Are Young Women Going to Lose Out?" *Modern China* 10, no. 3 (July): 317–43.

———. 1994. "Women, Consumerism and the State in post–Mao China." *Asian Studies Review* 17, no. 3 (April): 73–83.

Howard, Joshua H. 2004. *Workers at War: Labor in China's Arsenals, 1937–1953*. Stanford, CA: Stanford University Press.

———. 2011. "History of Child Labor in China." In *Child Labour's Global Past, 1650–2000*, ed. Kristoffel Lieten and Elise van Nederveen Meerkerk, 501–25. Bern and New York: Peter Lang.

———. 2013. "The Politicization of Women Workers at War: Labour in Chongqing's Cotton Mills during the Anti-Japanese War." *Modern Asian Studies* 47, no. 6 (November): 1888–1940.

Hsiung, Ping-Chun. 2001. "The Women's Studies Movement in China in the 1980s and 1990s." In *Education, Culture, and Identity in Twentieth-Century China*, ed. Glen Peterson, Ruth Hayhoe, and Yongling Lu, 430–49. Ann Arbor: University of Michigan Press.

Hsiung, Ping-Chun, and Yuk-Lin Renita Wong. 1998. "Jie Gui—Connecting the Tracks: Chinese Women's Activism Surrounding the 1995 World Conference on Women in Beijing." *Gender & History* 10, no. 3: 470–97.

Hsu, Sara. 2016. "High Income Inequality Still Festering in China." *Forbes*, November 18. http://www.forbes.com/sites/sarahsu/2016/11/18/high-income-inequality-still-festering-in-china.

Hu, Chi-hsi. 1974. "The Sexual Revolution in the Kiangsi Soviet." *China Quarterly*, no. 59: 477–90. http://www.jstor.org/stable/652453.

Hu, Siao-chen. 2008. "The Construction of Gender and Genre in the 1910s New Media: Evidence from The Ladies' Journal." In *Different Worlds of Discourse: Transformations of Gender and Genre in Late Qing and Early Republican China*, ed. Nanxiu Qian, Grace S. Fong, and Richard J. Smith, 349–82. Leiden: Brill.

———. 2010. "War, Violence, and the Metaphor of Blood in Tanci Narratives by Women Authors." In *The Inner Quarters and Beyond: Women Writers from Ming through Qing*, ed. Grace S. Fong and Ellen Widmer, 249–80. Leiden and Boston: Brill.

Hu, Ying. 2000. *Tales of Translation: Composing the New Woman in China, 1899–1918*. Stanford, CA: Stanford University Press.

———. 2002. "Naming the First 'New Woman.'" In *Rethinking the 1898 Reform Period: Political and Cultural Change in Late Qing China*, ed. Rebecca E. Karl and Peter Gue Zarrow, 180–211. Cambridge, MA: Harvard University Asia Center; distributed by Harvard University Press.

———. 2004. "Writing Qiu Jin's Life: Wu Zhiying and Her Family Learning." *Late Imperial China* 25, no. 2: 119–60.

———. 2007. "Qiu Jin's Nine Burials: The Making of Historical Monuments and Public Memory." *Modern Chinese Literature and Culture* 19, no. 1 (April): 138–91.

———. 2008. "'Tossing the Brush'? Wu Zhiying (1868–1934) and the Uses of Calligraphy." In *Different Worlds of Discourse: Transformations of Gender and Genre in Late Qing and Early Republican China*, ed. Nanxiu Qian, Grace Fong, and Richard Joseph Smith, 57–85. Leiden: Brill.

———. 2009. "'How Can a Daughter Glorify the Family Name?' Filiality and Women's Rights in the Late Qing." *Nan Nü—Men, Women & Gender in Early & Imperial China* 11, no. 2 (March): 234–69.

———. 2011. "Gender and Modern Martyrology: Qiu Jin as Lienü, Lieshi, or Nülieshi." In *Beyond Exemplar Tales: Women's Biography in Chinese History*, ed. Joan Judge and Ying Hu, 121–36. Berkeley: Global, Area, and International Archive, University of California Press.

———. 2012. "Women's Characters: Calligraphy as a Source for Women's History." In *Overt and Covert Treasures: Essays on the Sources for Chinese Women's History*, ed. Clara Wing-chung Ho, 435–60. Hong Kong: Chinese University Press.

———. 2016. *Burying Autumn*. Cambridge, MA: Harvard University Asia Center; distributed by Harvard University Press.

Hua, Chang-ming. 1984. "Peasants, Women and Revolution—CCP Marriage Reform in the Shaan-Gan-Ning Border Area." *Republican China* 10, no. 1 (November): 1–24.

Huang, Philip C. 1985. *The Peasant Economy and Social Change in North China*. Stanford, CA: Stanford University Press.

———. 1990. *The Peasant Family and Rural Development in the Yangzi Delta, 1350–1988*. Stanford, CA: Stanford University Press.

———. 2001. *Code, Custom, and Legal Practice in China: The Qing and the Republic Compared*. Stanford, CA: Stanford University Press.

———. 2005. "Divorce Law Practices and the Origins, Myths, and Realities of Judicial 'Mediation' in China." *Modern China* 31, no. 2 (April): 151–203.

Huang, Xin. 2014. "In the Shadow of Suku (Speaking-Bitterness): Master Scripts and Women's Life Stories." *Frontiers of History in China* 9, no. 4 (December): 584–610.

Huang, Yingying, and Suiming Pan. 2014. "Government Crackdown of Sex Work in China: Responses from Female Sex Workers and Implications for Their Health." *Global Public Health* 9, no. 9 (October): 1067–79.

Huang, Yuqin. 2011. "Labour, Leisure, Gender and Generation: The Organization of 'Wan' and the Notion of 'Gender Equality' in Contemporary Rural China." In *Women, Gender and Rural Development in China*, ed. Tamara Jacka and Sally Sargeson, 49–70. Cheltenham: Edward Elgar.

Hubbard, Joshua A. 2014. "Queering the New Woman: Ideals of Modern Femininity in The Ladies' Journal, 1915–1931." *Nan Nü—Men, Women & Gender in Early & Imperial China* 16, no. 2 (September): 341–62.

Hung, Chang-Tai. 1993. "Reeducating a Blind Storyteller: Han Qixiang and the Chinese Communist Storytelling Campaign." *Modern China* 19, no. 4 (October): 395–426.

Hunter, Jane. 1984. *The Gospel of Gentility: American Women Missionaries in Turn-of-the-Century China*. New Haven, CT: Yale University Press.

Huntington, Rania. 2005. "Ghosts Seeking Substitutes: Female Suicide and Repetition." *Late Imperial China* 26, no. 1: 1–40.

Huters, Theodore. 2005. *Bringing the World Home: Appropriating the West in Late Qing and Early Republican China*. Honolulu: University of Hawai'i Press.

Hyatt, Irwin T. 1976. *Our Ordered Lives Confess: Three Nineteenth-Century American Missionaries in East Shantung*. Cambridge, MA: Harvard University Press.

Hyde, Sandra Teresa. 2007. *Eating Spring Rice: The Cultural Politics of AIDS in Southwest China*. Berkeley: University of California Press.

Ip, Hung-Yok. 2003. "Fashioning Appearances: Feminine Beauty in Chinese Communist Revolutionary Culture." *Modern China* 29, no. 3 (July): 329–61.

Ip, Penn Tsz Ting. 2017. "Desiring Singlehood? Rural Migrant Women and Affective Labour in the Shanghai Beauty Parlour Industry." *Inter-Asia Cultural Studies* 18, no. 4 (December): 558–80. https://doi.org/10.1080/14649373.2017.1387415.

Isett, Christopher Mills. 2007. *State, Peasant, and Merchant in Qing Manchuria, 1644–1862*. Stanford, CA: Stanford University Press.

Israel, John. 1966. *Student Nationalism in China, 1927–1937*. Stanford, CA: Published for the Hoover Institution on War, Revolution, and Peace by Stanford University Press.

———. 1998. *Lianda: A Chinese University in War and Revolution*. Stanford, CA: Stanford University Press.

Israel, John, and Donald W. Klein. 1976. *Rebels and Bureaucrats: China's December 9ers*. Berkeley: University of California Press.

Jacka, Tamara. 1997. *Women's Work in Rural China: Change and Continuity in an Era of Reform*. Cambridge and New York: Cambridge University Press.

———. 2005. "Finding a Place: Negotiations of Modernization and Globalization among Rural Women in Beijing." *Critical Asian Studies* 37, no. 1: 51–74.

———. 2006a. "Approaches to Women and Development in Rural China." *Journal of Contemporary China* 15, no. 49: 585–602.

———. 2006b. *Rural Women in Urban China: Gender, Migration, and Social Change*. Armonk, NY: M. E. Sharpe.

———. 2008. "Increasing Women's Participation in Village Government in China." *Critical Asian Studies* 40, no. 4.

———. 2009. "Cultivating Citizens: Suzhi (Quality) Discourse in the PRC." *positions: east asia cultures critique* 17, no. 3: 523–35.

———. 2010. "Women's Activism, Overseas Funded Participatory Development, and Governance: A Case Study from China." *Women's Studies International Forum* 33, no. 2: 99–112.

———. 2012. "Migration, Householding and the Well-Being of Left-Behind Women in Rural Ningxia." *China Journal* 67 (January): 1–22.

———. 2013. "Chinese Discourses on Rurality, Gender and Development: A Feminist Critique." *Journal of Peasant Studies* 40, no. 6: 983–1007.

———. 2014. "Left-behind and Vulnerable? Conceptualising Development and Older Women's Agency in Rural China." *Asian Studies Review* 38, no. 2: 186–204.

Jacka, Tamara, Andrew B. Kipnis, and Sally Sargeson. 2013. *Contemporary China: Society and Social Change*. Cambridge and Port Melbourne, Victoria: Cambridge University Press.

Jacka, Tamara, and Sally Sargeson, eds. 2011. *Women, Gender and Rural Development in China*. Cheltenham: Edward Elgar.

Jacobs, Andrew. 2015. "Sex Expert's Secret Is Out, and China's Open to It." *New York Times*, March 6. http://www.nytimes.com/2015/03/07/world/asia/chinese-advocate-of-sexuality-opens-door-into-her-own-private-life.html.

Jaschok, Maria. 1989. *Concubines and Bondservants*. London and Atlantic Highlands, NJ: Zed Books.

Jaschok, Maria, and Suzanne Miers, eds. 1994. *Women and Chinese Patriarchy: Submission, Servitude and Escape*. Hong Kong and London: Hong Kong University Press; Zed Books.

Jaschok, Maria, and Jingjun Shui. 2000. *The History of Women's Mosques in Chinese Islam: A Mosque of Their Own*. Richmond: Curzon.

———. 2011. *Women, Religion, and Space in China: Islamic Mosques & Daoist Temples, Catholic Convents & Chinese Virgins*. New York: Routledge.

Jeffreys, Elaine. 1997. "'Dangerous Amusements': Prostitution and Karaoke Halls in Contemporary China." *Asian Studies Review* 20, no. 3 (April): 43–54.

———. 2004a. *China, Sex and Prostitution*. London and New York: RoutledgeCurzon.

———. 2004b. "Feminist Prostitution Debates: Are There Any Sex Workers in China?" In *Chinese Women, Living and Working*, ed. Anne E. McLaren, 83–105. London and New York: RoutledgeCurzon.

———. 2006. "Over My Dead Body! Media Constructions of Forced Prostitution in the People's Republic of China." *PORTAL Journal of Multidisciplinary International Studies* 3, no. 2 (November).

———. 2012. *Prostitution Scandals in China: Policing, Media and Society*. New York: Routledge.

———. 2015. *Sex in China*. Malden, MA: Polity.

Jiang, Jin. 2009. *Women Playing Men: Yue Opera and Social Change in Twentieth-Century Shanghai*. Seattle: University of Washington Press.

Jiang, Pei, and Wei Wang. 2016. "Tradition, Revolution and Gender: An Analysis of Wife-Initiated Divorce in North China's Revolutionary Bases from 1941–1949." *Frontiers of History in China* 11, no. 1 (March): 66–92.

Jin, Yihong. 2006. "Rethinking the 'Iron Girls': Gender and Labour during the Chinese Cultural Revolution." Translated by Kimberley Ens Manning and Lianyun Chu. *Gender & History* 18, no. 3 (November): 613–34.

Jing, Jun, ed. 2000. *Feeding China's Little Emperors: Food, Children, and Social Change*. Stanford, CA: Stanford University Press.

Johnson, Kay Ann. 1983. *Women, the Family, and Peasant Revolution in China*. Chicago: University of Chicago Press.

———. 2016. *China's Hidden Children: Abandonment, Adoption, and the Human Costs of the One-Child Policy*. Chicago: University of Chicago Press.

Johnson, Tina Phillips. 2011. *Childbirth in Republican China: Delivering Modernity*. Lanham, MD: Lexington.

Judd, Ellen R. 1989. "Niangjia: Chinese Women and Their Natal Families." *Journal of Asian Studies* 48, no. 3: 525.

———. 1994. *Gender and Power in Rural North China*. Stanford, CA: Stanford University Press.

———. 2002. *The Chinese Women's Movement between State and Market*. Stanford, CA: Stanford University Press.

———. 2010. "Family Strategies: Fluidities of Gender, Community and Mobility in Rural West China." *China Quarterly* 204: 921–38.

Judge, Joan. 1997. "Citizens or Mothers of Citizens? Reimagining Femininity in Late Qing Women's Textbooks." *TICES Kokusai Tōhō Gakusha Kaigi Kiyō/Transactions of the International Conference of Eastern Studies* 42: 102–14.

———. 2001. "Talent, Virtue, and the Nation: Chinese Nationalisms and Female Subjectivities in the Early Twentieth Century." *American Historical Review* 106, no. 3 (June): 765–803.

———. 2002. "Reforming the Feminine: Female Literacy and the Legacy of 1898." In *Rethinking the 1898 Reform Period: Political and Cultural Change in Late Qing China*, ed. Rebecca E. Karl and Peter Gue Zarrow, 158–79. Cambridge, MA: Harvard University Asia Center; distributed by Harvard University Press.

———. 2004. "Blended Wish Images: Chinese and Western Exemplary Women at the Turn of the Twentieth Century." *Nan Nü—Men, Women & Gender in Early & Imperial China* 6, no. 1 (March): 102–35.

———. 2005. "Between Nei and Wai: Chinese Women Students in Japan in the Early Twentieth Century." In *Gender in Motion: Divisions of Labor and Cultural Change in Late Imperial and Modern China*, ed. Bryna Goodman and Wendy Larson, 121–43. Lanham, MD: Rowman & Littlefield.

———. 2008a. "Mediated Imaginings: Biographies of Western Women and Their Japanese Sources in Late Qing China." In *Different Worlds of Discourse: Transformations of Gender and Genre in Late Qing and Early Republican China*, ed. Nanxiu Qian, Grace S. Fong, and Richard J. Smith, 147–66. Leiden: Brill.

———. 2008b. *The Precious Raft of History: The Past, the West, and the Woman Question in China.* Stanford, CA: Stanford University Press.

———. 2009. "A Translocal Technology of the Self: Biographies of World Heroines and the Chinese Woman Question." *Journal of Women's History* 21, no. 4: 59–83.

———. 2012. "A Kaleidoscope of Knowledge about Women: The Chinese Periodical Press, 1872–1918." In *Overt and Covert Treasures: Essays on the Sources for Chinese Women's History*, ed. Clara Wing-chung Ho, 461–85. Hong Kong: Chinese University Press.

———. 2015. *Republican Lens.* Berkeley: University of California Press.

"Judicial Interpretation of Marriage Law Sparks Debate." 2011. *Women of China* [中国妇女], November 8. http://www.womenofchina.cn/html/report/3379-1.htm.

Kan, Karoline. 2017. "China, Where the Pressure to Marry Is Strong, and the Advice Flows Online." *New York Times*, June 18, sec. Asia Pacific. https://www.nytimes.com/2017/06/18/world/asia/china-advice-columnists-online-relationships.html.

Kang, Wenqing. 2009. *Obsession: Male Same-Sex Relations in China, 1900–1950.* Hong Kong: Hong Kong University Press.

Kang, Xiaofei. 2006. *The Cult of the Fox: Power, Gender, and Popular Religion in Late Imperial and Modern China.* New York: Columbia University Press.

———. 2014. "Women and the Religious Question in Modern China." In *Modern Chinese Religion: 1850–Present*, ed. Vincent Goossaert, John Lagerwey, and Jan Kiely, 1:491–559. Leiden: Brill.

Kang, Youwei. 1958. *Ta T'ung Shu, the One-World Philosophy of K'ang Yu-Wei.* Translated with introduction and notes by Laurence G. Thompson. London: Allen & Unwin.

Kao, Chen-Yang. 2009. "The Cultural Revolution and the Emergence of Pentecostal-Style Protestantism in China." *Journal of Contemporary Religion* 24, no. 2 (May): 171–88.

Kapp, Robert A. 1973. *Szechwan and the Chinese Republic; Provincial Militarism and Central Power, 1911–1938.* New Haven, CT: Yale University Press.

Karl, Rebecca E. 2002a. "'Slavery,' Citizenship, and Gender in Late Qing China's Global Context." In *Rethinking the 1898 Reform Period: Political and Cultural Change in Late Qing China*, ed. Rebecca E. Karl and Peter Gue Zarrow, 212–44. Cambridge, MA: Harvard University Asia Center; distributed by Harvard University Press.

———. 2002b. *Staging the World: Chinese Nationalism at the Turn of the Twentieth Century.* Durham, NC: Duke University Press.

———. 2012. "Feminism in Modern China." *Journal of Modern Chinese History* 6, no. 2 (December): 235–55.

Keating, Pauline B. 1997. *Two Revolutions: Village Reconstruction and the Cooperative Movement in Northern Shaanxi, 1934–1945.* Stanford, CA: Stanford University Press.

Kim, Ho-dong. 2004. *Holy War in China: The Muslim Rebellion and State in Chinese Central Asia, 1864–1877.* Stanford, CA: Stanford University Press.

Kim, Sung won, Vanessa L. Fong, Hirokazu Yoshikawa, Niobe Way, Xinyin Chen, Huihua Deng, and Zuhong Lu. 2010. "Income, Work Preferences and Gender Roles among Parents of Infants in Urban China: A Mixed Method Study from Nanjing." *China Quarterly* 204: 939–59.

King, Dean. 2010. *Unbound: A True Story of War, Love, and Survival.* New York: Little, Brown.

King, Michelle T. 2014. *Between Birth and Death: Female Infanticide in Nineteenth-Century China.* Stanford, CA: Stanford University Press.

King, Richard. 2013. *Milestones on a Golden Road: Writing for Chinese Socialism, 1945–80.* Vancouver: UBC Press.

King, Richard, Zhun Li, and Yigong Zhang, eds. 2010. *Heroes of China's Great Leap Forward: Two Stories.* Honolulu: University of Hawai'i Press.

Ko, Dorothy. 1997. "The Written Word and the Bound Foot: A History of the Courtesan's Aura." In *Writing Women in Late Imperial China*, ed. Ellen Widmer and Kang-i Sun Chang, 74–100. Stanford, CA: Stanford University Press.

———. 2001. *Every Step a Lotus: Shoes for Bound Feet.* Berkeley: University of California Press.

———. 2005. *Cinderella's Sisters: A Revisionist History of Footbinding.* Berkeley: University of California Press.

———. 2012. "Cinderella's Sisters." *ChinaFile*, March 2. http://www.chinafile .com/library/books/Cinderellas-Sisters.

Kung, James Kai-sing, and Daniel Yiu-fai Lee. 2010. "Women's Contributions to the Household Economy in Pre-1949 China: Evidence from the Lower Yangzi Region." *Modern China* 36, no. 2 (March): 210–38.

Kuo, Margaret. 2012a. *Intolerable Cruelty: Marriage, Law, and Society in Early Twentieth-Century China.* Lanham, MD: Rowman & Littlefield.

———. 2012b. "The Construction of Gender in Modern Chinese Law: Discrepant Gender Meanings in the Republican Civil Code." *Frontiers of History in China* 7, no. 2 (March): 282–309.

Laing, Ellen Johnston. 2003. "Visual Evidence for the Evolution of 'Politically Correct' Dress for Women in Early Twentieth Century Shanghai." *Nan Nü: Men, Women and Gender in China in Early and Imperial China* 5, no. 1 (April): 69–114.

———. 2004. *Selling Happiness: Calendar Posters and Visual Culture in Early-Twentieth-Century Shanghai*. Honolulu: University of Hawai'i Press.

———. 2013. "Picturing Men and Women in the Chinese 1911 Revolution." *Nan Nü—Men, Women & Gender in Early & Imperial China* 15, no. 2 (September): 265–316.

Lake, Roseann. 2015. "Why Is It So Hard for Unmarried Women in China to Go See a Gynecologist?" *Jezebel*, September 10. http://jezebel.com/why-is-it-so-hard-for-unmarried-women-in-china-to-go-se-1729393595.

Lam, Tong. 2011. *A Passion for Facts: Social Surveys and the Construction of the Chinese Nation State, 1900–1949*. Berkeley: University of California Press.

Lan, Hua R., and Vanessa L. Fong, eds. 1999. *Women in Republican China: A Sourcebook*. Asia and the Pacific. Armonk, NY: M. E. Sharpe.

Lan, Xiaoxiu 蓝小修. 2015. "The Two-Child Policy and the Way Out for Chinese Women" [二孩政策下看中国女性的出路]. October 30. http://mp.weixin.qq.com/s/Jhhm-TcPd6rkl9i4vKd12A.

Larson, Wendy. 1998. *Women and Writing in Modern China*. Stanford, CA: Stanford University Press.

Lary, Diana. 2010. *The Chinese People at War: Human Suffering and Social Transformation, 1937–1945*. New York: Cambridge University Press.

———. 2015. *China's Civil War: A Social History, 1945–1949*. Cambridge: Cambridge University Press.

Lary, Diana, and Stephen R. MacKinnon, eds. 2001. *The Scars of War: The Impact of Warfare on Modern China*. Vancouver: UBC Press.

Laughlin, Charles A. 2002. *Chinese Reportage: The Aesthetics of Historical Experience*. Durham, NC: Duke University Press.

Lee, Haiyan. 2007. *Revolution of the Heart: A Genealogy of Love in China, 1900–1950*. Stanford, CA: Stanford University Press.

Lee, James Z., and Cameron D. Campbell. 1997. *Fate and Fortune in Rural China: Social Organization and Population Behavior in Liaoning, 1774–1873*. New York: Cambridge University Press.

Lee, James Z., and Feng Wang. 1999. *One Quarter of Humanity: Malthusian Mythology and Chinese Realities, 1700–2000*. Cambridge, MA: Harvard University Press.

Lee, Leo Ou-fan. 1999. *Shanghai Modern: The Flowering of a New Urban Culture in China, 1930–1945*. Cambridge, MA: Harvard University Press.

Lee, Lily Xiao Hong.1994. *The Virtue of Yin: Studies on Chinese Women*. Broadway, NSW, Australia: Wild Peony.

Lee, Lily Xiao Hong, and Sue Wiles. 1999. *Women of the Long March*. St. Leonards, NSW, Australia: Allen & Unwin.

Leith, Suzette. 1973. "Chinese Women in the Early Communist Movement." In *Women in China*, ed. Marilyn Young, 47–71. Ann Arbor: Center for Chinese Studies, University of Michigan.

Leung, Angela Ki Che. 1993. "To Chasten Society: The Development of Widow Homes in the Qing, 1773–1911." *Late Imperial China* 14, no. 2: 1–32.

———. 2006. "Dignity of the Nation, Gender Equality, or Charity for All? Options for the First Modern Chinese Women Doctors." In *The Dignity of Nation: Competition and Honor in East Asian Nationalism*, ed. S. Chien and John Fitzgerald, 71–91, 219–26. Hong Kong: Hong Kong University Press.

Levine, Steven. 1989. "Mobilizing for War: Rural Revolution in Manchuria as an Instrument for War." In *Single Sparks: China's Rural Revolutions*, ed. Kathleen Hartford and Steven M. Goldstein, 151–75. Armonk, NY: M. E. Sharpe.

Li, Changli. 2010. "The Social Consequences of the May Fourth Movement." *Chinese Studies in History* 43, no. 4 (Summer): 20–42.

Li, Danke. 2010. *Echoes of Chongqing: Women in Wartime China*. Urbana: University of Illinois Press.

Li, Ke. 2015. "'What He Did Was Lawful': Divorce Litigation and Gender Inequality in China." *Law & Policy* 37, no. 3 (July): 153–79.

Li, Lillian M. 1991. "Life and Death in a Chinese Famine: Infanticide as a Demographic Consequence of the 1935 Yellow River Flood." *Comparative Studies in Society and History* 33, no. 3 (July): 466–510.

Li, Xiaojiang 李小江. 2001. "From 'Modernization' to 'Globalization': Where Are Chinese Women?" *Signs* 26, no. 4: 1274–78.

———. 2003. 让女人自己说话:亲历战争 [Let Women Speak for Themselves: Personal Experiences of War]. 北京: 生活•讀書•新知三联书店.

———. 2016. 女性乌托邦: 中国女性/性别研究二十讲 [Women Utopia: Women's and Gender Studies in New China (20 topics)]. 社会科学文献出版社.

Li, Xiaojiang, and Xiaodan Zhang. 1994. "Creating a Space for Women: Women's Studies in China in the 1980s." *Signs* 20, no. 1: 137–51.

Li, Yu-ning, ed. 1992. *Chinese Women through Chinese Eyes*. Armonk, NY: M. E. Sharpe.

Liang, Samuel Y. 2010. *Mapping Modernity in Shanghai: Space, Gender, and Visual Culture in the Sojourners' City, 1853–98*. Milton Park, Abingdon, Oxon, and New York: Routledge.

Liao, Sara Xueting. 2016. "Precarious Beauty: Migrant Chinese Women, Beauty Work, and Precarity." *Chinese Journal of Communication* 9, no. 2 (April): 139–52.

Liaw, H. Ray. 2008. "Women's Land Rights in Rural China: Transforming Existing Laws into a Source of Property Rights." *Pacific Rim Law & Policy Journal* 17, no. 1 (January): 238–64.

Lien, Ling-ling. 2001. "Searching for the 'New Womanhood': Career Women in Shanghai, 1912–1945." PhD diss., University of California, Irvine.

———. 2006. "Leisure, Patriotism, and Identity: The Chinese Career Women's Club in Wartime Shanghai." In *Creating Chinese Modernity: Knowledge and Everyday Life, 1900–1940*, ed. Peter Zarrow, 213–40. New York: Peter Lang.

Lim, Louisa. 2017. "How Class in China Became Politically Incorrect." *BLARB (Blog, Los Angeles Review of Books)*, July 12. http://blog.lareviewofbooks.org/chinablog/class-china-became-politically-incorrect.

Lin, Chun. 2001. "Whither Feminism: A Note on China." *Signs* 26, no. 4: 1281–86.

———. 2006. *The Transformation of Chinese Socialism*. Durham, NC: Duke University Press.

Lin, Shing-ting. 2013. "'Scientific' Menstruation: The Popularisation and Commodification of Female Hygiene in Republican China, 1910s–1930s." *Gender & History* 25, no. 2: 294–316.

Lin, Wei-hung. 1975. "Activities of Women Revolutionists in the Tung Meng Hui Period (1905–1912)." *China Forum* 2, no. 2: 245–99.

Link, E. Perry. 1981. *Mandarin Ducks and Butterflies: Popular Fiction in Early Twentieth-Century Chinese Cities*. Berkeley: University of California Press.

Lipkin, Zwia. 2006. *Useless to the State: "Social Problems" and Social Engineering in Nationalist Nanjing, 1927–1937*. Cambridge, MA: Harvard University Asia Center; distributed by Harvard University Press.

Littell-Lamb, Elizabeth. 2011. "Caught in the Crossfire." *Frontiers: A Journal of Women Studies* 32, no. 3 (September): 134–66.

Little, Mrs. Archibald. 1899. *Intimate China: The Chinese as I Have Seen Them*. London: Hutchinson & Co.

———. 1909. *In the Land of the Blue Gown*. New York: Appleton.

Litzinger, Ralph. 2013. "The Labor Question in China: Apple and Beyond." *South Atlantic Quarterly* 112, no. 1 (December 21): 172–78.

Liu, Fei-wen. 2011. "Text, Practice, and Life Narrative: Bridal Lamentation and a Daughter's Filial Piety in Changing Rural China." *Modern China* 37, no. 5 (September 1): 498–527.

Liu, Fengshu. 2014. "From Degendering to (Re)gendering the Self: Chinese Youth Negotiating Modern Womanhood." *Gender & Education* 26, no. 1 (January): 18–34.

Liu, Jennifer. 2013. "Defiant Retreat: The Relocation of Middle Schools to China's Interior, 1937–1945." *Frontiers of History in China* 8, no. 4 (January 1): 558–84.

Liu, Jieyu. 2007a. *Gender and Work in Urban China: Women Workers of the Unlucky Generation*. London and New York: Routledge.

———. 2007b. "Gender Dynamics and Redundancy in Urban China." *Feminist Economics* 13, no. 3/4 (October 7): 125–58.

———. 2017. *Gender, Sexuality and Power in Chinese Companies: Beauties at Work*. London: Palgrave Macmillan.

Liu, Kwang-ching, and Richard J. Smith. 1980. "The Military Challenge: The Northwest and the Coast." In *Late Ch'ing, 1800–1911, Part 2*, ed. Denis Crispin Twitchett, John King Fairbank, and Kwang-ching Liu, 11:2:202–73. The Cambridge History of China. Cambridge and New York: Cambridge University Press.

Liu, Lydia He. 1994. "Female Body and Nationalist Discourse: Manchuria in Xiao Hong's Field of Life and Death." In *Body, Subject & Power in China*, ed. Angela Zito and Tani E. Barlow, 157–77. Chicago: University of Chicago Press.

Liu, Lydia He, Rebecca E. Karl, and Dorothy Ko, eds. 2013. *The Birth of Chinese Feminism: Essential Texts in Transnational Theory*. New York: Columbia University Press.

Liu, Min. 2011. *Migration, Prostitution, and Human Trafficking: The Voice of Chinese Women*. New Brunswick, NJ: Transaction Publishers.

Liu, Wenming. 2012. "The Rise of a 'New Women's History' in Mainland China." *Chinese Studies in History* 45, no. 4 (Summer): 71–89.

Lodwick, Kathleen L. 1996. *Crusaders against Opium: Protestant Missionaries in China, 1874–1917*. Lexington: University Press of Kentucky.

Loyalka, Michelle Dammon. 2012. *Eating Bitterness: Stories from the Front Lines of China's Great Urban Migration*. Berkeley: University of California Press.

Lu, Weijing. 2004. "Beyond the Paradigm: Tea-Picking Women in Imperial China." *Journal of Women's History* 15, no. 4: 19–46.

———. 1998. "Uxorilocal Marriage among Qing Literati." *Late Imperial China* 19, no. 2: 64–110.

Lu Xun. 1980a. "Anxious Thoughts on 'Natural Breasts.'" In *Lu Xun: Selected Works*, trans. Yang Xianyi and Gladys Yang, 2:353–55. Beijing: Foreign Languages Press.

———. 1980b. "In Memory of Miss Liu Hezhen." In *Selected Works of Lu Hsun*, 2:267–72. Beijing: Foreign Languages Press.

———. 1999 [1923]. "What Happens after Nora Leaves Home?" In *Women in Republican China: A Sourcebook*, ed. Hua R. Lan and Vanessa L. Fong, 176–81. Armonk, NY, and London: M. E. Sharpe.

———. 2017. *Jottings under Lamplight*, ed. Eileen Cheng and Kirk A. Denton. Cambridge, MA: Harvard University Press.

Luo Suwen 罗苏文. 1996. 女性与近代中国社会 [Women and Modern Chinese Society]. Shanghai: Renmin chubanshe.

———. 2011. *Gaolang qiao ji shi: Jindai Shanghai yige mianfang zhi gongyequ de xingqi yu zhong jie 1700–2000* [高郎桥纪事: 近代上海一个棉纺织工业区的兴起与终结 (1700–2000); [Chronicle of Gaolangqiao: The Rise and Fall of a Cotton Spinning and Weaving Industrial District in Modern Shanghai]. Shanghai: Shanghai renmin chubanshe.

Luo, Yunjuan, and Hao Xiaoming. 2007. "Media Portrayal of Women and Social Change." *Feminist Media Studies* 7, no. 3: 281–98.

Luo, Wei, and Zhen Sun. 2015. "Are You the One? China's TV Dating Shows and the Sheng Nü's Predicament." *Feminist Media Studies* 15, no. 2 (March 4): 239–56.

Lutz, Jessie Gregory, ed. 2010. *Pioneer Chinese Christian Women: Gender, Christianity, and Social Mobility*. Bethlehem, PA: Lehigh University Press.

Lynch, George. 1901. *The War of the Civilisations, Being the Record of a "Foreign Devil's" Experiences with the Allies in China*. London: Longman's.

Ma, Yuxin. 2003. "Male Feminism and Women's Subjectivities: Zhang Xichen, Chen Xuezhao, and The New Woman." *Twentieth-Century China* 29, no. 1 (November 1): 1–37.

———. 2005a. "Constructing Manchukuo Womanhood to Service Japanese Imperialism." *Journal of the Georgia Association of Historians* 24: 80–105.

———. 2005b. "Women Journalists in the Chinese Enlightenment, 1915–1923." *Gender Issues* 22, no. 1 (Winter): 56–87.

———. 2007. "Women Suffragists and the National Politics in Early Republican China, 1911–1915." *Women's History Review* 16, no. 2 (June): 183–201.

———. 2010. *Women Journalists and Feminism in China, 1898–1937*. Amherst, NY: Cambria.

Ma, Zhao. 2014. "Female Workers, Political Mobilization, and the Meaning of Revolutionary Citizenship in Beijing, 1948–1950." *Frontiers of History in China* 9, no. 4 (December): 558–83.

———. 2015. *Runaway Wives, Urban Crimes, and Survival Tactics in Wartime Beijing, 1937–1949*. Cambridge, MA: Harvard University Asia Center; distributed by Harvard University Press.

MacKinnon, Stephen R. 2001. "Refugee Flight at the Outset of the Anti-Japanese War." In *The Scars of War: The Impact of Warfare on Modern China*, ed. Diana Lary and Stephen R. MacKinnon, 118–34. Vancouver: UBC Press.

———. 2008. *Wuhan, 1938: War, Refugees, and the Making of Modern China*. Berkeley: University of California Press.

Mak, Karin T. 2010. *Red Dust*. Documentary film.

———. 2014. "Until Our Last Breath: Voices of Poisoned Workers in China." In *Listening on the Edge: Oral History in the Aftermath of Crisis*, ed. Mark Cave and Stephen M. Sloan, 166–82. New York: Oxford University Press.

Makley, Charlene E. 2007. *The Violence of Liberation: Gender and Tibetan Buddhist Revival in Post-Mao China*. Berkeley: University of California Press.

Mann, Susan. 1992. "Women's Work in the Ningbo Area, 1900–1936." In *Chinese History in Economic Perspective*, ed. Thomas G. Rawski and Lillian M. Li, 243–71. Berkeley: University of California Press.

———. 1997. *Precious Records: Women in China's Long Eighteenth Century*. Stanford, CA: Stanford University Press.

———. 2007. *The Talented Women of the Zhang Family*. Berkeley: University of California Press.

———. 2008. "Dowry Wealth and Wifely Virtue in Mid-Qing Gentry Households." *Late Imperial China* 29, no. 1S: 64–76.

———. 2010. "The Lady and the State: Women's Writings in Times of Trouble during the Nineteenth Century." In *The Inner Quarters and Beyond: Women Writers from Ming through Qing*, ed. Grace S. Fong and Ellen Widmer, 283–313. Leiden and Boston: Brill.

Manning, Kimberley Ens. 2006a. "The Gendered Politics of Woman-Work: Rethinking Radicalism in the Great Leap Forward." *Modern China* 32, no. 3 (July 1): 349–84.

———. 2006b. "Making a Great Leap Forward? The Politics of Women's Liberation in Maoist China." *Gender & History* 18, no. 3 (November): 574–93.

———. 2010. "Embodied Activisms: The Case of the Mu Guiying Brigade." *China Quarterly* 204: 850–69.

Manning, Kimberley Ens, and Felix Wemheuer, eds. 2011. *Eating Bitterness: New Perspectives on China's Great Leap Forward and Famine*. Vancouver: UBC Press.

Mao, Zedong. 1990. *Report from Xunwu*. Translated by Roger R. Thompson. Stanford, CA: Stanford University Press.

———. 1995. *Mao's Road to Power: Revolutionary Writings 1912–1949, vol. 3: From the Jinggangshan to the Establishment of the Jiangxi Soviets*, ed. Stuart R. Schram. Armonk, NY: M. E. Sharpe.

———. 1997. *Mao's Road to Power: Revolutionary Writings, 1912–49: vol. 4: The Rise and Fall of the Chinese Soviet Republic, 1931–34*, ed. Stuart R. Schram. Armonk, NY: Taylor and Francis.

———. 1999 [1919]. "Concerning the Incident of Mao Zhao's Suicide." In *Women in Republican China: A Sourcebook*, ed. Hua R. Lan and Vanessa L. Fong, 80–83. Armonk, NY, and London: M. E. Sharpe.

———. 2015. *Mao's Road to Power: Revolutionary Writings 1912–1949, vol. 8: From Rectification to Coalition Government 1942–July 1945*, ed. Stuart R. Schram and Timothy Cheek. New York and London: Routledge.

"Marriage Law of the People's Republic of China, Amended April 28, 2001." http://www.npc.gov.cn/englishnpc/Law/2007-12/13/content_1384064.htm. Accessed June 19, 2017.

May, Shannon. 2010. "Bridging Divides and Breaking Homes: Young Women's Lifecycle Labour Mobility as a Family Managerial Strategy." *China Quarterly* 204: 899–920.

McCarthy, Simone. 2017. "China's Sexual Harassment Problem," December 4. https://supchina.com/2017/12/04/chinas-sexual-harassment-problem.

McElderry, Andrea. 1986. "Woman Revolutionary: Xiang Jingyu." *China Quarterly* 105 (March): 95.

McElroy, Sarah Coles. 2001. "Forging a New Role for Women: Zhili First Women's Normal School and the Growth of Women's Education in China, 1901–21." In *Education, Culture, and Identity in Twentieth-Century China*, ed. Glen Peterson, Ruth Hayhoe, and Yongling Lu, 348–74. Ann Arbor: University of Michigan Press.

McLaren, Anne E. 2008. *Performing Grief: Bridal Laments in Rural China*. Honolulu: University of Hawai'i Press.

McMahon, Keith. 2002. *The Fall of the God of Money: Opium Smoking in Nineteenth-Century China*. Lanham, MD: Rowman & Littlefield.

Meisner, Maurice J. 1999. *Mao's China and After: A History of the People's Republic*. New York: Free Press.

Merkel-Hess, Kate. 2016a. *The Rural Modern: Reconstructing the Self and State in Republican China*. Chicago: University of Chicago Press.

———. 2016b. "The Public Health of Village Private Life: Reform and Resistance in Early Twentieth Century Rural China." *Journal of Social History* 49, no. 4 (August 11): 881–903.

Meyer, Kathryn. 2014. *Life and Death in the Garden: Sex, Drugs, Cops, and Robbers in Wartime China*. Lanham, MD: Rowman & Littlefield.

Meyer, Richard J. 2005. *Ruan Ling-yu: The Goddess of Shanghai*. Hong Kong: Hong Kong University Press.

Meyer-Fong, Tobie. 2011. "Women and War in 19th Century China." Lecture. University of Mary Washington, April 6.

———. 2013. *What Remains: Coming to Terms with Civil War in 19th Century China*. Stanford, CA: Stanford University Press.

Michael, Franz H. 1966. *The Taiping Rebellion; History and Documents*. University of Washington Publications on Asia. Seattle: University of Washington Press.

"Migrant Workers and Their Children." 2015. *China Labour Bulletin*. http://www.clb.org.hk/content/migrant-workers-and-their-children.

Millward, James A. 1998. *Beyond the Pass: Economy, Ethnicity, and Empire in Qing Central Asia, 1759–1864*. Stanford, CA: Stanford University Press.

———. 2007. *Eurasian Crossroads: A History of Xinjiang*. New York: Columbia University Press.

Mitter, Rana. 2013. *Forgotten Ally: China's World War II, 1937–1945*. Boston: Houghton Mifflin Harcourt.

Mittler, Barbara. 2004. *A Newspaper for China?: Power, Identity, and Change in Shanghai's News Media, 1872–1912*. Cambridge, MA: Harvard University Asia Center; distributed by Harvard University Press.

———. 2007a. "Gendered Advertising in China: What History Do Images Tell?" *European Journal of East Asian Studies* 6, no. 1 (March): 13–41.

———. 2007b. "In Spite of Gentility: Women and Men in Linglong (Elegance), a 1930s Women's Magazine." In *The Quest for Gentility in China: Negotiations beyond Gender and Class*, ed. Daria Berg and Chloë Starr, 208–34. London and New York: Routledge.

Miyazaki, Ichisada. 1976. *China's Examination Hell: The Civil Service Examinations of Imperial China*. New York: Weatherhill.

Modern Girl around the World Research Group. 2008. *The Modern Girl around the World: Consumption, Modernity, and Globalization*, ed. Alys Eve Weinbaum et al. Durham, NC: Duke University Press.

Mungello, D. E. 2008. *Drowning Girls in China: Female Infanticide since 1650*. Lanham, MD: Rowman & Littlefield.

Murphy, Rachel. 2014. "Sex Ratio Imbalances and China's Care for Girls Programme: A Case Study of a Social Problem." *China Quarterly* 219 (September): 781–807.

Muscolino, Micah S. 2015. *The Ecology of War in China: Henan Province, the Yellow River, and Beyond, 1938–1950*. New York: Cambridge University Press.

Nedostup, Rebecca. 2009. *Superstitious Regimes: Religion and the Politics of Chinese Modernity*. Cambridge, MA: Harvard University Asia Center.

Ngo, Thi Minh-Hoang. 2009. "A Hybrid Revolutionary Process: The Chinese Cooperative Movement in Xiyang County, Shanxi." *Modern China* 35, no. 3 (May 1): 284–312.

Nie, Jing-Bao. 2005. *Behind the Silence: Chinese Voices on Abortion*. Lanham, MD: Rowman & Littlefield.

Nivard, Jacqueline. 1984. "Women and the Women's Press: The Case of the Ladies' Journal (Funü Zazhi) 1915–1931." *Republican China* 10, no. 1 (November 1): 37–55.

"*Nüboshi yanjiu 'xiaojie' jin shinian: Ni yiwei tamen zui zaihu qian?*" [女博士研究'小姐' 近十年：你以为她们最在乎钱?; A Woman PhD researches "Misses" for Almost a Decade: Do You Think That What They Care about Most Is Money?]. February 28, 2017. http://news.sohu.com/20170217/n481032339.shtml.

Ono, Kazuko. 1989. *Chinese Women in a Century of Revolution, 1850–1950*. Stanford, CA: Stanford University Press.

Orliski, Constance. 2003. "The Bourgeois Housewife as Laborer In Late Qing And Early Republican Shanghai." *Nan Nü — Men, Women & Gender in Early & Imperial China* 5, no. 1 (April 1): 43–68.

Osburg, John. 2013. *Anxious Wealth: Money and Morality among China's New Rich*. Stanford, CA: Stanford University Press. http://site.ebrary.com/lib/ucsc/Doc ?id=10674432.

Osnos, Evan. 2012. "China's No. 1 Matchmaker." *New Yorker*, May 14. http://www.newyorker.com/magazine/2012/05/14/the-love-business.

Otis, Eileen. 2016. "China's Beauty Proletariat: The Body Politics of Hegemony in a Walmart Cosmetics Department." *positions: east asia cultures critique* 24, no. 1 (February): 155–77.

———. 2012. *Markets and Bodies: Women, Service Work, and the Making of Inequality in China*. Stanford, CA: Stanford University Press.

Ownby, David. 2015. "Redemptive Societies in the Twentieth Century." In *Modern Chinese Religion II: 1850–2015*, ed. Vincent Goossaert, John Lagerwey, and Jan Kiely, 2:685–727. Leiden: Brill.

Pan, Yihong. 1997. "Feminism and Nationalism in China's War of Resistance against Japan." *The International History Review* 19, no. 1: 115–30.

Pang, Ching Lin, Sara Sterling, and Denggao Long. 2014. "Cosmopolitanism, Mobility and Transformation: Internal Migrant Women in Beijing's Silk Street Market." *Asian Anthropology* 13, no. 2 (December): 124–38.

Pang, Laikwan. 2005. "Photography, Performance, and the Making of Female Images in Modern China." *Journal of Women's History* 17, no. 4 (Winter): 56–85.

Parish, William L., and Martin King Whyte. 1978. *Village and Family in Contemporary China*. Chicago: University of Chicago Press.

Payne, Robert. 1947. *China Awake*. New York: Dodd, Mead.

Peck, Graham. 1950. *Two Kinds of Time*. Boston: Houghton Mifflin.

Pepper, Suzanne. 1999. *Civil War in China: The Political Struggle, 1945–1949*. Lanham, MD: Rowman & Littlefield.

Perdue, Peter C. 2005. *China Marches West: The Qing Conquest of Central Eurasia*. Cambridge, MA: Belknap Press of Harvard University Press.

Perry, Elizabeth J. 1980. *Rebels and Revolutionaries in North China, 1845–1945*. Stanford, CA: Stanford University Press.

———. 1993. *Shanghai on Strike: The Politics of Chinese Labor*. Stanford, CA: Stanford University Press.

———. 2002. *Challenging the Mandate of Heaven: Social Protest and State Power in China*. Asia and the Pacific. Armonk, NY: M. E. Sharpe.

Pietz, David Allen. 2002. *Engineering the State: The Huai River and Reconstruction in Nationalist China, 1927–1937*. New York: Routledge.

———. 2015. *The Yellow River: The Problem of Water in Modern China*. Cambridge, MA: Harvard University Press.

Platt, Stephen R. 2012. *Autumn in the Heavenly Kingdom: China, the West, and the Epic Story of the Taiping Civil War*. New York: Knopf.

Pomeranz, Kenneth. 2000. *The Great Divergence: Europe, China, and the Making of the Modern World Economy*. Princeton Economic History of the Western World. Princeton, NJ: Princeton University Press.

———. 2005. "Women's Work and the Economics of Respectability." In *Gender in Motion: Divisions of Labor and Cultural Change in Late Imperial and Modern China*, ed. Bryna Goodman and Wendy Larson, 239–63. Lanham, MD: Rowman & Littlefield.

Prazniak, Roxann. 1986. "Weavers and Sorceresses of Chuansha: The Social Origins of Political Activism among Rural Chinese Women." *Modern China* 12, no. 2 (April 1): 202–29.

———. 1999. *Of Camel Kings and Other Things: Rural Rebels against Modernity in Late Imperial China*. Lanham, MD: Rowman & Littlefield.

Pripas-Kapit, Sarah. 2015. "Piety, Professionalism and Power: Chinese Protestant Missionary Physicians and Imperial Affiliations between Women in the Early Twentieth Century." *Gender & History* 27, no. 2 (August 1): 349–73.

Pruitt, Ida. 1967. *A Daughter of Han: The Autobiography of a Chinese Working Woman*. Stanford, CA: Stanford University Press.

Pun, Ngai. 2005. *Made in China: Women Factory Workers in a Global Workplace.* Durham, NC, and Hong Kong: Hong Kong University Press: Duke University Press.
———. 2007. "Gendering the Dormitory Labor System: Production, Reproduction, and Migrant Labor in South China." *Feminist Economics* 13, no. 3–4 (July 1): 239–58.
Pun, Ngai, and Jenny Chan. 2013. "The Spatial Politics of Labor in China: Life, Labor, and a New Generation of Migrant Workers." *South Atlantic Quarterly* 112, no. 1 (December 21): 179–90.
Pun, Ngai, and Lu Huilin. 2010. "Unfinished Proletarianization: Self, Anger, and Class Action among the Second Generation of Peasant-Workers in Present-Day China." *Modern China* 36, no. 5 (September 1): 493–519.
Pun, Ngai, Shen Yuan, Guo Yuhua, Lu Huilin, Jenny Chan, and Mark Selden. 2016. "Apple, Foxconn, and Chinese Workers' Struggles from a Global Labor Perspective." *Inter-Asia Cultural Studies* 17, no. 2 (April 2): 166–85.
Pusey, James Reeve. 1983. *China and Charles Darwin.* Cambridge, MA: Council on East Asian Studies, Harvard University.
Qi, Liyan. 2017. "Journey to the Rest: China's Migrant Workers Top 280 Million." *Wall Street Journal,* April 30. https://blogs.wsj.com/chinarealtime/2017/04/30/journey-to-the-rest-chinas-migrant-workers-top-280-million.
Qian, Nanxiu. 2004. "'Borrowing Foreign Mirrors and Candles to Illuminate Chinese Civilization': Xue Shaohui's Moral Vision in the Biographies of Foreign Women." *Nan Nü—Men, Women & Gender in Early & Imperial China* 6, no. 1 (March): 60–101.
———. 2008. "The Mother Nüxue Bao versus the Daughter Nüxue Bao: Generational Differences Between 1898 and 1902 Women Reformers." In *Different Worlds of Discourse: Transformations of Gender and Genre in Late Qing and Early Republican China,* ed. Nanxiu Qian, Grace Fong, and Richard Joseph Smith, 257–92. Leiden: Brill.
———. 2010. "Xue Shaohui and Her Poetic Chronicle of Late Qing Reforms." In *The Inner Quarters and beyond: Women Writers from Ming through Qing,* ed. Grace S. Fong and Ellen Widmer, 339–72. Leiden and Boston: Brill.
———. 2015. *Politics, Poetics, and Gender in Late Qing China: Xue Shaohui and the Era of Reform.* Stanford, CA: Stanford University Press.
Qiu, Jin. 1998. "Excerpts from Stones of the Jingwei Bird (1905–1907)." In *Writing Women in Modern China: An Anthology of Women's Literature from the Early Twentieth Century,* ed. Amy D. Dooling and Kristina M. Torgeson, 43–78. Modern Asian Literature Series. New York: Columbia University Press.
Qiu, Peipei. 2013. *Chinese Comfort Women: Testimonies from Imperial Japan's Sex Slaves.* Vancouver: UBC Press.
Rankin, Mary Backus. 1971. *Early Chinese Revolutionaries; Radical Intellectuals in Shanghai and Chekiang, 1902–1911.* Cambridge, MA: Harvard University Press.
———. 1974. "Elite Reformism and the Chinese Women's Movement: Evidence from the Kiangsu and Chekiang Railway Demonstration, 1907." *Ch'ing-Shih Wen-T'i* 3, no. 2: 29–42.
———. 1975. "The Emergence of Women at the End of the Ch'ing: The Case of Ch'iu Chin." In *Women in Chinese Society,* ed. Margery Wolf and Roxane Witke, 39–68. Stanford, CA: Stanford University Press.

Ransmeier, Johanna S. 2017. *Sold People: Traffickers and Family Life in North China.* Cambridge, MA: Harvard University Press.

Rawski, Evelyn Sakakida. 1979. *Education and Popular Literacy in Ch'ing China.* Michigan Studies on China. Ann Arbor: University of Michigan Press.

"Reality Check: Are Women Welcome in Chinese Politics?" 2017. *BBC News*, October 25, sec. Asia. http://www.bbc.com/news/world-asia-41652487.

Reardon-Anderson, James. 2005. *Reluctant Pioneers: China's Expansion Northward, 1644–1937.* Stanford, CA: Stanford University Press.

Remick, Elizabeth. 2014. *Regulating Prostitution in China: Gender and Local State-building, 1900–1937.* Redwood City, CA: Stanford University Press.

Richardson, Nicole. 2012. "The Nation in Utero: Translating the Science of Fetal Education in Republican China." *Frontiers of History in China* 7, no. 1 (March 1): 4–31.

Roberts, Rosemary A. 2010. *Maoist Model Theatre: The Semiotics of Gender and Sexuality in the Chinese Cultural Revolution (1966–1976).* Leiden and Boston: Brill.

Rocha, Leon Antonio. 2010. "Xing: The Discourse of Sex and Human Nature in Modern China." *Gender & History* 22, no. 3 (November 1): 603–28.

Rofel, Lisa. 1999. *Other Modernities: Gendered Yearnings in China after Socialism.* Berkeley: University of California Press.

———. 2007. *Desiring China: Experiments in Neoliberalism, Sexuality, and Public Culture.* Durham, NC: Duke University Press.

Rogaski, Ruth. 1997. "Beyond Benevolence: A Confucian Women's Shelter in Treaty-Port China." *Journal of Women's History* 8, no. 4: 54–90.

———. 2004. *Hygienic Modernity: Meanings of Health and Disease in Treaty-Port China.* Berkeley: University of California Press.

Rohlf, Gregory. 2016. *Building New China, Colonizing Kokonor: Resettlement to Qinghai in the 1950s.* Lanham, MD: Lexington Books.

Rong, Tiesheng. 1986. "The Women's Movement in China Before and After the 1911 Revolution." In *The Chinese Revolution of 1911: New Perspectives*, ed. Chun-tu Hsueh and Xing Huang, 139–74. Hong Kong: Joint Publishing (HK).

Rowe, William T. 2001. *Saving the World: Chen Hongmou and Elite Consciousness in Eighteenth-Century China.* Stanford, CA: Stanford University Press.

Ruwitch, John. 2017. "Women Fail to Crack China's Glass Ceiling as Party Picks New Leaders." *Reuters*, October 26. https://www.reuters.com/article/us-china-congress-women/women-fail-to-crack-chinas-glass-ceiling-as-party-picks-new-leaders-idUSKBN1CU19I.

Sakamoto, Hiroko. 2004. "The Cult of 'Love and Eugenics' in May Fourth Movement Discourse." *positions: east asia cultures critique* 12, no. 2 (September): 329–76.

Sang, Tze-lan Deborah. 2003. *The Emerging Lesbian: Female Same-Sex Desire in Modern China.* Chicago: University of Chicago Press.

Santos, Gonçalo D., and Stevan Harrell, eds. 2017. *Transforming Patriarchy: Chinese Families in the Twenty-First Century.* Seattle: University of Washington Press.

Sargeson, Sally. 2012. "Why Women Own Less, And Why It Matters More in Rural China's Urban Transformation." *China Perspectives* 2012, no. 4 (December): 35–42.

Sargeson, Sally, and Song Yu. 2011. "Gender, Citizenship and Agency in Land Development." In *Women, Gender and Rural Development in China*, ed. Tamara Jacka and Sally Sargeson, 25–48. Cheltenham: Edward Elgar.

Schein, Louisa. 1997. "Gender and Internal Orientalism in China." *Modern China* 23, no. 1 (January 1): 69–98.

———. 2000. *Minority Rules: The Miao and the Feminine in China's Cultural Politics*. Durham, NC: Duke University Press.

Schneider, Helen M. 2011. *Keeping the Nation's House: Domestic Management and the Making of Modern China*. Vancouver: UBC Press.

———. 2012. "Mobilising Women: The Women's Advisory Council, Resistance and Reconstruction during China's War with Japan." *European Journal of East Asian Studies* 11, no. 2 (September): 213–36.

———. 2013. "Women and Family Education Reform in Wartime China, 1937–45." *Chinese Historical Review* 20, no. 2 (November 1): 180–201.

Schwarcz, Vera. 1986. *The Chinese Enlightenment: Intellectuals and the Legacy of the May Fourth Movement of 1919*. Berkeley: University of California Press.

Schwartz, Benjamin I. 1964. *In Search of Wealth and Power: Yen Fu and the West*. Cambridge, MA: Belknap Press of Harvard University Press.

Selden, Mark. 1995. *China in Revolution: The Yenan Way Revisited*. Socialism and Social Movements. Armonk, NY: M. E. Sharpe.

Sergeant, Philip W. 1911. *The Great Empress Dowager of China*. New York: Dodd, Mead. http://catalog.hathitrust.org/api/volumes/oclc/5704652.html.

Service, John S. 1974. *Lost Chance in China; The World War II Despatches of John S. Service*, ed. Joseph Esherick. New York: Random House.

Shan, Shili 單士釐. 1911. *Guixiu zhengshi zaixu ji* [閨秀正始再續集], vol. 1. [China]: Gui'an Qian shi 歸安錢氏.

Shao, Qin. 2013. *Shanghai Gone: Domicide and Defiance in a Chinese Megacity*. Lanham, MD: Rowman & Littlefield.

Shea, Jeanne L. 2005. "Sexual 'Liberation' and the Older Woman in Contemporary Mainland China." *Modern China* 31, no. 1 (January 1): 115–47.

Sheehan, Brett. 2006. "The Modernity of Savings, 1900–1937." In *Everyday Modernity in China*, ed. Madeleine Yue Dong and Joshua L. Goldstein, 121–55. Seattle: University of Washington Press.

Shemo, Connie. 2010. "'To Develop Native Powers': Shi Meiyu and the Danforth Memorial Hospital Nursing School, 1903–1920." In *Pioneer Chinese Christian Women: Gender, Christianity, and Social Mobility*, ed. Jessie Gregory Lutz, 292–311. Bethlehem, PA: Lehigh University Press.

———. 2011. *The Chinese Medical Ministries of Kang Cheng and Shi Meiyu, 1872–1937: On a Cross-Cultural Frontier of Gender, Race, and Nation*. Bethlehem, PA, and Lanham, MD: Lehigh University Press; Rowman & Littlefield.

Shen, Hsiu-Hua. 2008. "The Purchase of Transnational Intimacy: Women's Bodies, Transnational Masculine Privileges in Chinese Economic Zones." *Asian Studies Review* 32, no. 1 (March 1): 57–75.

Sheng, Keyi. 2012. *Northern Girls: Life Goes On*. Camberwell, Victoria: Penguin.

Shepherd, John R. 2016. "The Qing, the Manchus, and Footbinding: Sources and Assumptions under Scrutiny." *Frontiers of History in China* 11, no. 2 (June 8): 279–322.

Sheridan, Mary. 1976. "Young Women Leaders in China." *Signs* 2, no. 1: 59–88.

———. 1984. "Contemporary Generations: Zhao Xiuyin: Lady of the Sties." In *Lives: Chinese Working Women*, ed. Mary Sheridan and Janet W. Salaff, 204–35. Bloomington: Indiana University Press.

Sheridan, Mary, and Janet W. Salaff, eds. 1984. *Lives: Chinese Working Women.* Bloomington: Indiana University Press.

Shi, Lili. 1933. "The Modern Girl's Outward Appearance and Essence." *Linglong,* 3, no. 99: 882–83. Columbia University Libraries Online Exhibitions/Linglong Women's Magazine. https://exhibitions.cul.columbia.edu/exhibits/show/ling long/about_linglong/woman/modern.

Shih, Shumei. 2001. *The Lure of the Modern: Writing Modernism in Semicolonial China, 1917–1937.* Berkeley: University of California Press.

Shiroyama, Tomoko. 2008. *China during the Great Depression: Market, State, and the World Economy, 1929–1937.* Cambridge, MA: Harvard University Asia Center.

Shue, Vivienne. 2006. "The Quality of Mercy: Confucian Charity and the Mixed Metaphors of Modernity in Tianjin." *Modern China* 32, no. 4 (October 1): 411–52.

Siu, Helen F. 1990. "Where Were the Women?: Rethinking Marriage Resistance and Regional Culture in South China." *Late Imperial China* 11, no. 2: 32–62.

Smedley, Agnes. 1945. *Battle Hymn of China.* New York: Knopf.

———. 1976. *Portraits of Chinese Women in Revolution.* Old Westbury, NJ: Feminist Press.

Smith, Aminda M. 2013a. "The Dilemma of Thought Reform: Beijing Reformatories and the Origins of Reeducation through Labor, 1949–1957." *Modern China* 39, no. 2 (March 1): 203–34.

———. 2013b. *Thought Reform and China's Dangerous Classes: Reeducation, Resistance, and the People.* Lanham, MD: Rowman & Littlefield.

Smith, Norman. 2007. *Resisting Manchukuo: Chinese Women Writers and the Japanese Occupation.* Vancouver: UBC Press.

———. 2012. *Intoxicating Manchuria: Alcohol, Opium, and Culture in China's Northeast.* Vancouver: UBC Press.

Smith, S. A. 2002. *Like Cattle and Horses: Nationalism and Labor in Shanghai, 1895–1927.* Durham, NC: Duke University Press.

Smith, Steve. 1994. "Class and Gender: Women's Strikes in St. Petersburg, 1895–1917 and in Shanghai, 1895–1927." *Social History* 19, no. 2: 141–68.

Sommer, Matthew H. 2005. "Making Sex Work: Polyandry as a Survival Strategy in Qing Dynasty China." In *Gender in Motion: Divisions of Labor and Cultural Change in Late Imperial and Modern China,* ed. Bryna Goodman and Wendy Larson, 29–54. Lanham, MD: Rowman & Littlefield.

———. 2010. "Abortion in Late Imperial China: Routine Birth Control or Crisis Intervention?" *Late Imperial China* 31, no. 2: 97–165.

———. 2015. *Polyandry and Wife-Selling in Qing Dynasty China: Survival Strategies and Judicial Interventions.* Berkeley: University of California Press.

Song, Shaopeng 宋少鹏. 2015. "女权？还是要讲讲资本主义和社会主义" [Women's Rights? We Still Need to Talk about Capitalism and Socialism]. March 6. http://m.guancha.cn/songshaopeng/2015_03_06_311232.shtml.

Spakowski, Nicola. 2005. "Women's Military Participation in the Communist Movement of the 1930s and 1940s: Patterns of Inclusion and Exclusion." In *Women in China: The Republican Period in Historical Perspective,* ed. Mechthild Leutner and Nicola Spakowski, 129–71. Münster: Lit.

———. 2009. *Mit Mut an die Front: die militärische Beteiligung von Frauen in der kommunistischen Revolution Chinas; (1925–1949).* Köln [u.a.]: Böhlau.

———. 2011. "'Gender' Trouble: Feminism in China under the Impact of Western Theory and the Spatialization of Identity." *positions: east asia cultures critique* 19, no. 1 (March): 31–54.

Spence, Jonathan D. 1969. *To Change China: Western Advisers in China, 1620–1960.* Boston: Little, Brown.

———. 1981. *The Gate of Heavenly Peace: The Chinese and Their Revolution, 1895–1980.* New York: Viking Press.

———. 1996. *God's Chinese Son: The Taiping Heavenly Kingdom of Hong Xiuquan.* New York: Norton.

Stanley, John R. 2010. "Establishing a Female Medical Elite: The Early History of the Nursing Profession in China." In *Pioneer Chinese Christian Women: Gender, Christianity, and Social Mobility,* ed. Jessie Gregory Lutz, 274–91. Bethlehem, PA: Lehigh University Press.

Stapleton, Kristin. 2000. *Civilizing Chengdu: Chinese Urban Reform, 1895–1937.* Cambridge, MA: Harvard University Asia Center.

———. 2008. "Hu Lanqi: Rebellious Woman, Revolutionary Soldier, Discarded Heroine, and Triumphant Survivor." In *The Human Tradition in Modern China,* ed. Kenneth James Hammond and Kristin Eileen Stapleton, 157–76. Lanham, MD: Rowman & Littlefield.

———. 2016. *Fact in Fiction: 1920s China and Ba Jin's Family.* Stanford, CA: Stanford University Press.

Starr, Chloë. 2007. "The Aspirant Genteel: The Courtesan and Her Image Problem." In *The Quest for Gentility in China: Negotiations beyond Gender and Class,* ed. Daria Berg and Chloë Starr, 155–75. London and New York: Routledge.

Steele, Valerie, and John S. Major. 1999. *China Chic: East Meets West.* New Haven, CT: Yale University Press.

Stevens, Sarah E. 2003. "Figuring Modernity: The New Woman and the Modern Girl in Republican China." *NWSA Journal* 15, no. 3 (October 1): 82–103.

Stockard, Janice E. 1989. *Daughters of the Canton Delta: Marriage Patterns and Economic Strategies in South China, 1860–1930.* Stanford, CA: Stanford University Press.

Stranahan, Patricia. 1983. *Yan'an Women and the Communist Party.* China Research Monograph, no. 26. Berkeley: Institute of East Asian Studies, University of California, Berkeley Center for Chinese Studies.

———. 1998. *Underground: The Shanghai Communist Party and the Politics of Survival, 1927–1937.* Lanham, MD: Rowman & Littlefield.

Strand, David. 2011. *An Unfinished Republic: Leading by Word and Deed in Modern China.* Berkeley: University of California Press.

Stross, Randall E. 1986. *The Stubborn Earth: American Agriculturalists on Chinese Soil, 1898–1937.* Berkeley: University of California Press.

Su Ping 苏平, and Xu Yuzhen 徐玉珍, eds. 1991. 延安之路 [The Road to Yan'an]. 北京: 中国妇女出版社.

Sudo, Mizuyo. 2006. "Concepts of Women's Rights in Modern China." Translated by Michael G. Hill. *Gender & History* 18, no. 3 (November): 472–89.

Sun, Lung-kee. 1997. "The Politics of Hair and the Issue of the Bob in Modern China." *Fashion Theory: The Journal of Dress, Body & Culture* 1, no. 4 (December): 353–65.

Sun, Shuyun. 2006. *The Long March: The True History of Communist China's Founding Myth*. New York: Doubleday.

Sun, Wanning. 2004. "The Maid in China: Opportunities, Challenges and the Story of Becoming Modern." In *Chinese Women, Living and Working*, ed. Anne E. McLaren, 65–82. London and New York: RoutledgeCurzon.

———. 2008. "Men, Women and the Maid: At Home with the New Rich." In *The New Rich in China: Future Rulers, Present Lives*, ed. David S. G. Goodman, 213–28. Abingdon and New York: Routledge.

———. 2009a. "Symbolic Bodies, Mobile Signs: The Story of the Rural Maid in Urban China." *Asian Studies Review* 33, no. 3 (September 1): 275–88.

———. 2009b. "Suzhi on the Move: Body, Place, and Power." *positions: east asia cultures critique* 17, no. 3 (December): 617–42.

———. 2014. "'Northern Girls': Cultural Politics of Agency and South China's Migrant Literature." *Asian Studies Review* 38, no. 2 (April 3): 168–85.

Sun, Xiaoping. 2008. "New Life: State Mobilization and Women's Place in Nationalist China, 1934–1949." PhD diss., University of California, Santa Cruz.

Sun, Yi. 2011. "Reading History in Visual Rhetoric: The Changing Images of Chinese Women, 1949–2009." *Chinese Historical Review* 18, no. 2 (September 1): 125–50.

Supreme Court of the People's Republic of China. 2017. "Interpretation of the Supreme People's Court on Several Issues Concerning the Application of the Marriage Law of the People's Republic of China (II) (2017 Amendment)" [最高人民法院关于适用《中华人民共和国婚姻法》若干问题的解释(二)(2017修正)]. http://www.pkulaw.cn/fulltext_form.aspx?Db=chl&Gid=290789. Accessed July 19, 2017.

Tao Yi. 1999. "Commentary on Miss Zhao's Suicide." In *Women in Republican China: A Sourcebook*, ed. Hua R. Lan and Vanessa L. Fong, 83–85. Armonk, NY, and London: M. E. Sharpe.

"Tao Yi 陶毅（民国时期江南才女" [Tao Yi: Talented Jiangnan Woman of the Republican Era]._百度百科. https://baike.baidu.com/item/%E9%99%B6%E6%AF%85/35775. Accessed August 25, 2017.

Tatlow, Didi Kirsten. 2011. "Chinese Law Could Make Divorced Women Homeless." *New York Times*, September 7, sec. Asia Pacific.

———. 2015. "Costs, Not Just Law, Deterred Chinese Couples from Another Child." *New York Times*, October 29.

———. 2017. "As China Prepares for New Top Leaders, Women Are Still Shut Out." *New York Times*, July 16, sec. Asia Pacific.

Tatlow, Didi Kirsten, and Michael Forsythe. 2015. "In China's Modern Economy, a Retro Push Against Women." *New York Times*, February 20.

Teng, Emma. 1998. "An Island of Women: The Discourse of Gender in Qing Travel Writing about Taiwan." *International History Review* 20, no. 2 (June 1): 353–70.

———. 2004. *Taiwan's Imagined Geography: Chinese Colonial Travel Writing and Pictures, 1683–1895*. Cambridge, MA: Harvard University Asia Center; distributed by Harvard University Press.

———. 2013. *Eurasian: Mixed Identities in the United States, China, and Hong Kong, 1842–1943*. Berkeley: University of California Press.

Thaxton, Ralph. 2008. *Catastrophe and Contention in Rural China: Mao's Great Leap Forward Famine and the Origins of Righteous Resistance in Da Fo Village*. Cambridge and New York: Cambridge University Press.

Thorborg, Marina. 1978. "Chinese Employment Policy in 1949–78 with Special Emphasis on Women in Rural Production." In *Chinese Economy Post-Mao: A Compendium of Papers Submitted to the Joint Economic Committee, Congress of The United States*, ed. United States Joint Economy Committee, Congress of the United States. Washington, DC: U.S. Government Printing Office.

Tien, H. Yuan. 1987. "Abortion in China: Incidence and Implications." *Modern China* 13, no. 4 (October 1): 441–68.

Tillman, Margaret Mih. 2014. "Engendering Children of the Resistance: Models of Gender and Scouting in China, 1919–1937." *Cross-Currents* (December). https://cross-currents.berkeley.edu/e-journal/issue-13/tillman.

Tong, Xin. 2008. "Women's Labor Activism in China." *Signs* 33, no. 3: 515–18.

Topley, Marjorie. 1975. "Marriage Resistance in Rural Kwangtung." In *Women in Chinese Society*, ed. Margery Wolf and Roxane Witke, 67–88. Studies in Chinese Society. Stanford, CA: Stanford University Press.

Tran, Lisa. 2015. *Concubines in Court: Marriage and Monogamy in Twentieth-Century China*. Lanham, MD: Rowman & Littlefield.

Tsai, Weipin. 2006. "Having It All: Patriotism and Gracious Living in Shenbao's Tobacco Advertisements, 1919–1937." In *Creating Chinese Modernity: Knowledge and Everyday Life, 1900–1940*, ed. Peter Zarrow, 117–45. New York: Peter Lang.

Tsang, Eileen Yuk-ha. 2017. "Neither 'Bad' nor 'Dirty': High-End Sex Work and Intimate Relationships in Urban China." *China Quarterly* 230 (May): 1–20.

Tsui, Brian. 2018. *China's Conservative Revolution: The Quest for a New Order, 1927–1949*. Cambridge: Cambridge University Press.

Uretsky, Elanah. 2016. *Occupational Hazards: Business, Sex, and HIV in Post-Mao China*. Stanford, CA: Stanford University Press.

Verschuur-Basse, Denyse. 1996. *Chinese Women Speak*. Westport, CT: Praeger.

Wakeman, Frederic E. 1996. *The Shanghai Badlands: Wartime Terrorism and Urban Crime, 1937–1941*. Cambridge, UK, and New York: Cambridge University Press.

Walker, Kathy Le Mons. 1993. "Economic Growth, Peasant Marginalization, and the Sexual Division of Labor in Early Twentieth-Century China Women's Work in Nantong County." *Modern China* 19, no. 3 (July 1): 354–86.

———. 1999. *Chinese Modernity and the Peasant Path: Semicolonialism in the Northern Yangzi Delta*. Stanford, CA: Stanford University Press.

Wang, Danning. 2010. "Intergenerational Transmission of Family Property and Family Management in Urban China." *China Quarterly* 204: 960–79.

Wang, Di. 2004. "'Masters of Tea': Teahouse Workers, Workplace Culture, and Gender Conflict in Wartime Chengdu." *Twentieth-Century China* 29, no. 2 (April 1): 89–136.

Wang, Gary. 2011. "Making 'Opposite-Sex Love' in Print: Discourse and Discord in Linglong Women's Pictorial Magazine, 1931–1937." *Nan Nü—Men, Women & Gender in Early & Imperial China* 13, no. 2 (December 1): 244–347.

Wang, Lingzhen. 2004. *Personal Matters: Women's Autobiographical Practice in Twentieth-Century China*. Stanford, CA: Stanford University Press.

———. 2013. "Gender and Sexual Differences in 1980s China: Introducing Li Xiaojiang." *Differences: A Journal of Feminist Cultural Studies* 24, no. 2 (Summer): 8–21.

Wang, Qi, Min Dongchao, and Bo Ærenlund Sørensen, eds. 2016. *Revisiting Gender Inequality: Perspectives from the People's Republic of China*. Houndmills, Basingstoke, Hampshire, and New York: Palgrave Macmillan.

Wang, Xiying, and Daniel Nehring. 2014. "Individualization as an Ambition Mapping the Dating Landscape in Beijing." *Modern China* 40, no. 6 (November 1): 578–604.

Wang, Zheng. 1996. "A Historic Turning Point for the Women's Movement in China." *Signs* 22, no. 1 : 192–99.

———. 1997. "Maoism, Feminism, and the UN Conference on Women: Women's Studies Research in Contemporary China." *Journal of Women's History* 8, no. 4.

———. 1999. *Women in the Chinese Enlightenment: Oral and Textual Histories*. Berkeley: University of California Press.

———. 2001. "Call Me 'Qingnian' but Not 'Funu': A Maoist Youth in Retrospect." In *Some of Us: Chinese Women Growing up in the Mao Era*, ed. Xueping Zhong, Zheng Wang, and Bai Di, 27–52. New Brunswick, NJ: Rutgers University Press.

———. 2005. "Gender and Maoist Urban Reorganization." In *Gender in Motion: Divisions of Labor and Cultural Change in Late Imperial and Modern China*, ed. Bryna Goodman and Wendy Larson, 189–209. Lanham, MD: Rowman & Littlefield.

———. 2006. "Dilemmas of Inside Agitators: Chinese State Feminists in 1957." *China Quarterly* 188: 913–32.

———.2010a. "Creating a Socialist Feminist Cultural Front: Women of China (1949–1966)." *China Quarterly* 204 (December): 827–49.

———. 2010b. "Feminist Networks." In *Reclaiming Chinese Society: The New Social Activism*, ed. You-tien Hsing and Ching Kwan Lee, 101–18. London and New York: Routledge.

———. 2015. "Detention of the Feminist Five in China." *Feminist Studies* 41, no. 2 (June): 476–82.

———. 2017. *Finding Women in the State: A Socialist Feminist Revolution in the People's Republic of China, 1949–1964*. Oakland: University of California Press.

Washington, R. A. 2012. "The Largest Migration in History." *Economist*, February 24. https://www.economist.com/blogs/freeexchange/2012/02/china.

Wasserstrom, Jeffrey. 1984."Resistance to the One-Child Family." *Modern China* 10, no. 3 (July 1): 345–74.

Watson, Rubie S. 1984. "Women's Property in Republican China: Rights and Practice." *Republican China* 10, no. 1 (November 1): 1–12.

———. 1986. "The Named and the Nameless: Gender and Person in Chinese Society." *American Ethnologist* 13, no. 4: 619–31.

Wee, Sui-lee. 2017. "After One-Child Policy, Outrage at China's Offer to Remove IUDs." *New York Times*, January 7. http://www.nytimes.com/2017/01/07/world/asia/after-one-child-policy-outrage-at-chinas-offer-to-remove-iuds.html.

———. 2018. "Wanted at Chinese Start-Ups: Attractive Women to Ease Coders' Stress." *New York Times*, April 24, sec. Business Day. https://www.nytimes.com/2018/04/24/business/china-women-technology.html.

Welland, Sasha Su-Ling. 2006. *A Thousand Miles of Dreams: The Journeys of Two Chinese Sisters*. Lanham, MD: Rowman & Littlefield.

Wemheuer, Felix. 2014. *Famine Politics in Maoist China and the Soviet Union*. New Haven, CT: Yale University Press.

Wesoky, Sharon R. 2011. "Engendering the Local: Globalization, Development and the 'Empowerment' of Chinese Rural Women." In *Women, Gender and Rural Development in China*, ed. Tamara Jacka and Sally Sargeson, 190–207. Cheltenham: Edward Elgar.

———. 2015. "Bringing the Jia Back into Guojia: Engendering Chinese Intellectual Politics." *Signs* 40, no. 3: 647–66.

———. 2016. "Politics at the Local–Global Intersection: Meanings of Bentuhua and Transnational Feminism in China." *Asian Studies Review* 40, no. 1 (January 2): 53–69.

West, Jackie, M. Zhao, X. Chang, and Y. Cheng, eds. 1999. *Women of China: Economic and Social Transformation*. New York: St. Martin's Press.

Westad, Odd Arne. 2003. *Decisive Encounters: The Chinese Civil War, 1946–1950*. Stanford, CA: Stanford University Press.

"What Happens after Nora Walks Out." 2017. *China Channel*, September 29. https://chinachannel.org/2017/09/29/lu-xun-nora.

"Where Are Gay Rights and Feminism Headed in China? Leading Activist Li Maizi Speaks Out." *SupChina*, August 4, 2017. http://supchina.com/2017/08/04/gay-rights-feminism-headed-china-leading-activist-li-maizi-speaks.

White, Chris. 2014. "'To Rescue the Wretched Ones': Saving Chinese Slave Girls in Republican Xiamen." *Twentieth-Century China* 39, no. 1 (January): 44–68.

White, Sydney D. 1997. "Fame and Sacrifice the Gendered Construction of Naxi Identities." *Modern China* 23, no. 3 (July 1): 298–327.

White, Tyrene. 2006. *China's Longest Campaign: Birth Planning in the People's Republic, 1949–2005*. Ithaca, NY: Cornell University Press.

Whyte, Martin King, ed. 2003. *China's Revolutions and Intergenerational Relations*. Ann Arbor: Center for Chinese Studies, University of Michigan.

Widmer, Ellen. 2006. *The Beauty and the Book: Women and Fiction in Nineteenth-Century China*. Cambridge, MA: Harvard University Asia Center; distributed by Harvard University Press.

———. 2007. "Gentility in Transition: Travels, Novels, and the New Guixiu." In *The Quest for Gentility in China: Negotiations beyond Gender and Class*, ed. Daria Berg and Chloë Starr, 21–44. London and New York: Routledge.

———. 2010. "Retrieving the Past: Women Editors and Women's Poetry, 1636–1941." In *The Inner Quarters and Beyond: Women Writers from Ming through Qing*, ed. Grace S. Fong and Ellen Widmer, 81–105. Leiden and Boston: Brill.

Williams, Sue. 1997 [1989]. *China in Revolution: Battle for Survival, 1911–1936*. WinStar Home Entertainment.

Wilson, Verity. 1999. "Dress and the Cultural Revolution." In *China Chic: East Meets West*, by Valerie Steele and John S. Major, 167–86. New Haven, CT: Yale University Press.

Witke, Roxane. 1970. "Transformation of Attitudes towards Women during the May Fourth Era of Modern China." PhD diss., University of California, Berkeley.

———. 1973a. "Mao Tse-Tung, Women and Suicide." In *Women in China*, ed. Marilyn Young, 7–31. Ann Arbor: Center for Chinese Studies, University of Michigan.

———. 1973b. "Woman as Politician in China of the 1920s." In *Women in China*, ed. Marilyn Young, 33–45. Ann Arbor: Center for Chinese Studies, University of Michigan.

———. 1975. "Chiang Ch'ing's Coming of Age." In *Women in Chinese Society*, ed. Margery Wolf and Roxane Witke, 169–92. Stanford, CA: Stanford University Press.

———. 1977. *Comrade Chiang Ching: Roxane Witke*. Boston: Little, Brown.

Wolf, Margery. 1972. *Women and the Family in Rural Taiwan*. Stanford, CA: Stanford University Press.

———. 1985. *Revolution Postponed: Women in Contemporary China*. Stanford, CA: Stanford University Press.

"Women's Fertility Desires in Liaoning Province against the Background of the Comprehensive Second Child Policy" [全面二胎政策背景下辽宁省女性生育意愿情况]. Accessed July 24, 2017. https://www.wenjuan.com/s/bE7Zbu.

Woon, Yuen-Fong. 1999. "Labor Migration in the 1990s: Homeward Orientation of Migrants in the Pearl River Delta Region and Its Implications for Interior China." *Modern China* 25, no. 4 (October 1): 475–512.

Wu, Guo. 2014. "Speaking Bitterness: Political Education in Land Reform and Military Training under the CCP, 1947–1951." *Chinese Historical Review* 21, no. 1 (May 1): 3–23.

Wu, Ka-ming. 2015a. "Paper-Cuts in Modern China: The Search for Modernity, Cultural Tradition, and Women's Liberation." *Modern China* 41, no. 1 (January 1): 90–127.

———. 2015b. *Reinventing Chinese Tradition: The Cultural Politics of Late Socialism*. Urbana: University of Illinois Press.

———. 2018. "Elegant and Militarized: Ceremonial Volunteers and the Making of New Women Citizens in China." *Journal of Asian Studies* 77, no. 1: 205–23.

Wu, Shengqing. 2009. "Gendering the Nation: The Proliferation of Images of Zhen Fei (1876–1900) and Sai Jinhua (1872–1936) in Late Qing and Republican China." *Nan Nü—Men, Women & Gender in Early & Imperial China* 11, no. 1 (June 1): 1–64.

Wu, Xiujie. 2008. "Men Purchase, Women Use: Coping with Domestic Electrical Appliances in Rural China." *East Asian Science, Technology and Society* 2, no. 2 (June 1): 211–34.

Wu, Yi-Li. 2000. "The Bamboo Grove Monastery and Popular Gynecology in Qing China." *Late Imperial China* 21, no. 1: 41–76.

———. 2010. *Reproducing Women: Medicine, Metaphor, and Childbirth In Late Imperial China*. Berkeley: University of California Press.

Wyman, Judith. 2000. "Opium and the State in Late-Qing Sichuan." In *Opium Regimes: China, Britain, and Japan, 1839–1952*, ed. Timothy Brook and Bob Tadashi Wakabayashi, 212–27. Berkeley: University of California Press.

Xia, Xiaohong. 2008. "Tianyi Bao and He Zhen's Views on 'Women's Revolution.'" Translated by Hu Ying. In *Different Worlds of Discourse: Transformations of Gender and Genre in Late Qing and Early Republican China*, ed. Nanxiu Qian, Grace Fong, and Richard Joseph Smith, 293–314. Leiden: Brill.

Xia, Yun. 2013. "Engendering Contempt for Collaborators: Anti-Hanjian Discourse following the Sino-Japanese War of 1937–1945." *Journal of Women's History* 25, no. 1: 111–34.

Xiao, Hong. 1979. *The Field of Life and Death and Tales of Hulan River: Two Novels*. Translated by Howard Goldblatt and Ellen Yeung. Bloomington: Indiana University Press.

———. 1986. *Market Street: A Chinese Woman in Harbin*. Translated by Howard Goldblatt. Seattle and London: University of Washington Press.

Xiao, Hui Faye. 2014. *Family Revolution: Marital Strife in Contemporary Chinese Literature and Visual Culture*. Seattle: University of Washington Press.

Xiao, Meili. 2018. "China Must Combat On-Campus Sexual Harassment: An Open Letter," January 8. https://supchina.com/2018/01/08/china-must-combat-on-campus-sexual-harassment-an-open-letter.

Xiao, Yun 肖云. 2003. 我的母亲: 长征中最小的女红军 [My Mother: The Youngest Member of the Red Army on the Long March]. 北京: 中国文联出版社.

Xie, Bingying. 2001. *A Woman Soldier's Own Story: The Autobiography of Xie Bingying*. Translated by Lily Chia Brissman and Barry Brissman. New York: Columbia University Press.

Xinhua. 2007. "All China Women's Federation Survey Shows Violence in One Third of Families" [全国妇联调查显示:三成家庭存在家庭暴力_时政频道_新华网]. November 25. http://news.xinhuanet.com/politics/2007-11/25/content_7141041.htm.

Xinran. 2002. *The Good Women of China: Hidden Voices*. Translated by Esther Tyldesley. New York: Pantheon.

Xu, Feng. 2009. "Chinese Feminisms Encounter International Feminisms." *International Feminist Journal of Politics* 11, no. 2 (June 1): 196–215.

Yan, Hairong. 2006. "Self-Development of Migrant Women and the Production of Suzhi (Quality) as Surplus Value." In *Everyday Modernity in China*, ed. Madeleine Yue Dong and Joshua L. Goldstein, 227–59. Seattle: University of Washington Press.

———. 2008. *New Masters, New Servants: Migration, Development, and Women Workers in China*. Durham, NC: Duke University Press.

———. 2013. "'What If Your Client/Employer Treats Her Dog Better Than She Treats You?': Market Militarism and Market Humanism in Postsocialist Beijing." In *Global Futures in East Asia: Youth, Nation, and the New Economy in Uncertain Times*, ed. Ann Anagnost, Andrea Arai, and Hai Ren, 150–73. Stanford, CA: Stanford University Press.

Yan, Yunxiang. 2003. *Private Life under Socialism: Love, Intimacy, and Family Change in a Chinese Village, 1949–1999*. Stanford, CA: Stanford University Press.

———. 2011. "The Individualization of the Family in Rural China." *Boundary 2* 38, no. 1 (January 1): 203–29.

Yang, Bin, and Shuji Cao. 2016. "Cadres, Grain, and Sexual Abuse in Wuwei County, Mao's China." *Journal of Women's History* 28, no. 2: 33–57.

Yang, Binbin. 2011. "The Individualization of the Family in Rural China." *Boundary 2* 38, no. 1 (January 1): 203–29.

———. 2012. "Disruptive Voices: Three Cases of Outspoken 'Exemplary Women' from Nineteenth-Century China." *Nan Nü—Men, Women & Gender in Early & Imperial China* 14, no. 2 (December): 222–61.

Yang, Daqing. 2000. "The Challenges of the Nanjing Massacre." In *The Nanjing Massacre in History and Historiography*, ed. Joshua A. Fogel, 133–79. Berkeley: University of California Press.

Yang, Erche Namu, and Christine Mathieu. 2003. *Leaving Mother Lake: A Girlhood at the Edge of the World*. Boston: Little, Brown.

Yang, Guobin. 2016. *The Red Guard Generation and Political Activism in China*. New York: Columbia University Press.

Yang, Jie. 2011. "Nennu and Shunu: Gender, Body Politics, and the Beauty Economy in China." *Signs* 36, no. 2: 333–57.

Yang, Jisheng. 2012. *Tombstone: The Great Chinese Famine, 1958–1962*. New York: Farrar, Straus & Giroux.

Yang, Rae. 1997. *Spider Eaters: A Memoir*. Berkeley: University of California Press.

Yang Xingmei 杨兴梅. 2000. "观念与社会：女子小脚的美丑与近代中国的两个世界" [Ideas and Society: The Aesthetics of Bound Feet and Two Worlds of Modern China]. *Modern Chinese History Studies* [近代史研究], no. 4 (5386).

———. 2010. "以王法易风俗：近代知识分子对国家干预缠足的持续呼吁" [Using the State to Change Customs: The Intellectuals' Continuing Appeal for State Intervention in Foot Binding]. *Modern Chinese History Studies* [近代史研究], no. 1 (5466).

Yao Fei 姚霏. 2009. "近代中国女子剪发运动初探 (1903–1927)—以 '身体'为视角的分析" [A Preliminary Exploration of the Movement for Women to Cut Their Hair in Modern China (1903–1927)—Using the "Body" as an Analytical Perspective]. 史林, no. 2: 52–61.

Yao Fei 姚霏, and Ma Pei 马培. 2015. "抗战宣传画中的女性形象研究" [Research on Poster Images of Women during the Anti-Japanese War]. 妇女研究论坛, no. 3 (July): 41–49.

Ye, Jingzhong, Huifang Wu, Jing Rao, Baoyin Ding, and Keyun Zhang. 2016. "Left-behind Women: Gender Exclusion and Inequality in Rural-Urban Migration in China." *Journal of Peasant Studies* 43, no. 4 (July 3): 910–41.

Ye, Weili. 2001. *Seeking Modernity in China's Name: Chinese Students in the United States, 1900–1927*. Stanford, CA: Stanford University Press.

———. 2006. "The Death of Bian Zhongyun." *Chinese Historical Review* 13, no. 2 (September 1): 203–40.

Ye, Weili, and Xiaodong Ma. 2005. *Growing up in the People's Republic: Conversations between Two Daughters of China's Revolution*. New York: Palgrave Macmillan.

Yeh, Catherine Vance. 1998. "Reinventing Ritual: Late Qing Handbooks for Proper Customer Behavior in Shanghai Courtesan Houses." *Late Imperial China* 19, no. 2: 1–63.

———. 2006. *Shanghai Love: Courtesans, Intellectuals, and Entertainment Culture, 1850–1910*. Seattle: University of Washington Press.

Yeh, Wen-Hsin. 2007. *Shanghai Splendor: Economic Sentiments and the Making of Modern China, 1843–1949*. Berkeley: University of California Press.

Yen, Hsiao-pei. 2005. "Body Politics, Modernity and National Salvation: The Modern Girl and the New Life Movement." *Asian Studies Review* 29, no. 2 (June 1): 165–86.

Yip, Hon-ming. 2012. "Between Drawing and Writing: Prostitutes in the Dianshizhai Pictorial." In *Overt and Covert Treasures: Essays on the Sources for Chinese Women's History*, ed. Clara Wing-chung Ho, 487–542. Hong Kong: Chinese University Press.

Young, Ernest P. 1977. *The Presidency of Yuan Shih-Kai: Liberalism and Dictatorship in Early Republican China*. Ann Arbor: University of Michigan Press.

Young, Helen Praeger. 2001. *Choosing Revolution: Chinese Women Soldiers on the Long March.* Urbana: University of Illinois Press.

———. 2005. "Threads from Long March Stories: The Political, Economic and Social Experience of Women Soldiers." In *Women in China: The Republican Period in Historical Perspective*, ed. Mechthild Leutner and Nicola Spakowski, 172–93. Münster: Lit.

Young, Louise. 1998. *Japan's Total Empire: Manchuria and the Culture of Wartime Imperialism.* Berkeley: University of California Press.

Yu Chien ming 游鑑明. 1996. "Jindai Zhongguo Nüzi Tiyuguan Chutan" [近代中國女子體育觀初探; A Probe into Views of Women's Physical Education in Modern China]. *Xin Shixue* [新史學] 7, no. 4 (December): 119–56.

———. 2005. "Female Physical Education and the Media in Modern China." In *Women in China: The Republican Period in Historical Perspective*, ed. Mechthild Leutner and Nicola Spakowski, 482–506. Münster: Lit.

———. 2009. 運動場內外: 近代華東地區的女子體育(1895–1937) [On and Off the Sports Field: Women's Physical Education in Modern, Eastern China 1895–1937]. Taipei 臺北: Institute for Modern History, Academia Sinica 中央研究院近代史研究所.

Yu Chien ming, 游鑑明, Jiurong Luo 羅久蓉, and Haiyuan Qu瞿海源, eds. 2004. *Fenghuo Suiyuexia de Zhongguo Funü Fangwen Jilu* [烽火歲月下的中國婦女訪問紀錄; Records of Interviews with Chinese Women about a Fiery Era]. Zhongyang Yanjiuyuan Jindaishi Yanjiusuo Koushu Lishi Congshu 85. Taibei: Zhongyang yanjiuyuan jindaishi yanjiusuo.

Yue, Ai, Yaojiang Shi, Renfu Luo, Jamie Chen, James Garth, Jimmy Zhang, Alexis Medina, Sarah Kotb, and Scott Rozelle. 2017. "China's Invisible Crisis: Cognitive Delays among Rural Toddlers and the Absence of Modern Parenting." *China Journal*, no. 78 (July): 50–80.

Zamperini, Paola. 2010. *Lost Bodies: Prostitution and Masculinity in Chinese Fiction.* Leiden and Boston: Brill.

Zanasi, Margherita. 2006. *Saving the Nation: Economic Modernity in Republican China.* Chicago: University of Chicago Press.

Zarrow, Peter Gue. 1988. "He Zhen and Anarcho-Feminism in China." *Journal of Asian Studies* 47, no. 4 (November): 796–813.

———. 1990. *Anarchism and Chinese Political Culture.* New York: Columbia University Press.

Zavoretti, Roberta. 2017. *Rural Origins, City Lives: Class and Place in Contemporary China.* Seattle: University of Washington Press.

Zeldin, Wendy. 2011. "China: Supreme People's Court Issues Third Interpretation of Marriage Law/Global Legal Monitor." Library of Congress, September 19. http://www.loc.gov/law/foreign-news/article/china-supreme-peoples-court-issues-third-interpretation-of-marriage-law.

"Zeng Yong (曾咏)." *Baidu.* Accessed August 23, 2017. https://baike.baidu.com/item/%E6%9B%BE%E5%92%8F/4654900?fr=aladdin.

Zhang, Hong. 2007. "China's New Rural Daughters Coming of Age: Downsizing the Family and Firing Up Cash-Earning Power in the New Economy." *Signs* 32, no. 3: 671–98.

Zhang Jishun 张济顺. 2015. 远去的都市: 1950年代的上海 [A City Displaced: Shanghai in the 1950s]. Beijing: Shehui kexue wenxian chuban she.

Zhang, Jun, and Peidong Sun. 2014. "When Are You Going to Get Married? Parental Matchmaking and Middle-Class Women in Contemporary Urban China." In *Wives, Husbands, and Lovers: Marriage and Sexuality in Hong Kong, Taiwan, and Urban China*, ed. Deborah Davis and Sara Friedman, 118–44. Stanford, CA: Stanford University Press.

Zhang, Shiying. 2012. "Subversive Laughter." *Chinese Studies in History* 46, no. 1 (Fall): 30–70.

Zhang, Weiguo. 2009. "'A Married out Daughter Is Like Spilt Water'? Women's Increasing Contacts and Enhanced Ties with Their Natal Families in Post-Reform Rural North China." *Modern China* 35, no. 3 (May 1): 256–83.

———. 2013. "Class Categories and Marriage Patterns in Rural China in the Mao Era." *Modern China* 39, no. 4 (July 1): 438–71.

Zhang, Ye. 2004. "Migrant Women Negotiate Foreign Investment in Southern Chinese Factories." *Signs* 29, no. 2: 540–43.

Zhang, Yun. 2015. "Nationalism and Beyond: Writings on *Nüjie* and the Emergence of a New Gendered Collective Identity in Modern China." *Nan Nü* 17, no. 2 (March 24): 245–75.

Zhao Fei 姚霏. 2015. "抗战动员与性别实践 [Mobilization of Anti-Japanese War and Gendering Practice: Women's Participation in Medical Aid During the Anti-Japanese War]." 妇女研究论坛, no. 3 (July): 50–59.

Zhao, Kiki. 2016. "Chinese Who Violated One-Child Policy Remain Wary of Relaxed Rules." *New York Times*, February 8. http://www.nytimes.com/2016/02/09/world/asia/china-one-child-policy-hukou.html.

Zhao, Mi. 2014. "From Singing Girl to Revolutionary Artist: Female Entertainers Remembering China's Socialist Past (1949–the Present)." *Twentieth-Century China* 39, no. 2 (May): 166–90.

Zhao, Sile. 2015. "The Inspirational Backstory of China's 'Feminist Five.'" *Foreign Policy*, April 17. https://foreignpolicy.com/2015/04/17/china-feminist-bail-interview-released-feminism-activist.

Zheng, Su. 1997. "Female Heroes and Moonish Lovers." *Journal of Women's History* 8, no. 4.

Zheng, Tiantian. 2008. "Commodifying Romance and Searching for Love: Rural Migrant Bar Hostesses' Moral Vision in Post-Mao Dalian." *Modern China* 34, no. 4 (October 1): 442–76.

———. 2009. *Red Lights: The Lives of Sex Workers in Postsocialist China*. Minneapolis: University of Minnesota Press.

Zheng, Yangwen. 2005. *The Social Life of Opium in China*. Cambridge, UK: Cambridge University Press.

Zhong, Xueping. 2006. "Who Is a Feminist? Understanding the Ambivalence towards Shanghai Baby, 'Body Writing' and Feminism in Post-Women's Liberation China." *Gender & History* 18, no. 3: 635–660.

———. 2011. "Women Can Hold Up Half the Sky." In *Words and Their Stories: Essays on the Language of the Chinese Revolution*, ed. Ban Wang, 227–47. Leiden and Boston: Brill.

Zhong, Xueping, Wang Zheng, and Bai Di, eds. 2001. *Some of Us: Chinese Women Growing up in the Mao Era*. New Brunswick, NJ: Rutgers University Press.

Zhongguo renmin zhengzhi xieshang huyi, Quanguo weiyuanhui, and Wenshi xiliao yanjiu weiyuanhui 中国人民政治协商会議, 全国委员会, and 文史資料研究委

員會. 1961. *Xinhai geming huiyi lu* [辛亥革命回憶錄; Memoirs of the 1911 Revolution]. 北京: 中華書局.

Zhou, Shuxuan. 2015. "Suku and the Self-Valorization of Chinese Women Workers: Before, During, and after Enterprise Privatization." *Frontiers of History in China* 10, no. 1: 145–67.

Zhu, Ping. 2014. "The Phantasm of the Feminine: Gender, Race and Nationalist Agency in Early Twentieth-Century China." *Gender & History* 26, no. 1 (April): 147–66.

Zhuang, Pinghui. 2017. "How a Domestic Helper Became China's Hottest Writer." *South China Morning Post*, May 1. http://www.scmp.com/news/china/policies -politics/article/2091964/how-domestic-helpers-tale-hardship-made-her-chinas.

Zito, Angela. 2006. "Bound to Be Represented: Theorizing/Fetishizing Footbinding." In *Embodied Modernities: Corporeality, Representation, and Chinese Cultures*, ed. Fran Martin and Larissa Heinrich, 21–41. Honolulu: University of Hawai'i Press.

———. 2007. "Secularizing the Pain of Footbinding in China: Missionary and Medical Stagings of the Universal Body." *Journal of the American Academy of Religion* 75, no. 1: 1–24.

Zoe. 2016. "女男厕所比例真的要3: 2了? 女权主义者约谈住建部" [Do We Really Need a 3:2 Ratio of Women's to Men's Toilets?].女声网 (Reposted from 女权之声), December 5. http://www.genderwatch.cn:801/detail.jsp?fid=305821&cnID=90020.

Zuo, Jiping. 2003. "From Revolutionary Comrades to Gendered Partners: Marital Construction of Breadwinning in Post-Mao Urban China." *Journal of Family Issues* 24, no. 3: 314–37.

———. 2004. "Feminization of Agriculture, Relational Exchange, and Perceived Fairness in China: A Case in Guangxi Province." *Rural Sociology* 69, no. 4: 510–31.

———. 2013. "Women's Liberation and Gender Obligation Equality in Urban China: Work/Family Experiences of Married Individuals in the 1950s." *Science & Society* 77, no. 1 (January): 98–125.

———. 2014. "Understanding Urban Women's Domestic-Role Orientation in Post-Mao China." *Critical Sociology (Sage Publications, Ltd.)* 40, no. 1 (January): 111–33.

———. 2016. *Work and Family in Urban China: Women's Changing Experience Since Mao*. n.p.: Palgrave Macmillan.

Zuo, Jiping, and Yanjie Bian. 2001. "Gendered Resources, Division of Housework, and Perceived Fairness—A Case in Urban China." *Journal of Marriage and the Family* 63, no. 4: 1122–33.

Zuo, Xijia. 2008. "A Widow's Journey During the Taiping Rebellion: Zuo Xijia's Poetic Record." Translated by Grace S. Fong. *Renditions* 70 (Autumn): 49–58.

"Zuo Xijia (左锡嘉)." *Baidu*. Accessed November 6, 2013. http://baike.baidu.com/ link?url=UW7b9PbTWpRap7kP89N7ihUQLUzl0etzSSxycWr3gn_EldR5O42 pTe1giASv5pCJ.

Zurndorfer, Harriet T. 2005. "Gender, Higher Education, and the 'New Woman': The Experiences of Female Graduates in Republican China." In *Women in China: The Republican Period in Historical Perspective*, ed. Mechthild Leutner and Nicola Spakowski, 451–81. Münster: Lit.

———. 2013. "Wartime Refugee Relief in Chinese Cities and Women's Political Activism." In *New Narratives of Urban Space in Republican Chinese Cities: Emerging Social, Legal and Governance Orders*, ed. Billy K. L. So and Madeleine Zelin, 65–91. Leiden: Brill.

Index

About the Author

Gail Hershatter is Distinguished Professor of History at the University of California, Santa Cruz, and a former president of the Association for Asian Studies. Her books include *The Workers of Tianjin* (1986; Chinese translation, 2016), *Personal Voices: China Women in the 1980s* (1988, with Emily Honig), *Dangerous Pleasures: Prostitution in Twentieth-Century Shanghai* (1997; Chinese translation, 2003), *Women in China's Long Twentieth Century* (2007), and *The Gender of Memory: Rural Women and China's Collective Past* (2011; Chinese translation, 2017).

CRITICAL ISSUES IN WORLD AND INTERNATIONAL HISTORY
Series Editor: Morris Rossabi

Printed in the USA
CPSIA information can be obtained
at www.ICGtesting.com
LVHW011108030923
757095LV00010B/698

9 781442 215696